# TAKING POPULAR MUSIC SERIOUSLY

As a sociologist Simon Frith takes the starting point that music is the result of the play of social forces, whether as an idea, an experience or an activity. The essays in this important collection address these forces, recognising that music is an effect of a continuous process of negotiation, dispute and agreement between the individual actors who make up a music world. The emphasis is always on discourse, on the way in which people talk and write about music, and the part this plays in the social construction of musical meaning and value. The collection includes nineteen essays, some of which have had a major impact on the field, along with an autobiographical introduction.

# ASHGATE CONTEMPORARY THINKERS ON CRITICAL MUSICOLOGY SERIES

The titles in this series bring together a selection of previously published and some unpublished essays by leading authorities in the field of critical musicology. The essays are chosen from a wide range of publications and so make key works available in a more accessible form. The authors have all made a selection of their own work in one volume with an introduction which discusses the essays chosen and puts them into context. A full bibliography points the reader to other publications which might not be included in the volume for reasons of space. The previously published essays are published using the facsimile method of reproduction to retain their original pagination, so that students and scholars can easily reference the essays in their original form.

**Titles published in the series**

Critical Musicology and the Reesponsibility of Respose
*Lawrence Kramer*
Music and Historical Critique
*Gary Tomlinson*

**Titles to follow**

Music, Performance, Meaning
*Nicholas Cook*
Sound Judgment
*Richard Leppert*
Reading Music
*Susan McClary*

# Taking Popular Music Seriously

Selected Essays

SIMON FRITH
*Tovey Professor of Music, University of Edinburgh, UK*

ASHGATE CONTEMPORARY THINKERS ON
CRITICAL MUSICOLOGY SERIES

ASHGATE

Published by
Ashgate Publishing Limited
Gower House
Croft Road
Aldershot
Hampshire GU11 3HR
England

Ashgate Publishing Company
Suite 420
101 Cherry Street
Burlington, VT 05401-4405
USA

Ashgate website: http://www.ashgate.com

ISBN 978-0-7546-2679-4

**British Library Cataloguing in Publication Data**
Frith, Simon
    Taking popular music seriously : selected essays. -
    (Ashgate contemporary thinkers on critical musicology series)
    1. Popular music - History and criticism 2. Popular music -
    Social aspects
    I. Title
    781.6'4

**US Library of Congress Control Number:** 2006940013

Reprinted 2008

Printed and bound in Great Britain by TJI Digital, Padstow, Cornwall

# Contents

# Acknowledgements

The author and publisher wish to thank the following for permission to use copyrighted material:

Cambridge University Press for 'The Magic That Can Set You Free' in R. Middleton and D. Horn ed., *Popular Music 1*, 1981, pp. 159–68; 'Pop Music' in S. Frith *et al* ed., *The Cambridge Companion to Pop and Rock,* 2001, pp. 93–107; 'Towards an Aesthetic of Popular Music' in R. Leppert and S. McClary eds, *Music and Society. The Politics of Composition, Performance and Reception,* 1987, pp. 133–49.

Constable and Company Ltd for 'Youth and Music' in *The Sociology of Rock*, 1978, pp. 37–58.

Manchester University Press for 'Hearing Secret Harmonies' in C. MacCabe ed., *High Theory/ Low Culture. Analysing Popular Television and Film*, 1986, pp. 53–76.

Media, Culture and Society for 'Art *vs* Technology: the Strange Case of Popular Music', **8**, 1986, pp. 107–22.

Methuen and Co. Ltd. for 'Playing With Real Feeling. Making Sense of Jazz in Britain', *New Formations,* **4**, 1988, pp. 7–24; 'Adam Smith and Music', *New Formations,* 1992, **18,** pp. 67–83.

New Statesman for 'Afterthoughts' August 23 1985.

Popular Music for 'Look! Hear! The Uneasy Relationship of Music and Television', **21/3**, 2003, pp. 277–90.

Routledge for 'The Suburban Sensibility in British Rock and Pop' in R. Silverstone ed., *Visions of Suburbia,* 1997, pp. 269–79; 'Music and Everyday Life' in M. Clayton *et al* ed., *The Cultural Study of Music*, 2003, pp. 92–101; 'Why Do Songs Have Words?' in A.L. White ed., *Lost in Music. Culture, Style and the Musical Event*, 1987, pp. 77–106; 'What Is Bad Music?' in C.J. Washburne and M. Derno eds, *Bad Music. The Music We Love To Hate,* 2004, pp. 15–36.

Sage Publications, Inc. for 'The Industrialization of Popular Music' in J. Lull ed., *Popular Music and Communications,* 1992 edition, pp. 49–74; 'Music and Identity' in S. Hall and P. du Gay eds, *Questions of Cultural Identity*, 1996, pp. 108–27.

Screen Education for 'Rock and Sexuality' (with Angela McRobbie) in *Screen Education*, **29**, 1978/79, pp. 1–19; 'Formalism, Realism and Leisure: the Case of Punk' originally published as 'Music for Pleasure' in *Screen Education*, **34**, 1980, pp. 163–74.

University of California Press for 'The Discourse of World Music' in G. Born and D. Hesmondhalgh ed., *Western Music and Its Others*, 2000, pp. 305–23.

# Introduction

Although this volume is appearing in a series devoted to 'critical musicology' it will be obvious from the essays that follow that I am not in any conventional sense a musicologist. I was trained in sociology and approach music as a sociologist. My starting point is that whether as an idea, an experience or an activity, music is the result of the play of social forces. And it is the play of social forces (rather than musical notes) that these essays address.

I studied sociology as a graduate student at the University of California, Berkeley, in the late 1960s and as a neophyte lecturer at the University of Warwick in the early 1970s (teaching a subject is the best way of learning it). In these places, at that time, it was probably inevitable that my approach to music was influenced in equal part by Marxism and symbolic interactionism, 'a somewhat barbaric neologism', in the words of the man who coined the phrase, Herbert Blumer. Blumer (who chaired the Berkeley Sociology Department while I was there) suggests that:

> Symbolic interactionism rests in the last analysis on three simple premises. The first premise is that human beings act towards things on the basis of the meanings that the things have for them. The second premise is that the meaning of such things is derived from, or arises out of, the social interaction that one has with one's fellows. The third premise is that these meanings are handled in, and modified through, an interpretative process used by the person in dealing with the thing he encounters.[1]

From this (and, in particular, from Blumer's student, Howard S. Becker, whose 1950s work on 'the dance musician' was still inspirational for me in the 1960s) I understood that music is an effect of a continuous process of negotiation, dispute and agreement between the individual actors who make up a music world. One aspect of this argument became especially significant in my own work: the emphasis on discourse, on the way in which people talk and write about music, and the part this plays in the social construction of musical meaning and value.

Marxism, meanwhile, was a rather vague academic label by the time I was a graduate student. In broad terms I understood that to study contemporary music was to study a culture industry, a term first developed by the Frankfurt School in Germany (and, in particular, by the music scholar, T.W. Adorno) as part of its critique of mass society in the 1930s (I was taught the Sociology of Culture at Berkeley by a Frankfurt exile, Leo Lowenthal). The starting point of my *Sociology of Rock* was the Marxist approach to mass culture: music involved processes of production and consumption mediated by ideology. But my approach differed from mass culture critique in two respects.

---

1    Herbert Blumer: *Symbolic Interactionism. Perspective and Method*, Englewood Cliffs NJ: Prentice-Hall Inc 1969, 1–2.

First, Adorno's characteristic pessimism (and its underpinning philosophical and psychoanalytic positions) were replaced by a more cheerful belief in the possibilities of class struggle at the cultural level, by an activist's optimism derived theoretically from Adorno's fellow German intellectuals, Walter Benjamin and Bertolt Brecht, and from the Italian political theorist, Antonio Gramsci. I was influenced here by the work of Stuart Hall and his colleagues at the Centre for Contemporary Cultural Studies in Birmingham, whose seminars I attended when I arrived at nearby Warwick in the early 1970s.

Second, I had an empirical (rather than theoretical) view of Marxist methodology (the result of having written a PhD thesis in historical sociology, on working class education in Britain in the mid-nineteenth century). I was more interested in how capitalism worked materially than in the abstract arguments about ideology and structure that dominated left-wing university debate in Britain at that time. I thought that being a Marxist sociologist of music meant making sense of day-to-day decision making in the music market in economic rather than philosophical terms. It meant examining music by reference to its means of production and to the situations of power (and powerlessness) in which music makers and listeners lived. In the *Sociology of Rock* (the source of the first essay selected here) I was therefore interested in understanding youth (and therefore youth music) as a category in the organisation of work (and leisure) rather than for its speculative ideological or symbolic meaning.

Even in this abridged version of my intellectual formation it is clear that there was a tension between the two positions to which I subscribed. On the one hand, I assumed that the social meaning of music was determined, in the last instance, by material factors—by the economic logic of a music industry, by the power of a dominant class. On the other hand, I was fascinated by the way people made music and musical arguments for themselves, inventively, in the situations in which they found themselves. In trying to resolve (or perhaps ignore) the contradictions here I rejected what was still academic common sense when I started writing (among musicologists and Marxists alike), the suggestion that we could distinguish between music that was entirely determined by commercial forces and music that was entirely autonomous, between pop (whose meaning was exhausted by an analysis of its money-making purpose) and art (that could be studied without any reference to sociology at all). I rejected the notion that because pop music was commercial it couldn't be art, just as I assumed that art music was the result, in its own way, of economic and political forces.

One reason such assumptions about the differences between serious and popular music made no sense to me at all was because I began writing about music at precisely the moment when a new way of doing pop, rock, was taking social, musical and cultural shape. And what was fascinating about rock from both my sociological and fan perspectives was that it was both straightforwardly commercial (rock albums were by the end of the 1960s the most profitable musical commodities ever) *and* self-consciously anti-commercial and arty. Rock interested me academically as a discourse in which the contradictions at issue for all music-making in a capitalist society were constantly, self-consciously, addressed. This interest is apparent in the next three essays collected here. 'The Magic That Can Set You Free', an examination of rock's founding ideology, was published in the launch issue of *Popular Music*, then a year book but soon to become the academic journal which did more than any other to establish serious popular music studies. 'Rock and Sexuality' was written with Angela McRobbie, a pioneer in the development of feminist cultural studies. 'Formalism, Realism and Leisure: the Case of Punk' was an early take on a research project I'd begun with Howard Horne on the role of art schools in British popular culture.

Each of these essays had a polemical purpose. Each challenged developing orthodoxies: that rock was a new kind of folk music, that rock was sexually liberating, that punk was the sound of the dole queue. And each addressed the defining characteristic of popular musicology: that it is popular! Rock was first theorised by practitioners rather than academics, by journalists, musicians and audiences, by record companies and their PR departments, by radio producers and deejays. The key to an understanding of popular music was, I had come to realise, not high but low theory. The importance of such writers as Dave Laing and Charlie Gillett in Britain, Greil Marcus and Robert Christgau in the USA, lay less in their books (which are, in fact, of the highest academic standard) than in their weekly journalism, their everyday engagement with music and musical institutions as critics and reporters. They were the models for my own attempt to combine the academic study of popular music with rock journalism.

One aspect of this, which I think I would have missed if I had been just an academic, was everyday dealing with record companies (the source of my supply of records, concert tickets, press packs, etc). Record company practices were, I realised, more peculiar—more irrational—than my Marxist assumptions had led me to expect. This led me to research the history of the music industry, to rethink rock in a long historical framework. The next two essays here, 'Art *vs* Technology: the Strange Case of Popular Music' and 'The Industrialization of Popular Music', came out of this work. They turned out to be quite influential pieces (at least in terms of citation), perhaps because they so explicitly challenged the prevailing belief in rock's musical and artistic 'authenticity'. What music industry history revealed to me, though, was that rock discourse, its very claim to being different, could be traced back through earlier musical movements, such as jazz, and forward through later musical movements, such as world music. Such continuities are the subject of the next three essays collected here.

By the millennium the first rock generation was in its fifties and belief that rock was a special sort of popular culture was essentially nostalgic. The academic study of popular music (as reflected in the pages of *Popular Music* and at conferences of the International Association for the Study of Popular Music) was now the study of all kinds of genre from all kinds of place and time. What increasingly interested sociological scholars was *how* music mattered to people rather than what sort of music it was. This question is explored in the essays here on 'pop' as a musical category, on music and television and on music and everyday life.

In the 1990s, as my musical tastes as listener and critic became more eclectic, my academic interests became increasingly focused on issues of musical value, on the everyday processes of musical judgement, on the ways in which people just know (within genres) that one artist or recording is better than another. These questions had always been involved in my interest in musical discourse, but they had also always been something of a challenge to sociological methodology. To understand the social and discursive practices through which people respond to music as good or bad necessarily involves paying attention to what they perceive to be *in* the music. The issues here are explored in the final group of essays collected here. 'Why Do Songs Have Words' was my first attempt to consider what pop songs mean to people *as songs*. 'Hearing Secret Harmonies' examines the way in which film music both draws on and shapes people's ability to be moved by various musical devices. 'Towards an Aesthetic of Popular Music' was my first attempt to move from functional to aesthetic analysis or, rather, to suggest that a theory of musical value could be constructed on the basis of an understanding of music's social purposes. 'Adam Smith and Music' examines eighteenth-century philosophical and musicological arguments about rhetoric and performance as ways of understanding the relationship between aesthetics and ethics, an issue further explored, in more individualised terms, in 'Music and Identity'. Finally, 'What Is Bad Music?' brings these sometimes abstract arguments down to earth, rooting them in our routine experiences of musical abuse!

I hope that the cumulative effect of all these essays is to convince readers that a sociologist can have useful and illuminating insight into the ways in which musical values and meanings work. Whether this counts as 'critical musicology' I'm not sure. There is little here on specific pieces of music, nothing that could be considered formal analysis. On the other hand, I am convinced that musicologists must take account of the sociological understanding of the musical worlds in which pieces of music become possible in the first place, just as sociologists cannot understand these musical worlds fully without reference to music and how it works. Reading through the essays again I realise that underlying my various changes of interest and approach is a continuing belief in a modified Marxist dictum: people make their own music, but only in the circumstances in which they find themselves. This not only has methodological consequences—as a sociologist of music one has to pay attention always to the dialectic of necessity and invention—but also phenomenological implications. Music is a material practice offering a transitory experience of the ideal.

# Complete Bibliography

**Books**

*The Sociology of Rock*, Constable, 1978.

*Sound Effects, Youth, Leisure and the Politics of Rock'n'Roll*, Pantheon, New York, 1981.

(with Howard Horne) *Art into Pop*, Methuen, 1987.

*Music for Pleasure, Essays on the Sociology of Pop*, Polity, Cambridge and Routledge, New York, 1988.

ed. *Facing the Music. A Pantheon Guide to Popular Culture*, Pantheon, New York, 1988 and Mandarin, London, 1989.

ed. *World Music, Politics and Social Change*, Manchester University Press, 1989.

ed. (with Andrew Goodwin) *On Record. Pop, Rock and the Written Word*, Pantheon, New York and Routledge, London, 1990.

ed. (with Andrew Goodwin and Lawrence Grossberg) *Sound and Vision: Music. Video. Television*, Routledge, 1993.

ed. (with Tony Bennett, Lawrence Grossberg and John Shepherd) *Rock and Popular Music: Politics, Policies and Institutions*, Routledge, 1993.

ed. *Music and Copyright*, Edinburgh University Press, 1993.

*Performing Rites. On the Value of Popular Music*, Harvard University Press/Oxford University Press, 1996.

ed. (with Will Straw and John Street) *The Cambridge Companion to Rock and Pop*, Cambridge University Press, 2001.

ed. *Popular Music. Critical Concepts in Media and Cultural Studies*, Routledge, 2004, 4 volumes.

ed. (with Lee Marshall) *Music and Copyright*, Edinburgh University Press/Routledge (USA), 2004.

**Articles**

'Popular Music 1950–1980' in George Martin ed., *Making Music*, F. Muller, 1983, 18–48.

'Art *vs* Technology. The Strange Case of Popular Music', *Media, Culture and Society*, 8(3) 1986, 263–80.

'The Making of the British Record Industry 1920–1964', in J. Curran, A. Smith and P. Wingate eds., *Impacts and Influences. Essays on Media Power in the Twentieth Century*, Methuen, 1987, 278–90.

'The Industrialisation of Popular Music', in J. Lull ed., *Popular Music and Communication*, Sage, 1987, 53–77.

'The Aesthetics of Popular Music', in R. Leppert and S. McClary eds., *Music and Society*, Cambridge University Press, 1987, 133–49.

'Copyright and the Music Business' *Popular Music*, 7(1) 1987, 1–19.

'What is Good Music?', *Canadian University Music Review*, 10(2) 1990, 92–102.

'The Cultural Study of Popular Music', in L.Grossberg at al eds., *Cultural Studies*, Routledge, 1991, 174–186.

'From Beatles to Bros. Twenty-Five Years of British Pop' in N. Abercrombie and D. Warde eds., *Social Change in Contemporary Britain*, Polity, 1992, 40–53.

'Adam Smith and Music', *New Formations*, 18, 1992, 67–83.

'Representatives of the People: Voices of Authority in Popular Music' in *Mediterranean Music Cultures and their Ramifications*, Sociedad Espanola de Musicologia, 1994.

'What is Bad Music?' *Musiken ar 2002* (Rapport nr.11), Kungl. Musikaliska Akademien Stockholm, 1994, 3–27.

'Reviving the Folk', Essay Review, *Popular Music*, 13(3) 1994, 345–53.

'The Academic Elvis' in R. King and H. Taylor eds. *Dixie Debates. Perspectives on Southern Culture*, Pluto Press, 1996, 99–114.

'Music and Identity' in S. Hall and P. du Gay eds. *Questions of Cultural Identity*, Sage, 1996, 108–27.

'Entertainment' in J. Curran and M. Gurevitch ed. *Mass Media and Society*, (2nd edition), Edward Arnold, 1996, 160–76.

'Does Music Cross Boundaries?' in A. Van Hemel ed., *Trading Culture: GATT, European Cultural Policies and the Transatlantic Market*, Boekmanstichting, 1996, 157–63.

'The Suburban Sensibility in British Rock and Pop' in R. Silverstone ed., *Visions of Suburbia*, Routledge, 1996, 269–79.

'Popular Music Policy and the Articulation of Regional Identities: the Case of Scotland and Ireland', *Music in Europe*, European Music Office, Bruxelles, September 1996, 98–103.

'Vaerdisporgsmalet inden for populaemusik' in C. Madsen and B.M. Thomsen eds., *Tidsen Former*, Aarhus University Press, 1997, 92–112.

'Shaping the Future' *Finnish Music Quarterly*, 2/99, 28–30.

'Politics and the Experience of Music', *Sosiologisk arbok*, 1999, 1–15.

'La Constitucion de la Musica Rock como Industria Transnacional', in L.Puig and J.Talens ed., *Las culturas del rock*, Pre-Textos/Fundacion Bancaja (Spain), 1999, 11–30.

'Power and Policy in the British Music Industry' in Howard Tumber ed., *Media Power, Professionals and Policy*, Routledge 2000, 70–83.

'The Discourse of World Music' in Georgina Born and David Hesmondhalgh eds., *Western Music and Its Other*, University of California Press, 2000, 305–22.

'Music Industry Research: Where Now? Where Next? Notes from Britain', *Popular Music*, 19(3), 2000, 387–93.

'The Centre Writes Back. A Response to YOUNG', *YOUNG. Nordic Journal of Youth Research*, 8(3) 2000, 47–51.

'Film Music Books: a review article', *Screen*, 41(3) 2000, 334–38.

'L'industrializzazione della musica e il problema dei valori', in J-J. Nattiez ed., *Enciclopedia della musica . Volume primo: Il Novecento*, Torina: Einaudi, 2001, 953–65.

'Note introduttive', F.D'Amato ed., *Sound Tracks. Tracce, convergenze e scenari degli studi musicali*, Roma: Meltemi, 2001, 11–23.

'Music and Everyday Life', *Critical Quarterly*, 44(1) 2002, 35–48.

'An Essay on Criticism', T. Carson, K. Rachlis and J. Salamon eds., *Don't Stop 'til You Get Enough. Essays in Honor of Bob Christgau*, Austin, Texas: Nortex Press, 2002, 65–9.

'Illegality and the Music Industry' in M. Talbot ed.: *The Business of Music*, Liverpool University Press, 2002, 195–216.

'Fragments of a Sociology of Rock Criticism' in Steve Jones ed.: *Pop Music and the Press*, Philadelphia: Temple University Press, 2002, 235–46.

'Gatherings' in *New Routes. A World of Music from Britain*, British Council, 2002, 10–13.

'Look! Hear! The Uneasy Relationship of Music and Television', *Popular Music* 21(3) 2002, 249–62.

'Globalizaçâo E Fluxo Cultural: O Caso Da Música Rock Anglo-Americana', *Forum Sociológico*, 7/8, 2002, 127–43.

'Music and Everyday Life', Martin Clayton, Richard Middleton and Trevor Herbert ed: *The Cultural Study of Music: A Critical Introduction*, London and New York: Routledge, 2003, 92–101.

'Does British music still matter? A reflection on the changing status of British popular music in the global music market', *European Journal of Cultural Studies*, 7(1), 2004, 43–58.

'"And I guess it doesn't matter anymore." European Thoughts on American Music', Eric Weisbard ed: *This is Pop. In Search of the Elusive at the Experience Music Project*, Cambridge MA and London: Harvard University Press, 2004, 15–25.

'Why does music make people so cross?' and 'Reply to Gary Ansdell and Bent Jensen', *Nordic Journal of Music Therapy*, 13(1) June 2004, 66–71; 78–80.

(with Martin Cloonan and John Williamson): 'What is music worth? Some reflections on the Scottish Experience', *Popular Music*, 23 (2), May 2004, 213–21.

'Reasons to be cheerful. A review essay' *Popular Music*, 23 (3), 2004, 363–72.

'What is bad music?' Christopher J. Washburne and Maiken Derno ed. *Bad Music*, New York and London: Routledge, 2004, 15–36.

'The best disco record: Sharon Redd: "Never Give You Up"' Alan McKee ed. *Beautiful Things in Popular Culture*, Oxford: Blackwell, 2007, 193–203.

# CHAPTER 1

# Youth and music

A lively, regular and varied social programme is vital to the building of Young Socialist branches. Every branch should aim to hold
a regular discothèque to attract hundreds of youth in the area ...
(*Young Socialist*, 3 April 1976.)

Young people's interest in music is taken for granted by everyone
these days, and although post-war sociologists were initially surprised
that teenagers should 'frequently and spontaneously' express a love
of music, they already knew that young people had their own leisure
pursuits and that one of the most popular was dancing. A 1951 survey of British leisure, commenting on 'the importance of dancing as
a means of spending leisure', added that

> a large majority of dancers are young people, mostly between the
> ages of 16 and 24 ... drawn from the working and lower middle
> classes.

These authors went on to voice familiar fears of teenage hedonism:

> Modern ballroom dancing may easily degenerate into a sensuous
> form of entertainment, and if self-control is weakened with
> alcohol it is more than likely that it will do so, which might easily
> lead at least to unruly behaviour and not infrequently to sexual
> immorality.[1]

Concern for the young at play can be traced back to the nineteenth
century, when a variety of institutions appeared to regulate the leisure
of proletarian youth. By the 1930s remarks on the 'independence' and
even 'affluence' of young workers were commonplace, but although
jazz, particularly as a form of dance music, was seen to have a special
appeal to the young, neither it nor any other form of popular music
was seen as an expression of a youth culture.[2]
    The full integration of pop music and youth culture was a develop-
ment of the 1950s and was symbolised by a new form of music, rock
'n'roll, and a new form of youth, teddy boys. If the young had always
had idols – film stars, sportsmen, singers such as Frank Sinatra and
Johnnie Ray – the novelty of rock'n'roll was that its performers

*38*                           *The consumption of rock*

were 'one of themselves', were the teenagers' own age, came from
similar backgrounds, had similar interests. The rise of rock'n'roll
was accompanied by the development of a generation gap in dancing,
as dance halls advertised rock'n'roll nights or became exclusively
rock'n'roll venues. In 1954 it was estimated that nine-tenths of
London's teenagers spent some of their leisure time listening to
records, and among the more visible features of the new world of
teenage consumption were the self-service record 'Browseries' and
'Melody Bars'. When Abrams' teenage consumer report came out in
1959 its statistics on music reflected findings that were being made
simultaneously by sociologists.[3]

Abrams showed that music and activities involving music absorbed
a significant part of young expenditure, and in 1961 Coleman's
mammoth survey of American adolescents confirmed that music was
their most popular form of entertainment and that rock'n'roll was
their most popular form of music. The importance of rock in young
people's lives became an axiom of British youth research. In her
1964–5 survey of 15- to 19-year-olds in Glasgow, Jephcott noted that
'pop in any form was an almost universal interest . . . the word
"pop" brought a sigh of relief – "Here's something we *want* to talk
about".' The young's interest in pop determined the television programmes they watched, the magazines they read, the cafés they went
to, the 'necessary tools' – transistor, record player, tape recorder,
guitar – they sought to own.[4]

Jephcott did her research at the time of the beat boom (Lulu and
the Luvvers were a local community group!) but there is no evidence
to suggest that her findings should be confined to the mid-sixties.
Researchers in the 1970s have replicated Coleman's findings that pop
is central to the teenage social system, and a recent survey of the
British literature on adolescent leisure concluded that 'music is in
many ways the central activity of the British youth culture, from
which many subsidiary activities flow'. White's account of young
workers in Wembley is a good illustration of this point. He shows
that it is the presence of 'their music' that attracts young people to
pubs and discos and youth clubs, and that:

> Home-made entertainment means only one thing – music. Front
> rooms are occasionally leased from parents for planned parties,
> but generally this home music-making involves an impromptu
> visit, a couple of young people going round to a friend's house.
> Baby-sitting provides a good opportunity for listening to new LPs.
> And the young workers do listen. This is quite different from the
> overpowering musical wallpaper of the Village Inn [a pub], almost
> an act of worship.[5]

*Youth and music*                                             *39*

Abrams' 1959 study has never been repeated in so clear a form, but the importance of youth's consumption of musical products has continued to be emphasised in market research. A national teenage survey in 1974 confirmed that the majority of 15- to 24-year-olds go dancing and buy records regularly, own their own record players and radios, and have an overwhelming musical preference for rock music and Top Thirty pop. This pattern of music use is not confined to British youth or even to capitalist youth, although if in America and Britain it was the advent of rock'n'roll that signalled the arrival of musical youth culture, for most European countries it did not emerge clearly until the success of the Beatles in the 1960s.[6]

While there can be no doubting the importance of music for the young, these surveys, sociological or not, are descriptive: music's presence in youth culture is established, but not its purpose. Jephcott suggests that if music is a universal teenage interest, it is also a superficial one – the impression left by her research is of a culture in which music is always heard but rarely listened to.[7] This impression is given statistical support by this finding in the Schools Council's 1968 survey of young school-leavers:

*Table 4:*
*Percentage saying that pop music was important to themselves/to their children/to their pupils*

|          | boys | girls |
|----------|------|-------|
| Children | 20   | 35    |
| Parents  | 41   | 64    |
| Teachers | 38   | 71    |

*Source:* Schools Council (1968), pp. 167–90.

These figures suggest that young people assess the music in their lives as much less significant than its constant noise makes it sound to outsiders, and it is time now to examine youth's use of music in more detail.

## The use of music

In 1972 I conducted a survey of 14- to 18-year-olds at a comprehensive school in Keighley, Yorkshire, and I want to begin this section with a brief summary of the results.[8]          *Primary proof*

In general terms, the pupils in my sample were all in much the same situation: as school children, they were not affluent – pocket money averaged from 50p for the 14-year-olds to £1·50 for the sixth-formers, supplemented by varying part-time earnings – but most had their own rooms, and most owned the basic tools for music playing – radios, record players and/or recorders. The children were similar, too, in their general attitudes to music: they were 'quite' rather than 'very' interested in it; devoted 'some' time, but not 'a lot', to talking about it; spent a proportion of their income on it, but not an overwhelming one. On the whole, though, they all listened to music as a normal part of their daily lives, and the shared knowledge involved was reflected in the ease with which all my sample could comment on all genres of rock – a question on T. Rex, for example, was answerable by everyone, fan or not, and even the two classical-music devotees knew what T. Rex records sounded like. A basic experience of rock was common to all these young people, whatever their class or academic background, and the findings that most interested me were the different patterns of music use and taste *within* this framework.

Firstly, there was a distinct sixth-form culture, a pattern of rock use shared by all the sixth-formers to whom I spoke (mostly but not necessarily middle-class in background) which merged into student culture and was already being adopted by the academic pupils below them. These pupils bought albums rather than singles, had 'progressive' rather than 'commercial' tastes, were not involved in the trappings of rock (if they did, in a desultory way, watch *Top of the Pops* and listen to Radio 1, *The Old Grey Whistle Test* was the only show they made a special effort to see), and went to performance-based gigs – folk clubs, rock concerts – more than to discos or dances. The ideological essence of this culture was its individualism. Typical replies to questions about influences on taste were:

> I like what I like, no one changes my opinions on music . . .
> I like what I like, not what I'm told or influenced to like . . .

Choosing records was an individual decision of some importance: albums were never bought spontaneously or on spec and sixth-formers rejected the idea that records were chosen to fit an image or group identity; they didn't accept that they had an image ('I am myself') or else accepted it only reluctantly ('I suppose I have, although I don't readily admit it'; 'I hope not'; 'I do not *want* an image'). The role of the musically knowledgeable in informing and stimulating rock interest was acknowledged – boys were more likely than girls to play the role of opinion leader – but, in the end, musical taste was individual. Records were listened to, appreciated and criticised in terms of their meaning – lyrics were an important but not the only source of such meaning – and music was praised in terms of its originality, sincerity and beauty, or condemned for its triviality, banality, repetition. 'Rubbish' was the favourite pejorative word for

*Youth and music*                                                   *41*

'commercial trash which gets in your head and you can't escape and it does nothing for you except make you puke'.

Such sixth-formers experienced youth culture as a culture with an articulated set of values different from those of an older generation; they saw themselves as 'rebelling against unreasonable ideas and conventional ways of doing things'. Their fear was that even youth culture was not a true or meaningful expression of individuality:

> Rock music is unfortunately fashionable and its followers are exploited. It is very hard to separate true opinion from 'conditioned response'.

In sharp contrast to this was the lower-fifth culture of the pupils who bought singles and watched *Top of the Pops*, were regulars at youth clubs and discos but rarely went to concerts, who emphasised beat and sound in their tastes rather than meaning, who identified with a specific youth style and its music, and whose standard mode of criticism of other tastes was abuse:

> T. Rex are shit. I've heard kids whistle better than that group. Music, it's all the same, no difference in rhythm or sound. They're all a set of puftas, Bolan with all his make-up and god knows what his wife thinks about wearing glitter under his eyes. Other groups wear it but don't go round talking like a puff. T. Rex ARE CRAP.

But having established that there were distinct rock cultures, I must be careful not to misinterpret the differences. What was involved was ideology, the way people talked about music, more than activity, the way they actually used it. The apparent lyric *vs* beat difference, for example, conceals the fact that the sixth-formers did dance! They danced the same sort of self-taught 'freak' and 'mod' and 'bop' styles as the other pupils and shared their appreciation of the standard dance music like Motown.[9]

If sixth-formers used music for dancing and background as often as for concentrated listening, so the lower fifth-formers were aware of lyrics, could remember and appreciate them, had some notion of songs' meanings – 'love is much better to sing about than a football team' – and responded to the messages and stories of rock and soul singles.

Similarly, I don't want to exaggerate the difference between the individualism of the sixth-formers and the group identities of the lower fifth. The latter were aware of the playfulness of their groups – 'the image changes – it's just for laughs' – and conscious of their individuality within them. Group styles were a matter of convenience

*42*                         *The consumption of rock*

and all the pupils could make an instant equation of group and music even when they did not fit themselves *into* such groups:

> I have assorted friends – some hairies, some crombie boys and girls. I can sit and listen to both sorts of music and don't mind either. . . .

> I'm in between a skinhead and a hippie. I wear 'mod' clothes but I listen to both kinds of music. . . .

> I wear skinhead clothes, but I don't just like that type of music. . . .

And consider these two more extended comments from lower-stream fourth-formers:

> I don't know what youth culture means. I think it means what you are – skin, grebo, or hairie. I am none of these. Beat that, I think. The groups have different outlooks on sex, drugs and politics. The lot of it is different views to that of my parents. My brother was a skinhead gang leader for three years. Music is not important to any group, to me music is what I like, not everybody else's opinion.

> I think that music makes up for 75% of youth culture and that the music you like depends on the cult you're in. This idea of cult is taken too far. Teenagers can't be split into hating each other with a few in the middle just because they have different viewpoints. But they are.

On the other hand, one of the most militant groups among 15- and 16-year-olds was that of the future sixth-formers, the self-identified hairies and hippies, with their missionary zeal for progressive rock and a hatred of commercial pop:

> Rock music, progressive and heavy are fantastic. If they were not there life would not be worth living. They are the backbone behind music as a whole – showing us what it should really be like.

It was from this group that the most assertive statements of image and shared tastes came. If group identity is part of teenage culture for conventional reasons – 'if you like soul or reggae music and they like rock you will both wear different clothes and you may split up to go with your own group' – then even people with an ideology of individual taste become a group of individualists and need the symbols and friends and institutions to assert themselves as a group:

## Youth and music 43

I listen at home most of the time, in my room. I don't often go to parties. Don't go to clubs 'cos I haven't anyone to go with and the clubs round here aren't the places which I enjoy going to. Dances are a bit like clubs, the people that go aren't the sort of people I mix with well. Discos are the same, my sort of people don't go there. I love concerts but it's difficult for me to get to them or get tickets. I go when I can. I listen alone or with a friend most. There's not a lot of people in our village which like progressive music.

One of the paradoxes in my survey was that the group which most stressed individual musical choice also most stressed the importance of shared musical taste for friendship – music served as the badge of individuality on which friendship choices could be based. One of the ironies was that because music was taken as a symbol of a cluster of values, the most individualistic groups were the ones most thrown by their musical heroes changing direction. This was particularly a problem for the hairies because they differentiated themselves from the masses as a self-conscious elite by displaying exclusive musical tastes. When one of their acts went commercial ('sold out') and became part of mass taste there was great bitterness:

What do you think of T. Rex? I do not usually think of them. It puts me off my meals whenever I think about T. Rex. They were once good when called Tyrannosaurus Rex – Next Best Thing to Beatles and Stones. T. Rex are very bopperish. It's all the same music like Tamla. N.B. Marc Bolan and Micky Finn are *Two of a kind*. Puff Puff Puff.

There are two other points I must make about different uses of music. Firstly, there were some pupils whose musical cultures were quite different from those I've described, either because they were not essentially youth-cultural (a small group of Pakistani pupils whose tastes were entirely for Pakistani performers, a brass-band fanatic, the two classical musicians) or because they were subscribers to a musical cult that really was the centre of their lives – there was a soul freak in my sample, and a couple of rock'n'rollers, who had quite distinct patterns of record buying, dancing and magazine reading.

Secondly, the class/academic cultural differences were interwoven with age and sex differences. One aspect of the difference between sixth-form and lower-fifth culture was that sixth-formers were older. It was clear in my survey that the maximum involvement in youth groups and their symbols occurred in the fourth year, when most pupils had some such identity; by the fifth year most were claiming non-membership and by the sixth there were no admitted group

*44*                           *The consumption of rock*

members at all. There were also distinctions between the sexes. Girls
were more interested in dancing and tended to be more concerned
with rock lyrics, especially with the words of love. They were all
aware of the special female features of pop culture – fan clubs, *Fab
208*, star personalities – even if only a small minority were interested
enough to get involved in them. I shall return to the sex division in
youth cultures in the next chapter.

I want to conclude this section with a qualitative description of the
pupil cultures I found in Keighley. Alison and her friends were a
group of sixth-formers and students who had a busy and self-con-
tained social life, meeting weekly at the folk club (most of them picked
at guitars themselves), at parties in each others' houses, at concerts
or the bar at the local universities, at selected pubs. The group tended
to come from middle-class backgrounds (the local professional and
management class) and this had some effect on the material basis of
their leisure – they had access to cars, for example, which made them
mobile – but they were not particularly well off in terms of income,
spent a large proportion of non-school time studying and were consequently at home a lot. Working-class sixth-formers fitted into this
culture without much difficulty.

Music was used as a background to their lives, radio and records
were always on. The records were LPs, chosen carefully and individually and often saved for after hearing a friend's copy; there was much
mutual listening and temporary exchanging of records and few people
in the group had a large record collection, although a crucial musical
role was played by older brothers and sisters and friends who had
more records, knew what was happening and turned the group on to
new sounds. The overall result was an eclecticism of taste, with individuals developing their own specialisms – folk, heavy, singer/song-
writer; they were aware of general rock trends but not particularly
interested in them.

This group was conscious of itself as a group and differentiated
itself clearly from the culture of its parents, but what really dominated its members' lives was a sense of possibility. They were all pre-
paring to move on – to universities and colleges, to new towns and
opportunities, to new sexual and social experiences; they were all
aware that the group itself was transitional and temporary, that individuals had to maintain their individualism within it. They were
articulate and self-aware and valued these qualities in music, to which
they turned for support as well as for relaxation. They most valued
music that was most apparently 'artistic' – technically complex or
lyrically poetic – and tastes here went with other interests, in the
other arts, in politics, in religion. There were few direct restraints on
the activities of this group except the members' shortage of money;

*Youth and music* **45**

they were successful at school and at home and rarely clashed with authority. But their life was already a career and the importance of exams and qualifications was fully realised. The resulting tensions made music all the more important – as the context for bopping, relaxing, petting, falling in love and shouting a temporary 'Fuck the world!'.

Craig and his friends were in their last year at school, fifth-formers itching to get out. They would leave school without skill or qualification but had been used to failure for years and school was not so much oppressive now as irrelevant. Their lives already revolved around the possibilities of (unskilled) work – most members of the group were already working part-time – and their leisure reflected this expectation. The group went out (no bother about studying) to the youth club, to the pubs that would take them, to the chippy and the bus station and the streets. None of this group were militantly members of any particular gang, but they had skinhead friends and relations, could run casually with them and with the emerging groups of mods and crombies and smoovies and knew which side they were on in a bundle; Friday night, for example, was the traditional time for a trip to Bradford, the boys for a fight, the girls for a dance at the Mecca.

This group had plenty of free time but little money or mobility and their leisure was consequently focused on public places, putting them in constant confrontation with the controllers of those spaces – police and bus conductors and bouncers. But home wasn't much freer and so the boys went out most nights, doing nothing, having a laugh, aware that this was their youth and that their future would be much like the past of their working-class parents. Music was a pervasive part of their lives, in their rooms and clubs, on the juke-box, at the disco. Sometimes, when they had the money, they'd buy that single that was really great. They knew the big names and what was in the charts and what was good to dance to, though they didn't really follow it. The point was that when they were in their group they had their music and knew what it was without thinking much. And they knew what they hated, that hairy stuff, heavy rock – 'it's crackers the way it's arranged – isn't it?' – though that mattered more at school than on the streets, where they were grown up already, went drinking with their brothers and their mates. Music was for the girls really, wasn't it? It was the girls who stayed home and listened more, who even had their favourites pinned on the wall still and sometimes told the boys what to buy for their girl friends.

David's and Peter's friends were younger, in the fourth form, but committed to the academic route. They saw their futures stretching out through the sixth form and college – which was how David's parents and teachers saw it too, though Peter's had their doubts. They were young yet, lacked the resources and the mobility and the permission for student life. In chafing about this they were more aggressively hip, at school, in the youth club and most of all at home, where they'd gather their friends and sit round the record player like it was Moses or something, bringing messages from on high. It was important for this lot to distinguish themselves from everybody, teachers, parents, peers. They were hippies, hairies, in their clothes and attitudes and tastes and drugs, and they worked at it, read the music press, got passionate about their records and about the evils of commercialism. They were an élite, a group apart from the masses even if they were in the same school and youth club and street.

Most of these kids made it into the sixth form, no sweat, and entered that culture easily, the greater freedom and success accompanying a looser hipness so that their interests remained but their expression was less aggressive. Some, though, did not. Peter failed his O-levels. The school wouldn't have him in the sixth and wouldn't even give him a reference for the tech. He found his life-style incompatible with the unskilled work his father and brothers did, so he lived on the dole mostly, not articulate enough to say what he really wanted but hearing it in the music, which seemed like the right life if he could get it together. He dreamt about that in the cafés by day and the hippie pub by night, did a little dealing and always turned on his friends, still at school or home for the vac. He knew everything that was going on and believed more than ever what they'd all once believed, that 'rock is a real boost from reality', and he needed to believe it too, now more than ever.

## Sociological explanations

I have presented a general and a particular description of young people's use of music and I want next to consider the existing sociological explanations of the importance of music in youth cultures. The first comes from adolescence theorists. With their concern for the problems of socialisation and transition, they focus on peer-groups as the social context in which children learn to be adults. Music is seen to be important to peer-groups for two reasons: it is a means by which a group defines itself, and it is a source of in-group status.[10]

The most vivid example of music functioning to define group identity is in Colin Fletcher's account of how rock'n'roll transformed Liverpool street gangs into beat groups, as every gang nurtured its own musicians, provided its own fans and started to fight its battles on stage with the 'wild and basic sound' of Mersey Beat:

*Youth and music* **47**

This thumping sound made the clubs relatively complete as the new adolescent world, a whole new source of status within them selves. Adolescents had a music, a number of dances, a 'place of their own'.[11]

This quote brings out the two aspects of musical identity: it distinguishes young from old, but it also distinguishes one peer-group from another:

What about me? I dig mod clothes but I don't wear them. I like the Beatles but don't rave over them. I listen to Blue Beat music but don't dance the Blue Beat way. I wear my hair long and sometimes use hair lacquer, but I don't sport a Blue Beat hat. I dig everything a mod raves over but I don't hunt with a mod pack. Recently I asked a typical mod boy what title I should come under. Sizing me up he said, 'You're not one of those in-between mods and rockers called mids. There's an Ivy League style about your suits and your appearance differs from the mid. I would put you under the title of – a Stylist.'[12]

Teenage styles reflect the need of all adolescents to 'belong' and one aspect of group identity is its stylistic precision:

True skinheads look neat. Their clothes are smart and expensive. Their boots are always polished to perfection. Their favourite clothes are Levi Sta-Prest, Harrington jackets, Jaytex (shirts), Bens (shirts), Crombies (coats), Blue-beats (hats), Doc's (Dr Marten's boots), Royals' (shoes), Monkey boots (girls' boots), Fred's (Fred Perry shirts), Toniks (two-tone suits).[13]

Another is that everyone gets put into a group, even if only negatively; *Sniffin' Glue*, the punks' magazine, refers to other groups as 'footballs' and 'discos', for example. Each group has its music, which can and must reflect the finest nuances: 'as skinheads become smoothies and skinhead girls begin to go out with smoothies they start to like T. Rex and Slade better than Motown'.[14]

This is a description of the Halloween dance in her village from one of my Keighley sample:

Just as in the youth club the two rival gangs sit at opposite ends of the room. The band will begin to play and everybody is waiting for everybody else to get up and dance. Then some girls will get up and dance and gradually the floor will fill up with people dancing. Suddenly the record will change to a rock record and

*48*                          *The consumption of rock*

everybody makes their way back to the seats as the rockers get up
and stand in a circle ready to start their dance. The older folk stand
and look amazed as they start to dance, they most probably never
seen anything like it before because they are doing cartwheels and
splits in the middle of the circle. As their type of music dies away
into the background, a Tamla Motown record comes on and all
the mods get up and go into a circle and begin to dance. This
carries on for most of the night, it's like one big dancing contest,
trying to be better than the other. They have nothing against each
other, they do it for fun and everybody enjoys themselves either
laughing at them or laughing at the people's faces.

And after supper there are old-time dances for older people and
the kids join in and 'pretend that they are on *Come Dancing*'.

In such a village the division into groups seems random (indeed,
the groups fought together against neighouring skinheads and rockers) and in general adolescent identities can be based on a variety of
symbols, including fine musical differences within a single musical
taste – Elvis *vs* Cliff, the Beatles *vs* the Stones, Donny Osmond *vs*
David Cassidy. Even the slightest differences between groups can
be matters of passionate argument and musical identity takes on a
variety of references – one of the most visible is the phenomenon of
everyone at a rock concert dressing like the star.[15]

The second use of music-as-identity is to distinguish the young
from the old, to identify a place or occasion or time as youth's property. Music – played on transistor radios, record players, portable
cassettes – becomes the easiest way for the young to maintain and
display their control of their rooms, clubs and street corners, of their
pubs and discos. The demands made of it – in terms of noise and
beat and flash – are general rather than specific. If the noise is right,
any noise will do – although familiarity is valued, hence the use of
the charts. Music is the context for rather than the focus of youthful
leisure. This is most noticeable in the central institution of teenage
culture, the dance. It may be true, as Patterson has argued, that the
impact of black dancing records – ska and soul and reggae – has reflected the needs of a newly violent and hedonistic white youth
culture, but it is also true that the real focus of dances is the youthful
displays and interactions which revolve around the 'exchange and
mart' of sexual partners, and such displays long pre-date rock'n'roll.
The music is the accompaniment of an activity, not its expression, or,
as a 15-year-old in my sample put it:

And if the older people want to begin looking for a wife or husband, they have to go to Bradford Mecca.[16]

## Youth and music                                    49

Although adolescent theorists claim to understand the functions
of youth music  they are not sanguine about its effects. Do teenage
symbols express teenage concerns or do they manipulate them?
There has always been a fear that the teenageness of teenage culture
has rested on false idols, that the posters and the stars, the beat and
the love lyrics and the rest of this world of teenage fantasy are a false
expression of real needs. Teenage culture is seen as filling a need, but
not really fulfilling it.[17]

(My own research suggests that teenagers are much hipper about *Primary*
themselves and their world than the traditional adolescent image
allows) They know how commercial rock works, even as they enjoy
it. My sample's comments on T. Rex revealed an awareness (no
doubt informed by the sneers of the hairies) of the relationship between record-making and money-making. (In response to a question   *qualitative*
asking if they would like to be rock stars, there was only one fantasy
along the lines of 'Yes, because you could enjoy yourself, you would
be on TV and you would get lots of girl friends and fans.') Mostly
there was realistic assessment of rock as a job something like the
army – hard work but plenty of travel!

Adolescence theorists' evaluation of teenage culture rests on their
understanding of adolescent needs. If the use of music can be explained as answering a need, it can also be judged according to how
well it does so. The problem with this model, as I suggested in the last
chapter, is that adolescent needs are defined in social-psychological
terms, and related to the abstract difficulties of social transition.
Leisure is not related to work or, indeed, given any material setting –
school leaving, for example, does not, according to these theorists,
have any major effects on youth's leisure needs; rather, 'it is leisure
that provides the continuity between school and work'. Similarly,
although most of the studies of adolescence are studies of working-
class teenagers, the suggestion is that the analysis is classless; all
adolescents have the same needs and create the same peer-group
systems, music therefore fulfils the same purpose for all of them.[18]

This conclusion has been strongly criticised by Graham Murdock.
In his own subtle interpretation of the use of music by secondary-
school pupils, Murdock emphasises the sharp class differences within
youth's use of similar musical symbols. He suggests that, as a source
of peer-group status and identity, music must be contrasted with
working-class street culture as well as with conformist school culture.
He describes a pattern of music use similar to the one I found in
Keighley: middle-class children interested in the 'underground' and
concerned with lyrics, 'the source of those values, roles and meanings
which the school undervalues'; working-class children interested in
dance music and concerned with the beat – they got their 'alternative

*50*                              *The consumption of rock*

meanings from street peer groups rooted in the situational cultures of working-class neighbourhoods' and music served them simply as a background and 'small coin of social exchange'. From such taste differences sprang the different media uses – *Top of the Pops* vs *The Old Grey Whistle Test* – and Murdock builds up a convincing picture of class differences maintained and even exaggerated by the different uses of a supposedly common youthful means of expression.[19]

There are difficulties, however, in the very neatness of Murdock's conclusions. Obviously I don't doubt the significance of class-based differences in rock use – my own research has similar implications and American sociologists have come up with the same general findings – but I do doubt the precision of Murdock's relationships. The evidence that working-class pupils are less interested in music than their middle-class colleagues, for example, can equally support findings that their taste choices are completely random! Whatever the differences within youth culture, the statistical evidence of an interest crossing class boundaries remains impressive. The readership of the music press, for example, whether the *New Musical Express* and *Melody Maker* or *Fab 208*, includes a roughly similar percentage of readers from each class, as does the audience for Radio 1. Age remains a much better indicator of music use than class.[20]

The problem is to explain the differences within a broadly similar pattern of music use, and Murdock misinterprets some of the differences he found. His research, like mine, was based on a survey of school children, young people in a very particular situation. His sample was poor, for example, and in terms of pocket money working-class children are certainly poorer than their middle-class peers – to what extent is their lesser involvement in music a matter of resources? Some of Murdock's distinctions, as he himself suggests, were related to sex rather than class differences, and how should the argument that middle-class pupils lack the freedom of the streets and base their leisure on the home be extended to students? But the central claim of Murdock's argument is that youth cultures get their meaning from their class base rather than from a universal state of adolescence. In the end, criticism must focus on the definition of class involved.

Murdock classified his pupils according to the occupations of their parents. While this is a good indicator of their likely class futures, it does mean that for the children themselves class was defined as a matter of family culture rather than of productive role: their class characteristics were the results of values and attitudes learnt at home and shaped by school, community and mass media; they were not the results of their own roles in production or in the labour process. Murdock's explanation of class differences in music use is in terms of

*Youth and music*                     *51*

how class *values* structure responses to adolescent problems. Murdock brings class into the sociology of youth via the notion of youth sub-cultures: if all young people have a need for status and autonomy, how these needs are expressed and experienced depends on their different class-cultural backgrounds. I want to turn now to sub-cultural explanations of youth music.

*Sub-cultural explanations*

Characteristically, the teds' association with rock'n'roll came to public attention with the outbreak of rock'n'roll riots, disturbances in cinemas featuring rock'n'roll films. In the public mind teds and nastiness merged together in an uneasy blur of primitive rhythms and primitive behaviour. The sub-cultural account of rock takes off from this lead: youth's use of music is related to the behaviour of specific deviant groups. Sub-cultural theorists take teds, for instance, as an example of 'Lumpenproletariat youth'. Their lack of job satisfaction, their 'status frustration', made their leisure important – 'they seek from it the excitement, self-respect and autonomy which are so conspicuously absent from work'. But in their preoccupation with 'toughness, excitement, fate, autonomy and status' the teds were no different from other lower-class adolescents – it was just that their dependence on this culture was more 'intense and comprehensive' and their use of cultural symbols, clothes and music, was thus more jealously defended.[21]

The thrust of the sub-cultural approach is that youth music is a symbol which expresses the underlying leisure values of the group which uses it. The first difficulty with this explanation of rock is that the symbolic objects involved are usually provided by commercial interests rather than generated by the youth groups themselves. If the teds responded to rock'n'roll with passion, it was hardly teddy-boy music by either origin or even style (that connection only developed later with rock'n'roll revival and rocker culture). To interpret music as symbol, it is no good looking at how music is produced; the sociologist must show how youth groups give music its real meaning in the act of consumption, and the mods, the ultimate consumer group, have been taken as the model of a youth sub-culture.

It was the mods who first used music as an exclusive symbol, something with which to distinguish themselves from the conformist young:

They met at the Scene in Ham Yard off Great Windmill Street in London's West End, an all-night club where groups played, but whose main attraction was Guy Stevens' record sessions. Stevens'

*52*                     *The consumption of rock*

collection of obscure black American records was the basis of
mods' musical tastes and a cornerstone of the soul boom of the
mid-sixties. At a time when it was commonplace to hear the
Beatles and hip to listen to Jimmy Reed, John Lee Hooker and
Howlin' Wolf, Stevens was playing James Brown and Otis Redding,
Don Covay, Solomon Burke, the Miracles, the Impressions and
Major Lance.[22]

The mods' sociological image is confusing: on the one hand the
moral-panic-inducing thugs of Margate and rocker-bashing, on the
other hand the pill-popping all-night dancers and all-day consumers
of Carnaby-Street style. Sub-culturalist theories seek to focus this
double image. The description of the frustrated prole, pouring his
needs into leisure, remains, but emphasis is put on the resulting mod
style, a more self-conscious and creative mode of expression than
ted style, more arrogant, narcissistic, cynical and tense. The mods
came on like winners and consumption for them was as much a playground as a last resort; if sociologists have failed to ask the obvious
questions (Why the scooters? Where did the money come from?)
they have been able to make an elaborate reading of the nuances of
mod style.[23]

**But** the second difficulty with sub-cultural accounts of music is
that, as a symbol, it becomes completely subsumed in the much more
general notion of style. This is most obvious in the analysis of the
skinhead sub-culture. They were rough kids again, displaced from
working-class communities and occupations and seeking the
'magical recovery of community' through leisure, but they weren't
much interested in musical expression – ' "Reggae" was important
for only a few months in 1969, but it was soon rejected as "West
Indian music".' This doesn't appear to faze the sub-cultural theorists
one bit, they simply replace music in their analysis with football![24]

Teds, mods and skins are the three teenage groups that have been
examined in the most detail by sub-cultural sociologists. Their findings rest on the theories outlined in the last chapter: these kids'
uses of leisure are understood by reference to their lack of job
satisfaction, their alienation from the community. Music (or football) is a symbolic expression of this dissatisfaction and alienation,
and the particular styles adopted, rock'n'roll, soul, reggae – even
when provided by commerce – can be read for their signs of youthful
'cultural space winning'. By their very nature the members of these
sub-cultures are rarely articulate about their lives but the good
sociologist can extrapolate the true meaning of their activities and
styles.[25]

The trouble with this approach is the narrowness of its focus. In interpreting music as a *symbol* of leisure values, sub-culturalists fail to make sense of it as an *activity*, one enjoyed by the vast number of non-deviant kids. The error is clear in the suggestion that for some young people football is a substitute for music. The only way football could be such a substitute is at the symbolic level of group identity – via badges, heroes, talking-points; it can't be the same as an activity. Skinhead identity may not have been based on musical taste, but that didn't stop skins listening to music and enjoying all the usual music-based activities. Indeed, football-based identity soon became a part of rock as Slade, for example, and even David Cassidy made effective use of football chants and songs.[26]

Sub-cultural theory rests on a false freezing of the youthful world into deviants and the rest. As my Keighley survey made clear, the fact is that kids pass through groups, change identities and play their leisure roles for fun. Observing sociologists are wrong to elevate the most visibly different leisure styles above the less apparent sexual and occupational differences in leisure activities. The exact role of music for these sub-cultures remains unclear and it is worth contrasting them with deviant groups which are truly focused on music.[27]

Jock Young has argued that whereas 'delinquent youth culture' is centred on leisure because its members are marginal to the labour market in terms of skills and opportunities, bohemian youth culture is centred on leisure because its members have deliberately rejected the rewards of work:

> Like the delinquent he focuses his life on leisure, but unlike the former his dissociation is a matter of choice rather than a realistic bowing to the inevitable. Moreover, his disdain for society is of an articulate and ideological nature. He evolves social theories which uphold subterranean values as authentic guides to action, and which attempt to solve the problem of the domination of the ethos of productivity.[28]

Music had a special importance for hippie culture ('pop music is an essential element of the "underground" and a central preoccupation of most adolescent hippie groups') and because of its ideology, hippie rock was more than just hippie music by adoption. In Richard Mills's words, music was given a 'missionary purpose', it could carry hippie values into the heart of the commercial beast, it could spread

> the ubiquitous notion of 'turning on', the sudden intuition, the transcending of rational standards and structured judgements – there was mystical illumination or there was nothing – and the

*54*                            *The consumption of rock*

explicit linking of mental and physical dimensions – to be 'smiling and bopping about and not questioning, to know what it is to be alive'.

In seeking to transform the experience and use of rock music, hippie culture also sought to transform its production: for hippie groups music came out of the community, the distinction between performer and audience was blurred even in the experience of performance – music was an experience of community as well as its expression:

> Pop groups thus held a key position within the culture. They helped minister and uphold that experience of transformation which underlay it, provided the forms and rituals through which its goals and values found expression, and, in the process, established the minimal degree of social and economic organisation necessary to sustain them. All these factors gave them a position of leadership which partly strengthened, and partly itself flowed from, their final role, that of negotiating between the different realities of the hip and the straight.[29]

In the long run this role, as missionaries in the commercial world, proved almost impossible for hippie musicians to sustain. In California, where hippie ideology was most powerful, the violence of the Altamont Festival of 1969 was taken as the final sign that a community could not be based on music use alone – the world of the hip could only be the world of the commercial hip. Nevertheless, in a more politicised form, the hippie argument still inspires many a struggling revolutionary rock band.[30]

My purpose at this stage is not to criticise the hippie ideology of music but to suggest that in sub-cultural theory the hippies' articulate use of rock as a symbol of leisure, an expression of the opposition to the 'ethos of productivity', is taken to be an example of the use of music that is made by all youth sub-cultures. But the hippies really did have an ideology of leisure; their music was created to express a worked-out position. Their position can be directly contrasted to that of, say, the teds.

In his detailed empirical study of teddy boys Fyvel points out that if music is teenagers' 'most vivid link with contemporary culture', for teds it was the only area where they were 'at one' with society: 'tunes are the one subject where you can be sure of getting them to talk'. Fyvel suggests that 'his love for pop music appears to be the chink in the teddy boy's armour of non-participation'. If teds were against hard work and getting on:

## Youth and music 55

Sweat and toil to learn music is one of the few exceptions. A boy willing to devote every day to practice in a band is not derided for his pains. Even in the toughest Ted circles, musical ambition is generally regarded as legitimate.

This echoes Mills's comments on the hippie musician negotiating between the hip and the straight, but the hippie was armed with an ideology, the teddy boy was not: rock'n'roll wasn't a symbol of the teddy boys' independence but of their continued dependence on the world of the teenage consumer.[31]

In my survey of Keighley it was clear that music was important as a symbolic expression of values only for those young people who were rejecting their given class cultures, whether middle-class pupils rejecting academic success or working-class pupils rejecting the street, and the 'hairies' equally rejected the values of commerce. In his study of working-class boys in London Willmott described 'another kind of rebel' than the traditional criminal deviant:

He was alone, playing records by Billie Holiday and Miles Davis. He says of his parents, 'They couldn't understand me in a hundred years. Like most ordinary East End people, their idea of living is to have a steady job and settle down with a nice little wife in a nice little house or flat, doing the same things every day of your life. They think the sorts of thing I do are mad.' What sort of things? 'Well, I might decide to take the day off and go up the park and sit and meditate. Or go round my friend's pad for an all-night session. A group of us drink whisky and smoke tea and talk about what's happiness and things like that.' He says that he and his friends regularly take Purple Hearts too: 'It may seem sinful to some people. But we're just young people who like to enjoy ourselves and forget the Bomb.' He reads Jack Kerouac, Norman Mailer, James Baldwin – 'That's the sort of thing I dig. I suppose I'm really searching.'

Willmott makes the point that such 'rebels' were rare in his sample, but their importance for rock (and rock's importance for them) must not be underestimated, nor can the use of music involved simply be explained as an expression of a middle-class sub-culture. Anyone who grew up in the 1960s knows the importance of such local 'hip' figures, not just in turning us on to blues and politics and poetry, but also in acting as the link between the culturally adventurous of both classes. From this group (particularly from its creatively successful version in art colleges) came the majority of British rock musicians.[32]

Ironically, it is also this group which, excluded from most

*56*                              *The consumption of rock*

sociological accounts of adolescence, most clearly uses music as a
source of autonomy and status. For most young people leisure is not
enjoyed in self-conscious opposition to work but as an aspect of it,
their work and leisure complement each other; only for hippies,
hairies and equivalent groups does it make sense to read rock for
values. Such groups are ideologically based and claim their music as
meaningful; it is crucial to their position that they make music and
don't just consume it in their 'free time'; a contempt for commerce
and for commercial leisure is essential to their mode of rebellion and
differentiates it sharply from the mainstream youth use of music,
whatever deviant styles the latter may adopt. In Keighley's youth
culture rock was important and meaningful *in itself* for only a few
pupils; only for a rebel like Peter was it not just, as it was for most of
his peers, leisure's garnish.

This contrast, between music as the focus of leisure and music as
the accompaniment of leisure, can be made equally by looking at
another kind of leisure 'deviant' – people who are deviant not in the
way they value music, but in the way they consume it. Some such
musical deviants are straightforward fanatics, fans gone to extremes
for Elvis, the Beatles, country music, whatever. In this they are
hardly different from fanatics of other artifacts, whether trains, the
English Civil War or pre-Raphaelite paintings, and are not usually
part of youth culture. Then there are the people who share their peers'
tastes but take them to extremes, for whom membership of a commercially provided fan club is not enough, but whose life revolves
around their idol to the extent of imitation (the Bowie boys who dyed
bits of their hair green), sexual pursuit (groupies) or compulsive
flaunting of their idolatory (the Roller girls).[33]

For such groups the object of attention is a star rather than a genre,
but there are, equally, musical fanatics. Britain has a long tradition
of jazz, blues, soul and other musical freaks – hence fanzines (and
rock critics). Such groups are composed of scholars, interested in
fact and document, functioning less as a group than as a network of
communication, but such purists may meet to play and listen to their
music (as did the Stones and other early sixties blues fans) in their
own clubs, pubs and halls. Britain is scattered with jazz clubs and folk
clubs, with rock'n'roll nights and country evenings. For their participants music is more than a casual accompaniment of leisure, it is
leisure's purpose.[34]

The most interesting of such groups in youth culture is that revolv-
ing around Northern Soul and its life of all-night dancing to obscure
black music. It has been estimated that this scene has 25,000 adher-
ents (I had one in my Keighley sample), many of whose leisure time
is concerned entirely with soul music:

*Youth and music*                                **57**

I can't stand to be with anyone who doesn't like soul. . . .
My whole life centres around soul. . . .
I couldn't imagine going out with a girl who didn't like soul. . . .
I like Black films and I like the life-style that they depict.
Soul has given me so much that me and my girl have contemplated
    adopting a black baby. . . .

The Northern Soul scene draws its members from the same sources
as the non-musical deviant youth groups. It has continuities with
both the mods (in its emphasis on dancing, its use of pills, its soul
cult) and the skinheads (in its self-conscious anti-progressive and pro-
working-class stance) but the differences reveal what a sub-culture
looks like when it's *really* focused on music![35]
In the last chapter I suggested that sociologists of youth, whether
approaching young people as consumers, adolescents or deviants,
end up with a sociology of choice. In looking at the explanations of
youth's use of music we can see some of the difficulties that result
from this focus on choice. While adolescence theorists, for example,
provide a theory of youth's leisure 'needs' they can't account for the
particular forms in which these needs are expressed and satisfied or
explain the undoubted pattern of different youth cultures. The sub-
culturalists do claim to understand such differences, but they explain
them by reference to values: leisure choices are seen as expressions
of leisure values, which can then be related to the vaguely defined
class position which produces such values. But this argument is not
helpful for an understanding of rock. The music is explained as a
symbol but not as an activity, and because leisure groups are frozen
into 'sub-cultures' most young people vanish from the analysis altogether. The sub-culturalists may be able to make sense of the music
of groups engaged in a deliberate value rebellion (though the source
of such rebellion remains unexplained) but for most young people
music just doesn't have such importance as either symbol or activity,
as can be illustrated by comparison with those groups which really
are deviant in their musical consumption.
Most of the pupils in my survey saw their leisure not as a matter of
choice but of opportunity (the commonest response in all youth surveys to the question, 'What is there to do here in your free time?', is
'Nothing!'). Opportunity was defined in very narrow terms. One girl
explained to me where skinheads went at night: there were not many
places besides pubs and youth clubs, and the latter were closing as the
skins started fights and did damage. Anyway, they were boring and
nothing exciting ever did happen unless a fight started. In detail,
there was the Holycroft disco (7p admission); Churchill House disco
(25p, but stopped because of violence); Temperance Hall disco (25p);

*58*                        *The consumption of rock*

Victoria Hall for an occasional dance (25p–50p); and Haworth, Oxenhope and some school youth clubs. Otherwise, two pubs, the Star and the Rodney, and the latter tended to fling kids out for being under age. This girl and her skinhead friends were well aware of the effects of labelling: 'just by being dressed mod style we get blamed without any evidence at all'.

I want to consider leisure opportunities in rather more general terms than this. If we are to understand youth use of music and the particular patterns of leisure involved, if we are to bring class into the analysis of youth culture, then we must look at leisure as a relationship between choice and constraint. In the next chapter I will discuss how the consumption of rock is affected by youth's relation to production.

# Notes and references

1. Rowntree and Lavers, *English life and leisure*, 280, 282. Ch. X has a
   general discussion of dancing as a form of leisure; for case histories
   of young people see pp. 108–21. For post-war sociology of youth see
   Logan and Goldberg, 'Rising eighteen in a London suburb', and note
   the lack of any reference to music in Stewart, 'The leisure activities of
   grammar school children'.
2. See Gillis, 61–6, 128–31, 138–48; Roberts, R., 155–6; *The new survey
   of London life and labour*, vol. IX, 140–61, 195–217, 295–6. For the
   development of dance halls after the First World War see Rust, 89–93.
   For jazz as young music see Leonard, *Jazz and the white Americans*,
   54–5, 68 and Newton, *The jazz scene*, 229–51.
3. See Hopkins, 426, 431–3. For 'Swoonatra' see Pleasants, *The great
   American popular singers*, 182; for teds, Rock and Cohen, 'The teddy
   boy', 289; for dancing, Rust, 117–18; for youth and records, the BBC
   research cited in Belson, *The impact of television*, 38–45; for sociology,
   Venness, *School leavers*, 118 (her research was done in 1956).
4. Abrams showed that teenagers spent £2m annually on records – only
   2% of their total expenditure but 42·5% of the total expenditure on
   records. This was easily the biggest domination of a consumer market
   by teenagers, and more than 25% of Abrams' 16–24 year olds had been
   to a dance at least once in the previous week, compared with 4% for
   the rest of the adult population. For American adolescents and music
   see Coleman, *The adolescent society*, 4, 22. For Britain see Venness –
   she discusses how record and music listening had become a 'regular
   pastime' in the previous decade; Carter, *Home, school and work*, 306;
   Jephcott, *Time of one's own*, 59–66, 69, 91. Willmott's contemporaneous study of adolescent boys in London doesn't have an explicit discussion of the teenage use of music, its presence was taken for granted
   – see Willmott, *Adolescent boys of East London*, e.g., 22.
5. D. White, 'The young workers', *New Society*, 1 June 1972, 460; C. S.
   Smith, 'Adolescence', Smith, M. A., ed., *Leisure and society in
   Britain*, 154. And see Sugarman, 'Involvement in youth culture', and
   Brown and O'Leary, 'Pop music in an English secondary school
   system'.
6. Carrick James Market Research, *National survey among teenagers and
   young adults, aged 11–24*, Nov. 1974. And see the IPC's *Marketing
   Manual*, 1975, Table A.8.15 and BMRB's *Target group index*, 1976, vol.
   34. For Europe see Bontink, ed., *New patterns of musical behaviour*.
   Countries with post-1962/3 youth musics include Finland, Hungary,
   Poland, Denmark, Yugoslavia, Austria, Sweden and Belgium. For

*216*                         *Notes and references*

German youth see UNESCO, *Music and tomorrow's public*, vol. II, pp. 168–179.

7. Jephcott, 59–60.

8. My sample was 105 pupils from one of Keighley's two comprehensive schools and was representative of the school's social and academic mix. In the town as a whole only upper-middle-class children were creamed off to direct-grant or public schools. I also talked to pupils' friends who were at the other comprehensive school or had already started at college and university.

9. In a small survey of teacher trainees in Bradford in 1971 (36 students) Paddy Rogers found that the majority (23) stressed music's importance as a source of relaxation. Only 10 students preferred listening to dancing (most enjoyed both equally), the majority went dancing regularly, and of the 30 who thought pop 'valuable' half saw it as a source of escape and only 12 stressed its 'positive' effects. (private communication)

   An article in *Music Week*, 25 May 1974 ('Record industry backs out of student campaign') suggests that record companies had been over-promoting 'heavy' rock on campuses at the expense of the 'entertainment' music that students really wanted.

10. For a useful survey of the adolescence literature see Smith, M. A. ed. For the emphasis on peer groups see e.g., Coleman, Jephcott and Willmott.

11. C. Fletcher, 'Beats and gangs on Merseyside', Raison, ed., *Youth in New Society*', 158. This is not quite the picture of Liverpool that comes through in Williams, A., *The man who gave the Beatles away* – he suggests that the beat groups complemented the gangs and, if anything, increased their violence.

12. Quoted in Hamblett and Deverson, *Generation X*, 20.

13. 14 year old girl quoted in the West Riding County Council Education Committee's *Schools Bulletin*, July 1971. *Cf.* a contemporary American comment from a junior high school boy: 'freaks always wear Lees, greasers wear Wranglers, and everyone else wears Levis.' – quoted in Alison Lurie, 'The dress code', *New York Review of Books*, 25 Nov. 1976.

14. Quote from a fifth form girl in my Keighley sample.

15. See the pictures of Slade and Faces fans in Gold, ed., *Rock on the road*.

16. Orlando Patterson, 'The dance invasion', *New Society*, 15 Sept. 1966. For a brilliant description of the dance as an institution see G. Mungham, 'Youth in pursuit of itself', Pearson and Mungham, eds. and *cf.* Leigh, *Young people and leisure*, 139.

17. For an early statement of such angst see Ray Gosling, 'Dream Boy', *NLR*, 3, 1960 and *cf.* Jephcott and Leigh.

18. Quote from P. Harrison, 'Growing up ordinary', *New Society*, 18 Sept. 1975, 633.

19. Murdock and Phelps, *Mass media and the secondary school*, and *cf.* G. Murdock and R. McCron: 'Scoobies, skins and contemporary pop', *New Society*, 29 March 1973.

20. For America see J. Robinson and P. Hirsch: 'It's the sound that does

## *Youth and music* 217

it', *Psychology Today*, Oct. 1969, 43 and, for differences by class and race within a student population, Skipper, 'How popular is popular music?'. For the 'randomness' of pop tastes see Corrigan, *Schooling the Smash Street kids* – he found that pupils apparently similar in their class backgrounds and academic abilities but in different schools, had diametrically opposed musical tastes, one group preferring heavy rock, the other traditional pop singers like Tom Jones.

The JICNRS *National Readership Survey* for 1976 reveals the following readership patterns for July 1975–June 1976:

| | Social Group | | | | | | | | | | | |
|---|---|---|---|---|---|---|---|---|---|---|---|---|
| % of group reading | | | | | | | | | | | | |
| | A | | B | | C1 | | C2 | | D | | E | |
| | m | f | m | f | m | f | m | f | m | f | m | f |
| NME | 3 | 3 | 3 | 2 | 5 | 2 | 4 | 2 | 4 | 2 | 2 | 1 |
| MM | 4 | 3 | 4 | 2 | 5 | 2 | 4 | 2 | 4 | 2 | 2 | 1 |
| Sounds | 1 | 1 | 2 | 1 | 2 | 1 | 2 | 1 | 2 | 1 | 1 | – |
| Fab 208 | – | – | – | 1 | – | 1 | – | 1 | – | 1 | – | 1 |

These figures have been roughly the same since 1970.

BBC Audience Research figures suggest that age differences are much more significant than class differences in determining listening habits. Most shows reach similar percentages of middle-class and working-class listeners – the only slight trend being for the day-time strip shows to reach a slightly higher proportion of the working-class audience. There is a pattern of working-class listeners listening to more hours of Radio 1 per week, but not to different programmes and *Top of the Pops* (20·6%/22·0%) and *Old Grey Whistle Test* (2·7%/2·4%) reach very similar proportions of the middle- and working-class audiences. These figures cover October 1976, but this pattern of media use has been observed since the mid-sixties.

For expenditure patterns see BMRB's *Target Group Index*, 1976, vol. 34. Detailed market research conducted for IPC into the readership of the music press suggested that the most significant differences in musical preferences and habits within the general youth market depended on age (15-17-year-olds *vs* 21–24-year-olds) and sex – see Taylor, Nelson and Associates Ltd., *Final Stage of the Research into the Market for 'Pop Music' Magazines*, ms, January 1973.

21. Rock and Cohen, 310–11, 316–17; Jefferson, 'The ted'.
22. Pidgeon, *Rod Stewart and the changing Faces*, 9 and *cf.* Herman, *The Who*, 19–27.
23. For mods as hooligans see P. Barker, 'The Margate offenders', Raison, ed.; for mods as consumers see Wolfe, *The Pump House gang* and Twiggy, *Twiggy*, 16–19; for mods as sub-culture see S. Cohen, *Folk devils and moral panics*, ch. 6 and D. Hebdige, 'The meaning of mod', WPCS, 7, 1975.
24. Quote from *The Paint House*, 12; for skinheads as sub-culture see Clarke, 'The skinheads and the study of youth culture'.

*218*                          *Notes and references*

25. We can expect the current moral panic about punks to produce in due course sub-cultural readings of safety pins, hennaed hair and the Sex Pistols, although one novel feature of the punks is their readiness to be their own sociologists – see the ideology of the punk fanzine, *Sniffin' Glue*, for example.

26. For the football argument see Pete Fowler's stimulating and influential 'Skins Rule', Gillett, ed., *Rock File* and Chris Lightbown's 'Kids, soccer and pop', *New Society*, 11 July 1974. For a shoddy and misleading application of the argument see I. Taylor and D. Wall, 'Beyond the skinheads', Pearson and Mungham, eds. For football symbols entering rock see S. Frith, 'Cum on feel the noize', Gold, ed. Although sub-culturalists claim to be able to read the symbols of youth culture only one has 'read' music with any subtlety or depth – see Willis, *Profane culture* and *cf.* Monod, 'Juvenile gangs in Paris'.

27. For useful critiques of sub-cultural assumptions see G. Murdock and R. McCron, 'Consciousness of class and consciousness of generation' in WPCS, 7, 1975, 203–6 and 'Youth and class: the career of a confusion', Pearson and Mungham, eds., 24–6.

28. Young, *The drug takers*, 147 and *cf.* his 'The hippie solution', Taylor I. and Taylor, L., eds., *Politics and deviance*, 188. For hippie ideology see Neville, *Play power* and S. Hall, 'The hippie: an American moment', Nagel, ed., *Student power*.

29. Mills, *Young outsiders*, 123–41.

30. See, for example, Ian Walker's interview with the Derelicts in *The Leveller*, 2, 1976: 'Music [after the revolution] would play that role of binding people together, enabling them to communicate at a rare and high level: the replacement of individualism by collectivism.'

31. Fyvel, *The insecure offenders*, 71–81, 240.

32. Willmott, 175–6 and *cf.* Newton on jazz fans, 223–5. For a good description of the working-class drop-out coffee-bar hippie see T. O'Brien, 'Young Nick', *New Society*, 17 Feb. 1972, and *cf.* Willis, Nuttall, *Bomb culture*, Rapoport and Rapoport, *Leisure and the family life cycle*, 144–70.

33. See B. Rogers, 'Rock around the years', *S. Telegraph Magazine*, 28 Nov. 1976, on British Elvis fans; A. Bailey, 'Apple scruffs come to dinner', *RS*, 24 Dec. 1970, on Beatles fans; P. Fowler, 'Fighting off the Martians', *LIR*, Oct. 1975, on Bowie and Ferry fans.

34. For 'weird scenes' *cf. MM*'s 1974 series – e.g., 'Nashville cats', 18 May, on country clubs and 'Where Irish eyes are smiling', 1 June, on Irish clubs. For music, as opposed to star, fans see R. Katz, 'Behind a painted smile', *Sounds*, 27 July 1974, on the Tamla Motown fan club, and L. Henshawe, 'When a fan club is not a fan club', *MM*, 27 July 1974.

    A fanzine is a privately published non-profit-making magazine devoted to a particular genre and circulating among that genre's devotees. There are 50–100 such magazines in Britain, covering everything from old time music to punk.

35. Quotes from Northern Soul fans interviewed by Dave Godin for *Black Music*'s special feature on 'The strange world of northern soul', June

## *Music and leisure*                *219*

1974, 13. See also *Black Music* January and November 1975 and Gordon Burns, 'A hard week's night', *Sunday Times Colour Supplement*, 29 Feb. 1976, and *cf.* the brief Southern disco cult in 1975–6 for forties music and dress.

One group with an interesting 'deviant' use of music is young blacks. In material terms black youth are like *lumpenproletariat* white youth, only more so – marginal in terms of their lack of jobs and training and low social status – but their music, reggae, has emerged from the politics and culture of Jamaica and expresses a racial and political consciousness which is neither youthful nor British. The use of reggae by Britain's black youth involves contradictions not explicable in terms of sub-culture, though for an attempt see Hebdige, 'Reggae, rastas and rudies'. For black youth see 'The black youth speak', *Race Today*, April 1975; for black youth and music see Carl Gayle, 'The reggae underground', *Black Music*, July 1974 and C. McGlashan, 'From Babylon to Brixton' in Gold, ed.

# Bibliography of major sources cited in the text

Abrams, Mark, *The teenage consumer*, London 1959

Belson, W.A., *The impact of television*, London 1967

Bontinck, I., ed., *New patterns of musical behaviour*, Vienna 1974

Brown, R.L., and O'Leary, M., 'Pop music in an English secondary school system', *American Behavioural Scientist*, 14, 1971

Carter, M.P., *Home, school and work*, London 1962

Clarke, John, 'The skinheads and the study of youth culture', *CCCS Occasional Papers*, 23, Birmingham University 1973

Cohen, Stan, *Folk devils and moral panics*, London 1973

Coleman, James S., *The adolescent society*, New York 1961

Fyvel, T.R., *The insecure offenders*, London 1963

Gillett, Charlie, ed., *Rock file*, London 1972

Gillis, John R., *Youth and history*, New York 1974

Gold, Mick, ed., *Rock on the road*, London 1976

Hamblett, Charles, and Deverson, Jane, *Generation X*, London 1964

Hebdige, Dick, 'Reggae, rastas and rudies', *CCCS Occasional Paper*, 24, Birmingham University 1974

Herman, Gary, *The Who*, London 1971

Hopkins, Harry, *The new look*, London 1963

Jefferson, Tony, 'The ted: a political resurrection', *CCCS Occasional Paper*, 24, Birmingham University 1973

Jephcott, P., *Time of one's own*, Edinburgh 1967

Leigh, John, *Young people and leisure*, London 1971

Leonard, Neil, *Jazz and the white Americans*, London 1964

Logan, R.F., and Goldberg, E.M., 'Rising eighteen in a London suburb', *Brit. J. Sociology*, 4. 1953

Mills, Richard, *Young outsiders*, London 1973

Monod, Jean, 'Juvenile gangs in Paris', *J. Research in Crime and Delinquency*, 4, 1967

Murdock, Graham, and Phelps, Guy, *Mass media and the secondary school*, London, 1973

Nagel, Julian, ed., *Student Power*, London 1969

Neville, Richard, *Play power*, London 1970

Newton, Francis, *The jazz scene*, London 1961

Nuttall, Jeff, *Bomb culture*, London 1970

Pearson, Geoff, and Mungham, Geoff, eds., *Working-class youth culture*, London 1976

Pidgeon, John, *Rod Stewart and the Changing Faces*, London 1976

Pleasants, Henry, *The great American popular singers*, New York 1974

Raison, T., ed., *Youth in New Society*, London 1966

Rapport, Rhona and Robert, *Leisure and the family life cycle*, London 1975

Roberts, Robert, *The classic slum*, London 1973

Rock, Paul, and Cohen, Stanley, 'The teddy boy', in *The age of affluence, 1951–*

*1964*, eds., Bogdanov, V., and Skidelsky, R., London 1970

Rowntree, B.S., and Lavers, G.R., *English life and leisure*, London 1951

Rust, Francis, *Dance in society*, London 1969

Smith, Cyril S., *Young people at leisure*, Manchester 1967

Smith, Micheal A., *et al.*, eds., *Leisure and society in Britain*, London 1973

Sugarman, Barry, 'Involvement in youth culture, academic achievement and conformity in school', *Brit. J. Sociology*, 18, 1967

Taylor, Ian, and Taylor, Laurie, eds, *Politics and deviance*, London 1973

UNESCO, *Music and tomorrow's public*, ed., E. Helm, Paris 1975

Veness, Thelma, School leavers, London 1962

Williams, Alan, *The man who gave the Beatles away*, London 1975

Willis, Paul, *Profane culture*, London 1978

Willmott, Peter, *Adolescent boys of east London*, London 1969

Wolfe, Tom, *The Pump house gang*, New York 1968

Young, Jock, *The drug takers*, London 1971

# CHAPTER 2

## 'The magic that can set you free': the ideology of folk and the myth of the rock community

Rock, the saying goes, is 'the folk music of our time'. Not from a sociological point of view. If 'folk' describes pre-capitalist modes of music production, rock is, without a doubt, a mass-produced, mass-consumed, commodity. The rock–folk argument, indeed, is not about how music is made, but about how it works: rock is taken to express (or reflect) a way of life; rock is *used* by its listeners as a folk music – it articulates communal values, comments on shared social problems. The argument, in other words, is about subcultures rather than music-making; the question of *how* music comes to represent its listeners is begged. (I develop these arguments further in Frith 1978, pp. 191–202, and, with particular reference to punk rock, in Frith 1980.)

In this article I am not going to answer this question either. My concern is not whether rock is or is not a folk music, but is with the effects of a particular account of popular culture – the ideology of folk – on rock's interpretation of itself. For the rock ideologues of the 1960s – musicians, critics and fans alike – rock 'n' roll's status as a folk music was what differentiated it from routine pop; it was as a folk music that rock could claim a distinctive political and artistic edge. The argument was made, for example, by Jon Landau in his influential role as reviews editor and house theorist of *Rolling Stone*. Rock 'n' roll, he wrote, 'was unmistakeably a folk-music form. Within the confines of the media, these musicians articulated attitudes, styles and feelings that were genuine reflections of their own experience and of the social situation which had helped produce that experience' (Landau 1972, p. 130).

There were two components to the rock–folk argument: firstly, the music was an authentic 'reflection of experience'; secondly, the music reflected the experience of a community – there was no distinction of social experience between performers and audiences. In Landau's words: 'there existed a strong bond between performer and audience, a natural kinship, a sense that the stars weren't being imposed from above but had sprung up from out of our own ranks. We could identify with them without hesitation' (ibid. p. 21).

The cultural claims made for rock by the end of the 1960s (in Carl Belz's *The Story of Rock*, for example) derived from the assertion that the music was the authentic expression of a youth community. But this was not a sociological assertion. The rock claim was that if a song or record or performance had, in itself, the necessary signs of authenticity, then it could be interpreted, in turn, as the sign of a real community – the musical judgement guaranteed the sociological judgement rather than vice versa. There was no need to provide an independent, non-musical description of the rock 'community', nor to describe how such a community came to make music for itself. What was at issue was a set of musical conventions.

Rock ideologues like Jon Landau claimed their music as folk in order to distinguish it from the rest of pop: rock was popular music that was not 'imposed from above', that did not fake emotion. 'Folk', in other words, did not describe musical production but musical values, and these values were derived from a critique of commercialism: the description of folk creation (active, collective, honest) was, in fact, an idealised response to the experience of mass consumption (fragmented, passive, alienating). If, in practice, it is difficult to discover the historical moment at which folk music turned into mass music, we can see how the development of commercial popular music pushed musical scholars into a re-examination of non-commercial popular music. And it was the scholars who first made a sharp distinction between 'folk' and 'pop' songs; the distinction was not always apparent to the people themselves (in the 1930s, for example, song collectors in the US rural South quite often recorded 'authentic' versions of songs learned from the radio a few weeks before).

The ideology of folk that was developed at the end of the nineteenth century reflected not existing musical practices but a nostalgia for how they might have been. The first folk collectors discovered and selected those songs that supported the arguments with which they began. As Sir Hubert Parry put it, folk music 'grew in the heart of the people before they devoted themselves so assiduously to the making of quick returns; and it grew there because it pleased them to make it, and what they made pleased them; and that is the only way good music is ever made' (quoted in Pearsall 1973, p. 208). The argument was that folk music was a music made directly, spontaneously, by the rural communities themselves; it was the music of working people and expressed their communal experience of work. There was no distinction between folk artist and folk audience – this point remained central to A. L. Lloyd's post-war definition of folk: 'the main thing is that the songs are made and sung by men [*sic*] who are identical with their audience in standing, in occupation, in attitude to life, and in daily experience' (Lloyd 1975, p. 346).

Folk songs – 'real, raw, rank and file music', to use Dave Harker's language – are, then, a direct contrast to pop songs – bland, escapist, artificial, produced only for the money. The problem with this argument is that, without a material analysis of how specific songs have actually been made and used, it is circular: an aesthetic judgement that folk songs are more 'authentic' than pop songs is the basis for the contrast between means of production (community creation v. commercial exploitation) which is used to explain why folk songs are more authentic than pop songs. Armed with this ideology it was easy enough for 1960s rock fans to hear their music as more authentic than pop too; to claim that even if their music was commercial, it nevertheless symbolised a community.*

The folk argument entered rock via the American folk 'revival' of the 1940s and 1950s. This too was bound up with rural romanticism, with a search for values and ways which could be opposed to urban commerce and corruption. The post-war New York interest in blues and bluegrass echoed the turn-of-the-century British interest in British rural music. But if Cecil Sharp and his co-collectors were, in a sense, fearful of the urban proletariat and its music, in the USA rural nostalgia was informed by populism. In the radicals' version of folk ideology, folk music was not a source of regret (as 'organic communities' of the past were compared to the class conflicts of the present) but a source of inspiration, a way of countering the debilitating effects of the mass media and enthusing the working class with 'folk consciousness'. In the 1930s the American communist party adopted rural music as the most suitable means of expression for the urban workers; the party's intellectuals became 'people's artists' by singing folk songs dressed in Oakie clothes (see Denisoff 1971).

The American folk revival was based on a contradiction. The 'spontaneous folk creations' it celebrated were the result of musical judgements made by outsiders, by urban performers (the British folk 'tradition' was, similarly, constructed in the first place by bourgeois scholars). What was at issue was a definition of 'the people', and in the 1930s communist party music policy shifted from making 'a *new kind* of song, which will be so identified with the workers that nobody can take it from them', to using 'native folk consciousness and tradition – a treasury of the people's art'. The political problem was how to use music to attract people into an organisation, to develop their class consciousness; and if the tactics changed – from developing a new form of workers' music to using an old form – the cultural position did

---

* The most interesting recent statement of the folk argument is Harker 1980. Harker has done important historical work in clarifying the ideological bases of the British folk movement, but his own account of musical meaning is still derived from this argument.

162    *Simon Frith*

not: 'correct' songs were still correct in as far as they built a sense of class solidarity. The authenticity of music was, despite the folk language, still being judged by its effects rather than its sources. Even Woody Guthrie, in social terms the model performer for 1960s rock-folk, made his music for an urban, educated audience rather than for the rural workers about whom he sang – none of Guthrie's songs was found among the Oakies and Arkies who fled the Dustbowl; their lives were already dominated by the commercial sounds of the radio and phonogram.

The radical tradition of American folk music was primarily the creation of a group of metropolitan, left-wing bohemians: their account of 'the people' was as rooted in myth and their own circumstances as was that of their more respectable, bourgeois, folk predecessors. Nevertheless, it was within the folk movement that musicians kept alive a popular music that was defined, politically and musically, in opposition to commercial pop. American folk music may have ended up, in Denisoff's sour words, as simply 'what was listened to at the informal gatherings and social affairs, at the hootenannies given by radicals', but the conventions of these gatherings were drawn on by rock musicians to justify their own claims of musical authenticity.

'Sing the truth as simply as you can', advised the Almanac Singers, 'and repeat it as many times as it has to be repeated.' The folk emphasis was on lyrics and their plain presentation; the central musical instrument was the voice and it was by reference to vocal conventions that sincerity could be judged. In people's music there were no stars or hits, no distinctions between performers and audiences, and this too was established by musical convention, by the norms of collective performance – the use of repetition and chorus and clichéd melody, the lack of vocal flourish, the restriction of instruments (guitars, piano) to accompaniment. The folk community was the community created by the musical performance itself; folk consciousness was the effect of folk singing. By the end of the 1940s such singing was almost entirely confined to college campuses, but even at these middle-class hootenannies students could get, in Irwin Silber's ringing words, 'a sense of the real America'.

The folk revival in the 1950s revived folk institutions – clubs, coffee houses, festivals – and it was in these settings that the 1960s folk community was defined. It was an ideological community, bound by its attitude to music-making itself. In the folk clubs there was, in theory, no separation of performer and listener – anybody could get up and sing. The aesthetic emphasis was less on technique than on truth, and the musical 'honesty' of performers was measured by what they did not do. As folk singer Jean Ray remembers:

*'The magic that can set you free'*    163

Young people in the sixties who had any touch on the pulse of folk music couldn't be satisfied with going and doing all the external movements of selling a song like pop singers do, with hand movements and all. It became taboo to do that. You were just to stand up straight and deliver your message. No frills. No fancy phoney stuff. (Quoted in Eliot 1979, p. 51)

Marc Eliot suggests that in the mid-sixties the New York folk scene turned its attention from 'the romance of politics to the politics of romance'; this change involved a new argument about the relationship of performer and audience, a new definition of authenticity. In 1965 Phil Ochs told a *Village Voice* interviewer that 'I'm writing to make money. I write about Cuba and Mississippi out of an inner need for expression, not to change the world. The roots of my songs are psychological not political' (quoted in ibid. p. 93).

In the original New York folk scene, folk songs were a form of political propaganda – their aim was to invoke solidarity, to draw listeners into organisations; by the mid-sixties, folk singers were more concerned to express their individual discontent with events than to organise political responses. The criteria of sincerity began to shift from raw signs to marks of artifice; the resulting separation of artist and audience was confirmed by the development of folk-rock. Performers moved from the clubs to the studios; their records began to mean more than their appearances. This did not undercut rock's folk claims. For rock fans, Bob Dylan was a more 'authentic' singer after he went electric than before.

The political version of folk ideology obscured its own contradiction: on the one hand, folk music was an offensive weapon, an educational device, a way of driving bourgeois ideology out of working-class culture; on the other hand, folk expressed the working-class community, and this was the political significance of the folk 'tradition' – in Dave Harker's words, these songs 'must have articulated feelings and values which lay at the heart of working people's culture'. The 'authenticity' of folk songs was, then, judged in two ways: according to their musical value, and according to their class consciousness. Folk ideology equated the two measures, and it was according to this equation that folk performers could claim to represent the people, simultaneously instructing and learning from them. The people's class interests were, in other words, *mediated* through folk songs, and folk singers were a form of musical instrument, there to be played *by* the masses.

This was the position eventually rejected by singers like Bob Dylan and Phil Ochs. As they turned to rock 'n' roll, they denied that they 'represented' anyone but themselves. But the emphasis on truth remained – truth-to-self. 'The authentic folk singer', wrote Alan Lomax

164    *Simon Frith*

in a 1959 issue of *Sing Out!*, has 'to *experience* the feelings that lie behind his art', and it was this notion of authenticity – truth to experience rather than to class or organisation – that the 1960s folk performers retained as they became rock singer–song-writers. They combined the folk conventions of sincerity with literary devices drawn from beat poetry; their 'authenticity' was the result of a combination of soul-baring and poetic vision.

The paradox of rock ideology in the 1960s was that performers' claims to represent a community (unlike the usual 'plastic' pop singers) were supported by the marks of their individuality. The myth of community remains central to all the arguments about rock's cultural significance. Sociologically, rock's account of community has always been unsatisfactory. Reference is usually made (in Belz's book, for example) to the 'community of youth', but as youth is described only in terms of musical tastes, the resulting concept of community is vacuous – we are left only with windy phrases like 'the Woodstock generation'. This is not, in fact, how the myth of community works for popular music. The music (whether folk or pop or rock) is not made *by* a community, but provides particular sorts of communal *experience*. When the folk-rockers individualised the folk concept of authenticity, they changed the political principles of their performances, but they continued to offer an experience of community. This community was defined in terms of taste and sensitivity, rather than in terms of politics and ideology, but, in bringing in emotional and physical devices from rock 'n' roll, a singer like Bob Dylan intensified the effects of his music on his audiences. Such audiences may have come together only to enjoy his music, but such enjoyment came to define what community meant. As Greil Marcus put it, more generally:

We fight our way through the massed and levelled collective taste of the Top 40, just looking for a little something we can call our own. But when we find it and jam the radio to hear it again it isn't just ours – it is a link to thousands of others who are sharing it with us. As a matter of a single song this might mean very little; as culture, as a way of life, you can't beat it. (Marcus 1975, p. 115)

The rock 'community' refers not to an institution, to a set of people, but to a sensation.

The ideology of 1960s rock is still articulated in *Rolling Stone*. Its reviewers still consider whether this artist, this piece of music, has the right sense of rock communion; artistic excellence for *Rolling Stone* still lies in the authentic expression of the old myth. The rock experience – 'the magic that can set you free', to quote the recurrent editorial phrase with which the paper was launched – describes the uplifting adolescent moment against which all subsequent rock 'n' roll experiences are to be judged, but where this moment came from, what it meant, is not examined. It is enough to name it – punk, for example, was eventually welcomed by the paper because it offered the authentic rock 'n' roll *buzz*: the Clash were just like the Stones! These days *Rolling Stone* is a consumer guide for adults. Its readers want to consume a particular sort of experience – the 1960s experience of rock togetherness – and the paper's task is to find the musicians who can provide that experience and to explain the art with which they do it. It is the 'authenticity' of their art that guarantees the experience of rock 'n' roll community.

Rock 'n' roll started as a working-class music not just in terms of its form and content, but also in terms of its use. It was rooted in the music of travelling black and white dance bands, in a style of pleasure that was defined not by the criteria of professional entertainment, but by the urgencies of the proletarian week-end. The rock 'n' roll experience depended on a mutually nourishing relationship between the audience and the musicians, but not on shared lives. Rock 'n' roll singers were not folk, and neither were they just *symbols* of achievement, punk signs of what anyone could do. They were, more importantly, *displaying* their mastery over their lives; they were workers whose efforts were subsumed in excitement and grace, who achieved, in Roland Barthes's terms, 'the sublimation of labour by its magical effacement'. And they were workers whose efforts could be judged; their dancing audiences were not mindless. Rock 'n' roll mastery meant the mastery of movement, speed, abundance, space.

When rock became a recorded form it retained these leisure meanings but in different settings – as party music, driving music, music of the road and the street, music in control of senses and circumstances. The paradox of rock 'n' roll leisure, the effect of its success in intensifying feeling, was that it offered a sense of freedom that was, simultaneously, a sense of rootlessness and estrangement. This was the traditional theme of American popular music, black and white, folk and commercial, from 'ain't it hard to stumble, when you got no place to fall', to 'freedom's just another word for nothing left to lose', and it was focussed in rock 'n' roll by the image of the youth rebel, the loner who cannot settle down because he's got no place to go.

This paradox – leisure as an experience of freedom so intense that it becomes, simultaneously, an experience of loneliness – is rooted in working-class experience of work – in alienation. Leisure has become the only setting for the experience of self, for the exploration of one's own skills and capacities, of the creative possibilities of relations with other people. But this experience is, by its very nature, fleeting, unreal. And rock 'n' roll was American working-class music, the music of a class that has rarely been symbolised as a class. American class experience is mediated through historical images of individual achieve-ment and failure; workers remember their past in terms of mobility rather than solidarity, self-sufficiency rather than socialism. Rock 'n' roll accounts of loneliness and rebellion *celebrated* the conditions that produced them.

The rock 'n' roll experience was an experience of community – teenage community, dance-hall friendships – but this was not really central to it. The music created its community by keeping other people out, and the resulting society was transient – people grew up, tastes changed, real friends and relations were elsewhere, at home and work. Rock 'n' roll made cultural sense not as an experience in itself, but in the context of a specific experience of work and power. When rock 'n' roll became rock in the 1960s it was removed from these contexts and drained of its original significance. Consciousness of class became a matter of self-indulgence; the rock 'n' roll experience was something which could be consumed; culture became commodity.

This is the process, often enough described (by historians of black music, for example), by which a 'folk culture' becomes mass culture. My point is that what has happened is less a change in the ways music is made than in the ways that it is used and interpreted; the move is not from 'folk' to 'mass' (both mystifying terms) but within class cultures (popular music, even when it is commercially made, involves a struggle for meaning – this is obvious in the history of punk, for example, or in the development of reggae). The usual way of analysing the ideological effects of the mass media is in terms of how they transform the collective organisations of working-class culture into the fragmented experiences of passive consumption. But the development of rock as a mass medium involved a different process: fantasies of community (drawn from images of the streets and lower-class city life) were sold to middle-class youth. The irony is that the ideology of folk was central to the resulting ideology of rock.

The rock–folk argument focussed on aesthetics: folk songs *worked* differently from pop songs; the folk experience was 'authentic', rooted in the experience of creation; the pop experience was unauthentic, involved only the act of consumption. In terms of musical practice (rather than scholarship or politics), the task, then, was not to develop the community that would create the right sort of music, but to use the right sort of music to communicate the lost sense of community. The emphasis (and this was obvious even in the radical aspects of the American folk revival) was on developing the appropriate conventions of performance. The use of these conventions enabled students and bohemians in their campuses and clubs to have a 'folk' experience of music without having to have a 'folk' experience of life. 'Community' became something that was created by the music, that described the *musical* experience. This was the argument that became central to the ideology of rock.

Most rock history is written in terms of a struggle between the people (musicians, fans) and the companies; the music develops through cycles of commercial control. But the most interesting question about rock is its class basis: how did rock 'n' roll, the working-class form of the 1950s, get institutionalised as a feature of middle-class, suburban youth culture?

Suburban culture is home-based, organised around family solidarity as parents and children work out their career strategies, commit themselves to sensible work at school, to the constructive use of leisure. Suburban youth learn the connection between effort and reward and live their lives as competitors – success is the measure of their self-worth. Their lives are disciplined and creative, rational and ambitious; they have to be, simultaneously, satisfied and dissatisfied with their lot. In this context, youth cultures, peer groups, are the setting not only for class competition, but also for an escape from the struggle, for irresponsibility, self-indulgence, fantasy. Music is a source of both an emotionally intensified sense of self (as artists are heard to articulate their listeners' own, private fears and feelings) *and* collective excitement, an illicit, immediate sense of solidarity and danger, an un-bourgeois innocence of caution, an uncalculated directness and honesty. Part of the middle-class use of rock, in short, has been as a way into working-class adolescence. What is on offer is the fantasy community of risk – such a use of music has a long history: in the 1920s and 1930s, middle-class adolescents were, for similar reasons, drawn to jazz.

The street culture that fascinates the suburban young is a romanticised version of the culture of working-class peer groups who, pushed around at home, school and work, claim their own territory literally, as they appropriate their material environment – streets and cafés and pubs and parks – from the people who really control it. For these teenagers the sense of class *is* the sense of place: it is their streets which must be defended, it is on the streets that status is won, that 'them' and 'us' are visible. This culture, again, has a long history, stretching back through a hundred years of city gangs. For such groups – more or less organised, more or less criminal, more or less desperate – music is little more than the background sound of activities, 'the small coin of social exchange', in Graham Murdock's words.

In understanding the myth of the rock community we have to understand how the street experience of leisure – dance-hall drunks, doing nothing, tedium and laughs, fighting and male fellow-feeling –

168    *Simon Frith*

has been sentimentalised, distanced, organised into the rock 'n' roll experience. Rock 'n' roll, in other words, has celebrated street culture both for its participants and for its suburban observers, and by the mid-1960s such a celebration meant more to the latter group. American observers at the time were prone to describe such celebrations in religious terms: rock concerts were ceremonies of the *spiritual* communion of youth. But this was to evade the complexity of the relationships between work and play, class and ideology, the fantastic and the real.

If working-class street culture is a romantic idea for 'rebel' suburban kids – a fantasy of spontaneous style and pleasure and excitement – so is the student community a romantic idea for 'rebel' street kids – a fantasy of self-exploration, sexual freedom, art and *Angst*. These are fantasies about leisure, about different ways of life, about different *possibilities* of community; and my final point is this: the importance of the myth of rock community is that it *is* a myth. The sociological task is not to 'expose' this myth or to search for its 'real' foundations, but to explain why it is so important. Just as the ideology of folk tells us little about how folk music was actually made but much about the folk scholars' own needs and fancies, so rock myths 'resolve' real contradictions in class experiences of youth and leisure. The significance of magic is that people believe in it.

### References

Belz, Carl, *The Story of Rock* (New York, 1969).
Denisoff, R. Serge, *Great Day Coming* (Urbana, 1971).
Eliot, Marc, *Death of a Rebel* (New York, 1979).
Frith, Simon, *The Sociology of Rock* (London, 1978).
    'Music for pleasure', *Screen Education*, 34 (1980), pp. 51–61.
Harker, Dave, *One for the Money: Politics and Popular Song* (London, 1980).
Laing, Dave (ed.), *The Electric Muse* (London, 1975).
Landau, Jon, *It's too Late to Stop now* (San Francisco, 1972).
Lloyd, A. L., *Folk Song in England* (London, 1975).
Marcus, Greil, *Mystery Train* (New York, 1975).
Pearsall, Ronald, *Victorian Popular Music* (Newton Abbot, 1973).

# CHAPTER 3

## Rock and Sexuality

From a sociological point of view, the most interesting film released in Britain last year was *Saturday Night Fever.* The film's effects on youth culture will be felt for many months to come: it established John Travolta as a teenybop pin-up, it brought a new self-consciousness to discos and disco dancing, it set Hollywood off on a rush of musical film/record/book packages, it gave rock moguls a new notion of exploitation. Indeed, there has been plenty of discussion of *Saturday Night Fever* as a phenomenon and of the film industry's increasing interest in making movies for the youth market. Even the left press has been concerned to treat the youthful appeal of *Saturday Night Fever* and its successor, *Grease.* But there has been little detailed analysis of how the ideology of these films works and the point of this article is to introduce such an analysis – not by writing about film as such, but by raising some questions about music. The contribution of sound to films' meaning is acknowledged but rarely discussed by film theorists. Colin MacCabe, for example, managed to examine *American Graffiti* in *Screen* without once mentioning its music. Our assumption is that we can't begin to understand the significance of a film like *Saturday Night Fever* without understanding the cultural and aesthetic conventions of its sound- track. It is equally clear to us that rock music must be included in any comprehensive course of media studies, and it is notable that books on rock are appearing in increasing numbers on the lists of educational publishers. The study of rock, whether as an aspect of film or as a form of ideology in itself, raises numerous questions, and in this article we can examine only one of them, but the importance of rock's representations of sexuality shouldn't be underestimated. *Saturday Night Fever,* for example, carries a more com- plex sexual message than is apparent in either its plot or dialogue, and the source of the complexity lies as much in its musical score as in its visual structure.

   Of all the mass media rock is the most explicitly concerned with sexual expression. This reflects its function as a youth cultural form: rock treats the problems of puberty, it draws on and articulates the psychological and physical tensions of adolescence, it accompanies the moment when boys and girls learn their repertoire of public sexual behaviour. If rock's lyrics mostly follow the rules of romance, its musical elements, its sounds and rhythms draw on other conventions of sexual representation, and rock is highly charged emotionally even when its direct concern is non-sexual. It is the ever present background of dancing, dating, courting. 'Rock'n'roll' was originally a synonym for sex and the music has been a cause of moral panic since Elvis Presley first swivelled his hips in public. It has equally been a cause for the advocates of sexual permissiveness – the Sixties counter- culturalists claimed rock as 'liberating', the means by which the young would free themselves from adult hang-ups and repression. For a large section of post-war youth, rock music has been the aesthetic form most closely bound up with their first sexual experiences and difficulties, and to understand rock's relationship to sexuality isn't just an academic exercise – it is a necessary part of understanding how sexual feelings and attitudes are learnt.

Unfortunately, knowing that rock is important is not the same thing as knowing how it is important. The best writers on the subject state the contradictions without resolving them. On the one hand, there is something about rock that is experienced as liberating – in Sheila Rowbotham's words, sixties youth music was 'like a great release after all those super-consolation ballads'. On the other hand, rock has become synonymous with a male-defined sexuality: 'Under my thumb,' sang the Stones, the archetypical rock group, 'stupid girl'. Some feminists have argued that rock is now essentially a male form of expression, that for women to make non-sexist music it is necessary to use sounds, structures and styles that cannot be heard as rock. This raises important questions about form and content, about the effect of male domination on rock's formal qualities as a mode of sexual expression. These are more difficult questions than is sometimes implied. Lyrics are not a sufficient clue to rock's meanings, nor can we deduce rock's sexual message directly from the male control of its conditions of production. Popular music is a complex mode of expression. It involves a combination of sound, rhythm, lyric, performance and image, and the apparently straightforward contrast that can be drawn, for example, between Tammy Wynette's *Stand By Your Man* (reactionary) and Helen Reddy's *I Am Woman* (progressive) works only at the lyrical level. It doesn't do justice to the overall meanings of these records: Tammy Wynette's country strength and confidence seem, musically, more valuable qualities than Helen Reddy's cute, show-biz self-consciousness. We will return to this comparison later.

There are few clues, then, in the existing literature as to *how* rock works sexually. Left accounts of popular music focus either on its political economy or on its use in youth sub-cultures. In the former approach, rock's ideological content is derived from its commodity form, rock is explained as just another product of the mass entertainment industry. But if we confine ourselves to this approach alone, we cannot distinguish between the sexual messages of, say, the Stranglers and Siouxsie and the Banshees. The contrast between the former's offensive attempts to reassert stereotypes of male domination and the latter's challenge to those stereotypes is lost if we treat them simply as equivalent best-selling products of multi-national record companies. The problem of analysing the particular ideological work of a particular piece of music is avoided with the assumption that all commodities have the same effect. In the sub-cultural approach rock's ideological meaning is derived, by contrast, from the culture of its consumers. The immediate difficulty here is that existing accounts of youth sub-cultures describe them as, on the one hand, exclusively male, and, on the other hand, apparently asexual. But even a good culturalist account of rock would be inadequate for our purposes. Rock is not simply a cultural space that its young users can win for their own purposes. Rock, as an ideological and cultural form, has a crucial role to play in the process by which its users constitute their sexuality. It is that process we need to understand.

Our difficulty lies in the ease with which the analysis of rock as an aesthetic form can slip past the comparatively straightforward sociologies of record production and consumption. An obvious indication of this problem is the complex reference to the term 'rock' iself. As rock fans we know what we mean by rock empirically but the descriptive criteria we use are, in fact, diverse and inconsistent. 'Rock' is not just a matter of musical definition. It refers also to an audience (young, white), to a form of production (com-

**4**

mercial), to an artistic ideology (rock has a creative integrity that 'pop' lacks). The result of this confusion is constant argument about whether an act or record is really rock and this is not just a matter of subjective disagreement. Records and artists have contradictory implications in themselves. The meaning of rock is not simply given by its musical form, but is struggled for. As a cultural product, a rock record has many layers of representation. The message of its lyrics may be undercut by its rhythmic or melodic conventions and, anyway, music's meanings don't reach their consumers directly. Rock is mediated by the way its performers are packaged, by the way it is situated as radio and dance music. Rock reaches its public via the 'gatekeepers' of the entertainment industry, who try to determine how people listen to it. The ideology of rock is not just a matter of notes and words.

One of the themes of this paper is that rock operates as both a form of sexual expression and as a form of sexual control. Expression and control are simultaneous aspects of the way rock works; the problem is to explain how rock gives ideological shape to its sexual representations. We reject the notion, central to the ideology of rock as counter-culture, that there is some sort of 'natural' sexuality which rock expresses and the blue meanies repress. Our starting point is that the most important ideological work done by rock is the *construction* of sexuality. We will describe rock's representations of masculinity and femininity and consider the contradictions involved in these representations. Our concern is to relate the effects of rock to its form — as music, as commodity, as culture, as entertainment.

## Masculinity and Rock

Any analysis of the sexuality of rock must begin with the brute social fact that in terms of control and production, rock is a male form. The music business is male run; popular musicians, writers, creators, technicians, engineers and producers are mostly men. Female creative roles are limited and mediated through male notions of female ability. Women musicians who make it are almost always singers; the women in the business who make it are usually in publicity; in both roles success goes with a male-made female image. In general, popular music's images, values and sentiments are male products. Not only do we find men occupying every important role in the rock industry and in effect being responsible for the creation and construction of suitable female images, we also witness in rock the presentation and marketing of masculine styles. And we are offered not one definitive image of masculine sexuality, but a variety of male sexual poses which are most often expressed in terms of stereotypes. One useful way of exploring these is to consider 'cock rock', on the one hand, and 'teenybop', on the other.

By cock rock we mean music making in which performance is an explicit, crude and often aggressive expression of male sexuality — it's the style of rock presentation that links a rock and roller like Elvis Presley to rock stars like Mick Jagger, Roger Daltrey and Robert Plant. The most popular exponents of this form currently are Thin Lizzy — their album *Live and Dangerous* articulates cock rock's values very clearly. Cock rock performers are aggressive, dominating, boastful and constantly seek to remind the audience of their prowess, their control. Their stance is obvious in live shows; male bodies on display, plunging shirts and tight trousers, a visual emphasis on chest hair and genitals — their record sales depend on years of

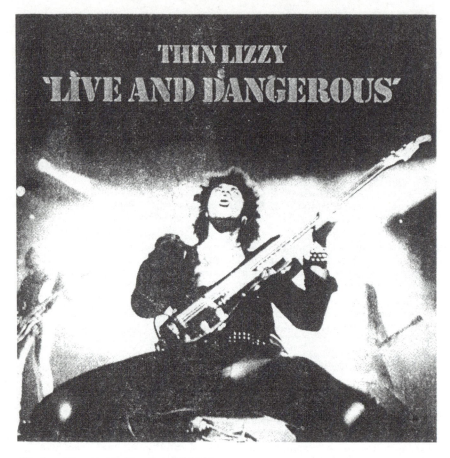

*Cock rock's macho imagery: Thin Lizzy*

such appearances. In America, the mid-west concert belt has become the necessary starting point for cock rock success; in Britain the national popularity of acts like Thin Lizzy is the result of numberless tours of provincial dance halls. Cock rock shows are explicitly about male sexual performance (which may explain why so few girls go to them — the musicians are acting out a sexual iconography which in many ways is unfamiliar, frightening and distasteful to girls who are educated into understanding sex as something nice, soft, loving and private). In these performances mikes and guitars are phallic symbols; the music is loud, rhythmically insistent, built round techniques of arousal and climax; the lyrics are assertive and arrogant, though the exact words are less significant than the vocal styles involved, the shouting and screaming. The cock rock image is the rampant destructive male traveller, smashing hotels and groupies alike. Musically, such rock takes off from the sexual frankness of rhythm and blues but adds a cruder male physicality (hardness, control, virtuosity). Cock rockers' musical skills become synonymous with their sexual skills (hence Jimi Hendrix's simultaneous status as stud and guitar hero). Cock rockers are not bound by the conventions of the song form, but use their instruments to show 'what they've got', to give vent to their macho imagination. These are the men who take to the streets, take risks, live dangerously and, most of all, swagger untrammelled by responsibility, sexual and otherwise. And, what's more, they want to make this clear. Women, in their eyes, are either sexually aggressive and therefore doomed and unhappy, or else sexually repressed and therefore in need of male servicing. It's the woman, whether romanticised or not, who is seen as possessive, after a husband, anti-freedom, the ultimate restriction.

Teenybop, in contrast, is consumed almost exclusively by girls. What they're buying is also a representation of male sexuality (usually in the form of teen idols) but the nature of the image and the version of sexuality on display is quite distinct from that of the cock rocker. The teenybop idol's image is based on self-pity, vulnerability, and need. The image is of the young boy next door: sad, thoughtful, pretty and puppy-like. Lyrically his songs are about being let down and stood up, about loneliness and frustration; musically his form is a pop ballad/soft rock blend; less physical music than cock rock, drawing on older romantic conventions. In teenybop, male sexuality is transformed into a spiritual yearning carrying only hints of sexual interaction (see Les McKeown's soft swaying hips). What is needed is not so much someone to screw as a sensitive and sympathetic soulmate, someone to support and nourish the incompetent male adolescent as he grows up. (See John Travolta's attraction to 'older women'.) If cock rock plays on conventional concepts of male sexuality as rampant, animalistic, superficial, just-for-the-moment, teenybop plays on notions of female sexuality as being serious, diffuse and implying total emotional commitment. In teenybop cults live performance is less significant than pin-ups, posters and television appearances; in teenybop music, women emerge as unreliable, fickle, more selfish than men. It is men who are soft, romantic, easily hurt, loyal and anxious to find a true love who fulfils their definitions of what female sexuality should be about.

The resulting contrast between, say, Thin Lizzy fans and David Soul fans is obvious enough, but our argument is not intended to give a precise account of the rock market. There are overlaps and contradictions, girls put cock rock pin-ups on their bedroom walls and boys buy teenybop records. Likewise there are a whole range of stars who seek to occupy both categories at once — Rod Stewart can come across just as pathetic, puppy-like and maudlin as Donny Osmond, and John Travolta can be mean and nasty, one of the gang. But our cock rock/teenybop comparison does make clear the general point we want to make: masculinity in rock is not determined by one all-embracing definition. Rather, rock offers a framework within which male sexuality can find a range of acceptable, heterosexual expressions. These images of masculinity are predicated on sexual divisions in the appropriation of rock. Thus we have the identity of the male consumer with the rock performer. Rock shows become a collective experience which are, in this respect, reminiscent of football matches and other occasions of male camaraderie — the general atmosphere is sexually exclusive, its euphoria depends on the absence of women. The teenybop performer, by contrast, addresses his female consumer as his object, potentially satisfying his sexual needs and his romantic and emotional demands. The teenybop fan should feel that her idol is addressing himself solely to her, her experience should be as his partner. Elvin Bishop's *Fooled Around*, a hit single from a couple of years ago, captures lyrically the point we're making:

7

'I must have been through about a million girls
I love 'em and leave 'em alone,
I didn't care how much they cried, no sir,
Their tears left me as cold as stone,
But then I fooled around and fell in love . . . '[1]

In rock conventions, the collective notion of fooling around refers explicitly to male experience, falling in love refers to the expectations of girls.

From this perspective, the cock rock/teenybop contrast is clearly something general in rock, applicable to other genres. Male identity with the performer is expressed not only in sexual terms but also in a looser appropriation of rock musicians' dominance and power, confidence and control. It is boys who become interested in rock as music, who become hi-fi experts, who hope to become musicians, technicians or music businessmen. It is boys who form the core of the rock audience, who are intellectually interested in rock, who become rock critics and collectors. (The readership of *Sounds*, *New Musical Express* and *Melody Maker* and the audience for the *Old Grey Whistle Test* are two thirds male; John Peel's radio show listeners are ninety per cent male.) It is boys who experience rock as a collective culture, a shared male world of fellow fans and fellow musicians. The problems facing a woman seeking to enter the rock world as a participant are clear. A girl is supposed to be an individual listener, she is not encouraged to develop the skills and knowledge to become a performer. In sixth form and student culture, just as much as in teenybop music, girls are expected to be passive, as they listen quietly to rock poets, and brood in their bed-sits to Leonard Cohen, Cat Stevens or Jackson Browne. Women, whatever their musical tastes, have little opportunity and get little encouragement to be performers themselves. This is another aspect of rock's sexual ideology of collective male activity and individual female passivity.

### Music, Femininity and Domestic Ideology

Male dominance in the rock business is evident in both the packaging and the musical careers of female rock stars. Even powerful and individual singers like Elkie Brooks can only find success by using the traditional show-biz vocabulary. Indeed, one of the most startling features of the history of British popular music has been the speed with which talented women singers, of all types, from Lulu through Dusty Springfield to Kate Bush, have been turned into family entertainers, become regulars on television variety shows, fallen into slapstick routines and taken their show-biz places as smiling, charming hostesses. Female musicians have rarely been able to make their own musical versions of the oppositional, rebellious hard edges that male rock can embody. Our argument is not that male stars don't experience the same pressures to be bland entertainers, but that female stars have little possibility of resisting such pressures. It may have been necessary for Cliff Richard and Tommy Steele to become all-round entertainers in the 1950s, but one of the consequences of the rise of rock in the 1960s was that mass success was no longer necessarily based on the respectable conventions of show-biz; sexual outrage became an aspect of rock's mass appeal. But for men only. The rise of rock did not extend the opportunities for

1 © Crabshawe Music 1975.

women; notions of a woman's musical place have hardly changed. The one new success route opened to women was to become the singer/songwriter/folkie lady – long haired, pure voiced, self-accompanied on acoustic guitar. But whatever the ability, integrity and toughness of Joan Baez, Judy Collins, Sandy Denny and the others, their musical appeal, the way they were sold, reinforced in rock the qualities traditionally linked with female singers – sensitivity, passivity and sweetness. For women rockers to become hard aggressive performers it was necessary for them, as Jerry Garcia commented on Janis Joplin, to become 'one of the boys'. Some women did make it this way – Grace Slick, Maggie Bell, Christine McVie – but none of them did it without considerable pain, frustration and, in the case of Janis Joplin herself, tragedy.

Perhaps the only way of resisting the pressures pushing women musicians into conventional stereotypes (and stereotyping is an inevitable result of commercialisation) was to do as Joni Mitchell did and avoid prolonged contact with the mass media. Since her success in the '60s, Joni Mitchell has consistently refused to do television appearances, rarely does concerts, turns down interviews with the music press and exerts personal control over the making and production of her records. She, like Joan Armatrading, is rewarded with an 'awkward' reputation and despite their artistic achievements, theirs is not the popular image of the woman musician. For that we have to look at a group like Abba. The boy/girl group is a common entertainment device in both pop and disco music (Coco, the Dooleys, on the one hand, Boney M and Rose Royce on the other), and Abba provide the clearest example of the sexual divisions of labour such groups involve: the men make the music (they write and arrange, play the guitars and keyboards), the women are glamorous (they dress up and sing what they're told, their instruments are their 'natural' voices and bodies). *Abba: the Movie* had a double plot; while a journalist pursued the men in the group, the camera lingered on Anna's bottom – it was the movie's key visual image. In rock, women have little control of their music, their images, their performances; to succeed they have to fit into male grooves. The subordination of women in rock is little different from their subordination in other occupations. As unskilled rock workers, women are a source of cheap labour, a pool of talent from which the successes are chosen more for their appropriate appearance than for their musical talents.

But the problems of women in rock reach much further than those of surviving the business. Oppressive images of women are built into the very foundations of the pop/rock edifice, into its production, its consumption and even into its musical structures. Pop music reaches its public via a variety of gatekeepers – the radio producers of BBC and commercial broadcasting, the television producers of *Top of the Pops* and the *Old Grey Whistle Test,* the film producers of *Saturday Night Fever* and *Grease.* Disc jockeys at discos and dances, writers in music papers and girls' magazines, compete to interpret musical meanings. The Bay City Rollers, for example, were taken by girls' magazines to represent vocally and visually their own persuasive sexual ideology, were heard to articulate the comic strip vocabulary of true love.

Teenage magazines have used pop star images, male and female, to illustrate their romantic fantasies and practical hints since their origin in the '50s. *Jackie,* for example, the highest selling girls' weekly magazine, interprets music for its readers exclusively in terms of romance. The magazine is dependent for its appeal on pop, carrying two or three large pop pin-ups each

9

week, but never actually deals with music.[2] It doesn't review records, never hints that girls could learn an instrument or form a band, should take music seriously as either a hobby or a career. Music is reduced to its stars, to idols' looks and likes. Head and shoulders shots loom out of the centre and back pages, symbols of dreamily smiling male mastery. Nothing else in *Jackie* is allowed such uncluttered space — even the cover girl has to compete for readers' attention with the week's list of features and offers. Pop stars in *Jackie's* account of them, are not just pretty faces. Romance rests on more than good looks; the stars also have 'personality'. Each pin-up uses facial expression and background location to tell readers something about the stars's character — David Essex's pert cheekiness, David Cassidy's crumpled sweetness, Les McKeown's reassuring homeliness. There is an obvious continuity in the visual appeal of teenybop idols, from Elvis Presley to John Travolta — an unformed sensuality, something sulky and unfinished in the mouth and jaw, eyes that are intense but detached. Sexiness, but sexiness that isn't physically rooted, that suggests a dreamy, fantasy fulfilment. These images tell us more about the ideology of female than male sexuality: the plot is revealed in the home settings of *Jackie's* photographs. Teenage music is not, after all, a matter of sex and drugs and carelessness. These stars are just like us, they're rich and successful and love their families, they come from ordinary pasts and have ordinary ambitions — marriage, settling down.

Girls are encouraged from all directions to interpret their sexuality in terms of romance, to give priority to notions of love, feeling, commitment, the moment of bliss. In endorsing these values girls prepare themselves for their lives as wives and mothers, where the same notions take on different labels — sacrifice, service and fidelity. In Sue Sharpe's words:

> 'Women mean love and the home while men stand for work and the external world ... women provide the intimate personal relationships which are not sanctioned in the work organisation ... women are synonymous with softness and tenderness, love and care, something you are glad to come home from work to.'[3]

Music is an important medium for the communication of this ideological message and its influence extends much further than our analysis of teenybop has so far made clear. The BBC's day-time music shows on Radio 1 and 2, for example, are aimed primarily at housewives and their emphasis is consequently on mainstream pop, on romantic ballads, and a lightweight bouncy beat. On these shows there is little new wave music, few of the progressive, heavy, punk or reggae sounds which creep into the playlists once the kids, the students, the male workers, are thought to be back from school and class and job. The BBC's musically interesting programmes are broadcast at night and the weekend, when men can listen, and this programming policy is shared by commercial stations. The recurrent phrase in radio producers' meetings remains: 'we can't really play *that* to housewives!'

Music has a function for women at work too, as Lindsay Cooper has pointed out.[4] Many employees provide piped music or Radio 1 for their female employees — indeed, piped music in a factory is a good indicator of a female workforce — and the service industries in which women work — offices, shops — also tend to have pop as a permanent backdrop. Music, like

2 A 1967 issue of *Petticoat* Magazine went so far as to urge girls to stop buying records and spend the money they saved on clothes, holidays and make-up. 'Borrow records from your boyfriend instead,' the magazine suggested.
3 *Just Like a Girl* Penguin 1976.    4 'Women, Music, Feminism' in *Musics* Oct 1977.

clean and pretty industrial design, is thought to soften the workplace, making it homely and personal, increasing female productivity and lessening female job dissatisfaction. Pop's romantic connotations are not only important for socialising teenagers, they also function to bring the sphere of the personal, the home, into the sphere of the impersonal, the factory. Music feminises the workplace, it provides women workers with aesthetic symbols of their domestic identity, it helps them discount the significance of the boring and futile tasks on which they're actually engaged. If talk, gossip, passing round photos and displaying engagement rings indirectly help women overcome the tedium of their work, then the pop music supplied by management is a direct attempt to foster a feminine culture, in order to deflect women from more threatening collective activities as workers. Women's music at work, as much as girls' music at home, symbolises the world that is 'naturally' theirs, the world of the emotions, of caring, feeling, loving and sacrificing.

There's a feature on Simon Bates's morning Radio 1 show in which listeners send in the stories they attach to particular records. Records are used as aural flashbacks, and they almost always remind Bates's listening women of one of the following moments: when we first met; a holiday romance I'll never forget; when we broke up; when I told him I was pregnant; when we got together again; when he first kissed me/proposed/asked me out. This request spot illustrates with remarkable clarity how closely music is linked with women's emotional lives and how important music is in giving sexual emotions their romantic gloss. The teenybop mode of musical appropriation has a general resonance for the ideology of femininity and domesticity. A similar argument could be made with reference to cock rock and male sexuality, showing how the values and emotions that are taken to be 'naturally' male are articulated in all male-aimed pop music. But music is, in significant respects, less important for male than for female sexual ideology. 'Maleness' gets much of its essential expression in work, manual and intellectual; it isn't, as 'femaleness' is for women, confined to the aesthetic, emotional sphere. Boys can express their sexuality more directly than girls. They are allowed to display physical as well as spiritual desire, to get carried away. The excitement of cock rock is suggestive not of the home and privacy but rather of the boozy togetherness of the boys who are, in Thin Lizzy's classic song, 'back in town'.

Of course male sex is no more 'naturally' wild and uncontrollable than feminine sexuality is passive, meek and sensitive. Both are ideological constructs, but there is a crucial difference in the way the ideologies and the musics work. Cock rock allows for direct physical and psychological expressions of sexuality: pop in contrast is about romance, about female crushes and emotional affairs. Pop songs aimed at the female audience deny or repress sexuality. Their accounts of relationships echo the picture strips in girls' comics, the short stories in women's magazines. The standard plots in all these forms are the same: the 'ordinary' boy who turns out to be the special man, the wolf who must be physically resisted to be spiritually tamed, and so on. Ideologies of love are multi-media products and teenage girls have little choice but to interpret their sexual feelings in terms of romance – few alternative readings are available.[5] This remains true even though we recog-

5 Although it would support this argument, we don't analyse lyrics. This has often been a crude way of assessing musical meaning and, anyway, an excellent study of lyrical messages already exists – T Goddard et al 'Popular Music' in J King and M Stott *Is This Your Life?* Virago 1977.

**11**

nise that pop music is not experienced as an ideological imposition. Music is used by young people for their own expressive purposes and girls, for example, use pop as a weapon against parents, schools and other authorities. At school they cover their books with pop pin-ups, carve their idols' names on their desks, slip out to listen to cassettes or trannies in the toilets. In the youth club, music is a means of distancing girls from official club activities. They use it to detach themselves from their clubs leaders' attempts to make them participate in 'constructive' pursuits. The girls sit round their record players and radios, at home and school and youth clubs, and become un-approachable in their involvement with their music. Music also gives girls the chance to express a collective identity, to go out *en masse,* to take part in activities unacceptable in other spheres. Unlike their brothers, girls have little chance to travel about together. As groups of girls they don't go to football matches, relax in pubs, get publicly drunk. Teenage girls' lives are usually confined to the locality of their homes; they have less money than boys, less free time, less independence of parental control. A live pop con-cert is, then, a landmark among their leisure activities. The Bay City Rollers' shows, for instance, used to give girls a rare opportunity to dress up in a noisy uniform, to enjoy their own version of football hooligan aggression.

These moments of teenybop solidarity are a sharp and necessary con-trast to the usual use of pop records in bedroom culture, as the music to which girls wash their hair, practice make-up and day-dream, as the back-ground music of domestic tasks — babysitting, housework — which girls un-like boys are already expected to do. But the ritual 'resistance' involved in these uses of music is not ideological. Rather, girls' use of teenybop music for their own purposes confirms the musical ideology of femininity. The vision of freedom on which these girls are drawing is a vision of the freedom to be individual wives, mothers, lovers, of the freedom to be glamorous, desirable sex objects for men.[6] For the contradictions involved in popular music's sexuality we have to look elsewhere, to the cock rock side of our ideal type distinction, to rock's ideological break with pop, to its qualities as beat music, its functions for dance.

### Rock contradictions

The audience for rock isn't only boys. If the music tends to treat women as objects, it does, unlike teenybop romance, also acknowledge in its direct physicality that women have sexual urges of their own. In attacking or ignoring conventions of sexual decency, obligation and security, cock rockers do, in some respects, challenge the ways in which those conventions are limiting — on women as well as on men. Women can contrast rock expression to the respectable images they are offered elsewhere — hence the feminist importance of the few female rock stars like Janis Joplin, hence the moral panics about rock's corrupting effects. The rock ideology of freedom from domesticity has an obvious importance for girls, even if it embodies an alternative mode of sexual expression.

There are ambiguities in rock's insistent presentation of men as sex objects. These presentations are unusually direct — no other entertainers flaunt their sexuality at an audience as obviously as rock performers. 'Is there

6 This argument is taken from the detailed analysis of girl culture in A McRobbie 'Working class girls and the culture of femininity' in Womens Studies Group *Women Take Issue* Hutchinson 1978.

anybody here with any Irish in them?' Phil Lynott of Thin Lizzy asks in passing on the *Live and Dangerous* LP, 'Is there any of the girls who would like a little more Irish in them?' Sexual groupies are a more common feature of stars' lives in rock than in other forms of entertainment and cock rock often implies female sexual aggression, intimates that women can be ruthless in the pursuit of *their* sex objects. Numerous cock rock songs – the Stones' for example – express a deep fear of women, and in some cases, like that of the Stranglers, this fear seems pathological, which reflects the fact that the macho stance of cock rockers is as much a fantasy for men as teenybop romance is for women.

Rock may be source and setting for collective forms of male toughness, roughness and noisiness, but when it comes to the individual problems of handling a sexual relationship, the Robert Plant figure is a mythical and unsettling model (in the old dance hall days, jealous provincial boys used to wait outside the dressing room to beat up the visiting stars who had attracted their women). Cock rock presents an ideal world of sex without physical or emotional difficulties, in which all men are attractive and potent and have endless opportunities to prove it. However powerfully expressed, this remains an ideal, ideological world, and the alternative, teenybop mode of masculine vulnerability is, consequently, a complementary source of clues as to how sexuality should be articulated. The imagery of the cheated, unhappy man is central to sophisticated adult-oriented rock and if the immediate object of such performers is female sympathy, girls aren't their only listeners. Even the most macho rockers have in their repertoire some suitably soppy songs with which to celebrate true (lustless) love – listen to the Stones' *Angie* for an example. Rock, in other words, carries messages of male self-doubt and self-pity to accompany its hints of female confidence and aggression. Some of the most interesting rock performers have deliberately used the resulting sexual ambiguities and ironies. We can find in rock the image of the pathetic stud or the salacious boy next door, or, as in Lesley Gore's *You Don't Own Me,* the feminist teenybopper. We can point too at the ambivalent sexuality of David Bowie, Lou Reed and Bryan Ferry, at the camp teenybop styles of Gary Glitter and Suzi Quatro, at the disconcertingly 'macho' performances of a female group like the Runaways. These references to the uses made of rock conventions by individual performers lead us to the question of form: how are the conventions of sexuality we've been discussing embodied in rock?

This is a complex question and all we can do here is point to some of the work that needs to be done before we can answer it adequately. Firstly, then, we need to look at the *history* of rock. We need to investigate how rock'n'roll originally affected youthful presentations of sexuality and how these presentations have changed in rock's subsequent development. Most rock analysts look at the emergence of rock'n'roll as the only event needing explanation. Rock'n'roll's subsequent corruption and 'emasculation' (note the word) are understood as a straightforward effect of the rock business's attempt to control its market or as an aspect of American institutional racism – and so Pat Boone got to make money out of his insipid versions of black tracks. But, from our perspective, the process of 'decline' – the successful creation of teenybop idols like Fabian, the sales shift from crude dance music to well-crafted romantic ballads, the late '50s popularity of sweet black music and girl groups like the Shirelles – must be analysed in equal detail. The decline of rock'n'roll rested on a process of 'feminisation'.

The most interesting sexual aspect of the emergence of British beat in the mid-sixties was its blurring of the by then conventional teenage dis-

**13**

tinction between girls' music – soft ballads – and boys' music – hard line rock'n'roll. There was still a contrast between, say, the Beatles and the Stones – the one a girls' band, the other a boys' band – but it was a contrast not easily maintained. The British sound in general, the Beatles in particular, fused a rough r&b beat with yearning vocal harmonies derived from black and white romantic pop. The resulting music articulated simultaneously the conventions of feminine and masculine sexuality, and the Beatles' own image was ambiguous, neither boys-together aggression nor boy-next-door pathos. This ambiguity was symbolised in Lennon and McCartney's unusual lyrical use of the third person – 'I saw *her* standing there', *'She* loves *you'.* In performance, the Beatles did not make an issue of their own sexual status, did not, despite the screaming girls, treat the audience as their sexual object. The mods from this period turned out to be the most interesting of Britain's post-war youth groups – offering girls a more visible, active and collective role (particularly on the dance floor) than in previous or subsequent groups and allowing boys the vanity, the petulance, the soft sharpness that are usually regarded as sissy. Given this, the most important thing about late sixties rock was not its well discussed, counter-cultural origins, but the way in which it was consolidated as the central form of mass youth music in its cock rock form, as a male form of expression. The 'progressive' music of which everyone expected so much in 1967-68 became, in its popular form, the heavy metal macho style of Led Zeppelin, on the one hand, and the technically facile hi-fi formula of Yes, on the other. If the commercialisation of rock'n'roll in the 1950s was a process of 'feminisation', the commercialisation of rock in the 1960s was a process of 'masculinisation'.

In the seventies, rock's sexual moments have been more particular in their effects but no less difficult to account for. Where did glam and glitter rock come from? Why did youth music suddenly become a means for the expression of sexual ambiguity? Rock was used this way not only by obviously arty performers like Lou Reed and David Bowie, but also by mainstream teenybop packages like the Sweet and by mainstream rockers like Rod Stewart. The most recent issue for debate has been punk's sexual meaning. Punk involved an attack on both romantic and permissive conventions and in their refusal to let their sexuality be constructed as a commodity some punks went as far as to deny their sexuality any significance at all. 'My love lies limp', boasted Mark Perry of Alternative TV. 'What is sex anyway?' asked Johnny Rotten, 'Just thirty seconds of squelching noises.' Punk was the first form of rock not to rest on love songs, and one of its effects has been to allow female voices to be heard that are not often allowed expression on record, stage or radio – shrill, assertive, impure individual voices, the sounds of singers like Poly Styrene, Siouxsie, Fay Fife of the Rezillos, Pauline of Penetration. Punk's female musicians have a strident insistency that is far removed from the appeal of most post-war glamour girls. The historical problem is to explain their commercial success, to account for the punks' interruption of the long-standing rock equation of sex and pleasure.[7]

These questions can only be answered by placing rock in its cultural and ideological context as a form of entertainment, but a second major task for rock analysts is to study the sexual language of its musical roots –

---

7 It is ironic that Tom Robinson's rock expression of gay pleasures and pressures, while made commercially possible by punk's sexual ambiguity, uses an orthodox musical form, many of the conventions of which are drawn from cock rock.

rhythm and blues, soul, country, folk and the rest. The difficulty is to work out the relationship of form and content. Compare, for example, Bob Dylan's and Bob Marley's current use of their supporting women singers. Dylan is a sophisticated rock star, the most significant voice of the music's cultural claims, including its claim to be sexually liberating. His most recent lyrics, at least, reflect a critical self-understanding that isn't obviously sexist. But musically and visually his back-up trio are used only as a source of glamour, their traditional pop use. Marley is an orthodox Rastafarian, subscribes to a belief, an institution, a way of life in which women have as subordinate a place as in any other sexually repressive religion. And yet Marley's I-Threes sing and present themselves with grace and dignity, with independence and power. In general, it seems that soul and country musics, blatantly sexist in their organisation and presentation, in their lyrical themes and concerns, allow their female performers an autonomous musical power that is rarely achieved by women in rock. We have already mentioned the paradoxes of a comparison of Tammy Wynette's *Stand By Your Man* and Helen Reddy's *I Am Woman*. The lyrics of *Stand By Your Man* celebrate women's duty to men, implore women to enjoy subordinating themselves to men's needs — lyrically the song is a ballad of sexual submissiveness. But the female authority of Tammy Wynette's voice involves a knowledge of the world that is in clear contrast to the gooey idealism of Helen Reddy's sound. 'Sometimes it's hard to be a woman,' Tammy Wynette begins, and you can hear that it's hard and you can hear that Tammy Wynette knows why — her voice is a collective one. 'I am woman,' sings Helen Reddy, and what you hear is the voice of an idealised consumer, even if the commodity for consumption in this instance is a packaged version of women's liberation.

This comparison raises the difficult issue of musical realism. It has long been commonplace to contrast folk and pop music by reference to their treatments of 'reality'. Pop music is, in Hayakawa's famous formula, a matter of 'idealisation/frustration/demoralisation'; a folk form like the blues, in contrast, deals with 'the facts of life'.[8] Hayakawa's argument rested on lyrical analysis but the same point is often made in musical terms — it is a rock critical cliché, for example, to compare the 'earthy' instrumentation of rhythm and blues with the 'bland' string arrangements of Tin Pan Alley pop. A L Lloyd rests his assessment of the importance of folk music (contrasted with the 'insubstantial world of the modern commercial hit') on its truth to the experience of its creators. If folk songs contain 'the longing for a better life', their essence is still consolation not escapism:

> 'Generally the folk song makers chose to express their longing by transposing the world on to an imaginative plane, not trying to escape from it, but colouring it with fantasy, turning bitter, even brutal facts of life into something beautiful, tragic, honourable, so that when singer and listeners return to reality at the end of the song, the environment is not changed but they are better fitted to grapple with it.'[9]

Such consolation was derived not just from folk songs' lyrical and aesthetic effects, but also from the collective basis of their creation and performance — women's songs, for example, became a means of sharing the common experience of sexual dependence and betrayal. This argument can be applied

8  S I Hayakawa 'Popular songs vs the facts of life' in B Rosenberg and D M White (eds) *Mass Culture* Free Press 1957.
9  A L Lloyd *Folk Song in England* Paladin 1975 p 170.

**15**

to the realistic elements of a commercial country performance like Tammy
Wynette's. But the problem remains: is musical realism simply a matter of
accurate description and consequent acceptance of 'the way things are', or
can it involve the analysis of appearances, a challenge to 'given' social
forms?

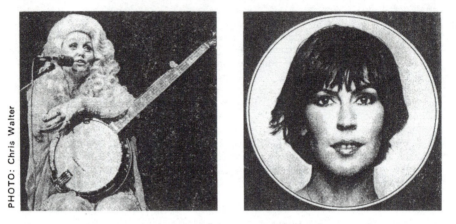

PHOTO: Chris Walter

*Rock's packaging of 'femininity': Dolly Parton, Helen Reddy*

In analysing the sexual effects of rock, a further distinction needs to
be made between rock realism – the use of music to express the experience
of 'real' sexual situations – and rock naturalism – the use of music to
express 'natural' sexuality. An important aspect of rock ideology is the
argument that sexuality is asocial, that is a means of spontaneous physical
expression which is beset on all sides by the social forces of sexual repression. Rhythm, for example, the defining element of rock as a musical genre,
is taken to be naturally sexual. What this means is unclear. What would be
the sexual message of a cock rock dancing class like *Honky Tonk Woman*
if its lyrics were removed? Rock's hard beat may not, itself, speak in terms
of male domination, power or aggression, but the question is whether it says
anything, in itself. Rock critics describe beat as 'earthy' or 'bouncy' or
'sensual' or 'crude', and so reach for the sorts of distinctions we need to
make, but such descriptive terms reflect the fact that rhythmic meaning
comes from a musical and ideological context. We can best illustrate the
complexities of musical sexuality with another comparison – between Kate
Bush's *Feel It* and Millie Jackson's *He Wants to Hear The Words*. Kate Bush
is the English singer/songwriter who became famous with *Wuthering
Heights*. *Feel It* is a track on her debut album *The Kick Inside* and is
lyrically a celebration of sexual pleasure:

> 'After the party, you took me back to your parlour
> A little nervous laughter, locking the door
> My stockings fall on the floor, desperate for more
> Nobody else can share this
> Here comes one and one makes one
> The glorious union, well, it could be love,

**16**

Or it could be just lust but it will be fun
It will be wonderful.'[10]

But, musically, the tracks draws on conventions that are associated not with physical enjoyment but with romantic self-pity. Kate Bush performs the song alone at her piano. She uses the voice of a little girl and sounds too young to have had any sexual experience – the effect is initially titillating, her experience is being described for *our* sexual interest. But both her vocal and her piano lines are disrupted, swooping, unsteady; the song does not have a regular melodic or rhythmic structure, even in the chorus, with its lyrical invocation of sexual urgency. Kate Bush sings the lyrics with an unsettling stress – the words that are emphasised are 'nervous', 'desperate', 'nobody else'. The effect of the performance is to make its listeners voyeurs, but what we are led to consider is not a pair of lovers but an adolescent sexual fantasy. The music contradicts the enjoyment that the lyrics assert. Kate Bush's aesthetic intentions are denied by the musical conventions she uses.

Millie Jackson is a black American musician who has made a career out of the celebration of adult sexual pleasure. Her performances are put together around long risqué raps and her stance, in the words of *Spare Rib*, is somewhere between 'Wages for Housework' and *Cosmopolitan. He Wants To Hear The Words* is a routine song on Millie Jackson's latest LP, *Get It Outcha' System.* She sings the songs to a new lover, 'he' is the man she lives with:

'He wants to hear the words, needs to know that it's for real.
He wants to hear me say that I love him in every way,
Though he knows he's got a hold on me and I will stay.
How can I tell him what I told you last night?'[11]

The song has a pretty tune, a gentle beat, and a delicate string arrangement. It has the conventional sound of an unhappy romantic ballad. But the passivity of this form is contradicted by the self-conscious irony of Millie Jackson's own performance. She gives the corny situation an interest that is not inherent in the song itself. She uses gospel conventions to express direct emotion, she uses her own customary mocking tone of voice to imply sexual need, and the effect is not to make the song's situation seem 'real' (the usual way in which great soul singers are said to transcend banal musical material) but to reverse its meaning. Millie Jackson is so obviously in control of her torn-between-two-lovers life that it is the man she lives with who becomes the figure of pathos – so desperate for deception, so easy to deceive. And Millie Jackson's contempt for her man's dependence on romance becomes, implicitly, a contempt for the song itself, and its own expression of romantic ideology. It is impossible to listen to her performance without hearing it as a 'performance'. Millie Jackson contradicts the sexual meaning of the song's musical form in her very use of it.

### Sexual Expression/Sexual Control

The recurrent theme of this article has been that music is a means of sexual expression and as such is important as a mode of sexual control. Both in its presentation and in its use, rock has confirmed traditional definitions of what constitutes masculinity and femininity, and reinforces their expression in leisure pursuits. The dominant mode of control in popular music (the mode which is clearly embodied in teenybop culture) is the ideology of romance, which is itself the icing on the harsh ideology of domesticity. Romance is the central value of show biz and light entertainment and in as far as pop musicians reach their public through radio, television and the press, they express traditional show biz notions of glamour, femininity and so forth.[12] These media are crucial for establishing the appeal of certain types of pop star (like Tom Jones, Gilbert O'Sullivan, Elton John) and – as we have already argued – they are particularly significant in determining the career possibilities of female musicians.

It was against this bland show business background that rock was, and is, experienced as sexually startling. Rock, since its origins in rock'n'roll, has given youth a more blatant means of sexual expression than is available elsewhere in the mass media and has therefore posed much more difficult problems of sexual control. Rock's rhythmic insistence can be heard as a sexual insistence and girls have always been thought by mass moralists to be especially at risk; the music so obviously denies the concept of feminine respectability. In short, the ideology of youth developed in the 1960s by rock (among other media) had as its sexual component the assumption that a satisfying sexual relationship meant 'spontaneity', 'free expression' and the 'equality of pleasure'. Sex in many ways came to be thought of as *best* experienced outside the restrictive sphere of marriage, with all its notions of true love and eternal monogamy. The point is, however, that this was a male defined principle and at worst simply meant a greater emphasis on male sexual freedom. Rock never was about unrestricted, unconfined sexuality. Its expression may not have been controlled through the domestic ideology basic to pop as entertainment, but it has had its own mode of control, a mode which is clearly embodied in cock rock and which can be related to the general ideology of permissiveness that emerged in the '60s, to the 'liberated' emphasis on everyone's right to sexual choice, opportunity and gratification.

One of the most important activities to analyse if we're going to understand how sexual ideology works is dancing. The dance floor is the most public setting for music as sexual expression, and it is the place where pop and rock conventions overlap. For teenybop girls music is for dancing, and rock, too, for all its delusions of male grandeur, is still essentially a dance form. Girls have always flocked to dance halls and their reasons haven't just been to find a husband: dance is the one leisure activity in which girls and young women play a dominant role. Dancing for them is creative and physically satisfying. But more than this dancing is also a socially sanctioned sexual activity – at least it becomes so when the boys, confident with booze, leave the bar and the corners to look for a partner from the mass of dancing girls. One function of dance as entertainment, from Salome to Pan's People, has been to arouse men with female display. That is not a function of most contemporary youth dancing, though. This remains an aspect of girls' own pleasure, even in the cattle market context of a provincial dance hall. The girls are still concerned to attract the lurking boys, but through their clothes, make-up and appearance – not through their dancing. This is equally true of boys' dances – their energy and agility is not being displayed to draw girls' attention and the most dedicated young dancers in Britain, the Northern soul fans, are completely self absorbed. Indeed Legs and Co's weekly attempts on *Top of the Pops* to impose 'dance-as-sexual-come-on' on current

12 For analysis of these values see R Dyer *Light Entertainment* BFI 1973.

**18**

dance music is embarrassing in its misunderstanding.

It is far from this perspective that we can begin to make sense of *Saturday Night Fever* as a musical. Ultimately it is not really a disco film. Its power is diluted by its pop elements – Travolta as teen idol, the love interest; the film closes on a Bee Gees ballad *How Deep is My Love* which could have been written at any time in the last fifty years. Nevertheless, there are moments when *Saturday Night Fever* is an accurate and revealing celebration of disco values. Take the rest of the Bee Gee soundtrack, which is in itself asexual. 'I'm a woman's man', they sing in *Stayin' Alive,* but they're singing it in falsetto harmonies, urgently but without passion, to a military beat and strummed impersonal strings. These rhythms are controlled electronically and no human urges; no hints of passion, get through. This is the disco convention: synthesisers and drum machines, robotic rhythms and disinterested vocals. The choreography of *Saturday Night Fever* is mostly clumsy. It follows old Hollywood musical rules, using cheerful conventions that don't make sense of the monotony of disco rhythms. Travolta himself dances them just right, though. He's not an inspired dancer by the film's own choreographic criteria, but he is a committed one – from the opening shots of his strut through the streets, Travolta's gaze on himself never falters. In the film's best dance sequence, the Bee Gees' *Night Fever* becomes the backing track for a crowd of isolated individuals. The alienation involved is so intense that the problem of expression and control is dissolved – the essence of disco sexual expression is complete control. Whatever happens John Travolta isn't going to let himself go. Disco music expresses a sexuality which is cool, restrained and understated. The social relations are traditional: the girls still dream of disco romance, while the boys weigh up the chances of a quick screw – but on the dance floors these concerns aren't evident. Narcissus rules.

The concept of narcissism, like that of realism, raises more difficult questions than we can answer here, but we do need to make one concluding point: rock's sexual effect is not just on the construction of femininity and masculinity. Rock also contributes to the more diffuse process of the sexualisation of leisure. The capitalist mode of production rests on a double distinction between work and pleasure, between work and home. The alienation of the worker from the means of production means that the satisfaction of his or her needs becomes focused on *leisure* and on the *family.* Under capitalism, sexual expression is constituted as an individual leisure need – compare this with pre-capitalist modes of production, in which sexual expression is an aspect of a collective relationship with nature. This has numerous consequences – the exchange of sex as a commodity, the exchange of commodities as sex – and means that we have to refer mass entertainment (films as well as music) to a theory of leisure as well as to a theory of ideology.

In writing this article we have been conscious of our lack of an adequate theory of leisure. Underlying our analysis of rock and sexuality have been some nagging questions. What would non-sexist music sound like? Can rock be non-sexist? How can we counter rock's dominant sexual messages? These issues aren't purely ideological, matters of rock criticism. The sexual meaning of rock can't be read off independently of the sexual meaning of rock consumption, and the sexual meaning of rock consumption derives from the capitalist organisation of production. So far we have described the ways in which rock constitutes sexuality for its listeners. Our last point is that sexuality is constituted in the very act of consumption.

**19**

# CHAPTER 4

## AFTERTHOUGHTS

○ ▲ ○ ▲ ○ ▲ ○

There was, it seems, a moment last summer (my source is a baffled Australian tourist) when the only pop stars left in Madame Tussaud's were David Bowie and Boy George (Michael Jackson was added later). "Gender bending" had got its final accolade; Britain's peculiar contribution to Western pop music was preserved, appropriately, in wax.

The Australians weren't the only people baffled. For more than a decade now American youth magazines like *Creem* have been filled with anxious readers' defenses of rock 'n' roll masculinity, and as a traveling rock critic last year I was repeatedly asked to explain Culture Club. I couldn't usually give much of an answer, just reply that the sexiest performer I'd seen was, in fact, a boy in Depeche Mode, a dyed blonde in mini-skirt and skimpy top. His shoulder straps kept slipping, leaving me, a "heterosexual" man, breathlessly hoping throughout the show to get a glimpse of his breasts.

In general, 1984 was a playful pop year. It began with Annie Lennox's appearance on the U.S. Grammy Awards Show, not with her usual close-cropped unisex look but in full drag, as a convincing Elvis Presley. It ended with the British record biz awards. Holly Johnson opened the envelope for Prince: "Oh yes, I've had telephone sex with him!" A huge bodyguard rose up (I thought he was going to thump Holly) and cleared a path for the little master, who walked daintily behind. Prince sings about incest, oral sex, pornography, obsessional lust, and masturbation.

Otherwise it was Frankie Goes to Hollywood's year. They made records about sexuality: Welcome to the Pleasure Dome! Their triumph was "Relax," a huge-selling single that was banned by the BBC for "sexual offensiveness," but the importance of the Frankie story wasn't its outrage but its coziness. Their very success made them part of the Radio 1 pop family—by the end of the year, Mike Read, the DJ who'd initiated the ban on "Relax," was the voice-over on Frankie's TV commercials. They had become family entertainment. What did it mean?

In 1978 Angela McRobbie and I wrote an article titled "Rock and Sexuality" for *Screen Education* (which is included in the present volume). It was not a very profound piece but it was, surprisingly, a "pioneering" attempt to treat rock's sexual messages analytically. It was reprinted in an Open University reader and is, to our embarrassment, still regularly cited. To our embarrassment because the piece was a jumble of good and bad arguments. We confused issues of sex and issues of gender; we never decided whether sexuality was a social fact or a social discourse.

Our aim was to counter the common assumption that rock 'n' roll somehow liberated sexual expression; we wanted to pick open terms like "raunchy," to challenge rock naturalism. Rock, we suggested, works with conventions of masculinity and feminity that situate both performers and audiences along clear gender lines—males as active participants, females as passive consumers. Musically, the distinction is marked by the contrast between "cock rock" and "teenybop."

In terms of who controls and consumes music, our points still seem valid. For all the current celebrations of the postpunk, postmodernist condition, teenage courtship rituals have changed remarkably little since the 1950s, and pop still plays much the same part in the organization of adolescent gender roles. We described a pattern of power in the music industry, men in charge, that hasn't altered since. Punk did have an effect on images of sex and romance, but it did little to improve women's career opportunities in or out of show biz. The most important female stars—Madonna, Cyndi Lauper, Tina Turner, Sade—are still important because of their complex (and contradictory) relationships to femininity. Male and female sexuality alike are still referred to male desires; if homosexual, bisexual, and asexual men can now use their confusions (and zest) as a source of pop success, lesbianism remains a secret.

And this is where the problems of our original piece start: our account of how music carries sexual meaning now seems awfully dated. We rejected rock naturalism but we retained the suggestion that sexuality has some sort of autonomous form which is expressed or controlled by cultural practice.

We were writing, ironically enough, just as the fashion in pop cultural analysis became do-it-yourself structuralism, and critics were quick to point out our "essentialist" view of sex. We were reminded that "cultural pro-

duction occurs always in relation to ideology and not to the 'real world' ";
we were instructed that rock is not about something other than itself—
sexuality—but is a "signifying practice" through which a particular "discourse of sexuality" is constituted. The task of criticism, in short, is not to
show how performers articulate a predefined ideology, but to trace the way
sexuality is constructed by the performing conventions themselves, by the
responses they compel listeners to make.

Take Frankie's "Relax." Everyone knew this was a "sexy" record, sexy
in a way most records aren't, but nobody could quite say why, as the BBC
found, to its discomfort, when it tried to explain the "Relax" ban. Sound
as such isn't offensive—BBC bannings always refer to lyrics. But the key
word in "Relax" was the innocent "come," and, in the end, the head of
Radio 1 had to refer his decision to what the group said about the record
in interviews, how they put pictures to it on the video. The record was
offensive for what it *represented*.

The irony of this is that a "deconstructive" reading of "Relax" reveals a
commonplace account of desire (which is why Frankie so quickly found
their place in the British pop establishment). "Relax" is a naughty record,
a singalong party pooper from the tradition that brought us Gary Glitter's
"Do You Wanna Touch Me" and Dave Dee, Dozy, Beaky, Mick, and Tich's
"Bend It." The original "Relax" video (which, seen on *The Tube* by Trevor
Horn, led to Frankie's ZTT contract) had a limited budget, crude camera
angles, and a tacky SM imagery that was much more unsettling than ZTT's
big-budget, snickering lust.

The ZTT "Relax" was a knowing record not just as a production number
but also as a marketing exercise—Frankie were the first pop group to be
sold by a huckster, Paul Morley, inspired by French critics Barthes and
Foucault. And Morley was, in turn, the child of a particular pop age. In the
1960s, when value judgments about music rested on notions of authenticity,
musicians were respected for their sexual honesty. Built into the original
rock aesthetic was the idea that sexual feelings/preferences/desires/anxieties
were either expressed (a good thing) or concealed (a bad thing). Sexuality
was either spoken out—lustily, painfully—or made false by pop's treacly,
romantic norms. The John Lennon story is the most complex example of
this opposition of romance and reality: having rejected pop's romantic lies,
Lennon could only authenticate his love of Yoko Ono by public accounts
of their sex life. And it's instructive too to remember that the Rolling Stones,
who now sound ridiculously camp, were once honored for their truthfulness
in revealing hidden, unrespectable desires.

Since David Bowie and early 1970s glam rock, the aesthetics of British
popular music have changed. Pop stars became valuable for their plasticity
and so their sexuality too became a matter of artifice and play, self-invention

and self-deceit. As rock entered its modernist, formalist stage, punk and disco became they key codes. The Bowie / Alice Cooper / Donna Summer / Malcolm McLaren / Blondie lessons in star-making were learned by everyone. These days, indeed, heavy metal bands, cock rockers writ large, are the most elaborately made-up groups of all.

Put together glam/punk/disco dressing up with the history of British youth posing (and, as Jon Savage has pointed out, every style, from teds to new romantics, took inspiration from the gay underworld), and you get a sociological explanation for Boy George. The general implications for rock and sexuality are, though, less clear. Sociologists themselves seem still wedded to the misconception that boys' concern for fashion somehow "feminizes" them (and it's hard not to assume that skinheads are more "masculine" than their more fancily dressed peers, even in this age of football terrace "casuals"). Rock critics, equally, still draw an instinctive line between the "natural" sexuality of rock tradition and the "artificial" sexuality of the gender benders. This has become obvious in 1985's New Authenticity movement (and the rise of Bruce Springsteen as a popular icon). Part of the appeal of the new generation of guitar/pub/roots bands (and the musicians are almost all male) is their restatement of old rock 'n' roll truths of sex and gender—rutting, romantic men, mysterious, deceptive women.

Such nostalgia can't undo the changes the 1970s made. The best evidence I know for this is Fred and Judy Vermorel's remarkable book, *Starlust*, "the secret fantasies of fans." These obsessive, devotional voices supply the missing strand in accounts of rock and sexuality: the consumer view.

The most misleading of our original arguments was the distinction we made between male activity and female passivity when, in fact, consumption is as important to the sexual significance of pop as production. Teenybop culture, for example, is as much made by the girls who buy the records and magazines as by the boys who play the music and pose for the pinups, and once we start asking how pop produces pleasure, then notions of passivity/ activity cease to make much sense. There's pleasure in being fucked as well as in fucking, and how these pleasures relate to gender is the question at issue. What's obvious in the Vermorels' book is that fan fantasies (however masochistic) are a form of vengeance—in dreams we control the stars who in our fandom seem to control us. What's equally apparent is that these private games with public faces are for many fans, male and female, a way of making sense of their own sexuality.

Pop stars' sexual games have changed the rock and sexuality questions. What is interesting now is not how the objects of desire are made and sold— as pinups, heroines, stars—but how sexual subjectivity works, how we use popular music and imagery to understand what it means to have desires, to be desirable. The most important effect of gender bending was to focus the problem of sexuality onto males. In pop, the question became, unusually, what do men want? And as masculinity became a packaging problem, then so did masculine desire—whether this was resolved by Boy George's espousal of chastity, by the careful shot of Marilyn's hairy chest during his drag appearance on *Top of the Pops*, or by the record company instructions to the director of Bronski Beat's first video: he had to make a promo clip that would be, simultaneously, obviously gay in Britain, obviously straight in the United States. In its attempt to make normal such "abnormal" men, the pop process simply drew attention to the fragility of sexuality itself.

Part of the fun of pop lies in this tension between reality and fakery, between experience and expression. *Smash Hits* became Britain's most successful music magazine precisely because of the delight it takes in the collision of pop star myth and mundaneness. Its editors know that pop's sexual come-on lies in the way stars tantalize us with the suggestion that we can get to know them as they *really* are (all those interviews). All fans dream of casual intimacy with their idols (I thus count Dylan, Jagger, and John Lennon among my friends), and even the most torrid sexual fantasy rests on the assumption that to fuck a star is to get to know them most intimately—their sexuality and reality are equated (an equation we make in everyday life too).

In the Vermorels' book the key term is "possession." Fans want to possess their idols just as they feel possessed by them. In material terms this comes out as manic consumer fetishism: every sight and sound of the star is collected, stored, inspected (and the replay button on the VCR adds a new dimension to what can be lovingly yours, again and again and again). In fantasy terms possession is, by its nature, erotic.

Pop effects are usually explained in terms of identity—the key words in most pop songs are "I" and "you," and in "Rock and Sexuality" we suggested that, for the most part, boys identify with the performing "I," girls with the addressed "you." But once we start looking at pop genres in detail, the play of identity and address becomes rather more complicated. Whether in the teenybop education of desire, sixth-form miserabilism (from Leonard Cohen to the Smiths), the Springsteenian community or torch singing, the best records (the ones that give most pleasure) are the ones that allow an ambiguity of response, letting us be both subject and object of the singers' needs (regardless of our or their gender).

And what's crucial to this, of course, is the grain of the voice, the articulation of sexuality, the body, through its timbre, texture, and pulse. Great voices, the ones that make us fans, are distinctive sounds that seem to hold in perfect balance words, rhythm, and personality. (One of the effects of video promotion has been a displacement of the pop voice—Simon LeBon simply isn't as evocative a singer as, say, Cliff Richard. On video, music can be mediated through the body directly; sexual representations are taken from established film codes like pornography and advertisement.)

Most pop songs are love songs but the critical problem is not, as I once thought, to contrast love as show-biz cliché (or romantic ideology) to real life, but to find out first what love is meant to mean. Obsession? Pain? Beautiful feelings? Power? Love songs give private desires a public language, which is why we can use them (and our uses are not necessarily gender divided).

The Vermorels show how much resentment there is in fans' feelings for their stars. Pop stars demand our attention and use their power (the weight of their public presence) to keep it. And the more their songs mean to us as private messages the more we can be unsettled by their public display. The voyeurism involved in pop concerts works both ways; it's not just the *stars'* emotions on show. The power struggle between stars and fans is what gives concerts their sexual charge.

In *Adam Bede*, George Eliot writes of her teenage heroine: "Hetty had never read a novel: how then could she find a shape for her expectations?" Nowadays our expectations are shaped by other media than novels, by film and television fictions, by pop stars and pop songs. Popular culture has always meant putting together "a people" rather than simply reflecting or expressing them, and the popularity of popular singers depends on their emotional force, their ability to build a mass following out of intensely personal desires. There's a way of reading pop history, then, that is profoundly depressing. Who, except for a Barry Manilow fan, could be heartened by his effect on his followers? But what's involved here is not just the appropriation of people's fantasy lives by some very silly love songs (and some very hackneyed porn imagery). The *Starlust* fantasies also express a kind of sexual utopianism, a dream world in which care and passion, abandon and affection can coexist.

What amazes me about pop history is how little the fantasies it has put into play have impinged on everyday life, how few demands they've made of it. The sixties, for all their bad press now, remain important, therefore, as an expression of hedonistic greed—which is why Frankie Goes to Hollywood videos returned, in the end, to hippie imagery, why Paul Morley remains caught on the cusp of provincial bohemianism and metropolitan poise. For him, as for many of us, Patti Smith was the key to the link between modernism and postmodernism, punk and beat, sexual liberation and sexual play. As children now of Barthes and Bowie rather than Marx and Coca-Cola, we may understand the discourse of sexuality better than we did in the 1960s, but the coordination of theory and practice seems as difficult as ever.

# CHAPTER 5

# FORMALISM, REALISM AND LEISURE
The case of punk [1980]

THE RECURRING PROBLEM for cultural theorists is to relate general accounts of ideology to the structures of particular media: it is difficult, for example, to find much in studies of film or television that seems directly applicable to an assessment of the cultural significance of popular music. In this [chapter] I want to suggest that the formalism versus realism debate in film studies is relevant to the analysis of pop music, but that in looking at pop in this way we come up against a neglected concept, leisure, which is, in turn, important for the analysis of other media.

The question common to studies of all media — and at the heart of the formalism/realism dispute — concerns ideology. How do different media work ideologically? What are their ideological effects and how are they achieved? At issue here is the concept of signification: how do different media organize the meanings with which and on which they work?

'Realist' theories assume that media operate with some degree of transparency: media images represent reality as if through a window or in a mirror; they are ideological to the degree that they are false. This can be measured against non-ideological representations, against experience. The argument is common in the sociology of television: news programmes are examined for bias, for false descriptions (of industrial conflict, for example); light entertainment is examined for stereotypes, for false images (of women, blacks and so forth). The political question is posed in terms of why media distort reality, and the answer is found not in media forms (which are examined only to see how distortion works) but in their controllers. Television news is bad because it is controlled by bad people, people who, for whatever reason (professionalism, political interest) have an ideological axe to grind.

SIMON FRITH

There are different degrees of control – from straight censorship to the vague 'feel' that producers have for 'good television' – but all have the same ideological effect: the reproduction of a false account of how the capitalist world works. The way to change this media message is to seize the technical means of message production, to take over the machines. Ideology is a problem of content and control; the media simply communicate the knowledge that is fed into them.

'Formalist' theories concentrate, in contrast, on the formal means of signification. Their assumption is that media images don't reflect or copy reality but construct it. Media forms are structures of meaning which bind us to an ideological account of the world; the very notion that we can judge such accounts against experience is 'an ideological effect of the realist discourse'. This approach is common in film studies: films are read not as distorted pictures of an independent reality, but as complex constructions of meaning which have 'a reality effect' – which makes us read them as if they were distorted pictures of an independent reality. The form has the same ideological effect whoever owns it. The political problem thus becomes not how to control a neutral process of production but how to read an ideological structure of signification; it is a question not of access, but of meaning. The ideological effect rests on the relationship between media texts and their readers.

## The problem of pop

I have given a deliberately crude account of a familiar debate in order to emphasise the problems of applying its terms (routine, in more sophisticated forms, in discussions of literature, film, television, the press) to music. There are obvious difficulties, for example, in describing musical texts in semiological terms: the theories of representation that film critics have taken from literary criticism aren't immediately available to music critics unless we reduce music to songs and songs to words. What does it mean to call a piece of music a 'classic realist text'? And, precisely because the content of music is not obvious, the question of the control of music is more confused than in, say, the politics of television. The state does seek to regulate musical communication – records are banned from radio, groups are banned from town halls – but this is a limited form of control (*Anarchy in the UK* was still a best seller) and, anyway, offence is almost always taken at the words involved. The Gang of Four, for example, were told to change the word 'rubbers' (contraceptives – a traditionally sensitive product for the BBC) to 'rubbish' in order to perform *At Home He's A Tourist* on *Top of the Pops*; the programme's producer had no other way of pinning down the subversiveness of the group's music.

It is difficult, then, to say how musical texts mean or represent, and it is difficult to isolate structures of musical creation or control. (Who owns

FORMALISM, REALISM AND LEISURE

the means of music making – the musicians? their record companies? broadcasters?) Music critics analyse pop not in terms of form and content but in terms of production and consumption: the argument is either that the ideological meaning of music lies in the way that it is commercially produced, in its commodity form; or that consumers create their own meanings out of the commodities on offer. Neither of these arguments is used in film and television studies, but the resulting disagreements do refer back to the aesthetic debates in Germany in the 1930s – the debates not about art and modernism, but about the mass media, about the political significance of cultural goods bought and sold in the market [see Bloch *et al*. 1977: 100–141].

The most convincing critique of mass culture is still that developed by the Frankfurt School. Adorno's was the original argument that the production of music as a commodity determines its cultural quality, that the standardisation of music is the source of its cultural effect. This subjection of creativity to commodity form (to 'capital discipline' in Horkheimer's words) was made possible, according to Adorno, by the technology of mass production, and he explained the popularity of mass music in psychological terms: the pleasure of mass culture is the pleasure of a particular kind of consumption – a passive, endlessly repeated confirmation of the world-as-it-is. The pleasure of art, in contrast, is the pleasure of imagination and involves an engagement with the world-as-it-could-be. This is a version of formalism. Adorno argued that the way a cultural text is produced (as a commodity) determines its significance. In particular, mass texts do their ideological work through their construction of an illusion of reality. Consumers 'experience' mass art as if they were grasping something for themselves but there is, in fact, no individual way into the construction of mass meaning. Subjectivity, in this context, means nothing more than market choice, and 'objectivity, the ability to evaluate mass culture, means nothing more than a mass of similar market choices.

The weakness of the argument lies in its account of consumption, its reduction of a complex social process to a psychological effect. Walter Benjamin's contrasting celebration of mechanical reproduction rested on the argument that because the artistic authority of cultural goods had been broken, their significance had become a matter of political dispute in which consumers did have a say: in the community of mass consumption everyone is an expert. The ideological significance of mass culture is determined, in other words, in the process of consumption itself. The grasping of particular works by particular audiences was, for Benjamin, a political rather than a psychological event; how such works got to the market was of less significance. Benjamin tended to treat the means of mass communication in technological terms, as ideologically neutral.

Critical accounts of popular music still depend on the Adorno/Benjamin positions. Out of Adorno have come, however crudely, analyses of the economics of entertainment and descriptions of cultural imperialism, in which the ideological effect of commercial music-making – the transformation of a

SIMON FRITH

creative people into a passive mass – is taken for granted. Out of Benjamin, however distantly, have come subcultural theories, descriptions of the struggle for the sign. Thus youth subcultures are said to make meanings out of records, products that have no cultural significance until they are consumed, until teenagers to go work on them. These arguments are not just a matter of high theory. Adorno's analysis (mediated through Marcuse) has been important for music consumers themselves. The ideological separation of rock and pop in the 1960s rested on it. Pop was 'rubbish', 'escapist', 'vacuous' or whatever because it was 'commercial', because it was produced only for the money. Rock was superior (and potentially subversive) in as far as it was made for uncommercial reasons and remained true to the youth culture or artist's vision from which it came. The crucial struggle for 1960s rock fans was between music and money, between music as art or folk culture and music as commodity.

In retrospect, now that rock is big business, the counter-cultural critique of pop seems naïve and/or dishonest, but the point is that the terms of the critique remain dominant. . . . The problem evaded in this approach, from Adorno onwards, is that records, pop and rock, like all cultural products, embody both use and exchange value and their ideological significance can't be reduced to exchange value alone. This explains the continued confusions in rock criticism. Rock's commodity form can't be denied . . ., but the problem is to what extent its commercial function determines its cultural meaning. It is with reference to this problem that music theorists can learn from the formalist/realist debates in theoretical work on other media. The subcultural solution to the problem is, without such a reference, too vague. It asserts that meanings are created out of commodities, but does not make clear how free such creation can be – what are the limits of records not as commodities but as texts, as signification structures with rules and restrictions of their own? In answering this question, subcultural studies of youth have, unfortunately, focused more on visual than on musical signs. . . .

## The case of punk

Punk is particularly important for this discussion because of its effect on cultural theorists. Before punk, popular music was rarely a matter of theoretical concern, and among organised socialists the line, in as far as there was one, tended towards folk purism. Within a few months of its public emergence in 1977, though, virtually every left paper agreed that Punk was a Good Thing. There were no doubts that it had transformed pop: it was credited with the success of Rock Against Racism [RAR] and the Anti-Nazi League carnivals and, in general terms, it was argued that popular music was now being made, heard and discussed in new ways. Punk took on this extraordinary significance because it seemed to focus three different arguments. The first was about the *audience*: punk was seen as a folk music and as a subcultural movement. The

FORMALISM, REALISM AND LEISURE

music was thus taken to represent or symbolise class consciousness – the consciousness of working-class youth. The second concerned the problem of *commodity production*, in that punk seemed to challenge capitalist control of mass music. There was an emphasis on do-it-yourself, on seizing the technical means of music production. Finally, it raised questions about *meaning*, about how music works; punk seemed to involve new sounds, new forms, new texts. By combining these positions, punk was able to ease the doubts of at least some of rock's previous critics. It seemed to be different from previous mass music in terms of how it was made *and* how it was used *and* how it meant. Now, three years later [in 1980], it is possible to examine the implications of these assumptions in more detail.

## Punk as folk

The political argument that punk represented working-class youth conscious-ness contained strong elements of opportunism – cultural politics often seemed to mean adopting youth styles in order to attract young people to adult issues; this was certainly an element in RAR's strategy. More impor-tant here, though, was the way that the argument drew on subcultural theory. The music was taken to articulate the values of the punk subculture and these, in turn, were read as a form of working-class consciousness – 'an oblique challenge to hegemony' in Dick Hebdige's words. In many ways the punks' music, their essentially masculine styles, were not much of a depar-ture from rock'n'roll tradition: class consciousness here meant a new variation of the established gestures of teenage bravado (gestures originally developed by teds, mods, skins and the rest). Indeed, the punk-as-folk position had to take on board an embarrassing amount of 'spontaneous' sexism and racism. The achievement of RAR in recruiting punks to the anti-racist struggle can't be over-estimated, because this was a matter of hard ideological work – RAR did not reflect some given punk consciousness. The political contradictions of punk ideology are obvious in Julie Burchill and Tony Parsons' *The Boy Looked at Johnny*: the book contained a dedication to Menachim Begin, for example, which the publishers – symptomatically, Pluto Press – felt bound to disclaim.

The left argument was that punk was a stage in the movement from class consciousness to class political consciousness: this depended on a description of punk as rank and file music, the direct expression of the way things were – a kind of realism. But even in terms of reflection theory, punk as sponta-neous expression of live experience, the argument did not make a lot of sense. The pioneering punk rockers themselves were a self-conscious, artful lot with a good understanding of both rock tradition and populist cliché; the music no more reflected directly back onto conditions in the dole queue than it emerged spontaneously from them. The musical 'realism' of punk was an effect of formal conventions, of a particular combination of sounds; more precisely, it was defined through its aural opposition to the 'unrealism' of mainstream pop and rock. The real/unreal distinction played on a series of musical connotations – ugly versus pretty, harsh versus soothing, 'raw' (lyrics constructed around simple syllables, a three-chord lack of technique, a 'primitive' beat) versus 'cooked' (rock 'poetry', virtuosity, technical complexity). These new conventions in fact drew on well known rock'n'roll signs – often established within the original American garage band meaning of punk rock – but they now took on a rather different currency. This shift was to a large extent achieved by the punk fanzines, which themselves had their stylistic origins (or at least parallels) in Andy Warhol's *Interview* magazine – the same 'artless' reproduction of every word spoken, the same sense of slapped together necessity, the same effect of realism as sly style.

Most of the left converts simply ignored these histories and rejected any suggestion that punk reality was *constructed*. Punk for them was simply a transparent image of a real youth condition. But even in its own terms, their account was unconvincing in that it had no basis in an independent analysis of that reality. As a result, the relationship between youth culture and youth politics, between punk ideology and socialist practice, remained extremely unclear. In this it proved even less politically developed than the attempt by the Weathermen to incorporate American street youth (and its musical tastes) into a political organisation, the RYM (Revolutionary Youth Movement), during the late 1960s. Their argument had involved two assumptions; that young people, from draftees to students, were similarly *exploited* because American capital faced a crisis of overproduction, and were similarly *oppressed* by the force of the State, whether in the army, in the classroom or on the streets [see Jacobs ed. 1970]. Although the political strategy was a failure and the assumptions were wrong, the Weathermen did at least attempt to theorise youth mobilisation. The apologists of British punk a decade later made little attempt to analyse the effects of changing social conditions on youth, to tackle the political complexities of how (or whether) to organise punks or to understand the aesthetic conventions of the music. Based on unconsidered notions that punk described young people's reality and expressed their boredom and rage, their arguments involved not cultural analysis but a purely rhetorical optimism.

## The problem of production

The punk argument about music production was drawn directly from debates in the 1960s. Punk opposed commercial music in two ways. First, it denounced multi-national record companies with a version of the assertion that 'small is beautiful' – punk music was, authentically, the product of small scale independent record and distribution companies. Secondly, punk demystified the production process itself – its message was that anyone can do it! The effect of this has been an astonishing expansion of local music making (for the results listen to John Peel's nightly show on Radio 1). In economic terms, then, punk is essentially petit-bourgeois. An important

FORMALISM, REALISM AND LEISURE

strand in its development has been a cultural version of consumerism; the idea is that record buyers have a right to maximum market choice, that record buying should involve customer expression rather than producer manipulation. Just as the hippie entrepreneurial spirit had found its expression in the shop-based Virgin Records a decade ago, so the most enterprising punk company – Rough Trade – is also, symptomatically, based on a shop. This consumerism has led to the creation of an 'alternative' production system that both parallels the established industry (alternative shops sell records made by alternative record companies and featured in the Alternative Charts) and is integrated into it. 'Independent' records, made by do-it-yourself companies, remain commodities.

Independence, in this context, seems to refer primarily to the question of artistic control (as in the Clash's anti-CBS records *Remote Control* and *Complete Control*). The punks, like hippie musicians before them, assume an opposition between art and business, between honesty and bureaucracy. This involves not only the Adorno argument about commodities, but also a romantic argument about creativity. Punk did not discuss the social relations of music production. Musicians were not seen as workers, as cultural employees akin to journalists, film technicians or actors: they were artists. Their music was progressive because it involved the direct expression of the people-as-artists; the punk task was to make everyone a star. Punk messages could be distorted by the process of commercial production, but only if this process was in the wrong hands (multi-national bureaucrats, boring old farts). This was the other side of punk realism and, again, the political problem is ownership. Punk truth could get through, but the means of music making had to be kept under control – by the musicians, by the kids.

### The problem of meaning

Although this was the most muddled strand in the argument, punk texts were clearly felt to challenge (by ridicule) pop and rock conventions of romance, beauty and ease: punk image (the safety pin) and sound (particularly of voices) had a shock effect. It soon became apparent, however, that punk was constricted by its realist claims, by its use of melodic structures and a rhythmic base which told-it-like-it-was *because* they followed rock'n'roll rules. The result of these limits to experiment was the emergence, after 1977, of a clear split: punk populism versus the punk avant-garde. The punk populists remain locked in their original position. They read teenage gestures and hear punk forms as the spontaneous expression of anti-hegemonic youth; they see the political problem as developing youth consciousness and preventing its symbols being commercialised. This is the standard left position: its clearest statements are in *Temporary Hoarding*, the RAR paper, where (usually adult) ideologists write in the populist punk style – not in reflection of a movement but in an attempt to sustain one. The punk avant-garde is more interested in musical meaning. These musicians (The Pop Group, Public Image Ltd, The

SIMON FRITH

Gang of Four, Scritti Politti, for example) expose textual structures in familiar ways (some of them have studied discourse theory) – by distancing themselves from their own performances and by juxtaposing terms from different
genres (musical montages of rock/reggae/funk/improvisation). They undermine the populist assumptions of transparency, mocking the idea of a direct
line from social experience to musical form, and expose the subjective claims
deeply embedded in all rock music.

Music is a medium in which the expression of emotion, feeling and belief
by performers can seem so direct (they talk straight at us) that powerful
conventions of 'subjective realism', or truth to feeling, have developed. These
are represented, most obviously, by the blues element in popular music –
rock, for example, drew on both blues and post-Dylan singer/songwriting
to develop its claims of authenticity, sincerity, depth of feeling and individuality. These terms were important for punk too; they lurk behind its realist
claims, its subcultural theory and its struggle for artists' control. The avant-
garde punks, in contrast, exploit 'artificial' musical forms – pop disco,
synthesisers – and challenge their listeners to hear them without using the
language of rock criticism, the terms of emotion, feeling, style. Meanwhile,
the rock critics are still struggling to listen to the music of Public Image Ltd
as a reflection of Johnny Rotten's 'abrasive personality'.

It is therefore possible to see the contrast between avant-garde punk and
traditional rock in the familiar cultural terms of the formalism/realism debate.
In setting up the distinction like this, as a rock critic trying to make sense
of post-punk rock texts, I am conscious of using the terms in a rather over-
simplified and idiosyncratic way. 'Realism' is an especially difficult term here
because in the analysis of other media (cinema, television, literature, the
visual arts) it denotes both particular sets of practices within cultural production (genres) and also a mode of analysis based on an epistemological assertion
about the relationship of 'text' to 'world'. The first sense doesn't apply in
music – there are no classic realist musical texts – and so we have to think
about the question of meaning without any of the usual critical shortcuts
created by the ambivalence of 'realism'. It is in this muddled and undevel-
oped area that the punk avant-garde is working – along with, for example,
certain schools of improvised music. Nevertheless, punk remains a commercial medium and my elevation of an 'avant-garde' is misleading – the problems
of production (rock as commodity) and consumption (the rock audience)
are unresolved by even the most 'objective' or 'deconstructed' musical text.
. . . Rock politics is never just a matter of meaning. This can be illustrated
by one specific struggle, Rock Against Sexism, which involves three different
problems. The first is the fight against sexist representation and stereotypes
in rock – whether songs, images, journalism or album sleeves. This is really
a question of education and propaganda, in which 'realist' assumptions are
quite appropriate. Secondly, there is the need to encourage female musicians
by providing places to play, gigs, contacts, workshops, and so on; this is a
practical struggle in which the control of music-making institutions is a key

170

FORMALISM, REALISM AND LEISURE

issue. Thirdly, at the theoretical level, musical signification needs to be explored in the attempt to explain how sexual representations work musically. Although these are different forms of intervention into different forms of struggle, they are obviously related: theories of rock meaning can only be developed through rock practice, and rock practice involves a relationship between musicians and audiences in a particular cultural institution. The ideology of rock, in short, is determined not by its texts – musical forms don't have eternal sexual meanings – but by its context. Rock music is an aspect of leisure.

## The problem of leisure

The concept of leisure provides another way of relating use and exchange value in the circulation of cultural goods and this approach has the great advantage of providing a historical and material account of needs and values. But it has been surprisingly little used by cultural theorists and it is worth making a simple point: the ideology of leisure in capitalist societies is that people (i.e. men) work in order to be able to enjoy their leisure – leisure is 'free' time, when people (i.e. men) do what they want, realise their individual interests and abilities; even in Marxist accounts there is an assumption that leisure values are determined in a purely ideological struggle. But the freedom involved in this account of leisure is deceptive, and not only in ideological terms. Leisure is necessary for capital: it is the time when labour is replenished physically and culturally, re-creation time, and it is the time when workers consume, when surplus value is realised. 'Free' time is structured not only by ideas but also by material forces, by the availability of goods and resources, by the effects of the labour process on people's capacities and desires. Leisure involves a tension between choice and constraint: it is an aspect of the general relationship between production and consumption. Leisure, in other words, is an effect of capital accumulation and it is in this setting that the meaning of cultural goods has to be analysed. This argument has long been made by social historians, who have shown how the imposition of rational work discipline meant, necessarily, the imposition of a rational leisure discipline: traditional forms of release and riot became bound by the timed routines of the industrial labour process. It was these routines that constituted the meaning of modern leisure, and the issues discussed by historians of nineteenth-century leisure remain important for the analysis of contemporary mass culture: it was then that leisure was established as a particular set of ideological and cultural relationships.

The first point to make is that there is a permanent strain between the need to control leisure (hence all the licences and licensing authorities) and the ideological importance of leisure as the time when people experience themselves as 'free' labourers – cultural conflict cannot be divided along simple class lines. Leisure commodities are not necessarily conductive to good

SIMON FRITH

order. Drink, for example, has been an issue of bourgeois dispute since Liberal manufacturers denounced Tory brewers, and a similar contradiction was obvious in the commercial exploitation of punk – private clubs put on the groups town halls banned, Virgin snapped up the Sex Pistols after EMI dropped them. As Marx noted, employers have quite different attitudes to their own workers, whose needs they attempt to limit, and to other people's, whose needs they attempt to extend.

Nineteenth-century leisure was organised through two sorts of bourgeois enterprise. The moral entrepreneurs saw leisure as a means to the end of self-improvement. Leisure was treated as an educational institution: rational recreation was encouraged for its useful effects. The argument is well illustrated by Sir James Kay-Shuttleworth's enthusiasm for music instruction in elementary schools. Songs, he declared, were 'an important means of forming an industrious, brave, loyal and religious working class. They might inspire cheerful views of industry and associate amusements . . . with duties' [cited in Bailey 1978: 46]. This emphasis on the moral significance of leisure remains embodied in state policy – in the use of subsidies to support particular high art forms, for example. Nineteenth-century leisure was defined along moral lines for the bourgeoisie as much as for the labourer, and the assumption that middle-class pleasures too must be functional lives on in the *Sunday Times* culture of joggers, gardeners and cooks. But the moral approach to leisure is complemented (and sometimes opposed) by commercial entrepreneurs churning out 'escapist' cultural commodities with reference not to their content but to their profitability. The logic of their production also puts a premium on order and routine, but through notions of professionalism, predictability and reduced commercial risk. Music hall proprietors weren't much interested in the morality of music, but they had their own concern for good order:

> It is one of the greatest nuisances possible to sensible people who go to places of amusement to divert their minds from politics and business alike to have the opinions of the daily papers reproduced in verse and flung at their heads by a music hall singer. Persons who go to a place of amusement to be amused, and these, we believe, form the steadily paying class, are too sensible to care to proclaim their private opinions by applauding mindless rubbish with a political meaning.
>
> [*The Era*, 28 November 1885; cited in Bailey 1978: 165]

This is a familiar assertion; we hear it most often these days from radio programmers, still giving people what they *really* want.

Working-class responses to the leisure provided contain their own contradictions. In working-class radical traditions, leisure was equally a time for improvement, political education and disciplined consciousness. Socialists have been as much concerned to encourage the rational use of free time as bourgeois moralists (in the temperance movement, for example) and the socialist distinction between escapist and improving leisure, the socialist critiques of commercial play and 'light' entertainment, remain potent. They surface, for example, in the punk denunciation of disco as 'mindless' hedonism. There is a tension between leisure as an individual activity (the realm of choice) and leisure as a collective activity (the realm of solidarity). State policies have always reflected a fear of public disorder – the dangers of dancing in the streets, class conspiracy, youthful anarchy. But the mass market depends on forms of collectivity, and leisure is crucially associated with the values of conviviality and comradeship. The public/private distinction has been mediated through the family: the home, as the refuge from work, has become an essential setting for most leisure consumption. Marx suggested that in capitalist social relations the worker 'feels himself at home only during his leisure', and the relationship works the other way round too – by the end of the nineteenth century workers were collecting household goods, going on family holidays and enjoying 'family entertainment'. The equation of leisure and home puts women in a double disadvantage: it is their labour which makes the home comfortable but they are excluded from the usual work/leisure distinction – women's pleasures, even more than men's, are confined to the household but this is, in fact, their place of work. The contradictions are obvious in, say, Radio 1's daytime programming – music to clean up and wash clothes by.

I have only had space here to skim the surface of the issues raised by studies of leisure, but the point I'm trying to make is that rock records aren't just commodities, they are *leisure* commodities. This is the context of their use value. To understand how leisure goods signify we have to refer them to the general meanings of leisure, meanings which have their own processes of construction and dispute: the ideology of rock comes from a relationship between form *and* use. The pleasure of rock is not just a textual matter. It reflects those wider definitions of the leisure experience embodied in concepts like 'entertainment', 'relaxation', and 'fun', which themselves emerged from a complex cultural struggle and rest on a structure of sexual differentiation. This is the structure Rock Against Sexism has to take on. Even the simplest of rock categories – like dance music or party music – are redolent with social significance: dances and parties are historically and socially specific institutions and their ideological meanings – as breaks from work, settings for sexual contact, expressions of solidarity – are not only articulated by different types of music (disco, the Rolling Stones) but, simultaneously, determine those musics' ideological effects.

The meaning of leisure is, nevertheless, essentially contradictory. The use value of entertainment derives from its intimations of fun, irresponsibility and fulfilment – leisure is an implicit critique of work. The ideology of leisure has to strike a balance between freedom and order, and so the experience of freedom must be real (otherwise leisure goods would have no use) but not disruptive of work routines. Leisure must give pleasure, but not too much. Pleasure, in turn, is not just a psychological effect, but refers

SIMON FRITH

to a set of experiences rooted in the social relations of production. It is important to stress that there cannot yet be *a* theory of pleasure, if only because the concept refers to too disparate a set of events – individual and collective, active and passive, defined against different situations of displeasure/pain/reality. I am not convinced that all these experiences can be explained in terms of sexuality. And it is also in this context that the importance of the bohemian tradition in rock (as in cultural history generally) needs explaining: bohemians articulate a particular kind of leisure critique of the work ethic. They are cultural radicals not just as the source of the formalist avant-garde, but also in institutional terms.

The problem of cultural politics, in short, is not just to organise subcultural resistance, to infiltrate the means of cultural production and to open closed texts, but to do these things with reference to the contradictions that are necessarily built into cultural consumption. It is this concept of 'consumption' that remains, in cultural analysis, the most difficult to define. It is, indeed, a term in a number of quite different discourses. It may, in each case, refer to the same activity (although even this is unclear – would it mean buying a record or listening to it?) but the concept means different things according to the analytic frameworks involved: in Marxist economic theory it refers to a moment in the circulation of value, in recent literary and film theory it refers to a kind of pleasure, in historical sociology it refers to an institutional process. Cultural theories of consumption are left in a muddle – 'passive consumption', for example, is a term used by theorists of all persuasions but as a rhetorical rather than as a theoretical device. My point is that we have to clarify the different meanings of 'consumption' before we can use the term adequately in the analysis of ideology.

## Bibliography

Bailey, P. (1978) *Leisure and Class in Victorian England*, London: Routledge and Kegan Paul.
Bloch, E. *et al.* (1977) *Aesthetics and Politics*, London: New Left Books.
Jacobs, Harold (ed.) (1970) *Weathermen*, San Francisco: Ramparts Press.

# CHAPTER 6

# ART VS TECHNOLOGY:
# THE STRANGE CASE OF
# POPULAR MUSIC

In early 1936 Cecil Graves, controller of programmes at the BBC, instructed his Head of Variety, Eric Maschwitz, and Director of Entertainment, Roger Eckersly, to keep crooning, 'this particularly odious form of singing', off the air waves.[1] In his memoirs of life in the BBC, written in 1945, Eckersly comments that crooners,

> seem from my experience to rouse more evil passions in certain breasts than anything else. I should very much like to point out that not all who sing with bands are crooners. There is a lot of difference between straight singing and crooning. The latter is an art of its own. I can't confess I like it, but I admire the skill with which the singer seems to pause for a split second either on top or below the note he is aiming at.
>
> (Eckersly, 1946: 144)

Crooning was a style of singing made possible by the development of the electrical microphone — vocalists could now be heard singing softly — and the source of a new sort of male pop star (Rudy Valee, Bing Crosby, Al Bowlly) whom the BBC found sentimental and 'effeminate'. (The association of crooning and sexual decadence was to be celebrated many years later in Dennis Potter's *Pennies from Heaven*.) The problem for the programme controllers was to define crooning in the first place and then to distinguish between 'good' and 'bad' crooning. Even after the war the Ted Heath Band couldn't get BBC broadcasts because their singer, Lita Roza, was defined as a crooner and therefore 'slush' (Heath, 1957: 94–5).

## THE ROCK ERA

Twenty years later, in 1966, Bob Dylan toured Britain with his new electric band. The Albert Hall concert was bootlegged so it is still possible to hear the slow hand-clapping between each number, the abuse hurled at the stage, and the shouting arguments between members of the audience. At the end of 'Ballad of a Thin Man' a voice rings clearly out: 'Judas!', 'I don't believe you', mutters Dylan as the chords start for 'Like a Rolling Stone'.

Fifteen years later, the pace of technological change is quickening. I had a call from a young band in Coventry who had entered the local battle of the bands sponsored by the Musicians' Union (slogan: Keep Music Live!). Their entry had been rejected — they use a drum machine. Was this official union policy? The answer was yes (although, of course, such policy is always open to debate and change). In the words of Brian Blain, the MU's publicity and promotion officer:

> In the first instance I would make the comment that the Union does seek to limit the use of synthesizers where they would be used to deprive orchestras of work. To this extent, in media engagements particularly and with touring concerts by singers of the calibre of Andy Williams etc, we do have a certain amount of success.
>
> However, I think it is to the Union's credit that we see the essential difference between that use of the synthesizer where it is clearly taking work away from 'conventional' musicians and its use in a self-contained band where there would not normally be any question of another conventional musician being used. In coming to this admittedly pragmatic view, we are merely following on a problem that keyboard instruments have always set an organization like this. Even the acoustic piano could be seen, in the beginning, as a displacement for a number of musicians and this has certainly been the case since the advent of the Hammond Organ.
>
> It is hopeless to look for a totally consistent view but I must say that I see a big difference between a synthesizer in a band, which at least requires a musician to play it, and a machine which takes the place of a musician.[2]

### Pop and authenticity

These disparate examples of the controversies caused by the changing techniques of music-making suggest three recurring issues. First, technology is opposed to nature. The essence of the BBC case against crooning was that it was 'unnatural'. 'Legitimate' music hall or opera singers reached their concert hall audiences with the power of their voices alone; the sound of the crooners, by contrast, was artificial. Microphones enabled intimate sounds to take on a pseudo-public presence, and, for the crooners' critics, technical dishonesty meant emotional dishonesty — hence terms like 'slushy'. Crooning

## ART VS TECHNOLOGY

men were particularly unnatural — their sexuality was in question and they were accused of 'emasculating' music. Even Eckersly contrasted crooning with 'straight' singing.

Second, technology is opposed to community. This argument, common on the folk scene in the early 1960s, proposes that electronic amplification alienates performers from their audiences. The democratic structure of the folk community was thus unable to survive a situation in which the singers came to monopolize the new means of communication — electrical power. By 'going electric' Bob Dylan embraced all those qualities of mass culture that the folk movement had rejected — stardom, commerce and manipulation.

Third, technology is opposed to art. The Musicians' Union's objection to drum machines is partly a conventional union position, defending members' job opportunities, but it reflects too a belief that the drummer is a musician in a way that the drum machine-programmer is not. One effect of technological change is to make problematic the usual distinction between 'musician' and 'sound engineer', with its implication that musicians are creative artists in a way that engineers are not. What matters here is not the difficult issue of creativity itself but, rather, the idea of self-expression. The argument that recurred in the pop press in the 1970s was that the production of electronic noises by synthesizers left no room for individual 'feel' or 'touch'. Gary Numan could tell readers of *Melody Maker*'s musicians' advice page exactly how to reproduce his sound in a way that Jeff Beck or even Keith Emerson could not. They could describe their techniques but not their final, on-the-spot judgement. All Numan had to do was write down the position of his various switches. This was the context in which synthesizers were heard as 'soul-less', and their most pointed use was on the soundtrack of *Clockwork Orange*. Beethoven's Ninth Symphony, as synthesized by Walter Carlos, was the musical symbol of the film's theme — the dehumanizing use of art as behaviour therapy — and the March from *Clockwork Orange* was later used, with effective irony, as the theme music for David Bowie's 1972 stage show.

What is at stake in all these arguments is the authenticity or truth of music; the implication is that technology is somehow false or falsifying. The origins of this argument lie, of course, in the mass culture criticism of the 1920s and 1930s, but what is interesting is the continuing resonance of the idea of authenticity within mass cultural ideology itself. The key disputes in the history of rock, for example, were all presented (even *sold*) in terms of authentic new stars replacing inauthentic old ones. On his first RCA LP Elvis Presley is pictured playing an acoustic guitar and the back sleeve blurb begins:

> Elvis Presley zoomed into big-time entertainment practically over-
> night. Born in Tupelo, Mississippi, Elvis began singing for friends and
> folk gatherings when he was barely five years old. All his training

109

THE ROCK ERA

has been self-instruction and hard work. At an early age, with not
enough money to buy a guitar, he practiced for his future stardom
by strumming on a broomstick. He soon graduated to a $2.98 instru-
ment and began picking out tunes and singing on street corners.

In the mid-1960s the by now conventional routines of teen pop were
challenged, in turn, by the 'authentic' moves of white rhythm'n'blues. In the
words of their official 1964 biography:

> The Stones picked up Rhythm'n'Blues, grappled with it, learned
> to 'feel' it. And once they'd made up their minds to stick with it,
> through the worst of times, nothing could shake them from their
> resolution. They were determined to express themselves freely,
> through their music.
> And they decided unanimously that they were going to make no
> concessions to the demands of the commercialism that they frankly,
> openly, despised.
>
> (The Rolling Stones, 1964: 13)

A dozen years later punk musicians shook the rock establishment with a
similar, if more apocalyptic, attitude. In the words of Caroline Coon in
*Melody Maker* in July 1976:

> There is a growing, almost desperate feeling that rock music should
> be stripped down to its bare bones again, taken by the scruff of its
> bloated neck and given a good shaking.
> It's no coincidence that the week the Stones were at Earls Court,
> the Sex Pistols were playing to their ever-increasing following at the
> 100 Club. The Pistols are the personification of the emerging British
> punk rock scene, a positive reaction to the complex equipment,
> technological sophistication and jaded alienation which has formed
> a barrier between fans and stars.
> Punk rock sounds basic and raw. It's meant to.
>
> (Coon, 1976: 14)

Each of these moments in rock history fused moral and aesthetic
judgements: rock'n'roll, rhythm'n'blues and punk were all, in their turn,
experienced as more truthful than the pop forms they disrupted. And in
each case authenticity was described as an explicit reaction to technology, as
a return to the 'roots' of music-making — the live excitement of voice/
guitar/drum line-ups. The continuing core of rock ideology is that raw sounds
are more authentic than cooked sounds.

This is a paradoxical belief for a technologically sophisticated medium and
rests on an old-fashioned model of direct communication — A plays to B

## ART VS TECHNOLOGY

and the less technology lies between them the closer they are, the more honest their relationship and the fewer the opportunities for manipulation and falsehoods. This model rests in turn on familiar aesthetic positions. From Romanticism rock fans have inherited the belief that listening to someone's music means getting to know them, getting access to their souls and sensibilities. From the folk tradition they've adopted the argument that musicians can represent them, articulating the immediate needs and experiences of a group or cult or community. It follows that if good music is, by either set of criteria, honest and sincere, bad music is false — and technological changes increase the opportunities for fakery. Take this typical newspaper story from 1985:

> When Frankie Goes to Hollywood take the stage in Newcastle tonight, midway through their first British tour, they will face a little technical problem: how to reproduce in a 90 minute live set the state-of-the-art sound of the hits that have taken them months to produce in the studio, using some of the most sophisticated hardware money can buy.
>
> Many groups have this problem nowadays. Some of them don't even try to solve it. Two weeks ago another Liverpool group, Dead or Alive, whose 'You Spin Me Round' currently tops the British pop charts, cancelled an appearance on Channel Four's rock programme, The Tube. They refused to go on without backing tapes, which would have contravened The Tube's 'live only' performance policy.
>
> This sorry tale will provide only a footnote in the long and quirkish history of fakery in pop music. There is a roll-call, stretching back 20 years, of groups who were packaged for their sex appeal and did little playing on their own 'hits'. Other groups were actually fabricated after the event, simply to put a marketable face on the honest but anonymous toil of session musicians and producers.
>
> (Brown, 1985)

What is intriguing here is the slide from 'fakery' in terms of technology to 'fakery' in terms of commercial manipulation. Two sorts of insincerity are confounded and we end up with only the anonymous session men who can call their work 'honest'. The muddle of critical terms involved in this sort of story, the implication that we can't 'trust' what we are hearing, reflects the confluence of three problems that technology now poses to the rock concept of authenticity.

First, there is the problem of aura in a complex process of artistic production: what or, rather, *who* is the source of a pop record's authority? The history of rock'n'roll rests on as complicated a set of assumptions about its authors as the history of film (and rock has its own version of *auteur* theory).

111

THE ROCK ERA

There is always a need for *someone* to be the author of a sound, the artist, but the relative artistic significance of writers/musicians/singers/producers/ engineers/arrangers keeps shifting. It is now possible for a publicist to be credited as a record's real author — think of Paul Morley's role in the selling of Frankie Goes to Hollywood. Frankie, the pop phenomenon of 1984, gained success with a gleeful celebration of their own artifice — Trevor Horn's production turned a plodding Liverpool group into a wrap-around, techno-flash disco sensation; the videos for 'Relax' and 'Two Tribes' offered camp versions of masculinity; the Frankie hype was delivered in wads of advertising copy. This was packaging as art and so pop theorist Paul Morley, who wrote the prose for Frankie and their label, ZTT, was credited as their real author. He even appeared on stage in the ZTT show, reading his copy over an Art of Noise backing tape.

Second, technological changes raise issues of power and manipulation: how does the ownership of the technical means of production relate to the control of what is produced? Do technical developments threaten or con-solidate such control?

Third, technology is seen to undermine the pleasures of music-making (and watching music-making). One important strand of rock common sense is that playing an instrument is a physical exercise, visibly involves the body, and is, above all, a matter of effort. This is reflected in the routine contrast of 'live' performance and 'dead' studio activity, and even now rock's core beliefs in energy and community can only be celebrated in concert (hence the importance of Bruce Springsteen). The guitarist became the symbol of rock because he (masculinity is a necessary part of the argument) communi-cates physically on stage even more obviously than the singer — the link between sound and gesture has become so familiar that audiences have even developed the 'air guitar', a way of sharing the guitarist's physical emotions without needing an instrument at all.

One reason why synthesizers, drum machines, tape recorders and so on are regarded as 'unnatural' instruments in performance is simply because playing them takes little obvious effort. Programming a computerized sampling device like a Fairlight engages the mind not the body and is not a spectator event. (Art music audiences, used to the action of orchestras and conductors, feel similarly insulted by computer musicians.) The explicit argument is that live performances allow for spontaneity, for performers' direct responses to their audiences; programmed instruments can't do this. But what really matters is not whether a show *is* spontaneous but, rather, whether it seems to be (the most celebrated live performers often have the most rigidly stylized acts — go and see James Brown on successive nights and see exactly the same 'improvisations'). Rock bands' use of 'artificial' aids are, therefore, hidden entirely (for example, the now routine use of backing-tapes) or disguised (electronic instrument manufacturers are skilled at producing devices that can be played as if they are normal keyboards or

ART VS TECHNOLOGY .

percussion — it's not really necessary to design a rhythm machine like a Syndrum or the Simmons Kit as something to be hit!). If the deception is discovered audiences do, indeed, feel cheated. I once watched Vince Clarke of Yazoo pretend to play his Fairlight (all he was really doing was loading and unloading floppy discs). When at last he got bored and walked away, the music played on and he was booed even more loudly than Bob Dylan at the Albert Hall.

## In praise of technology

For Yazoo's fans, as for Dylan's a couple of pop generations earlier, new technology meant a new means of crowd control; the direct line between star and fans was fatally disrupted. This is a familiar position in rock, as I've shown, but it is, in fact, a reversal of reality. A more dispassionate history of twentieth-century pop reveals two counter-theses.

### I. Technological developments have made the rock concept of authenticity possible

I can illustrate this by reference to pop's three central inventions. First, recording itself, from its beginnings at the turn of the century, enabled previously unreproducible aspects of performance — spontaneity, improvisation, etc — to be reproduced exactly and so enabled Afro-American music to replace European art and folk musics at the heart of western popular culture. This affected not just what sort of music people listened to (and listened to more and more after the First World War) but also how they listened to it, how they registered the emotional meanings of sounds, on the one hand, the musical shape of their own emotions, on the other. Recording made available the physical impact of an unseen performer, giving access to singers' feelings without those feelings having to be coded via a written score.

One immediate consequence was that star performers began to take over from composers as popular music's 'authors' (this was true in classical music too — Caruso was the first international recording star) but, more importantly, recording gave a public means of emotionally complex communication to otherwise socially inarticulate people — performers and listeners. The blues and hillbilly singers of the 1920s and 1930s were just as stylized, as rule bound, as the romantic songsmiths of the European middle-class tradition, but their rules could be learned and understood without the education and cultural training necessary to appreciate how classical music carries its meanings. The profound statements of pride, dread and defiance in a Robert Johnson blues, the subtle twists of desire and pain in a Billie Holiday song could be heard as truthful by listeners remote from these singers geographically, socially and in terms of cultural roots. I can still

113

remember the instant exhilaration of Little Richard's 'Long Tall Sally', which I heard for the first time when I was about ten years old, growing up in a small Yorkshire town, with no idea at all about who or what Little Richard was. That conversion to black music, similar to the experience of small town middle-class children before the war hearing Louis Armstrong for the first time, was being repeated, as a result of rock'n'roll, for teenagers all across Europe, and can't be explained away in terms of commercial cultural imperialism.

The second important invention, the electrical microphone, I have already discussed with reference to crooning, but its general effect was to extend the possibilities of the public expressions of private feelings in all pop genres. The microphone had the same function as the close-up in film history — it made stars knowable, by shifting the conventions of personality, making singers sound sexy in new ways, giving men a new prominence in big bands, and moving the focus from the song to the singer. The first pop singer to become a pin-up idol, Frank Sinatra, was well aware of the importance of amplification to his appeal. As John Rockwell writes:

> As a young singer, he consciously perfected his handling of the microphone. 'Many singers never learned to use one', he wrote later. 'They never understood, and still don't, that a microphone is their instrument.' A microphone must be deployed sparingly, he said, with the singer moving it in and out of range of the mouth and suppressing excessive sibilants and noisy intakes of air. But Sinatra's understanding of the microphone went deeper than this merely mechanical level. He knew better than almost anyone else just what Henry Pleasants has maintained: that the microphone changes the very way that modern singers sing. It was his mastery of this instrument, the way he let its existence help shape his vocal production and singing style, that did much to make Sinatra the preeminent popular singer of our time.
>
> (Rockwell, 1984: 51–2)

Sinatra was to remain sensitive to technical developments — in the 1950s he pioneered the use of the LP to build up moods and atmospheres in ways impossible on three-minute singles. From his perspective, technology was a tool to be used and one which could easily be misused. Sinatra famously dismissed Elvis Presley and rock'n'roll, agreeing with *New York Times* jazz critic, John S. Wilson, that 'singing ability is one of the least essential qualifications for success' in this new pop form:

> Recording techniques have become so ingenious that almost anyone can seem to be a singer. A small, flat voice can be souped

## ART VS TECHNOLOGY

up by emphasizing the low frequencies and piping the result through an echo chamber. A slight speeding up of the recording tape can bring a brighter, happier sound to a naturally drab singer or clean the weariness out of a tired voice. Wrong notes can be snipped out of the tape and replaced by notes taken from other parts of the tape.

(Levy, 1960: 111)

In fact, Elvis Presley neither corrupted nor transformed pop tradition — he was the culminating star of the technology of music-making made available by electrical recording and amplification. For Presley's fans he was much more immediately, *honestly* sexy than Frank Sinatra.

The third significant invention, magnetic tape, began to be used by record companies in the 1950s and eventually made possible the cutting/splicing/dubbing/multi-track recording of sounds, so that studio music became entirely 'artificial'. What for John S. Wilson was a form of fraud became, for 1960s rock musicians, a source of new creative ambitions. Most developments in recording technique — long players, hi-fidelity, magnetic tape, stereophonic sound, digital recording, compact discs, etc — have, in fact, been pioneered by the classical divisions of record companies, as producers and sound engineers have tried to find ways of capturing the audio-dynamics of live orchestral music. In pop, though, these techniques were soon used to the opposite effect: studios became the place to make music impossible to reproduce live, rather than to recreate the ideal concert experience. By the end of the 1960s the studio was, in itself, the most important rock instrument. The Beatles' 'Sergeant Pepper' LP symbolized the moment when rock musicians began to claim to be making complex artworks.

Progressive rock set a problem for the received ideas of authenticity: the rock'n'roll ideals of spontaneity, energy and effort were faced by new emphases on sensitivity, care and control. 1970s rock offered two solutions. On the one hand, effort and control were combined in the spectacular technological displays of art-rock groups like Pink Floyd and stadium rockers like Led Zeppelin; on the other hand, singer/songwriters like Paul Simon, Joni Mitchell and even John Lennon used studio devices and sonic collages to reveal themselves more openly, making music a matter of individual sensibilities that couldn't be engaged in the crude, collective setting of the concert hall. Punk was to rebel against the excessess of both technological and artistic self-display, but punk's very moralism suggested how closely by now rock aesthetics were entangled with ideas of honesty and dishonesty.

Punk only briefly interrupted the development of pop technology (a development that had, by the 1980s, led to the complete collapse of creative distinctions between musicians, producers and engineers) but it does illustrate my second historical thesis.

115

THE ROCK ERA

## II.  Technological change has been a source of resistance to the corporate control of popular music

This proposal, again, argues against orthodox pop history, so first I need to clarify my position: if we look at the history of inventions in the music industry — in terms of both production and consumption — those that catch on and are successfully marketed are the ones that lead, at least in the short term, to the decentralization of music-making and listening. To give a recent example, video tapes have become popular — video discs have not. The usual argument is that technological change is inspired by and makes possible the increased capitalist control of the market but, on the whole, recording technology has not worked like this. The music industry is essentially conservative, and uses new instruments to do old things more efficiently or cheaply rather than to do new things. This is obvious in the development of musical equipment, for example. Some devices have been invented in response to musicians' specific requests (the electric bass guitar, Marshall amps) but musicians have quickly found unexpected uses for the new instruments, and many electronic tools have been developed without any clear idea of what they might be used for at all — except, that is, as substitutes for existing instruments. Hence the importance to synthesizer firms of musicians who'll play their instruments and sell them by revealing their new possibilities.

It is because musicians (and consumers) have been able to use machines for their own ends that the mechanization of popular music has not been a simple story of capitalist take-over (or state control — see Bright, this issue). This has been true at all stages of pop history. Electrical amplification, for example, and, in particular, the development of the electric guitar in the 1930s, gave American musicians the freedom to travel and perform to large audiences without the capital expense of big bands, while the parallel development of recording broke the power of Vaudeville promoters and dance-hall owners to decide who could hear whom. The new industry gate-keepers, radio disc jockeys and record company A&R departments, had much less tight control on who could make music for a living — this was especially important for black music and musicians, and for making black music available to white listeners. Even the original 'synthetic' keyboard, the Hammond Organ, was first marketed as a do-it-yourself instrument — sounds you too can make at home! — and it is arguable that the creative process in rock, from The Beatles on, has been inspired by musicians struggling to make for themselves, on whatever equipment they can cobble together, sounds that originated in expensive studios. Far from being oppressed by the unequal distribution of technological power, musicians have been made inventive by it. Rock invention, then, is inseparable from both the use of technology and from musicians' attempts to control their own sounds.

116

## ART VS TECHNOLOGY

The most striking example of this was punk. Its ideology may have been anti-technology, but the late 1970s rush of home-made records and independent labels was dependent, in fact, on the lower cost of good quality recording equipment, on the availability of cheap but sophisticated electronic keyboards. The punk movement involved electronic musicians like Thomas Leer and Robert Rental, Cabaret Voltaire and the Human League; the most commercially successful independent label, Mute, has had, almost exclusively, an electro-pop roster.

Avant-garde music of all sorts has been made under the influence of punk electronics in the last decade. In the long term it turned out that the punk challenge to established modes of stardom and authority worked more clearly musically than sociologically. Punks did not replace the pop order of stars and followers, but post-punk musicians have challenged the idea of the finished product. In the 1980s, it has been commodity form rather than commodity status that has been under threat. Packaged songs, records and stars have all become the object of further play and manipulation.

One strand of such play has come from consumers themselves: home taping has given fans a new means of control over their sounds; they can compile LPs and radio shows for themselves; and use Walkmans to carry their soundscapes around with them. The record industry itself has treated home taping as the source of all its troubles. Behind the recurring campaigns for levies to be imposed on blank tapes is the suggestion that people are using them to acquire music illicitly, without paying for it, without even giving the musicians involved their just reward. Every blank tape sold, from this perspective, is a record not sold.

It is worth noting a couple of points about this argument. First, it rests on inadequate evidence. The effect of home taping is primarily deduced from record sales figures rather than from an investigation of the consumer choices that lie behind them. The patchy public research evidence there is (commissioned by Warners in the USA and by the Communist Party in Italy!) shows, not surprisingly, that home taping involves a particular commitment to music — it is done by the people who buy the most records, and the substitution effect (a tape bought means a record not bought) makes no sense to people spending as much money on music as they can. What emerges, rather, is the shifting significance of music within leisure. Records are being replaced not by tapes as such but by other leisure activities; music is being used differently and in different, more flexible forms (Warner Communications, 1982; Ala et al., 1985).

It's interesting too that the record industry's home taping fears emerged after the event. This is another example of the multinationals' ignorance of the implications of their own inventions. To repeat a point I've already made, record companies are essentially slow-thinking; research and development means devising ways of making more money out of people doing what they already do. No one in Britain anticipated the VTR boom —

117

THE ROCK ERA

Thorn-EMI decided not to invest in its initial development — while companies regularly mistake passing fads for lasting habits (hence Warners' fateful over-investment in Atari computer games). There are enough differences between different countries' uses of new technologies (why the home-based VTR pattern in Britain, the teen craze for video arcades in the USA?) and enough examples of products that don't sell despite massive capital investment, from quadrophonic sound systems to video discs, to suggest that consumers are not entirely malleable. In the record business, at least, the increasingly oligopolistic control of musical media is continually countered by the consumer preference for devices that can, in some sense, increase their control over their own consumption.

In musical terms the most interesting and influential 'folk' uses of new technology have been developed by black musicians and audiences in Jamaica and the USA. Jamaica is, perhaps, the clearest example of a society in which the opposition 'folk vs technology' makes no sense. Reggae is a folk form with records, studios, session musicians, and disc jockeys at its centre rather than live shows or collective sing-alongs. Jamaican DJs, in particular, pioneered the use of the record as a musical instrument, something to talk to and over, slow down and speed up, cut into and across, rather than as a fixed, finished good.

In the 1970s disco DJs in New York and elsewhere echoed (and were directly influenced by) these ideas. The most dramatic consequence was Brooklyn's hip-hop scene. This culture of rapping, scratch-mixing, graffiti, break dancing, etc, was, in traditional sociological terms, a street culture:

> Hip hop was originally born of kids evolving their own social networks, from crews to karate clubs, making their own dances, poetry, and music, in an attempt to make a harsh, cruel, often incomprehensible city a liveable environment. . . . In hip hop, mainstream fashion, art, language, leisure culture — mainstream values — are subverted by those who have been cast out of the status quo.
>
> (George et al., 1985: xvii)

But the means of this cultural enterprise were technological — the ghetto blaster, the turn-table — and everything, the subway train, the body, the record, became an object on which the hip-hop artist could go to work. Hip-hop music meant montage and collage:

> To phone Tommy Boy Records in February '84 was a treat. For as long as you were kept on hold there was the legendary 'Payoff Mix' in your ear, taking hip-hop cutting one step further into the realm of endless potential. It used the irresistible base of 'Play That Beat' to cut in fragments of 'Adventures on the Wheels of Steel', some James Brown soul power, 'Buffalo Gals', Funky Four's 'That's the

118

ART VS TECHNOLOGY

Joint', West Street Mob, The Supreme Team, Culture Club, Starski's 'Live at the Disco Fever', Little Richard's 'Tutti Frutti', exercise routines (heel-toe, heel-toe), Humphrey Bogart in *Casablanca*, 'Rockit', the Supremes' 'Stop in the Name of Love', 'Planet Rock', Indeep's 'Last Night a DJ Saved my Life' and more.

(Toop, 1984: 154)

All sounds could be grist to this mill, whether politicians' speeches, police sirens, bugged conversations, or the accidental effects of electronic distortion itself. As David Toop goes on to say:

The concurrent fashionability of scratch mixing and sampling keyboards like the Emulator and Fairlight has led to creative pillage on a grand scale and caused a crisis for pre-computer-age concepts of artistic property.

(Toop, 1984: 154)

Many of the best hip-hop records are not legally available. Their use of 'found sound' is, in record company terms, a form of piracy. The refusal to accept records as finished products threatens the basic organization of the music business as a profit-making enterprise — hence the virulent objections to home taping (and the systematic attempt to classify home-tapers and professional bootleggers together). Electronic technology undermines the idea of fixed objects on which copyright, the essential legal safeguard of art as property, rests. And so Malcolm McClaren's LP 'Duck Rock', a montage of sounds plucked from New York radio, South African townships and urban streets, shaped in Trevor Horn's studio, has to have an identifiable 'author' both in order to sell it and in order to assign its proceeds.

And this is where the final irony of the relationship between art and technology in the record business lies: record company profits are defended against new technology in the language of individual creativity. As Jon Stratton (1983) has shown, record industry personnel have long explained their activities and the 'irrational rationality' of music as a business in the ideological terms of Romanticism. What is happening now is that technology is disrupting the implicit equation of artists' 'ownership' of their creative work and companies' ownership of the resulting commodities — the latter is being defended by reference to the former. Copyright has become both the legal, ideological weapon with which to attack the 'pirates' and, increasingly, the source of multi-national leisure corporations' income, as they exploit the rights in their productions by licensing them for use by smaller companies and other media.

As John Qualen (1985) points out, the 'crisis' of the music industry in the last decade has concealed three significant shifts in the organization of profit-making since the late 1960s rock record boom. First, recording and

THE ROCK ERA

publishing companies are now integrated, and an increasing proportion of record company profits come, in fact, from their exploitation of their publishing copyrights via air play, the Performing Rights Society, etc. Second, the major record companies are, increasingly, licensing material from their back catalogues for use by independent TV and specialist music packagers. Third, record companies have begun to treat radio and TV use of records and videos not as advertisements for which they provide new material cheaply, but as entertainment services which should pay competitive prices for the recordings they use:

> In many ways the record industry is facing very similar problems to the film industry. Its base market is being eroded and fragmented (pre-recorded music sales are down, as are cinema admissions), costs are spiralling and the traditional distribution system is threatened by the new technologies.
> Though there will always be box-office biggies like *ET* (or *Relax* and *Thriller*), for the most part the earnings of the producers of films (pre-recorded music) will come not from their physical sale but from the exploitation by the producers of the rights they hold in their productions to broadcast and cable TV. The double advantage of this strategy for the record industry (which is far more vertically integrated than the film industry) is that, for the majors, it could eliminate the high cost of manufacturing and distribution.
>
> (Qualen, 1985: 16)

## Conclusion

The political claims of 1960s counter-culture used to be derided for the apparent contradiction between ideology and technology: how could the USA or Britain be 'greened' by Marshall amps and expensive stereo hi-fi systems? For the told-you-so school of mass cultural criticism the argument for technological progress doesn't amount to much. Look what happened, in the end, to Elvis Presley and the electric Bob Dylan, to punk and hip-hop — they were all, one way or another, *co-opted*. This is a familiar argument on the left but rests on its own dubious assumptions. Can musical truth, whether class or gender or ethnic or individual truth, really be guaranteed by acoustics? This seems to be a question that worries first world intellectuals, anxious, maybe, about the roots of their own culture, more than anyone else. Third world musicians, like black musicians in the USA, have rarely been reluctant to adapt their music to new technology (or new technology to their music) (see Laing, and Regev, this issue). Compare the intense American feminist debate about 'women's music'. Should feminists use folk and jazz forms, as more 'authentically' expressive? Or is punk and noise and electro-stridency the necessary source of a new voice?

## ART VS TECHNOLOGY

The debate here turns on who musicians want to reach and how they want to reach them as well as on the implicit ideologies of musical forms themselves, and this means entering the fray of the music market and pop taste, the role of songs and sounds in everyday life. To assume that what happens to stars and movements in the long term — co-option — discredits their disruptive impact in the short term is to misunderstand the politics of culture (and there is no doubting the momentary disruptive impact of Elvis Presley or the Rolling Stones, the Sex Pistols and X-Ray Spex). Technology, the shifting possibility of mechanical reproduction, has certainly been the necessary condition for the rise of the multinational entertainment business, for ever more sophisticated techniques of ideological manipulation, but technology has also made possible new forms of cultural democracy and new opportunities of individual and collective expression. It's not just that the 'aura' of traditional culture has been destroyed, but also that technological devices have been musicians' and audiences' most effective weapons in their continuous guerrilla war against the cultural power of capital and the state. Each new development in recording technology enables new voices to be heard and to be heard in new ways; and pop voices are systematically denied access to other public media. The history of pop is, in part, the history of different groups using the same means (records) for different ends (profits, art, the articulation of community, self-aggrandizement, protest, etc). Technology determines how the competition for a voice is organized but does not determine who will be heard or how what is heard is interpreted. My own belief is that capitalist control of popular music rests not on record company control of recording technology but on its recurring appropriation of fans' and musicians' ideology of art. That the economic arrangements of music production and consumption have not yet changed, despite their increasing lack of fit with the actual production and consumption process, reflects the continuing power of nineteenth-century ideas of creativity and truth.

### Notes

1 Thanks to Paddy Scannell for details of this dispute.
2 Letter from Brian Blain, 12 March 1981.

### References

Ala, N. et al. (1985) 'Patterns of Music Consumption in Milan and Reggio Emilia from April to May 1983', *Popular Music Perspectives*, 2.
Brown, M. (1985) 'Pop — How Live is Live?', *Sunday Times*, 17 March.
Coon, C. (1976) *1988: The New Wave Punk Rock Explosion*. London: Omnibus.
Eckersly, R. (1946) *The BBC And All That*. London: Sampson Low, Marston and Co.
George, N. et al. (1985) *Fresh*. New York: Random House.
Heath, T. (1957) *Listen To My Music*. London: Frederick Muller.

## THE ROCK ERA

Levy, A. (1960) *Operation Elvis.* London: André Deutsch.

Qualen, J. (1985) *The Music Industry.* London: Comedia.

Rockwell, J. (1984) *Sinatra.* New York: Random House.

The Rolling Stones (1964) *Our Own Story.* London: Corgi.

Stratton, J. (1983) 'Capitalism and Romantic Ideology in the Record Business',
    *Popular Music*, 3.

Toop, D. (1984) *The Rap Attack.* London: Pluto Press.

Warner Communications (1982) *Home Taping — A Consumer Survey.*

# CHAPTER 7

# *The Industrialization of Popular Music*

When I was a child I lived in dread of having to sing in public. This was a common forfeit in party games, but I'd do anything else humiliating in preference. Singing was too personal, too exposed an activity.

Singing still seems to me the rawest form of personal expression (which is why I love soul music) and music making, more generally, still seems the most spontaneously human activity. Without thinking much about it, people sing in the bath and on the playground, beat out rhythms on the dance floor, and whistle while they work. It is because of our experience of the *immediacy* of music making that its industrial production has always been somehow suspect. In fact, of course, people today work with piped-in music and skip to the beat of a ghetto blaster; they're more likely to listen to the radio than to sing in the bath. Most of the music we hear now, in public or private, has been mechanically produced and reproduced. It reaches us via an elaborate industrial process and is tied into a complex system of money making. And we take these "artificial" sounds for granted. A couple of years ago I went to see Al Green in concert in the Royal Albert Hall in London. At one point he left the stage (and his microphone) and walked through the audience, still singing. As he passed me I realized that this was the first time, in 30 years as a pop fan, that I'd ever heard a star's "natural" voice!

The contrast between music as expression and music as commodity defines twentieth-century pop experience and means that however much

50      Industrialization of Popular Music

we may use and enjoy its products, we retain a sense that the music industry is a bad thing—bad for music, bad for us. Read any pop history and you'll find in outline the same sorry tale. However the story starts, and whatever the authors' politics, the industrialization of music means a shift from active musical production to passive pop consumption, the decline of folk or community or subcultural traditions, and a general musical deskilling—the only instruments people like me can play today are their disc players and tape decks. The rise of the multinational leisure corporation means, inevitably, efficient manipulation of a new, global pop taste that reaches into every first, second, and Third World household like Coca Cola (and with the same irrelevance to real needs).

What such arguments assume (and they're part of the common sense of every rock fan) is that there is some essential human activity, music making, which has been colonized by commerce. Pop is a classic case of what Marx called alienation: Something human is taken from us and returned in the form of a commodity. Songs and singers are fetishized, made magical, and we can only reclaim them through possession, via a cash transaction in the marketplace. In the language of rock criticism, what's at issue here is the *truth* of music—truth to the people who created it, truth to our experience. What's bad about the music industry is the layer of deceit and hype and exploitation it places between us and our creation.

The flaw in this argument is the suggestion that music is the starting point of the industrial process—the raw material over which everyone fights—when it is, in fact, the final product. The "industrialization of music" can't be understood as something that happens *to* music but describes a process in which music itself is made—a process, that is, that fuses (and confuses) capital, technical, and musical arguments. Twentieth-century popular music means the twentieth-century popular record; not the record of something (a song? a singer? a performance?) that exists independently of the music industry, but a form of communication that determines what songs, singers, and performances are and can be.

We've come to the end of the record era now (and so, perhaps, to the end of pop music as we know it) and I'll return to the future later. What I want to stress here is that from a historical perspective rock and roll was not a revolutionary form or moment, but an evolutionary one, the climax of (or possibly footnote to) a story that begins with Edison's phonograph. To explain the music industry we have, then, to adopt a much wider time perspective than rock scholars usually allow. The pop business itself—the nature of its sales activities— is in a constant state of "crisis." Business analysts should, by contrast, keep cool. To be examining always the entrails of the "latest thing" is to mistake the trees for the forest, and, as I hope to show, there is more to be learned from the continuities in pop history than from the constantly publicized changes. "New things" are rarely as novel as suggested. In 1892, for example, "song slides" became a promotional craze for sheet music publishers. Pictures telling the story were, for years, a necessary sales aid for a new song sheet— they survived the coming of radio and talkies and had a measurable effect on the types of songs marketed and sold (Witmark & Goldberg, 1939). Video promotion doesn't just go back to 1930s jazz shorts!

To analyze the music industry through its history means focusing on three issues.

### The Effects of Technological Change

The origins of recording and the recording industry lie in the nineteenth century, but the emergence of the gramophone record as the predominant musical commodity took place after the 1914-1918 war. The history of the record industry is an aspect of the general history of the electrical goods industry, and has to be related to the development of radio, the cinema, and television. The new media had a profound effect on the social and economic organization of entertainment so that, for example, the rise of record companies meant the decline of the music publishing and piano-making empires, shifting roles for concert hall owners and live-music promoters.

### The Economics of Pop

The early history of the record industry is marked by cycles of boom (1920s), slump (1930s), and boom (1940s). Record company practices reflected first the competition for new technologies and then the even more intense competition for a shrinking market. By the 1950s the record business was clearly divided into the "major" companies and the "independents." Rock analysts have always taken the oligopolistic control of the industry for granted, without paying much attention to how the majors reached their position. What were the business practices

52      Industrialization of Popular Music

that enabled them to survive the slump? What is their role in boom times?

**A New Musical Culture**

The development of a large-scale record industry marked a profound transformation in musical experience, a decline in amateur music making, the rise of a new sort of musical consumption and use. Records and radio made possible both new national (and international, American-based) musical tastes and new social divisions between "classical" and "pop" audiences. The 1920s and 1930s marked the appearance of new music professionals—pop singers, session musicians, record company A & R people, record producers, disc jockeys, studio engineers, record critics, and so on. These were the personnel who both resisted and absorbed the "threat" of rock and roll in the 1950s and rock in the 1960s.

*The Making of a Record Industry*

The origins of the record industry are worth describing in some detail because of the light they cast on recent developments. The story really begins with the North American Phonograph Company which, in 1888, got licenses to market both Edison's phonograph and the Graphophone, a version of the phonograph developed by employees of the Bell Telephone Company. When Edison had predicted, 10 years earlier, how his invention would "benefit mankind," he had cited the reproduction of music as one of its capacities, but this was not the sales pitch of the North American Phonograph Company. They sought to rent machines (as telephones were rented) via regional franchises to offices—the phonograph was offered as a dictating device.

The resulting marketing campaign was a flop. The only regional company to have any success was the Columbia Phonograph Co. (Washington had more offices than anywhere else!). The company soon found that the phonograph was more successful as a coin-operated "entertainment" machine, a novelty attraction (like the early cinema) at fairs and medicine shows and on the vaudeville circuit. And for this purpose, "entertaining" cylinders were needed. Columbia took the lead in providing a choice of "Sentimental," "Topical," "Comic," "Irish," and "Negro" songs.

Meanwhile, Emile Berlinger, who in 1887-1888 was developing the gramophone, a means of reproducing sounds using discs, not cylinders, was equally concerned in making recordings—he needed to demonstrate the superiority of his machine over Edison's. The United States Gramophone Company was formed in 1893, and the following year Fred Gaisberg, who'd started there as a piano accompanist and thus taken charge of recording, was poached from Columbia to be Berlinger's recording director and talent scout. Berlinger, unlike Edison, regarded the gramophone as primarily a machine for home entertainment and the mass production of music discs such that "prominent singers, speakers or performers may derive an income from royalties on the sale of their phonautograms" (Gelatt, 1977, p. 13), and in 1897 Gaisberg opened the first commercial recording studio. For the next five years there was an intense legal struggle between disc and cylinder.

It is useful at this point to make the usual industry distinction between hardware and software: hardware is the equipment, the furniture, the "permanent" capital of home entertainment; software is what the equipment plays—particular records, tapes or discs. The invention, manufacture, and selling of hardware must, obviously, precede the manufacture and selling of software. What normally happens, then, is that hardware companies get involved in software production simply in order to have something on which to demonstrate their equipment—we can thus compare the early history of the record industry with the recent history of video. Video manufacturers too have been confused abut what video owners would, in practice, use them for. Software is, in fact, first regarded as a means of advertising hardware (where the initial profits lie)—think of the original marketing of stereo equipment, with records of train noises that could be heard to move from one speaker to the other!

At a certain moment in the development of a new electronic medium, though, the logic changes. If people begin buying records, any will do (train noises, the first compact disc releases, whatever one's tastes), just to have *something* to play. Then, as ownership of the new equipment becomes widespread, records are bought for their own sake, and people begin to buy new, improved players in order to listen to specific sounds. Records cease to be a novelty. In the record industry this switch began in the 1920s, the real boom time for companies making both phonographs and phonograph records. In the words of Edward Lewis, a stockbroker who helped Decca become a public company in 1928,

54      Industrialization of Popular Music

"a company manufacturing gramophones but not records was rather like making razors but not the consumable blades" (Lewis, 1956). In the video industry the switch means a changing source of the best profits—from the hardware makers (in Britain, for example, the home video market is pretty well exhausted; after its remarkable growth figures the manufacturers can now expect a steady decline in sales) to software (that is, film) rights, hence the interest of mass media moguls such as Rupert Murdoch in film companies: Their back catalogs are the basic resource for both home video users and cable television stations.

By the 1920s there were, in both Britain and the United States, numerous phonograph manufacturers competing for sales by references to technical advances, design qualities, a variety of gimmicks and, of necessity, by issuing their own records. At this stage record companies were part of the electrical goods industry, and quite separate in terms of financial control and ownership from previous musical entrepreneurs. They were owned and run by engineers, inventors, and stock market speculators that had little to do with song publishers, theater owners, agents and promoters, performers, and managers. They don't even seem to have been much interested in music. Gaisberg comments in his memoirs that "for many years Berlinger was the only one of the many people I knew connected with the gramophone who was genuinely musical" (Gaisberg, 1946, p. 25).

It follows that these companies' musical decisions, their policies on who and what to record, were entirely dependent on the judgments and tastes of the "live" music entrepreneur (just as the "new" form, pop video, has been dependent so far on the skills and tastes of existing short film—that is, advertisement—makers). Companies competed to issue material by the same successful stage and concert hall performers, to offer versions of the latest stage show hit or dance floor craze, a practice that continued into the 1950s and rock and roll with the "cover version." Few companies were interested in promoting new numbers or new stars, and there was a widely held assumption in the industry that while pop records were a useful novelty in the initial publicizing of phonographs, in the long run the industry's returns would depend on people wanting to build up permanent libraries of "serious" music. Fred Gaisberg, for example, the first A & R man, whose work soon took him from America to Britain and then across Europe and Asia, was, essentially, a classical music impresario. Record companies are making the same calculations today about compact discs as the sales potential of the back catalog is exhausted. People are once again being encouraged to build up "librar-ies" of music, and rock-identified labels, whether a major like WEA or independents like Virgin and Factory, have now established their own classical music divisions.

There is an irony here that has a continuing resonance: While each new technological change in mass music making is seen to be a further threat to "authentic" popular music, classical music is seen to benefit from such changes, which from hi-fidelity recordings to compact discs have, indeed, been pioneered by record companies' classical divisions. The record industry has always sold itself by what it could do for "serious" music. As Cyril Ehrlich points out, the gramophone began as not quite respectable (because of its public novelty use) and so an emphasis on its use for playing classical music was seen as necessary to sell it to middle-class families (Ehrlich, 1976). The early cinema went respectable with similar tactics—using classical music for its accompa-niment to silent films. The important point here is that in the history of electronic media, the initial "mass market" (this was true for radio, television, and video as well) is the relatively affluent middle-class household. The organization of the record industry around the pop record (and the pop audience) was a later development, a consequence, indeed, of the economic slump.

For anyone writing the history of the record industry in 1932, there would have been very little doubt that the phonograph was a novelty machine that had come and gone, just like the uneventful passing of the piano roll. Sales of records had dropped from 104 million in 1927 to 6 million; the number of phonograph machines manufactured had fallen from 987,000 to 40,000.

The 1930s slump was marked not just by an overall decline in leisure spending but also by a major reorganization of people's leisure habits. The spread of radio and arrival of talking pictures meant that a declining share of a declining income went toward records (just as in the late 1970s and early 1980s, when there was, after the rise in gas prices, less money overall to spend on new leisure time products like video record-ers and computer games). I won't go into the details of the slump here, but simply note its consequences. First, it caused the collapse of all small recording companies and reestablished the record business as an oligopoly, a form of production dominated by a small number of "major" companies. This wasn't just a matter of rationalization in the recording business itself—failing companies going bankrupt or being taken

56      Industrialization of Popular Music

over— but also involved the surviving companies covering the crisis in record sales by putting together more wide-ranging music interests.

The development of American radio had parallels with the history of the record industry. Various companies were working out how best to exploit a new medium (by carving up the patents) and were discovering that to persuade people to rent transmitters (and make money from advertisement sales) they'd also need to provide entertaining programs. By 1926, RCA was networking shows via its National Broadcasting Company. There was also an early broadcasting emphasis on "potted palm music" (to attract relatively affluent and respectable listeners), which meant that while radio did "kill" record sales it also left pockets of tastes unsatisfied. Early radio stations were not interested in black audiences and so the market for jazz and blues records became much more significant.

As radios replaced record players in people's homes the primary source of music profit shifted from record sales to performing rights and royalties, and the basic technological achievement of this period, the development of electrical recording by Western Electric, marked a fusion of interests among the radio, cinema, and record industries. Western Electric could claim a royalty on all electrical recordings and was the principal manufacturer of theater talkie installations. Film studios such as Warner's had to start thinking about the costs (and profits) of publishers' performing rights, and began the Hollywood entry into the music business by taking over the Tin Pan Alley publisher, Witmark, in 1928.

The following year RCA (with money advanced by GE and Westinghouse) took over the Victor Talking Machine Company and, with General Motors, formed GM Radio Corporation, to exploit the possibilities of car radio. The subsequent making (and unmaking) of the United State's electrical-entertainment corporations is too complicated to go into here, but in the resulting oligopoly, competition for sales got more intense and, quickly, changed its terms. The initial response to falling sales was a price war—records were sold for less and less and the assumption was that people would go for the cheapest record on the market, but this eventually came up against the "irrationality" of tastes—people's musical choices aren't just a matter of price. New sales tactics had to be developed and, for the first time, record companies, led by Decca, ran aggressive advertising campaigns in newspapers and on billboards:

Here they are—your favourites of radio, screen and stage—in their greatest performances of instrument and voice! Not obsolete records, cut in price to meet a market, but the latest, newest smash hits—exclusively DECCA. Hear them when you want—as often as you want—right in your own home. (Gelatt, 1977, p. 268)

Decca was the first company to realize that an investment in advertisement and promotion was more than justified by the consequent increase in sales. The peculiarity of record making is that once the break-even point is past, the accumulation of profit is stunningly quick. The costs of reproduction are a small proportion of the costs of producing the original master disc or tape. It follows that huge sales of one title are much more profitable than even cost-covering sales of lots of titles and that the costs of ensuring huge sales are necessary costs. Decca thus developed the marketing logic that was to become familiar to rock fans in the last 1960s: Promotion costs were established at whatever figure seemed necessary to guarantee huge sales. Only major companies can afford such risks (and have the necessary capital available) and the strategy is dependent also on a star system, on performers whose general popularity is guaranteed in advance.

In the 1930s the recording star system was dependent on a tie-in with film and radio (hence the arrival of Bing Crosby—again, Decca was the first company to realize how valuable he was). But in the 1980s, again in a time of recession, we saw very similar strategies being followed—an emphasis on a few superstars at the expense of the mass of groups just getting by, those stars in turn being marketed via films and film soundtracks and, more especially, with video promotion on MTV. Industry statistics suggest that the average of 4,000-5,000 new albums per year in the 1970s had become less than 2,000 per year in the 1980s.[1]

Aggressive selling and a star system in the 1930s meant a new recording strategy. Companies became less concerned to exploit existing big names, more interested in building stars from scratch, as recording stars; they became less concerned to service an existing public taste than to create new tastes, to manipulate demand. Electrical recording helped here. New crooning stars like Crosby could suggest an intimate, personal relationship with fans that worked best for domestic listeners: His live performances had to reproduce a recorded experience rather than vice versa, and jukebox programmers offered a direct way to control national taste. But radio mattered most of all, and by the end of the 1930s it was the most important musical medium. It gave record companies a means of promoting their stars and record companies provided radio stations with their cheapest form of programming. Media that had seemed totally incompatible—radio killed the record star—ended up inseparable.

The 1930s marked, in short, a shift in cultural and material musical power— from Tin Pan Alley to broadcasting networks and Hollywood studios, from the publisher/showman/song system to a record/radio/film star system—and the judgment of what was a good song or performance shifted accordingly—from suitability for a live audience to suitability for a radio show or a jukebox. It was in the 1930s that the "popularity" of music came to be measured (and thus defined) by record sales figures and radio plays. Popular music came to describe a fixed performance, a recording with the right qualities of intimacy or personality, emotional intensity or ease. "Broad" styles of singing taken from vaudeville or the music hall began to sound crude and quaint; pop expression now had to be limited to the two or three minutes of a 78rpm disc, and while musicians still had many of the same concerns—to write good tunes, to develop a hook, to sum up a feeling in a lyric, to give people something to whistle or dance to—the gatekeepers of this new music industry, the people who now determined what music was recorded, broadcast, and heard, were quite different from their predecessors in the music business. They were no longer directly connected to a public, trying to please it on the spot; their concern was a market, popularity as revealed by the sales that consumers delivered to advertisers. For the record industry (as for the film industry) the audience was essentially anonymous; popularity meant, by definition, something that crossed class and regional boundaries; the secret of success was to offend nobody. The record industry became a mass medium in the 1930s on the back of two assumptions; first, that the pop audience was essentially malleable; second, that pop music (and musicians) were, in cultural terms, vacuous. These assumptions were challenged after World War II by the rise of rock and roll.


### The Making of the Rock Industry

By 1945 the basic structure of the modern music industry was in place. Pop music meant pop records, commodities, a technological and commercial process under the control of a small number of larger companies. Such control depended on the ownership of the means of record production and distribution and was organized around the marketing of stars and star performances (just as the music publishing business had been organized around the manufacture and distribution of songs). Live music making was still important but its organization and profits were increasingly dependent on the exigencies of record making. The most important way of publicizing pop now—the way most people heard most music—was on the radio, and records were made with radio formats and radio audiences in mind.

The resulting shifts in the distribution of musical power and wealth didn't occur without a struggle. The declining significance of New York publishing houses and big city session musicians, the growing importance of radio programmers and record company A & R people, were marked by strikes, recording bans, disputes over broadcasting rights and studio fees, and, outside the United States, such disputes were inflected with the issue of "Americanization" (and anti-Americanism). The United States's influence on international popular music, beginning with the worldwide showing of Hollywood talkies, was accelerated by the U.S. entry into World War II—members of the service became the record industry's most effective exporters. By the end of the war the pop music people heard on radio and records across Europe—and even in parts of Southeast Asia—was either directly or indirectly (cover versions, copied styles) American. Hollywood's 1930s success in defining internationally what "popular cinema" meant was reinforced in the 1940s and 1950s by the American record industry's success in defining the worldwide sound of "popular music."

Outside the United States the ending of the war and wartime austerity and restraint meant a new boom for the record industry (in Britain, for example, Decca's turnover increased eightfold between 1946 and 1956). In the United States, postwar euphoria was short lived. By the end of the 1940s, television seemed to carry the same threat to the pop industry as radio had 20 years earlier. The industry's resistance to this threat and its subsequent unprecedented profits were due to technological and social changes that, eventually, turned the record industry into the rock business.

The technological developments that began with CBS's experiments with microgroove recording in the late 1940s and culminated with digital recording and the compact disc in the 1980s, had two objects: to improve recorded sound quality and to make record storage and preservation easier. For the electrical engineers who worked to give their companies a competitive edge in the playback market, the musical aspects of their experiments were straightforward. What they were trying to do was to make recorded sound a more accurate reproduction of "real" sound—from the start the new processes were marketed in the name of "high fidelity." But this sales talk of records reaching nearer and nearer to the "complete" experience of "live" music is just that— sales talk. Each new advance—stereo discs in the 1960s, compact discs' elimination of surface noise and wear in the 1980s—changes our experience of music (and some changes, such as quadraphonic, have been rejected by consumers despite their supposed superior truth-to-concert-experience). Hi-fi opened our ears to a new appreciation of dynamic range and subtlety. By the end of the 1960s, records, not concerts, defined the "best" sound. Nowadays both classical and popular musicians have to make sure that their live performances meet the sound standards of their records. The acoustic design of concert halls has changed accordingly, and rock groups take sound checks, sound mixers, elaborate amplification systems, and these days the use of taped material to enhance their "live" performances for granted. The increasing "purity" of recorded sound—no extraneous or accidental noises—is the mark of its artificiality. Prewar records were always heard as a more or less crackly mediation between listeners and actual musical events; their musical qualities often depended on listeners' own imaginations. To modern listeners these old discs (and particularly classical 78s) are "unlistenable"—we're used to treating albums as musical events in themselves.

A second point follows from this. All hi-fi inventions (and this includes the compact disc) have been marketed, at first, on the assumption that the consumers most concerned about sound quality and a permanent record library are "serious" consumers, consuming "serious" music. The late 1940s "battle of the speeds" between CBS's 33 1/3 LPs and RCA's 45 rpm records was resolved with a simple market division— LPs were for classical music collectors, 45s for pop, which continued to be organized in three-minute segments, as music of convenience and of the moment (a definition reinforced by the continuing significance of jukeboxes for pop sales).

Record companies' assumptions about "true" reproduction and pop triviality were, in the end, undermined by the invention that made hi-fi records feasible—magnetic tape. In the long term the importance of tape recording was to be its availability to domestic consumers:

> In 1969 the industry produced small, self-contained tape cassettes that could run backward or forward, record or replay, skip to specific selections, and hold as much as an LP. These mass-produced cassettes made all the advantages of tape—high quality sound, long wear and ease of storage—available, affordable, easy to use, and very popular. By 1970 cassettes accounted for nearly a third of recorded music sales, and in 1971 the value of tape players sold exceeded that of phonographs. (Toll, 1982, p. 74)

Hence arose the problem of home taping that, in the 1950s, was certainly not foreseen. Tape recording, initially developed by German scientists for broadcasting purposes in the war, was initially picked up not by the music biz but by radio stations (as a relatively cheap way of rerecording talk and jingles) and film studios (as an aid to making soundtracks), but record companies quickly realized tape's flexibility and cheapness too, and by 1950 tape recording had replaced disc recording entirely. This was the technological change that allowed new, independent producers into the market—the cost of recording fell dramatically even if the problems of large-scale manufacture and distribution remained. Mid-1950s United States indie labels such as Sun were as dependent on falling studio costs as late-1970s punk labels in Britain, the latter benefiting from scientific breakthroughs and falling prices in electronic recording.

But tape's importance wasn't just in terms of costs. Tape was an intermediary in the recording process. The performance was recorded on tape, the tape was used to make the master disc. And it was what could be done during this intermediary stage, to the tape itself, that transformed pop music making. Producers no longer had to take performances in their entirety. They could cut and splice, edit the best bits of performances together, cut out the mistakes, make records of ideal, not real, events. And on tape sounds could be added artificially. Instruments could be recorded separately; a singer could be taped, sing over the tape, and be taped again. Such techniques gave producers a new flexibility that enabled them to make records of performances, like a double tracked vocal, that were impossible live (though musicians and equipment manufacturers were soon looking for ways to get the same effects on stage). By the mid-1960s the development of multitrack recording enabled sounds to be stored separately on the same tape and altered in relationship to each other at the final mixing stage, rather than through the continuous process of sound addition. Producers could now work on the tape itself to "record" a performance that was actually put together from numerous, quite separate events, happening at different times and, increasingly, in different studios. The musical judgments, choices, and skills of producers and engineers became as significant as those of the musicians and, indeed, the distinction between engineers and musicians has become meaningless. Studio-made music need no longer bear any relationship to anything that can be performed live; records use sounds, the effects of tape tricks and electronic equipment, that no one has ever heard before as music (Frith, 1983). And the digital storage of sound has made its manipulation even easier. Computers can be used to isolate, extract, and distort any element from a digital recording (a drum sound, a bass note). Such "sampling" is now a norm of record production, though the legal implications in terms of authorship and "theft" remain unresolved.

It is a pleasing irony of pop history that while *classical* divisions of record companies have led the way in studio technology, their pursuit of authenticity has limited their studio imagination. It was *pop* producers, unashamedly using technology to "cheat" audiences (double tracking weak voices, filling out a fragile beat, faking strings) who, in the 1950s and 1960s, developed recording as an art form, thus enabling rock to develop as a "serious" music in its own right. The emergence of rock as art was symbolized by the Beatles' self-conscious studio artifact, *Sgt. Pepper's Lonely Hearts Club*.

The rise of rock depended too on a broader social change—the appearance of youth as the pop music market. This was partly the result of general demographic and economic trends—the increasing number of teenagers in the 1950s (a period of full employment) gave their consumer choices a new market weight—and partly reflected changes within the leisure industry itself. As television became the basic medium of family entertainment, previous leisure businesses such as the cinema, radio, dance halls, and theater went into decline. Teenagers were the one age group that still wanted to be out of the house and they began to take over public leisure spaces, to display a distinct teen culture in their own codes of dress and noise. These new leisure consumers were not, at first, catered to by the major leisure companies, and American teenagers had to find their style where they could—in black music, in certain Hollywood images. The resulting demands for records and clothes were first met by small, independent companies, looking for opportunities not already covered by the majors. Their success (and need for further advertisement outlets and promotion) opened the new market to media like radio and cinema desperately in need of it. The Elvis Presley story is typical. His commercial potential was first realized by his local independent label, Sun, but once his potential was realized (and his television appearances proved to the doubters that he could, indeed, be a national youth star) then he was quickly used as a way of selling records, cinema seats, magazines, merchandise, and advertising time on radio (which was adapting easily to Top 40 and rock and roll formats). From the industry perspective rock and roll was a means to an end. As music it was taken to be silly, gimmicky, and with a short shelf life; but as a way to control teenage spending, it couldn't be beaten. As deejay Dick Clark remembers,

> it was during this time that I decided to go into the record business. I got into talent management, music publishing, record pressing, label making, distribution, domestic and foreign rights, motion pictures, show promotion and teenage merchandise. (Frith, 1981, p. 96)

The record industry's post-Presley focus on youth had spectacular results. In 1955 U.S. record sales increased 30% (from their post war low point) to $277 million; in 1956 they reached $377 million; in 1957 $460 million; and in 1959 a peak of $603 million.

For the moment it seemed as if a sales plateau had been reached. The discovery of teenagers had given the industry a new lease on life but the exploitation of this market by a new network of teenage records/stars/films/TV shows/magazines/concerts/dance steps/radio shows had the effect of confining teenage culture and teenage music to a combination of vacuous fun and romantic self-pity. After the trashy, erotic excitement of the original rock and rollers, teen music had become, under the tutelage of the record biz, an aspect of white middle-class conformity, and it took the arrival of the Beatles to suggest how limited this market was, even in commercial terms. The Beatles revealed a "youth" market that crossed age and class lines, a "pop" market that confounded the distinctions between "serious" and "trivial" records. Beatles fans were the first generation to grow up with hi-fi sounds as the norm. They bought pop records to lay on sophisticated equipment, collected LPs, assumed that their stars would be available in stereo.

64        Industrialization of Popular Music

In the United States this market was first tapped not by local independent producers (though significant independent servicing companies were involved—FM radio stations, *Rolling Stone,* new promoters like Bill Graham) but by British acts, and the immediate result of this was the direct entry of the U.S. majors, CBS, RCA, and Warner's, into the British pop scene. They set up offices in London in pursuit of British musicians, not fans. The Beatles and Rolling Stones, Dave Clark, Herman's Hermits, and the rest of the British invasion groups were almost all signed to EMI or Decca, which made them vast profits, but by the end of the 1960s British rock groups such as Led Zeppelin, who made even vaster profits, were on American labels. By the end of the 1970s Decca itself had been taken over by the German-Dutch company, Polygram, and EMI had been reabsorbed by Thorn, the electrical goods manufacturer it had sold off 50 years earlier.

Rock, even more dramatically than rock and roll, reached sales levels previously thought impossible. In 1967 the American record industry passed the billion dollar annual sales mark for the first time. By 1973 annual sales had reached $2 billion, record companies were taking two million sales of single rock LPs for granted, and classical music's market share, 25% in the 1950s, had dropped to 5%. By 1978 the industry had reached sales of more than $4 billion. This was the industry I described in my book, *Sound Effects:* "music had become the most popular form of entertainment—the sales of records and tapes easily outgrossed the returns on movies or sport" (Frith, 1981, pp. 4-5).

The 1970s rock industry was focused almost exclusively on record sales. The major music corporations' profits derived from their manufacture and sale of vast numbers of vinyl discs and, as in the 1930s, the fixed costs of record making were such that the profit rate accelerated rapidly as sales rose. By the mid-1970s the potential sales figures of rock's superstars seemed limitless. All other aspects of the music business were subordinated to this record sales campaign. Live performance, radio and television appearances, music press interviews, photo sessions, and the like were all developed as promotional tools. Every rise in costs seemed to be justified by the resulting rise in sales:

By the end of the 1970s the average rock and roll album cost between $70,000 and $100,000 in studio time, and any "sweetening" (adding strings, for example) could add another $50,000 to the bill; promotion budgets began at around $150,000 and rose rapidly. At the beginning of the decade there was still some sense of "normal" production costs, "normal" sales and "normal" profits. Now the decision was made the other way round: the object became platinum sales—a million copies as a starting point. Company bosses began to turn their noses up at gold records—500,000 sales; studios and promotion costs were established at whatever would ensure platinum. (Frith, 1981, p. 147)

Throughout the 1970s, on the other hand, 80% of records released failed to cover their costs and so there developed a sharp distinction between "hit" groups, for whom the first sign of success meant a sudden surge of record company investment designed to realize the sales potential to the full, and "miss" groups, the majority, whose records were released without fanfare, vanished without a trace. The record industry can't control pop purchasers—partly because people's musical tastes are irrational, partly because some of the crucial gatekeepers in the business such as disc jockeys and journalists have their own interests to pursue. Record companies' usual strategy is, therefore, to release far too much product while trying to maximize the returns of success and to minimize the costs of failure. It's worth noting two points about this. First, stars are the best guarantors of success record companies can get, which is why established stars such as Stevie Wonder can negotiate such good deals when their contracts lapse: The record company ideal is to have a record go platinum before it's even released. Second, all record companies seek to exploit fully their fixed capital—the pressing plants, A & R departments, sales teams, and studios, which cost money whether they're being used or not. Record flops are made, then, with little additional costs for the companies, and just often enough a hit is released that covers all these costs anyway.

One of the most peculiar aspects of this business in the 1970s was that it was a hugely profitable corporate structure resting on two anti-corporate myths. Myth 1 pitched artists and their audiences against an industry that, supposedly, denied people access to their music with a series of greedy, profit-obsessed gatekeepers. Myth 2 celebrated independent labels as rock's real creative entrepreneurs—the majors were accused of simply taking over and homogenizing the original sounds and styles the indies developed. Neither of these myths made much sense about how the rock business actually worked—as a highly efficient organization of market servicing.

This involved, first of all, the steady professionalization of every facet of music making. Hucksters, amateurs, and gamblers were replaced by responsible team players—musicians, managers, promoters,

66      Industrialization of Popular Music

.pluggers, agents, and so on, who were paid not to take risks but to provide a fixed skill. The industry began to be dominated by lawyers and accountants and by the mid-1970s there was very little tension between musicians and the business. Rock performers were more likely to complain about companies not exploiting them properly than to object to being "commercialized."

Second, "independent" producers and label owners were part of this system. They became, in effect, talent scouts and market researchers for the major companies, while being driven, for survival, into dependent manufacturing and distribution deals. They were the main victims of the ever-increasing financial demands made by each professional in the system, made by the artists and producers and engineers and promotion crews. The costs of success were inflationary and it made sense to let the majors bear them.

The rock industry was, in short, not only profitable on an unprecedented scale, it also seemed all-enveloping. It was no longer possible to talk sensibly about the moguls' exploitation of the musicians (rock musicians were making enough money to be moguls), or the unfair competition between the majors and the independents ("independence" no longer described how small companies worked), or consumers' unmet demands—rock audiences wallowed in the music they got. There was no grit in the system, and when it did appear, as punk, it was in the form of a challenge not to the entertainment business as such but to the very idea of entertainment itself.

The punk argument was that rock no longer excited or challenged or threatened anyone. Something new was needed and, according to cyclical theorists, this was an inevitable turn of rock's wheel—independent labels develop new forms of music, the majors tame them, independent labels thus develop new forms of music, the majors tame them. But punk didn't feed into the industry this way. Its do-it-yourself ideology was both too radical for the record industry and too feeble. The punk musicians who wanted to be stars signed up to major labels anyway; the musicians who didn't want to be stars were no commercial threat.

The rock business faced a crisis at the end of the 1970s not because of punk or the cycle of business competition but because of "outside" technological and social changes parallel to those that gave birth to rock and roll in the first place. On the one hand, the demographic structure of Western countries was shifting (the number of teenagers fell, the number of people over 25 increased) while mass youth unemployment meant young people had less money to spend on leisure goods anyway. On the other hand, the spread of home taping, computer games, and video recording gave recorded music new sorts of competition for people's time and interest. In Britain, for instance, 1984 market research suggested that 97% of teenagers had access to tape recorders and that 85% used them to record music. By the same year 35% of households had videocassette recorders and 20% home computers, equipment that no one had in 1976. As the British Phonographic Industry commented on computer software (85% of which is "game-oriented"):

> The consumer profile is similar, especially in age group, to music buyers, and the pricing level of a game is only marginally more than a top price LP. There is strong evidence that recorded music purchasers are diverting some of their leisure spending to computer software. (BPI, 1985, p. 35)

This is the context for the end of the rock boom. Between 1973 and 1978 world record sales expanded from $4.75 to $7 billion, but in 1978-1979 there was a 20% drop in record sales in Britain, an 11% fall off in the United States. The growth rate of the rock business (which had reached 25% per year in 1976) was down to 5%-6%, and record companies had to stop assuming ever-increasing sales, an expanding number of platinum discs. The industry in the United States did recover in the mid-1980s, but as *Billboard* noted in 1984:

> The industry's total haul of gold and platinum albums declined for the third straight year. This supports the contention that the trade's recovery in '83 was due more to the runaway success of a handful of smash hits than to an across-the-board pickup in album sales.

The industry also benefited from the consumer shift from vinyl to compact discs, which have a much higher profit margin (especially as the bulk of CD sales so far have come from back catalog). The number of actual titles released remains much lower than it was in the mid-1970s.

68      Industrialization of Popular Music

### The Politics of Technology

Most explanations of change in the music industry are derived from general theories of corporate strategy and market control. As I summarized this in *Sound Effects:*

> Historians of American popular music argue that musical innovation has always come from outside the major record companies. "Independent" companies have been the outlet for the expression of new ideas and interests, and only when such ideas have been shown to be popular have the major companies used their financial advantages to take them over, to turn them into new, "safe" products. Innovation in such an oligopolistic industry is only possible because technological changes open gaps in existing market control, and if, in the long run, competition means creativity (the more sources of capital, the more chance of musical progress), in the short run, the music business is intensely conservative, more concerned with avoiding loss than risking profit, confirming tastes than disrupting them. Records are made according to what the public is known to want already. (Frith, 1981, p. 89)

What this analysis describes is a particular pattern of market competition—at one moment intense (new producers, new sounds, new media outlets, newly discovered audiences), at another moment stagnant (a small number of large companies producing a homogeneous product for a known consumer group). Technological change has a role in this cycle of competition and consolidation (it affects market conditions), but the underlying dynamo of pop history is human nature: People's musical "needs" are increasingly ill-met by conservative corporations until they burst out in a ferment of exciting new styles and stars (and new companies to market them).

I'm dubious about this model. It feeds into and derives from the 1960s rock delusion that it was possible, at moments, to have a mass produced music (rock and roll, British beat) that wasn't really "commercial," and there is little evidence today, as we've seen, that major and independent record companies are really competing with each other. As Heikki Hellman puts it:

> The pattern is rather that the smaller companies offer a test market for the competition between the larger companies, through which these companies can outline their music production. The smaller companies have gained a permanent and important although subordinate position in the music industry. The cycles have changed into symbiosis. (Hellman, 1983, p. 355).

This is not to say that there are no longer contradictions and struggles in the music business, but that they can't be reduced to a simple lineup of goodies and baddies (independent companies, bold musicians, and adventurous fans versus the multinationals, designer groups, and easy listeners). If there's one thing to be learned from twentieth-century pop history it is that technological inventions have unexpected consequences. The "industrialization of music" has changed what we do when we play or listen to music, and it has changed our sense of what "music" is, both in itself and as an aspect of our lives and leisure, but these changes aren't just the result of producer decisions and control. They also reflect musicians' and consumers' responses.

Music "machines" have not, in short, been as dehumanizing as mass media critics from both left and right perspectives have suggested. For a start, it was technological developments that made our present understanding of musical "authenticity" possible. Recording devices enabled previously unreproducible aspects of performance—improvization, spontaneity— to be reproduced exactly, and so enabled Afro-American music to replace European art and folk musics at the heart of Western popular culture (and the global reach of black American sounds is even more remarkable than the global reach of white American capital). This affected not just what sort of music people listened to but also how they listened to it, how they registered the emotional meanings of sounds and the musical shape of their own emotions. Recording gave a public means of communication to otherwise socially inarticulate people, and its continuing technical refinement, particularly since the development of the electrical microphone, has extended the possibilities of expression in all pop genres. Out of such developments came the star system— the marketing of individual performers as spuriously "knowable" friends and idols—but out of these same developments also came new means of self-definition, musical identities that could (as in "minority" cultures and subcultures) challenge the common sense of bourgeois ideology (Frith, 1986).

Technological change has also been the basic source of resistance to the corporate control of popular music. Examine the history of inventions in the recording industry and you find that those that catch on are the ones that lead, at least in the short term, to the decentralization of music making and listening—video tapes caught on, for example, video discs did not. The music industry uses new instruments and devices to do old things more efficiently or cheaply; it is musicians and consumers

70        Industrialization of Popular Music

who discover their real possibilities. The mechanization of popular music has not, then, been a simple story of capitalist takeover. Think, for example, of how Jamaican dub culture and New York hip-hop took over the technology of recording to undermine the status of the record as a finished product; scratching and mixing "found" sounds together, challenging the whole idea of copyright.

But the most significant example of new technological habits challenging old record company ways is home taping. Cassette recorders have given fans a new means of control over their sounds; they can compile LPs and radio shows for themselves, use a Walkman to carry their soundscapes around with them. And, for the industry, this is the source of all its troubles. Behind the recurring (and increasingly successful) campaigns for levies to be imposed on blank tapes is the suggestion that people are using them to acquire music illicitly, without paying for it, without even giving the musicians involved their just reward. Every blank tape sold is a record not sold. This is another example of the multinationals' inability to control the use of their own inventions (the effects of home taping were not anticipated) and their failure to grasp the point that to throw another electronic toy into the leisure market is to disrupt all consumer habits. The suggestion that blank tapes are simply replacing records is, therefore, misleading. What home taping signifies, rather, is the changing place of music in leisure generally. Records are being replaced not by tapes as such but by other leisure activities; music is being used differently and in different, more flexible forms.

If record companies often misread the future they also regularly mistake passing fads for lasting habits (hence Warner's fateful over investment in Atari computer games) and this raises a third point: how leisure pattern change can vary remarkably among countries even when they have similar entertainment setups. In 1975, for example, sales of Stereo 8 cartridges reached 25% of all recorded music sales in the United States but were statistically insignificant in Britain. By contrast, the "penetration" of videocassette recorders was an estimated 40% of households in Britain in 1984 and only 14% in the United States (no one in Britain had expected this VCR boom—Thorn-EMI even decided not to invest in its initial development). Britain, meanwhile, lags far behind both the United States and the rest of Northern Europe in cable TV connections. This has had the interesting consequence that Britain's first cable pop channel, Music Box, was in practice developed as a record promotion tool only in Holland and Belgium.

This is the context in which two terms of nineteenth-century ideology—nationalism and romanticism—have become crucial to the politics of twentieth-century technology. Countries are increasingly defending their music industries against the spread of cable and satellite broadcasting, against the marketing decisions of multinational communications groups, in the name of their "national heritage." The Dutch government demanded that Music Box give time to Dutch pop groups; the Swedish government uses blank tape levies to subsidize the production of Swedish music; the Canadians have a quota system for Canadian records on Canadian radio; Third World countries establish state-funded recording studios. And the irony is that the resulting "national" music is, more often than not, just a local variant of global style; the real idea is that small countries will generate international hits of their own.

Multinational profits are, meanwhile, being defended against new technology in the language of individual creativity. Home taping, scratch mixing, and the various forms of piracy have disrupted the equation of artists' "ownership" of their creative work and companies' ownership of the resulting commodities—the latter is being defended by reference to the former. Copyright has become the legal and ideological weapon with which to attack "illegal" copying, and the battle is being fought in the name of justice for the artist.

## Conclusion

> Rock is the sound of a commercial, the sound of people chasing each other on Miami Vice, the music to a World Series or a Broadway show. The 60s discovered that voice and that voice has now become the voice of corporate America. (Graham, 1986)

Record executives no longer wake up in the night worried they were the ones who turned down the next Michael Jackson. They've got a worse nightmare now: They sign up the next MJ and then make no money out of him! For every record they sell, 1,000 are copied on to tape by fans at home and 100,000 are produced illicitly in Singapore and Taiwan! His video clips are stolen from satellite services and the world is awash with unauthorized posters and tee-shirts!

72      Industrialization of Popular Music

Even by 1982 the piracy figures were daunting—66% of the Asian record and tape market, 30% in Africa and the Middle East, 21% in South America, 11% in Canada and the United States. European figures were lower (3% in Britain) but only by dint of expensive and time-consuming legal and detective work (and even in Eastern Europe "piracy" the ability of small producers and private consumers to use their own taping facilities to bypass state recording policy is now a major problem—even in the former East Germany there was more sophisticated recording equipment in private than in public hands). The western music industry will remain wary even of postcommunist Eastern bloc countries until they have established appropriate (i.e., Western) copyright laws. And if there's one thing we can predict with certainty it is that by the end of the century copying and reproducing equipment (developed relentlessly by Japanese electronic hardware firms) will be cheaper, better, and more widely owned. Not even the rise of the compact disc will solve this problem. Domestic digital recording equipment, blank CDs, the compact Walkman, and the rest of the necessary items for "home discing" are already developed.

What we have seen is, effectively, the "death of black vinyl." As John Qualen (1985) points out, the "crisis" in the music industry in the last decade has been marked by three important shifts in the organization of profit making. First, recording and publishing companies are now integrated, and an increasing proportion of record company profits come from the exploitation of publishing copyrights. Second, the majors now derive a regular source of income from licensing material from their back catalogs to independent TV and specialist music packagers. Third, record companies have begun to treat radio and TV use of records and videos not as advertisements for which they provide new material cheaply, but as entertainment services that should pay competitive prices for the recordings they use:

In many ways the record industry is facing similar problems to the film industry. Its base market is being eroded and fragmented (pre-recorded music sales are down, as are cinema admissions), costs are spiralling and the traditional distribution system is threatened by new technologies.

Though there will always be box-office biggies like *ET* (or *Thriller*), for the most part the earnings of the producers of films (pre-recorded music) will come not from their physical sale but from the exploitation by the producers of the rights they hold in their productions to broadcast and cable TV. The double advantage of this strategy for the record industry (which is far more vertically integrated than the film industry) is that, for the majors, it could eliminate the high cost of manufacturing and distribution. (Qualen, 1985, p. 16)

The move from record sales to rights exploitation as the basic source of music income has two implications. First, as Bill Graham (1986) suggests, it puts rock in corporate America. Already the biggest stars, like Michael Jackson and Bruce Springsteen, are being offered their biggest pay checks by companies keen to use their names in advertisements, and get their biggest concert returns not from ticket sales but from the tie-in merchandise. Companies are lining up to sponsor rock tours and TV shows. At the end of the 1980s the British group Sigue Sigue Sputnik even offered, only half-jokingly, to sell advertising space in the grooves between their LP tracks. Such multimedia tie-ins— record/film/advertisement/book/cable/clothes—change the purpose of pop, the reason why companies sign and develop their stars in the first place. Like films, the best-selling records of the 1990s will be made only when they've been presold as a sound/video/image packet—presold, that is, not to consumers directly, but to television shows and sponsors. The basic source of the multinational leisure corporations' income will be the licensing fees they charge for the use of their productions by other companies across all of the mass media. One interesting aspect of the new global leisure market is that it is not dominated by American-based corporations. CBS is now part of the Japanese SONY empire (as a hardware manufacturer looks to its software interests in classic fashion); RCA has been absorbed by the Bertlesmann Group (BMG), a German-based company whose central interests are publishing and distributing books and magazines. As the other two "majors" (Thorn-EMI and Polygram) are also based in Europe, WEA is the only American major label left, though the MCA-Geffen conglomerate is rather more a major these days than an independent.

Second, as the majors' interest in individual record buyers falls and the promotional drive shifts from radio to TV and video, new opportunities will arise for the independents. As Qualen says:

The one trend that is positive is the likelihood of the continued growth and expansion of the independent sector into the manufacture and distribution of black vinyl as the majors continue their process of withdrawal, as well as into

74        Industrialization of Popular Music

production by capitalizing on the possibilities for producing music with the aid of the new technologies and keeping in touch with the sound of the streets. (Qualen, 1985, p. 33)

And this reference to "the sound of the streets" brings me back to my starting point—music as human activity. The industrialization of music hasn't stopped people from using it to express private joys or public griefs; it has given us new means to do so, new ways of having an impact, new ideas of what music can be. Street music is certainly an industrial noise now, but it's a human noise too so it is perhaps fitting to conclude that the most exciting and political music of the early 1990s should be the hip-hop sounds of young urban black bands like Public Enemy, groups that are heavily dependent on both the latest technology and street credibility. The struggle for fun continues!

## Note

1. Thanks to Reebee Garofalo for these figures.

## References

BPI (1985). British phonographic industry yearbook. London: BPI.
Ehrlich, C. (1976). The piano: A history. London: Dent.
Frith, S. (1981). Sound effects. New York: Pantheon.
Frith, S. (1983). Popular music 1950-1980. In G. Martin (Ed.), Making music: The guide writing, performing, and recording. London: Muller.
Frith, S. (1986). Art vs. technology. Media, Culture and Society, 8.
Gaisberg, F. W. (1946). Music on record. London: Robert Hale.
Gelatt, R. (1977). The fabulous phonograph 1877-1977. London: Cassell.
Graham, B. (1986, May 30). Guardian, p.
Hellman, H. (1983). The new state of competition in the record industry. Sociologia, 20.
Lewis, E. (1956). No. C.I.C. London: Decca.
Qualen, J. (1985). The music industry. London: Comedia.
Toll, R. C. (1982). The entertainment machine. Oxford: Oxford University Press.
Witmark, I., & Goldberg, I. (1939). From ragtime to swingtime: The story of the house of Witmark. New York: Lee Furman.

# CHAPTER 8

## PLAYING WITH REAL FEELING:

### MAKING SENSE OF JAZZ IN BRITAIN

> Britain has several languages and a multiplicity of accents, but the *voice* that dominates British pop is a commercial construct, a phoney diction that says more about our slavish relationship to America than it does about popular expression.[1]

So writes Stuart Cosgrove in a 1987 *City Limits* feature on rock's thirty-sixth birthday. 'It was only with the emergence of Rock'n'Roll', explain Trevor Blackwell and Jeremy Seabrook, 'that the full impact of American culture thrust to the very heart of working-class experience',[2] and the search for a surviving British pop voice has been an obsessive theme of left cultural criticism ever since. But even before the impact of Elvis *et al.*, there was recurring anxiety about the effect of American music on working-class expression. Richard Hoggart brooded in his 1957 *The Uses of Literacy* on the decline of 'the open-hearted and big-bosomed' songs and singers of his pre-war childhood, while in 1946 Vaudeville historian Ernest Short noted that

> popular songs dating back to the turn of the century reflected the humorous outlook of the Cockney, the Lancashire lad, the Yorkshire lassies, the Tynesider, and the factory hand from 'Glasgie' rather than that of some alien with no firmer hold upon a traditional social atmosphere than an East Side New Yorker in the pay of Tin Pan Alley, as is so often the case today.[3]

For Mass-Observation in 1939 the Lambeth Walk was thus remarkable as a *revival* of community music:

> It proves that if you give the masses something which connects on with their own lives and streets, at the same time breaking down the conventions of shyness and stranger-feeling, they will take to it with far more spontaneous feeling than they have ever shown for the paradise-drug of the American dance-tune.[4]

This left dismissal of American pop as a 'paradise-drug' was matched by a conservative contempt for what Rudyard Kipling called 'the imported heathendom' of 'Americanized stuff', and even before the First World War there were, from this perspective, disturbing developments:

> With the passing of the old, healthy, sensual (but not sensuous) English dances came the rushing in of alien elements; chiefest and most deadly, the

cake-walk, a marvellous, fascinating measure of tremendous significance. The cake-walk tells us why the negro and the white can never lie down together. It is a grotesque, savage and lustful heathen dance, quite proper in Ashanti but shocking on the boards of a London hall.[5]

The twin themes of Americanization – corruption of working-class culture from above (the pop commodity, large-scale commerce), corruption of national culture from below (blacks, Jews, the masses) – are easily confused and it has become an orthodoxy of cultural studies that left and right responses to mass culture are in fact different facets of the same bourgeois defence. 'For there we have it', writes Iain Chambers.

The howls of protest and outrage that accompanied the flamboyant signs of a post-war recovery and, by the second half of the 1950s, a newly discovered consumerism were not only directed westwards across the Atlantic. The fundamental target was industrial society itself. . . . 'Educated' comment and opinion leaders, generally far removed from the daily workings and experience of post-war popular urban culture, claimed that it contained the alarming ability to 'level down' culture and sweep it away . . . By the 1950s, popular culture was clearly flourishing without the parochial blessing and participation of *that* culture. It was increasingly indifferent to the accusations launched against it from 'above'. Existing beyond the narrow range of school syllabuses, 'serious' comment and 'good taste', popular concerns broke 'culture' down into the immediate, the transitory, the experienced and the lived.[6]

For Chambers 1950s 'American' mass culture *was* urban British popular culture, its authenticity (its 'livedness') guaranteed by its 'heathendom': it was the black elements of the new pop music that made it relevant for the new experiences of age and class and community. In Dick Hebdige's words:

Just as the Afro-American musical language emerged from a quite different cultural tradition to the classical European one, obeyed a different set of rules, moved to a different time and placed a far greater emphasis on the role of rhythm, participation and improvisation, so the new economy based on the progressive automation and depersonalisation of the production process and the transformed patterns of consumption it engendered disrupted and displaced the old critical language. This new economy – an economy of consumption, of the signifier, of endless replacement, supercession, drift and play, in turn engendered a new language of dissent.[7]

Hebdige suggests that the British cultural establishment (the BBC, for example) attempted to neutralize pop's subversive language by making it available only after 'elaborate monitoring and framing procedures' – rock'n'roll was mediated by 'already-established "professional" presenters' like Pete Murray and David Jacobs. But this move was thwarted by the *materiality* of American goods, by the sound and look and shape of things. Just by being (by being desired) they mocked the values of their working-class users' supposed 'cultural heritage'.

The oppositions set up here – Afro-American vs. European music, 'popular urban' vs. 'educated' culture, the dissenting consumer vs. the established professional – underpin a new reading of pop culture: American sounds cross the sea to liberate not enslave us; the back-beat supplies the symbolic means of *resistance* to bourgeois hegemony. This is a cheering picture but increasingly misleading (the Tories are in favour of such American 'liberation' too – freeing market forces and all that) and in this article I want to make a counter-point: 'Americanization' means not the rise (or fall) of urban subcultures but the increasing importance of suburbia. I shall argue, in particular, that the 'dissenting' British use of black American music only makes sense in terms of middle-class ideology and that a 'European' sensibility has been just as important to the making of mass culture as US ways of doing things. I quite agree with Hebdige and Chambers that the so-called American 'take-over' really describes a series of local appropriations but the question is who is doing the appropriating and why.

## MAKING MUSIC SAFE FOR SUBURBIA – MINSTRELSY

White men put on black masks and became another self, one which was loose of limb, innocent of obligation to anything outside itself, indifferent to success . . . and thus a creature totally devoid of tension and deep anxiety. The verisimilitude of this *persona* to actual Negroes . . . was at best incidental. For the white man who put on the black mask modeled himself after a subjective black man – a black man of lust and passion and natural freedom which white men carried within themselves and harbored with both fascination and dread. (Nathan Irvin Huggins)[8]

In the 1984 issue of his magazine *Old Time Music* Tony Russell has an entertaining account of the making of Malcolm McLaren's hit version of 'Buffalo Gals'. Russell had put McLaren in touch with the East Tennessee Hilltoppers, an 'old-timey' family string-band, and Joel Birchfield's fiddling duly took its place in the mix, together with McLaren's own square-dance spiel, lifted directly from the work of New York caller, Piute Pete (as recorded on a 1949/50 Folkways LP). What McLaren didn't mention in his gleeful appropriation of American 'roots' music for his own eclectic ends was that back in the 1850s there were already men and women wandering London's streets in pursuit of a similar livelihood from mixed-up American sounds. These 'Ethiopian Serenaders' had switched from glees to minstrel songs under the influence of the visiting dancer, Juba. They learnt the latest transatlantic tunes from the barrel organists and, as one performer told Henry Mayhew, their favourite was 'Buffalo Gals', originally written as a minstrel number in 1844.[9]

Minstrelsy was the first American pop form to leave its mark on British musical culture, but in those pre-recording days it reached its audiences more often in local adaptations than as performed by the occasional visiting troupe. Peter Honri notes, for example, that his great-grandfather, a travelling showman in rural Northamptonshire, billed himself in the 1870s as The Original Black Cloud, Eccentric Jester and Funny Instrumentalist – the 'blackface' songs were just one strand of his act, and when Honri's grandfather,

Percy Thompson, began to perform with his father (at the age of 5) it was as both a clog dancer and a minstrel.[10]

The remarkably rapid rise of the minstrel show was as much an English as an American phenomenon, and while there were, no doubt, early complaints about 'foreign' influences, even the original minstrel songs were quickly absorbed into British ways of entertainment – as novelty numbers, as fashion markers, as standards. The music publishing company Francis, Day & Hunter was thus founded on Harry Hunter's songs for the Francis Brothers' Mohawk Minstrels (David Day was their business manager), while the Moore and Burgess troupe, which merged with the Mohawks in 1900, had by then given from nine to twelve performances weekly for more than forty years – in the 1880s it employed seventy performers, including eighteen vocalists, ten comedians, and twelve 'unrivalled clog and statuesque dancers'.[11]

Why were such shows so successful? What was the peculiar appeal to British audiences of these white people acting out black stereotypes? In straight commercial terms minstrels were valuable for their versatility – a minstrel show was a seamless package of pathos, humour, and glamour. 'Good clean entertainment in which sentiment and laughter blended', as John Abbott puts it, because what distinguished minstrel evenings from other variety nights was their air of uplift. By the 1850s minstrelsy was 'a form of family entertainment' in a way that music-hall was not; 'a husband and wife could take their children without fear of being asked embarrassing questions afterwards'. Both real and fake 'blackness' contributed to this. Minstrel songs, particularly the sentimental songs, were drawn more or less directly from spirituals and plantation laments, and writers like Stephen Foster and Leslie Stuart wrote ballads that were explicitly nostalgic; they gave melodic shape to the pervasive sense of homesickness that lay over the industrial landscape. British city audiences could identify with the pathos of black characters, could register their own yearning for rural simplicity, while being distanced from real blacks (from real working conditions) by the make-up and the comic turns. For the more exalted consumers the racial connotations of minstrelsy gave the music a moral quality too – the middle-class supporters of the anti-slavery movement were already patronizing the black performers who had begun to appear in the various stage versions of *Uncle Tom's Cabin*.[12]

Minstrel songs soon seemed so clearly expressive of British sensibility that some critics doubted their 'Americanness' anyway. Songwriter and *Illustrated News* editor Charles Mackay concluded after his US visit of 1857–8 that Americans 'have as yet done nothing in music'. The airs called 'negro melodies', concocted for the most part in New York, were merely '*rifacimenti*' of old English, Scottish, and Irish tunes. By then the structure and emotion of minstrel songs had made them ideal fodder for family piano performance – hence the success of Francis, Day & Hunter, and the fame of Stephen Foster, who became friendly with Charles Dickens and the music educator John Hullah, sharing their belief in the necessity of 'home music' for domestic bliss.[13]

In being Anglicized minstrel music had moved, then, from its early 'earthy robustness and frenzied excitement towards an appeal in refinement and sentimentality'. As Michael Pickering explains:

Much of the original appeal of negro delineators and minstrels had been founded on their singularity and quaintness, the catchiness of their tunes, and the way their odd comicality gave novel features to foolery and clowning. These attractions gradually waned, making minstrelsy's links with Afro-American culture itself even more tenuous. The comic parts became monopolised by the caricature of the 'negro' dandy with his constantly unrealised pretension to grandiloquence whereas the tatterdemalion plantation black became the object, in a much more concentrated fashion, of a sentimental pathos. Essentially 'the trend' was 'away from simplicity and primitive realism' towards a narrower seductive courting of senses and affects.[14]

Minstrelsy used blackface to 'bracket off a cultural space from the moral rules and regulated behaviour of mundane reality', but it did so in a way that was particularly important to the 'respectable' end of the leisure market. Professional British minstrels defined an entertainment that was less vulgar, less materialistic than music-hall, but with an equally satisfying emotional and dramatic range, and the suburban take-over of minstrel music did not mean that its racial messages were irrelevant. Rather, black Americans became deep coded as the 'other' of lower-middle-class relaxation, a source of musical access (less daunting than bourgeois concert forms) to one's heart and soul. This was to be highly significant for attitudes to jazz and blues. If the minstrels were an easy listening version of strong feeling, black masks were later put on with more excitement – by British jazz musicians in the 1930–50s, by British blues and soul bands in the 1960–80s. A performer like Mick Jagger didn't have to apply burnt cork (just slur his words); the underlying inspiration of 'the subjective black man' was obvious in the Rolling Stones' music (and success) anyway.

## TAKING CARE OF BUSINESS

I believe all the tendencies of modern living – of machine civilization – are to make crippled, perverted things of human beings. The machines are standardizing everything. There never was before such an era of standardization as there is today in the United States. It invades everything, crushing all the normal impulses of human beings. (Paul Whiteman)[15]

In November 1921, *Talking Machine News* (the world's 'oldest talking machine paper' and the first publication to review pop records) ran an aggressive editorial under the title 'Popular music on records – is there too much of it?' The paper supported the suggestion in the Canadian *Phonograph Journal* that the 'best music' was being submerged by 'the popular hits, the latest fox-trots and jazz blues' and that this was beginning to have an adverse effect on total record sales – people were inevitably getting bored with jazz; it was a sound that couldn't sustain their interest. *Talking Machine News* added that it was an American sound too and had therefore even less lasting value for Britons:

Jazz and ragtime have occupied the centre of the stage so long to the exclusion of things artistic, that it is high time they were buried further deep, whether in Canadian or American soil we care not.

The hostility of this trade paper (the journal of gramophone and record retailers) to the most popular music of the moment may seem surprising but the aesthetic objection to 'excessively syncopated song' reflected a commercial fear of being dependent on a fickle, shallow public taste. What would happen when times changed if the British music industry simply aped the Americans? (The same question was asked thirty years later about rock'n'roll.)

By July 1921 *Talking Machine News* was arguing that in their own interest dealers should try to improve public taste. There was now firm evidence of people turning against the 'unsavoury fare' inflicted by America and wanting something 'more refined and beautiful', and the paper gave its support to the campaign to prevent military bands playing jazz in public – this was 'degrading' the musicians and 'vitiating' the listeners. Dealers were advised to take advantage of the free tuition offered by The Gramophone Company. This would give them 'the foundations of a knowledge of musical works' so that they could advise customers and guide them 'in the right direction' – towards European light and classical music, away from American jazz and ragtime.

The 'Americanization' of music now referred to its mechanization, but for the British pop establishment anti-Americanism did not mean denying music's new meaning as recording and radio play but, rather, trying to develop its own way of doing things. This was most obvious in the most explicitly anti-American institution, the BBC. As Paddy Scannell points out, the BBC's music policy makers had to bow to two rules of radio as a mass medium: first, they were programming sounds for domestic consumption not social gatherings – music began to be defined in terms of its broadcast functions; second, every sound was now available to every licence-holder – radio music was a single field, and for the first time different tastes and taste publics had to be accounted for. This was when 'highbrow', 'middlebrow', and 'lowbrow' music began to be distinguished, when listeners placed themselves accordingly. The mass music paradox was, then, that as more people listened to more music in more private circumstances, so music became more important as a means of social (and ideological) identity (and certainly up to the end of the 1930s BBC audience identities were largely a matter of distinction *within* the middle classes).[16]

The BBC had an equally important part to play in the redefinition of what it meant to make music, in the reorganization of the music profession. Whatever the appeal of imported dance music or the impact of tin-pan alley tunes, the problem for British performers remained the same: how to take account of changing public tastes *in their own work*. For purists the issue might be *could* British musicians play jazz – no, thought Paul Whiteman, 'they lack the spontaneity, the exuberance, the courage' – but the real question was what happened to it when they did. If the 1920s dance craze meant a big demand for 'American' musicians, most of the new band members were, in fact, old musicians in new guises, moonlighting classical performers, seaside and music-hall players adapting once more to the trends, 'their Hungarian gypsy outfits discarded in favour of tuxedos and horn-rimmed spectacles'. They, like their listeners, depended on radio and records now to get a sense of how they were supposed to sound. But post-1918 'jazz' did also open opportunities to musicians who were untrained and unskilled by previous professional standards – the ability to improvise began to matter more than the ability to read, unusual instrumental sounds were as much in demand as the usual ones. In part, at least, the objection to the 1920s 'American invasion' came, then, from established players disgruntled by both the new demands on them and their new colleagues. As Cyril Ehrlich puts it:

> Pedants, accustomed to the manipulation of inanimate notes, and players for whom the ability to read all 'dots' at sight was the *sine qua non* of professional status, were equally outraged. Their distress was compounded by diverse prejudices and fears: moral disapproval, distaste for undignified cavorting, and apprehension at encroachment upon hard-won skills. Nothing could be more alien to their conception of music as written, studied, and instructed than the seemingly anarchic and untutored raw vitality of the new noise.[17]

Such attitudes were reflected in the initial reluctance of the Musicians Union (MU) to take the new dance music and musicians seriously, but in 1930 a dance band section was established, primarily in response to the BBC's continuing demand for such popular performers. It was easier (and more important) to negotiate minimum wages and conditions for dance broadcasts than with dance halls, and MU members were increasingly concerned that radio work was being taken by 'semi-pros' and 'aliens'. The former could be brought into the union, the latter had to be excluded, and as rank and file visitors already found it hard to get work permits, the MU's campaign now was to prevent foreign soloists sitting in with British bands. In 1935, after exchange deal negotiations with the American Federation of Musicians broke down, the union persuaded the Ministry of Trade 'to impose a notorious and quite untenable ban which but for a few exceptions denied the entry of American jazz musicians for the next twenty years' – the two unions did not come to mutually acceptable terms again until 1954.[18]

The single most effective anti-American music move in the inter-war years was, then, a matter of job protection rather than cultural elitism, though the Musicians Union did exploit highbrow assumptions. Its classical members were equally worried about foreign competition but had had to cede to the art music idea of individual genius – the government policy was that 'artists of clearly international standing will be admitted without conditions'. Now it was agreed that popular musicians were not 'of international standing'. They required labour permits that the union could challenge and almost always did – the few black jazz musicians to play in Britain between 1935 and 1955 did so illegally or, occasionally, slipped in under the guise of 'international classical' musician or 'solo variety' act.[19]

For professional musicians the American issue was straightforward – they might play American music (or their version of it) but this was all the more reason why real American musicians should be prevented from competing for the dance hall, radio, and recording work. Other sections of the British business had a more ambiguous position. The BBC, for example, was under constant pressure from local songwriters for protection and in 1936 set a quota of at least 20 per cent British tunes in dance broadcasts. But much of this pressure was informal. The Performing Rights Society did briefly campaign for such a quota but soon realized that this stance contradicted its international royalty collecting role and, anyway, Britain's largest music publishers, like Chappells and Francis, Day & Hunter, were already using licensing deals to become, in effect, Anglo-American companies. It was left to the newly formed Song Writers Guild to promote specific British interests.

In the record business, too, British and American interests were not easy to disentangle. As manufacturers British companies were dependent on American technology and patents, so that The Gramophone Company, for example, was explicitly founded in 1898 to exploit American inventions and to sell American products – it was funded by British investment but most of its senior management came from across the sea. It was soon assembling imported gramophone machine parts and selling records made in Hanover, but its only local resource was its London recording studio and even by the time of its merger with Columbia to form EMI in 1931 it was still essentially a marketing enterprise. Its role had been to provide British sounds for American equipment – the world-wide expansion of the recording industry had proceeded on the assumption that while the machines were international local music was the best way to sell them.[20]

For the early British companies national musical taste meant middle-class musical taste – The Gramophone Company was always reluctant to sell 'cheap' machines or music, and I have already noted the education service it offered to retailers (another aspect of this policy was the initial funding of *The Gramophone*). Memoirs of the first record producers, men like Fred Gaisberg and Joe Batten, make clear that they moved most easily in the European classical music world; for them the long-term success of a record label depended on its catalogue of concert hall stars (beginning with Caruso), and, as Cyril Ehrlich points out, this meant that record companies had much better relationships with the bourgeois music establishment than piano manufacturers had had – it was because gramophones were cheaper than pianos that they discouraged 'amateur fumblings' and restored proper criteria of musical excellence![21]

This comparison of piano and gramophone is a useful reminder that the development of music as a mass medium was not just a matter of mechanical production. Well into the 1920s the piano was a more popular domestic instrument than the record player and an equally important aspect of Americanization. The significance of ragtime, for example, was not just that it was the first black music to be widely published, but that it put the piano at the centre of public dance music as it was already for parlour song and (minstrel inflected) balladeers. It was piano manufacturers (led by the American Steinway company) who pioneered the music-marketing techniques later taken up by tin-pan alley; it was the player piano not the phonogram which was the first music 'machine' to be popular – piano rolls gave a better, longer, acoustic account of familiar music than the early discs.[22]

If the gramophone and wireless were first identified in Britain with the concert hall and up-market entertainment, the piano had long been sold as a truly 'popular' instrument, available for the pleasure of everyone, and this had important implications for mass music. The piano was, after all, a piece of family furniture, and even before the BBC defined the pleasures of the hearth the pop market had been conceived in terms of domesticity. Both broadcasters and record companies had, then, to adapt to *existing* marketing arrangements; they did not, initially, transform them. Here, for example, is the launching statement of *Popular Music Weekly*, a magazine from the early 1920s:

> POPULAR MUSIC WEEKLY needs no excuse for appearing at a moment when music and dancing is booming to the extent it is to-day; when all through the kingdom the people of all classes are catered for in the dancing halls, theatres and music-halls.

The editor explains that he has no thought of giving his readers 'songs of the past, beautiful as some of them may be'. The paper would be devoted, rather, to the 'latest' numbers – 'the great song and dance "hits" of the day will appear week by week'. But while the gramophone's importance is thus acknowledged – as a convenient means of musical dissemination and education – what still matters most is 'the homely piano'.

> POPULAR MUSIC WEEKLY is a paper pre-eminently for the home, and it is my earnest wish that it may provide you with constant happy evenings.
>
> There is nothing so jolly or so sociable as the little group clustered about the piano, singing the songs of the moment or happy amid the fun of a family dance.
>
> In my mind's eye I can see you so grouped, and as this, the first issue of my paper, passes into your hand I can already hear your feet upon the floor as the piano strikes up its tuneful strains, and as I lay down my pen I say: On with the dance, and let POPULAR MUSIC WEEKLY be your friend and partner!

What this captures is the essential *respectability* of the post-war pop world – the piano was an icon of the respectable working class, the record industry was being built on the basis of classical 'good taste', the BBC's musical mission was public 'improvement', professional musicians were united in defence of self-discipline. This was the setting in which 1920s American music was placed, the background against which it was heard as a threat – and a promise.


MAKING MUSIC SAFE FOR SUBURBIA – JAZZ

> The argument that England is England still is an intellectual one to which the musical nerves refuse to listen. If the composer imagines that he can treat present-day Surrey with its charabancs, filling stations, hikers, road houses, dainty tea rooms, and loudspeakers discoursing cosmopolitan jazz, in the way the Elizabethan composers treated the 'woodes so wilde' he is living in a narrow world of escape, incapable of producing anything more than a pretty period piece. (Constant Lambert)[23]

At first glance the 1920s jazz argument seems straightforward: 'true' jazz lovers thrilled at its power as the music of black America, 'synthetic' jazz entertainers played easy-on-the-air dance music for the middle-class night out. The early history of jazz in Britain is usually presented, then, as the 'taming' of subversive sounds by the leisure market. As jazz dancing, for example, became mainstream entertainment, so it took on the trappings of bourgeois culture – teachers and 'exhibitions', rules and competitions. The first British dance championship was held in London in 1923 and 'strict tempo' became the order of the day.[24]

The colour of jazz was a British issue from the start. 'We demand', wrote editor Edgar Jackson in an early (1926) issue of *Melody Maker*, 'that the habit of associating our music with the primitive and barbarous negro derivation shall cease forthwith, in justice to the obvious fact that we have outgrown such comparisons.' The assumption here – that 'negro' meant primitive, that jazz 'progress' meant its white take-over – was commonplace too among musicians. For Paul Whiteman it was a question of turning a 'folk' music into art. 'What folk form would have amounted to anything if some great writer had not put it into a symphony?' he asked. The 'elemental' had to be given a 'beautiful garment'. For Paul Specht, who claimed to have been playing 'classical jazz' long before Whiteman, it was a question of 'refining' black sounds, applying intelligence to instinct:

> I give full credit to and have always expressed admiration for the splendid Negro advance in swing music, but it is simply idle logic to issue any such claims that real 'swing music' originated with the Negro bands. The Negro players may be born with swing in their hearts, and such musical souls have outnumbered the white jazz players, but it took the scholarly, trained musicians like 'Ragtime Frank' Guarente, to first analyze the swing motif, and to add this faculty of improvisation to the rudiments of American jazz music as it was first written and then recorded on the phonograph disc by white musicians.[25]

These arguments were formalized in the first American jazz book, Henry Osgood's 1926 *So This Is Jazz*, and had a particular resonance for white British performers, struggling to assert their own creative authority. Jack Hylton, writing in *The Gramophone* in September 1926, declared the superiority of his own 'symphonic syncopation' – 'a pleasing combination of harmony, melody and rhythm' – to jazz, 'an unholy row'. He dismissed the suggestion that his style was just lifted from Whiteman. It was, rather, an explicitly British development: 'In the dance hall or on the gramophone record alike, it makes a subtle appeal to our British temperament. It is fast becoming a truly national music', satisfying 'the musical cravings of any normal person'. 'How I hate the word "jazz",' echoed Jack Payne in his 1932 autobiography. Jazz implied something crude while Payne's task as the BBC's first dance band leader was 'to put happiness and sunshine over the air'. His successor, Henry Hall, was similarly contemptuous of the 'cacophonous discords of hot music', while the BBC's first disc jockey, Christopher Stone, believed that the BBC 'lowered' itself by playing hot jazz, 'a primitive din'.[26]

For these writers black 'jazz' had to be distinguished from their own 'swing' in terms of the balance of rhythm and melody. For jazz to 'develop', rhythm (understood as something 'natural') had to come under the civilizing influence of a composed, harmonic score. 'Syncopation', Hylton explained in *Melody Maker* in January 1926, 'is the compromise between rhythm and harmony, between savagery and intellectualism. It is the music of the normal human being, and because of this it will live – progressively of course and gradually evolving new forms.' This argument was expanded in the first British jazz book, R. W. S. Mendl's 1927 *The Appeal of Jazz* – Mendl assured his anxious readers that jazz had developed by necessity well beyond the 'primitive artless stock' of the negro. Because jazz was, in itself, stimulating in rhythm but weak in melodic invention to survive as a popular form it had to become something else.[27]

These were the positions against which real jazz criticism was defined. Its tone of voice is encapsulated in Spike Hughes's 1933 *Daily Herald* review of Duke Ellington's first British appearance.

It has remained for us to discover . . . that Duke is something more than a bandleader specialising in what are vaguely called 'voodoo harmonies' and 'jungle rhythms'. He is in fact the first genuine jazz composer. This may come as a shock to people who associate jazz with the 'Rhapsody in Blue' or who consider jazz to be any noise made by a dance band in the background to conversation or an excuse for those ungraceful, hiking movements which pass for modern 'dancing'.

Jazz is not a matter of trite, unguarded melodies wedded to semi-illiterate lyrics, nor is it the brainchild of Tin Pan Alley. It is the music of the Harlem gin mills, the Georgia backyards and New Orleans street corners – the music of a race that plays, sings and dances because music is its most direct medium of expression and escape.[28]

Hughes's importance in British jazz criticism (as 'Mike' he started reviewing 'hot records' for *Melody Maker* in April 1931) was his pioneering analysis of *rhythm* (he was himself a bass player). By taking the beat seriously he changed people's understanding of where the 'art' of jazz lay and explained why black musicians were superior to whites: they had a far more sophisticated grasp of

Meeting of the No. 1 Rhythm Club, *circa* 1934

rhythmic language. Jazz would inevitably progress from folk to art, then, but such progress would always be on the basis of musical skills that were rooted in black history and experience.

As Jim Godbolt has shown, the Hughes line became dominant in inter-war British jazz writing and was particularly explicit in the pages of *Melody Maker*. Edgar Jackson, who had begun by dismissing black music, was soon favouring 'hot style' over 'popular' dance records, and as 'dance and popular rhythmic music' reviewer for *The Gramophone* (and hot record selector for Christopher Stone's BBC show) as well as *Melody Maker* editor, he became an influential black jazz advocate. This put *Melody Maker* itself (started by publisher Lawrence Wright as a trade paper for dance band musicians) in a paradoxical position: by 1927 it was championing hot sounds at the expense of the music played by most of its readers (and advertised in most of its display inches – in 1929 the paper was sold to Odhams). But the relabelling of dance music going on here was repeated everywhere in the record press – *The Gramophone Critic*, for example, which started in 1928, took the straight/hot jazz division for granted, and by the time of the second British jazz book, Stanley Nelson's 1934 *All About Jazz* (introduced by Jack Hylton), the real/fake distinction was part of musical common sense. Nelson started from the jazz progress-from-jungle-to-ballroom line but concluded that:

> most of the future development of jazz will come from the coloured race themselves and not from us. We have certainly played a great part in emancipating our present popular music from the crude form of the early cake-walks and we have standardised the instrumentation of the popular dance band. But our mania for order has led us into a cul de sac. We lack the spontaneity of the coloured people and their innate feel for the jazz idiom.[29]

Nelson noted that black musicians, unlike whites, did 'not seem to be influenced by any dictates of commercialism' and this assumption was now built into hot/popular, black/white discourse. In 1937 Harmon Grisewood, critically reviewing the BBC's 'swing programmes', tried to clarify for his colleagues the difference between authentic and inauthentic jazz. The former, he explained, was produced by black musicians for black audiences and was therefore 'a natural and emotional expression' – 'it was played for the love of the thing'. Its commercialization meant its corruption – hence the effete sound of 'decayed, sentimental dance music'. Good swing (which meant American swing – Grisewood's point was that British musicians couldn't play it) had therefore to stay in touch with the 'genuine article'. For the British Marxist critic Iain Lang, writing in 1943, the same point was given a more class-conscious edge; if jazz had given voice to the Afro-American proletariat, 'a kind of people which had never before been so powerfully articulate', its subsequent use as mass-produced entertainment for the middle classes was a mark of regression. The further a music moved away from its origins among the common people, the more it lost in expressiveness and integrity. As Ernest Borneman put it in 1946, at best jazz was the American negro's music of protest and assertion, at worst the white man's music of indolence and escape.[30]

The rhetorical shifts in inter-war jazz commentary are familiar from later responses to rock'n'roll: the initial treatment of the music as primitive and gimmicky, its survival dependent on its rapid assimilation into tried and tested forms of 'good' music; the later appreciation that such 'commercialization' is precisely what saps the sounds of their distinctive energy and truth. But there were problems with the latter position. Take the crucial idea of 'authenticity': how could a white British audience be other than 'entertained' by noises made meaningful only by their black American roots? How on earth could British *musicians* claim to play jazz for real?

The answer was to make the music a matter of feeling, expressive of personal not social identity, sensual not cultural need. Robert Goffin (in what he later claimed to be the first serious article on the subject) thus praised jazz in *Le Disque Vert* in 1919 for its appeal to 'the senses' – classical music appealed only to the mind. Spike Hughes, who marvelled at the 'remarkable technical precision' and discipline of jazz musicians, usually chose, nevertheless, to celebrate jazz's 'primitive' qualities, its 'direct expression of fundamental emotions'. Hughes's friend and fellow *Melody Maker* columnist, John Hammond, suggested in 1932:

> It is about time we got over terms such as hot music, corny, commercial, etc., all of the expressions of the white man. Either music is sincere or it isn't. If it is the latter, we can overlook it completely without bothering to characterize it. The reason I so greatly prefer the Negro's dance music must be obvious by now; he knows only how to play from the heart. 'Tis the white man, with his patent lack of sincerity, who has given jazz the malodorous name it possesses.[31]

How do we recognize 'playing from the heart' when we hear it? By its contrast to 'white' music – as Ernest Borneman pointed out, because Western art music signified order and control, syncopated rhythms came to signify disorder and abandon. Jazz worked here not as an alternative, autonomous culture, low meeting high, but as the 'other' defined by bourgeois culture itself, the 'low' produced by the high. 'Authentic' jazz feelings thus referred less to the musicians' state of mind than to the release of the listeners' own 'repressed' emotions – this argument is vividly made by John Wain's novel *Strike the Father Dead*, in which the role of jazz in British *middle-class* 'liberation' is made clear.

This accounts, I think, for the difficulty 1930s jazz writers had with the place of commerce in their music – black jazz might be distinguished from white jazz as something played for its own sake, but all jazz musicians were professionals and had to make some sort of living from their sounds. The purism of suburban British jazz fans, their contempt for commercial dance music, reflected the fact that this was the first British musical culture dependent on recordings (their attitudes were not shared whole-heartedly by the would-be jazz players hanging round Archer Street, taking whatever work came along). One consequence was a decided ambiguity about visiting stars' treatment of jazz as entertainment, but the suspicion of 'sell-out' that nagged at the fans marked really an anxiety about their own place as consumers in a supposedly uncommercial scene, and Roger Taylor suggests that in appropriating jazz as their own 'authentic experience', British audiences had, in the end, to appropriate it as *art* – a 'fantasy jazz' was thus put 'firmly within the grip of the aesthetics of Romanticism'.[32]

The question now was how jazz could make the move from folk to art without losing the qualities that made it an authentic means of expression in the first place. For many British '30s fans (most notoriously Philip Larkin) the answer was it couldn't – both Spike Hughes and Constant Lambert lost interest in jazz at the moment they were proclaiming Duke Ellington as a genius – but for other more modernist writers jazz 'primitivism' put it in advance of the avant-garde. Robert Goffin, for example, described jazz as 'the first form of surrealism' – its musicians had 'neutralis[ed] rational control in order to give free play to the spontaneous manifestations of the subconscious' – and British versions of this argument were developed in *Jazz Forum*, a magazine launched in 1946. Among its contributors was Toni Del Renzio who in the 1950s was a member of the Independent Group, involved in the promotion of pop art and the ICA's controversial jazz lectures. By then the art school appropriation of jazz was obvious. Writing in 1957, Paul Oliver concluded that jazz was the exact musical equivalent of modern art: it had 'broken with the orthodoxy of the past as emphatically as did the contemporaneous painting and sculpture of the first decade of the century', and in the exhilaration of collective improvisation experimental artists could grasp their own ideal of 'simultaneous unity and freedom'.[33]

Even before jazz became the sound of 1950s Bohemia it was clear that its British class base was not the proletariat. Harry Melvill, writing in *The Gramophone* in January 1924, commented that 'Will Vodery's Orchestra from the "Plantation" appearing at a private party, proved once more that black-faces, like Oriental china, blend admirably with eighteenth-century decoration', a judgement echoed in Evelyn Waugh's novels of the period, and the early '20s vogue for 'Blackbird' parties. What mattered here, though, was not that black music was a passing society fashion, but that its most articulate champions were highly cultured (Fred Elizalde, Spike Hughes, and Edgar Jackson were all ex-

Discographer and
enthusiast: Brian Rust

Cambridge students). Hot jazz was first heard, then, as 'elitist'. Hughes, for
example, was regularly attacked on *Melody Maker*'s letters page – hot music was
'alright for chaps at Oxford and Cambridge' but 'the Public' hadn't got time for
it – while the 'commercial' Henry Hall equated hot jazz with the 'advanced'
music of Schoenberg (both appealed to Jews) and claimed by contrast to
perform for 'errand boys and fireside folks who wanted a good time'.[34]

'Real' jazz remained an elite taste into the 1930s. Constant Lambert took it for
granted that Duke Ellington was only appreciated by 'the highbrow public',
while the restricted audience for Louis Armstrong's 1932 tour was reflected in
both box office takings and Fleet Street shock horror. Gerald Moore concluded
that Armstrong's music was 'not for the general public for whom his
enormously advanced work cannot possibly have any appeal', while Hannen
Swaffer in the *Daily Herald* described ordinary people walking out, leaving
'excited young men of the pseudo-intellectual kind . . . bleating and blahing in
ecstasy'.[35]

Jazz elitism was by now less a description of the slumming upper class than
the aspiring petty-bourgeoisie, who were soon organizing themselves (in good
suburban style) in rhythm clubs, celebrating jazz fandom as the culture of
collectors and scholars, people who took the music *seriously*. Such seriousness
was reflected in the BBC's 1937 redefinition of its popular music output as music
for dancing, music for entertainment, and music for the connoisseur. Jazz came
under the last label (even now it is more often heard on Radio 3 than Radios 1 or
2), and 'connoisseurship' is a good label for the use of jazz involved – a
painstaking passion, a yearning for sensuous, earthy experience equated now
with solemnly earned excitement and the 'furtive' release of real feeling. The
typical British jazz fan of the late 1930s was a swottish provincial schoolboy, a
Philip Larkin, who later wondered what happened to his fellow enthusiasts:

Sometimes I imagine them, sullen fleshy inarticulate men, stockbrokers, sellers of goods, living in 30-year-old detached houses among the golf courses of Outer London, husbands of ageing and bitter wives they first seduced to Artie Shaw's 'Begin the Beguine' or The Squadronnaires' 'The Nearness of You' . . . men in whom a pile of scratched coverless 78s in the attic can awaken memories of vomiting blindly from small Tudor windows to Muggsy Spanier's 'Sister Kate', or winding up a gramophone in a punt to play Armstrong's 'Body and Soul'; men whose first coronary is coming like Christmas; who drift, loaded helplessly with commitments and obligations and necessary observances, into the darkening avenues of age and incapacity, deserted by everything that once made life sweet.[36]

CONCLUSION

In his book on the Harlem renaissance Nathan Irvin Huggins suggests that white Americans took to minstrelsy in the mid-nineteenth century as a way of distancing themselves from European criticism of their vulgarity – this could still be enjoyed but was projected defensively now on to blacks. At the same moment that the British middle class began to criticize its own materialism by denouncing it as 'American', the American middle class was looking nervously to Europe for lessons in good taste. In 1853 the jury for musical instruments at New York's Crystal Palace Exhibition objected to the

> vulgar, tawdry decorations of American pianos, which show a great deal of taste, and that very bad. Not only do we find the very heroics of gingerbread radiating in hideous splendors, fit for the drawing-room of a fashionable hotel, adorned with spit-boxes among other savageries; but even the plain artistic black-and-white of the keys – that classic simplicity and harmonious distinction – is superseded for pearl and tortoise-shell and eye-grating vermilion abominations.[37]

The tone is exactly that of Albert Goldman on Elvis Presley, which reflects the fact that the major changes in the US music business too have always been argued in terms of civilization (Europe) vs. barbarity (Jews, blacks, workers), whether we examine the battle between the young tin-pan alley men and the established parlour song publishers at the turn of the century, or that between the young rock'n'rollers and the ASCAP establishment in the 1950s. The point is that so-called 'American' music emerges from these conflicts. It reaches the rest of the world as something that has *already* moved from the margins to the mainstream (this was true of minstrelsy and ragtime, jazz and rock'n'roll). To hear it as corrupting or subversive is, then, to *reinterpret* the sounds, to read one's own desires into them, and in Britain the dominant desires – the ones that set the terms of jazz (and rock) criticism, formed musicians' jazz (and rock) ambitions, determined what it meant to be a true jazz (or rock) fan – have been suburban. To understand why (and how) the worlds of jazz (and rock) are young men's worlds we have, for example, to understand what it means to grow up male and middle-class; to understand the urge to 'authenticity' we have to understand the strange fear of being 'inauthentic'. In this world, American music – black American music – stands for a simple idea: that everything *real* is happening elsewhere.

## NOTES

1 Stuart Cosgrove, 'Bad language', *City Limits* (25 June 1987), 16.
2 Trevor Blackwell and Jeremy Seabrook, *A World Still To Win* (London: Faber & Faber, 1985), 86–7.
3 Ernest Short, *Fifty Years of Vaudeville* (London: Eyre & Spottiswoode, 1946), 8; Richard Hoggart, *The Uses of Literacy* (Harmondsworth: Penguin, 1958), 163.
4 Mass-Observation, *Britain* (Harmondsworth: Penguin, 1939), 183–4. In the light of the recent activities of Red Wedge it is also interesting to read that

> · the working class has taken up the Lambeth Walk with more enthusiasm than anybody – a fact recognised and made use of by both the Communist Party and the Labour Party. In the latter case, it was partly due to a long discussion between a leader of M-O and the Transport House propaganda experts, who could not see the faintest connection between the Lambeth Walk and politics until the whole history of dancing and jazz had been gone into. (p. 169)

5 W. R. Titterton, *From Theatre to Music Hall* (1912), quoted in ibid., 148–9. Kipling quoted in Peter Bailey (ed.), *Music Hall. The Business of Pleasure* (Milton Keynes: Open University Press, 1986), xiv.
6 Iain Chambers, *Urban Rhythms* (London: Macmillan, 1985), 4–5.
7 Dick Hebdige, 'Towards a cartography of taste 1935–1962', *Block* 4 (1981), 53.
8 Quoted in Michael Pickering, 'White skin, black masks: "nigger" minstrelsy in Victorian Britain' in J. S. Bratton (ed.), *Music Hall Performance and Style* (Milton Keynes: Open University Press, 1986), 80, and see J. S. Bratton, 'English Ethiopians: British audiences and black face acts, 1835–1865', *Yearbook of English Studies* (1981), 127–42.
9 See Tony Russell, 'Haywire in the hills!', *Old Time Music*, 39 (1984), 5 and William W. Austin, *'Susanna', 'Jeanie', and 'The Old Folks at Home': The Songs of Stephen C. Foster from His Time to Ours* (New York: Macmillan, 1975), 31–2.
10 Peter Honri, *Working the Halls* (London: Futura, 1974), 19–20.
11 See Short, op. cit., 147–8 and John Abbott, *The Story of Francis, Day and Hunter* (London: Francis, Day & Hunter, 1952), chapter 1.
12 See Thomas L. Riis, 'The experience and impact of black entertainers in England, 1895–1920', *American Music*, 4, 1 (1986), and Abbott, op. cit., 5–6.
13 See Austin, op. cit., 48, 160–2, and cf. Colin MacInnes, *Sweet Saturday Night* (London: MacGibbon & Kee, 1967), 32–4.
14 Pickering, op. cit., 76.
15 Paul Whiteman and Mary Margaret McBride, *Jazz* (New York: J. H. Sears, 1926), 153–4.
16 Much of my argument here is drawn from Paddy Scannell's as yet unpublished history of the BBC's music policy, and see Simon Frith, 'The pleasures of the hearth: the making of BBC light entertainment', *Formations of Pleasure* (London: Routledge & Kegan Paul, 1983).
17 Cyril Ehrlich, *The Music Profession in Britain Since the Eighteenth Century* (Oxford: Clarendon Press, 1985), 201–4, and see Whiteman, op. cit., 74.
18 Jim Godbolt, *A History of Jazz in Britain 1919–50* (London: Quartet Books, 1984), 116.
19 For an overview of MU policy see Ehrlich, op. cit., 219–21.

20  See Geoffrey Jones, 'The Gramophone Company: an Anglo-American multinational, 1898–1931', *Business History Review*, 59, 1 (1985).
21  Cyril Ehrlich, *The Piano* (London: Dent, 1976) 185–6. And see Simon Frith, 'The making of the British record industry 1920–64', in James Curran, Anthony Smith, and Pauline Wingate (eds), *Impacts and Influences* (London: Methuen, 1987); Joe Batten, *Joe Batten's Book: The Story of Sound Recording* (London: Rockliff, 1956) and F.W. Gaisberg, *Music on Record* (London: Robert Hale, 1946).
22  Ehrlich, *The Piano*, 133, 171–2, and see Edwin M. Good, *Giraffes, Black Dragons and Other Pianos* (Stanford, NJ: Stanford University Press, 1982), 94–5, 175, 234.
23  Constant Lambert, *Music Ho!* (London: Faber & Faber, 1934), 177.
24  For a useful overview of this see Mark Hustwitt, '"Caught in a whirlpool of aching sound": the production of dance music in Britain in the 1920s', *Popular Music*, 3 (1983), and, for the inside story, Josephine Bradley, *Dancing Through Life* (London: Hollis & Carter, 1947).
25  Paul Specht, *How They Become Name Bands. The Modern Technique of a Dance Band Maestro* (New York: Fine Arts Publications, 1941), 121. And see Whiteman, op. cit., 283–4, Godbolt, op. cit., 28.
26  See Jack Payne, *This is Jack Payne* (London: Sampson Low Marston, 1932), 56–8, and Christopher Stone, *Christopher Stone Speaking* (London: Elkin, Mathews & Marrot, 1933), 95–6. Henry Hall quote courtesy of Paddy Scannell.
27  R. W. S. Mendl, *The Appeal of Jazz* (London: Philip Allan & Co., 1927), 71–3, 165. Hylton quoted in Edward S. Walker, 'Early English jazz', *Jazz Journal* (September, 1969), 24.
28  Quoted in Godbolt, op. cit., 102. For Ellington's similar importance for American jazz writers see Ron Wellman, 'Duke Ellington's music', *International Review of the Aesthetics and Sociology of Music*, 17, 1 (1986).
29  Quoted in Godbolt, op. cit., 153. See his chapter 3 for the *Melody Maker* story, and, for Hughes's critical career there, Chris Goddard, *Jazz Away From Home* (London: Paddington Press, 1979), 174–82.
30  Grisewood's argument courtesy of Paddy Scannell, and see Iain Lang, *Background to the Blues* (London: Workers Music Association, 1943), 18, and Ernest Borneman, *A Critic Looks at Jazz* (London: Jazz Music Books, 1946), 47.
31  Quoted in Goddard, op. cit., 178 and see Robert Goffin, *Jazz from Congo to Swing* (London: Musicians Press, 1946), 1, and Spike Hughes, *Opening Bars* (London: Pilot Press, 1946), 305–11.
32  See Roger L. Taylor, *Art, an Enemy of the People* (Hassocks: Harvester, 1978), 114.
33  Paul Oliver, 'Art aspiring', *Jazz Monthly*, 2, 12 (1957), 2–3, and see Goffin, op. cit., 3–4. For the problem of treating jazz as an art music see Mary Herron Dupree, '"Jazz", the critics and American art music in the 1920s', *American Music*, 4, 3 (1986), For jazz and the fine arts see Simon Frith and Howard Horne, *Art into Pop* (London: Methuen, 1987), ch. 3.
34  See Spike Hughes, *Second Movement* (London: Museum Press, 1951), 21. Hall quote courtesy of Paddy Scannell.
35  Moore quoted in Goddard, op. cit., 182–3, Swaffen in Godbolt, op. cit., 84–5.
36  Philip Larkin, *All What Jazz* (London: Faber & Faber, 1985), 28–9. For an entertaining account of rhythm club culture see Godbolt, op. cit., chs 8–9 and, for a sociological analysis, Francis Newton, *The Jazz Scene* (Harmondsworth: Penguin, 1961), ch. 13.
37  Quoted in Good, op. cit., 170 and see Nathan Irvin Huggins, *Harlem Renaissance* (New York: Oxford University Press, 1971), 254.

# CHAPTER 9

# THE SUBURBAN SENSIBILITY IN
# BRITISH ROCK AND POP

The suggestion that British pop sensibility is essentially suburban is hardly new. I have previously traced the suburban thread that runs through England's musical Bohemia from jazz to blues to rock, while Jon Savage has explored the suburban secrets of punk and Sarah Thornton described the suburban routes of rave. In England suburbanism is, it seems, equally implicated in folk revival and indie ideology, and what is the Last Night of the Proms if not a celebration of a suburban night out?[1]

I don't want to repeat these histories here, but pop's suburban sensibility is worth revisiting for three overlapping reasons.

First, because the working class remains so significant in the mythology of British pop culture. To cite an example to hand, in her MacTaggert Lecture to the 1995 Edinburgh Television Festival, Janet Street-Porter drew her media audience's attention to the contrast between the tired ideas of the middle-class middle-aged men of television and the vibrant creativity of the streetwise young people of pop. There is, in fact, very little difference between the class profiles of the television and music industries, and street wisdom is more a rhetorical than a material quality, but Street-Porter was only voicing common sense here – the common sense of both academic and media sociologists. Pop culture does seem different from television culture, and what interests me about this is not the gap between myth and reality but the way in which the myth – the rhetoric of class and street and grit – is itself the product of suburban dreams, suburban needs.

The resulting aesthetic confusion was apparent in the 1995 summer 'war' between Blur and Oasis. This was the first time since the 1960s that such a sales battle (whose new single would top the charts?) had interested news reporters and the narrative was quickly cast in 1960s terms – the north versus the south; working class versus middle class; rocker versus mod. But the analogies began to break down when more explicit comparisons were made: Blur versus Oasis as the Beatles versus the Stones. The problem here was both musical (Oasis are as obviously influenced by Lennon/McCartney as by Jagger/Richard) and social (it was the Beatles who were northern working class; the Stones southern petit bourgeois), and listening to the records made other comparisons seem more obvious (Blur as The Kinks; Oasis as Status Quo), and other precedents more telling – Blur work obviously and comfortably with the suburban sensibility that has always defined Britpop; Oasis work obviously and comfortably on the suburban awe that has always puffed up the proletarian lout. Both groups and their music, both groups and their Britishness, have to be understood in terms of the ideology of pop rather than the realities of class.

The second reason for exploring pop's suburban sensibility further is because it blurs distinctions that are otherwise taken for granted in sociological common sense – between high and low culture, art and pop, mass market and subculture. In this respect British pop ties in, perhaps unexpectedly, to another defining British cultural institution, the BBC. Again, it is hardly startling to point to the importance of the BBC to British identity, but it is worth stressing the essential suburbanity of this identity – in terms of both the domestic placing of the listener and viewer and the offered spectacle of the city: *In Town Tonight!*[2] And if cultural categories are therefore blurred – in the figure of the middle-brow – such blurring depends, in turn, on marking out other sorts of boundaries – regional, racial, social. Suburban culture, whether shaped by pop or the BBC, is white culture, white English culture, white south-eastern English culture; it describes, in the end, an urban phenomenon, the media domination of London, the concentrated site of both political and cultural power. The sub-urban sensibility with which I am concerned is sub-London sensibility. From this media perspective other English cities (and even Scottish, Northern Irish and Welsh cities) are themselves effectively suburban. The point about Oasis (and the Beatles), that is to say, is not that they are, in fact, from the north, but that they are seen and heard (from south of Watford) to be 'northern'.

And there is here a third reason for paying attention to pop sensibility, as a particularly fantastic account of the suburban experience. If suburban culture *tout court* seems essentially middle-brow, that is, in part, because the literature of suburbia has been essentially middle-brow, in the no-nonsense poetry of Betjeman, Larkin and the mocking Stevie Smith; in the plain fiction legacy of Bennett and Wells; in the genre *grande guignol* of an Ian McEwan or Ruth Rendall; in the comfortable humour of Richmal Crompton's William books. In mass cultural terms, while suburban mores do pervade the television screen, they do so in the bloodless terms of the sitcom and the commercial. In the last thirty years at least it has been pop music more than any other form that has articulated suburban pretension, suburban claustrophobia, suburban discontent. British pop draws on both the ironies and the secret desires of suburban literature but gives them a more grandiose setting, using rock, a musical form which is, after all, the sound of the metropolis. As Jon Savage puts it,

Pop (and rock's) rhetoric is of the inner city, but scratch the surface of most English pop stars, and you'll find a suburban boy or girl, noses pressed against the window, dreaming of escape, of transformation.[3]

And it is hardly surprising that the most incisive suburban fiction of recent times, Hanif Kureishi's *Buddha of Suburbia*, is driven by rock not literary dreams.

## SUEDE: SNARES AND THICKETS

Does you love only come, does your love only come,
Does he only come in a Volvo?

('Breakdown')

The most significant suburb in British pop history is probably Bromley, setting for Kureishi's novel, home of the quintessential suburban star, David Bowie, and the quintessential suburban fans, the Bromley Contingent (from whom later emerged both Siouxsie and the Banshees and Billy Idol). I don't want to rewrite the Bromley story here, but two aspects of Bowie's version of progressive rock and the Bromley Contingent's version of art-school punk are worth noting. First, both involved self-consciously aesthetic gestures (and pervasive references to such iconic art figures as Rimbaud and Baudelaire, Warhol and Wilde), gestures stylized less for their intrinsic artistic qualities than as a mark of social *difference* – this was art being used to irritate the philistine and to worry the conformist. 'I hated Bromley,' says Siouxsie.

I thought it was small and narrow-minded. There was this trendy wine bar called Pips, and I got

Berlin to wear this dog-collar, and I walked in with Berlin following me, and people's jaws just hit the tables. I walked in and ordered a bowl of water for him, I got the bowl of water for my dog. People were scared![4]

What was at stake here was what one might call *Bohemia in a bedroom*: an alternative lifestyle practised at home, and displayed as a kind of performance art at the bus stop and railway station, in select club backrooms and parents-are-away-for-the-weekend parties. (No wonder London's suburban art schools, ringing the capital like the outposts of a metropolitan mission, have been so important as pop hang-outs, safe havens for trying things on.)

The second aspect of the Bromley aesthetic I want to emphasize is the lure of the city – the metropolis at the end of the local railway line, a metropolis not to occupy but to visit, to visit as a matter of routine, at the weekend, for the occasion, in a gang. In pop terms London is a peculiar place. While they certainly offered the glimmering promise of sex and drugs and rock'n'roll, London's key music clubs, whether the Flamingo for mods in the 1960s or the Roxy for punks in the 1970s, whether Blitz for New Romantics in the 1980s or Shoom for raves in the 1990s, have actually been settings for the suburbanization of the city, as local obsessions and alliances were mapped on to Soho streets and basement dance floors. Suburban sensibility here concerns the enactment of escape (rather than escape itself) and the domestication of decadence. The affinity of suburbia with camp is obvious. As David Bowie has always understood, a suburban pop sensibility means a camp sense of irony, a camp knowingness, a camp mockery, a camp challenge: *do they really mean it?*

In recent pop history this question has been posed most interestingly by the group Suede. Suede emerged from a group initially formed in Haywards Heath around 1983 by Bowie obsessive Brett Anderson and bassist Mat Osman. In 1989, while they were university students in London, they recruited guitarist Bernard Butler (from Leyton) and drummer Simon Gilbert (from Stratford-upon-Avon). Musically, Suede stabilized around the classic singer/guitarist, lyricist/composer, front-man-sex-star/backroom-musical-genius-axis of Anderson and Butler, but emotionally Suede's key component was Anderson and Osman's teenage friendship. Even before they met,

'I knew of him,' Osman says. 'It's a small enough place that anyone who's slightly out of the ordinary is pretty well known. I met him at parties, when he used to look like a young stockbroker, with a striped shirt and tie-pins. You had this room full of people with huge bushes of hair, and Brett had this little block flick, a yellow suit: he looked like Tommy Steele's son.'[5]

The intended effect was David Bowie's *Let's Dance* look. As Jon Savage comments,

Now in their mid-20s, Osman and Anderson were teenagers in the early '80s: time of New Romantics, post-punk. . . . Both went wholesale for pop: 'You recreate yourself as an outsider,' says Osman. 'Because you know you're not going to have fun as the centre of the gang, you're immediately drawn to people like David Bowie. When you live in an environment where there is nothing elegant, nothing lasting, you're bound to be drawn to someone like that.'[6]

This sense of being on the margins of youth culture (and Osman's words here echo those of Berlin, remembering the Bromley Contingent in Jon Savage's study of punk culture, *England's Dreaming*) remained even as Suede became commercially successful. The group came to fame by playing on the media possibilities at each end of the Southern Line (Suede was first signed to a little label in Brighton; first got attention on London radio stations and in the metropolitan pop press). Suede was a *Melody Maker* cover story before a Suede record was released; the group became the national rock sensation of 1992–3 with a debut album, *Suede*, that charmed London critics and won the Mercury Music Prize. The second album, *Dog Man Star*, released in 1994, was equally effective (if rather more grandiloquent) but even before it reached the shops Bernard Butler had left the group, citing, as ever, 'musical differences'.

As a suburban success story Suede's pop career is familiar. The first non-cognoscenti knew of the group was probably from the billboard campaign for their debut album. It featured a blow-up of the cover picture, a photograph by Tee Corinne of an intense kiss – the lovers' nakedness is apparent; the lovers' gender is not. (The couple are, in fact, women but the casual passer-by was as likely to assume the advert featured two young men.) The image is artistic (rather than pornographic) – an elegant study of tenderness and inwardness not of lust and titillation – but shocking anyway, a glimpse of a sexuality not usually seen in the high street. Suede's hoarding claim to decadence was revealing in two ways: firstly, the picture worked as an artistic *representation* of the 'perverse' and not as the real thing (this was not a photo of Brett and Bernard kissing); secondly, the image was obviously romanticized, airbrushed, soft focused. As an advertising poster and CD cover it seemed less a picture of real life in the sexual twilight zone than a picture taken from a Book of Favourite Photographs in Brett's bedroom, and by the time *Dog Man Star* was released he was claiming 'Sleeve Concept and Art Direction' for himself. The *Dog Man Star* cover used another found gallery photo (by Joanne Leonard): a young man lies naked, arse up, on a bed beneath an open, tree-filled window; a sexual pose but (as male gay imagery goes) soft not hard. What the picture reveals is less Suede's sexual tastes than their aesthetic preferences, their ability to appreciate difference as art.

This message was reinforced by the other strands of the promotion process: the interviews (dominated by Brett) in which he proclaimed himself gay in spirit if not yet in the flesh; the look (emaciated, black garbed, floppy haired); the manners (nervy, awkward, laconic). Suede were sold as slightly dour, pretentious, intense and thus, in suburbia, as the boys next door.

In musical terms the most obvious reference point was David Bowie (*Dog Man Star* sounds like a Bowie title) in terms of both the songs' melodic construction (a kind of laconic melodrama) and Brett Anderson's tone of voice: pushing up against the pitch, shifting register, vocal self-regard, gloriously purple passages. Suede turned out to be the careening vehicle of expression for a narcissist; the line that comes through the rock beat and the guitar drive is, pathetically, 'Won't someone give me some fun?'

Lyrically, this means a vague romanticism, mood created through metaphor and simile not plot and character (like, say, Blur). Suede sing songs of feeling, but the feelings are derived from the lyrical images rather than imposed upon them, as if Anderson (as lyricist) is letting his life be shaped by the pop songs that rush around his head. Youth is thus an image of both possibility ('I'm 18!') and gloom (describing a quality that by its nature won't last); the youthful protagonists of Suede's songs are stuck in a vain attempt to stop time passing, and the essential boredom of suburbia becomes, oddly, a kind of utopia, a place where there's nothing to do except dream of other places. In the words of one of Suede's instant biographies,

For years, Brett, who claims that growing up in Haywards Heath excluded him 'from anything remotely interesting', dreamed of escape, a recurrent theme in Suede songs. He wanted to go somewhere glamorous and exciting where he could dress as he pleased without being victimised. The place was London.[7]

But Anderson's lyrics suggest a continuingly ambiguous attitude to the city, which is described less as a real place than as something made up in suburbia itself and imagined, inevitably, in media imagery, through Hollywood scenarios and sci-fi cartoons. The city, London, is not a place in which to live but a backcloth against which to imagine living. In this sort of suburban sensibility the twin engines of rock'n'roll power, sex and the motor car, are as much threat as pleasure. In Suede songs every sensual move is always already choreographed, a gesture in a pornographic video or pin-up, and the car stands as much for restraint as movement, windows closed against true life. Each moment of sexual satisfaction becomes a measure of the finitude of fantasy, and in this narrative the Wild Ones, far from driving dramatically into suburbia never get to leave it, never lose the sense that whatever is happening is happening elsewhere.

Suede, in short, celebrate (and their music is celebratory) suburban alienation, the sense of lives going nowhere, of activity reduced to 'lying in my bed, lying in my head'. This pop world is decidedly male – the footloose girl (Julie Christie in *Billy Liar*) remains the romantic icon – and determinedly adolescent: from Suede's perspective days don't pass but hang there, interminably; night means life but fleetingly; and 'home' is the term most riddled with unease.

## ALWAYS ON MY MIND

Suede's sensibility is familiar enough in recent British social history. We can hear echoes in their songs of suburban jazz fans' longing for real life in the 1930s and 1940s and suburban blues fans' reveries of dirty sex in the 1950s. And Suede's fans are obviously still engaged in the 1960s mod pursuit of elusive metropolitan pleasures and the 1970s punk rejection of buttoned-up cultural conformity. The group know this very well, dressing up their attitude self-consciously – as gesture, as style, as art.

It is not difficult to explain such suburban music sociologically. Reading backwards, that is to say, from music to society, from aesthetic to material circumstances, one can find a number of obvious sociological themes: mobility, difference, habitus. But then British suburbia is as much a product of pop as British pop is a product of suburbia. In articulating the suburban experience so powerfully over the last thirty years or so, rock musicians have developed a coming-of-age narrative which is convincing to teenagers wherever they live.

Simply as a matter of pop imagery 'suburbia' describes a way of living with a number of commonsense components. Suburban dwellers move there from somewhere else; suburban housing is designed for the small family; suburban lives are lived behind closed doors. There's no sense of excess here; no spill-over of cousins, aunts and uncles; no massing on street corners. These are single-class communities: people don't know each other but they know what they're like. Neighbours nod across the street, compare cars, keep their salaries to themselves. Suburbia is a place where people live but don't work; rest but don't play (the real jobs, the real shops, the real pleasures, are elsewhere). Geographically, suburbia is, in effect, an empty sign, a series of dots on the map from which people travel

– to the office, to the fleshpots, to the city. Suburban living is characterized by what it lacks – culture, variety, surprise – not by what it offers – safety, privacy, convenience.

What I'm outlining here is a pop fancy, of course – suburban communities are no more classless, genderless or cultureless than anywhere else in contemporary Britain – but the significance of suburbia in song is as an account of the situation of suburban youth; what is sociologically persuasive is the suggestion that to live in the suburbs is a different experience for children than for their parents. To grow up in suburbia is, indeed, to grow up *in* suburbia. Adults may go off each morning to work, each evening to play, but their children's world is the suburban world, the mother's world, the world of the play group, the park, the walk, the school. For teenagers the home is the place to escape from, not to retreat to, and if parents can live to all intents and purposes anonymously (with no obvious reason to know their neighbours at all), their children cannot: they've been in and out of each other's houses since kindergarten, gone through school in adjoining desks, staked out the locality in a grid of friendships and disdain. What may seem homogenous from the outside – the rows of identical residences; the shared commuting lifestyle; a kind of cultural blankness – is marked from the inside (where the children live) by the recurring problem of fine difference. And what was built to signify security – not least for the family: bring your children up in safety! – is, from these children's own point of view, an illusory edifice. The one thing they know for sure is that some day they'll have to leave, to make something of – for – themselves.

From another perspective, what sells suburbia to grown-ups – its stability as a place to go out from and return to – is precisely what is oppressive to the young: they can't just jump in the car. Except in the imagination, of course: it is suburban youth, more than anyone, who depend on the media as a window on the world that adults seem to occupy; it is the suburban teenager, more than anyone, for whom media dreams seem real, whether on screen or on record. It is not surprising, then, that rock and pop, as youth forms, should be obsessed with suburbia, nor that suburban experience should be, in its mass mediated form, defined by teenage mores.

This is the context in which British popular music has developed a distinctive account of time and a particular sense of space. At the heart of all youth pop lurks boredom – a state of mind which apparently defines both teenage experience and teenage talk about that experience. Boredom ostensibly refers to an absence of activity – nothing's happening; I've got nothing to do – but in suburbia it describes a more complex state: not only is nothing unexpected happening, but

I sense, uneasily, that I don't really know what it means for something to 'happen' anyway. On the one hand, then, boredom is a way of discounting suburban routine (as the repetition of everyday life is transmuted into the repetition of a 4:4 beat); on the other hand, boredom can only be abated by excitement, in an intensity of feeling, with a shock. In their songs, suburban pop artists like David Bowie and suburban pop groups like Suede move constantly between the mundane and the apocalyptic. And because teenage experience is still grounded in the home, the boredom/excitement axis is focused, narcissistically, on the most immediate adolescent anxieties. Sexuality, for example, becomes the site for fantasies of *going to extremes*, and it is taken for granted that the most intense sensations (sex and drugs and rock'n'roll) are those enjoyed furtively, fearfully, kept hidden from the family – the suburban Gothic, a form that describes not only the classic English detective novel and the horror novels of Stephen King but also a genre of teen movie, is familiar too in rock, in the music of, say, Siouxsie and the Banshees or The Cure.

Music is the art form most concerned with time, most interested in detaching us from the inevitability of time passing and from the dismay that time is standing still. Music imbues time, one might say, with both turbulence and grace. If suburban pop is conceived in boredom, then – as music in which routine becomes exciting – it is also written against the inexorable process of growing up/moving on/settling down. There's a distinctly nostalgic strain in the music (from The Kinks to Blur), an oblique longing for a kind of lost local innocence (the Village Green, the Ford Cortina) which in emotional practice seems to stand for childhood, for an idealized neighbourly life, for home.

Home operates here as the implicit term of comparison with the electric space of most suburban rock: the metropolis, the metropolis as both real city – a place at the end of a tube or train or bus ride – and mythical backcloth, with its neon-lit streets and shadowy alleys of adventure, exchange and disaster. London is central to suburban sensibility as being both accessible (the place where parents work and elder siblings play) and imaginary (the place which dreams are made of). London, after all, gives suburbia its social meaning – as a dependent community; and pop's suburban musicians (Suede, Blur) clearly have a different sensibility from their northern provincial equivalents (The Smiths, Pulp). For the former, London is, really and mythically, part of the locality; for the latter London is, resentfully and day-trippingly, somewhere else.

And for the suburban teenager too the distinction between public and private spaces is blurred: to grow up suburban is to use public spaces, to get out of the house and into the park, the railway station, and now, I guess, the multiplex and the mall; but such spaces are in effect occupied, marked out by a subcultural determination to draw boundaries against 'the public'. It is this way of taking over territory that is reflected in the suburban teenage use of London itself, in the weekend gatherings in clubs and on dance floors that have marked musical movements from Mod onwards.

In her book on music-making in Milton Keynes (a suburban settlement, to be sure) Ruth Finnegan suggests that sociologists should move away from describing people in occupational terms (what they do at work defines how they are at play) and take seriously cultural activities and interests as determining people's 'social pathways' through life (including, perhaps, their jobs).[8] From this perspective what is important about the suburban sensibility in British pop and rock is not the way it reflects the class structure but the way it maps out distinct attitudes, ways of culture (the Bohemian *versus* the conformist), that make sense simultaneously in terms of taste and sociability (musical tastes define friendship groups and vice versa) and which mark out divisions *within* a broadly shared class position.

These divisions are not easily categorized either in terms of high or low culture. If suburbia is, in itself, a product of the mass media (dependent culturally on radio and television and records, on newspaper and magazines) as well as mass planning, it is also the setting in which art is most important as a mark of social difference. The suburban pop dream (as is obvious for Suede) is to become a big star as a misunderstood artist; to turn suburban alienation into both aesthetic object and mass cultural commodity. And it could be argued (in defence of all these ridiculous pop boys) that because suburbia lacks a grand theorist (the proletariat can make sense of their lives with Marx, the bourgeoisie with Freud), youth pop, as *the* suburban art form, has filled the gap, feeding airwaves around the world with the sounds of boredom, grandeur, longing.

# NOTES

1 See Simon Frith and Howard Horne, *Art into Pop*, London: Methuen, 1987; Simon Frith, 'Playing with Real Feeling', *New Formations* 4 (1988); Jon Savage, *England's Dreaming*, London: Faber & Faber, 1991; Niall Mackinnon, *The British Folk Scene*, Milton Keynes: Open University Press, 1993; Sarah Thornton, *Club Culture: Music Media and Subcultural Capital*, London: Polity, 1995.

2 See Simon Frith, 'The Pleasures of the Hearth', in *Formations of Pleasure*, London: Routledge, .1983, and 'The High, the Low and the BBC', in Wilf Stevenson, ed., *All Our Futures: The Changing Role and Purpose of the BBC*, London: BFI Publishing, 1993.

3 Jon Savage, 'Suede', *Mojo* 3, January/February 1994.

4 Savage, *England's Dreaming*, pp. 183–4.

5  Savage, 'Suede'.
6  Ibid.
7  Chris Charlesworth, ed., *Suede*, London: Omnibus Press, 1993, p. 13.
8  Ruth Finnegan, *The Hidden Musicians*, Cambridge: Cambridge University Press, 1989.

# CHAPTER 10

# The Discourse of World Music

*When was the last time an ethnomusicologist went out to discover sameness rather than difference? When did we last encourage our students to go and do fieldwork not in order to come back and paint the picture of a different Africa but of an Africa that, after all the necessary adjustments have been made, is the "same" as the West?*
KOFI AGAWU

*The pioneers of [our] native rock did not step down here from a flying saucer, they emerged from the grain of the people, like the folklorists and the tangoists before them. Our rock is already part of the Argentinean musical tradition, despite those who view it solely as "foreign penetration." The [acoustic] guitar and the bandoneon were also imported to these pampas and it occurs to nobody to consider them aliens.*
MIGUEL GRINBERG

"World music" is an unusual pop genre in that it has a precise moment of origin.[1] In July 1987 eleven independent record companies concerned with "international pop" began meeting at a London pub, the Empress of Russia, to discuss how best to sell "our kind of material." As a press release issued at the end of the month explained: "The demand for recordings of non-Western artists is surely growing. This is where problems can start for the potential buyer of WORLD MUSIC albums—the High Street record shop hasn't got the particular record, or even an identifiable section to browse through, it doesn't show on any of the published charts, and at this point all but the most tenacious give up—and who can blame them?" The world music tag (and subsequent sales campaign) was designed "to make it easier to find that Malian Kora record, the music of Bulgaria, Zairean soukous or Indian Ghazals—the new WORLD MUSIC section will be the first place to look in the local record shop." From the start, therefore, world music described the commercial process in which the sounds of other people ("diverse forms of music as yet unclassifiable in Western terms") were sold to British record buyers, and the record companies involved were well aware of the descriptive problems involved: "Trying to reach a definition of WORLD MUSIC provoked much lengthy discussion and finally it was agreed that it means practically any music that isn't at present catered for by its own category, e.g.:

Reggae, jazz, blues, folk. Perhaps the common factor unifying all these WORLD MUSIC labels is the passionate commitment of all the individuals to the music itself."[2]

This story has by now the status of a myth. It is told by academic analysts to show that the very idea of world music was an assertion of Western difference, with core—Anglo-American—musics being protected from the encroachment of other sounds, and peripheral—non-Western—musics being assigned to their own shop display ghetto.[3] But this reading of the myth is misleading. The record companies involved were in the business of persuading consumers to distinguish themselves from the mainstream of rock and pop purchasers, to be different themselves. World music wasn't a sales category like any other; these record labels claimed a particular kind of engagement with the music they traded and promised a particular kind of experience to their consumers. As Jan Fairley notes, world music records were, on the one hand, sold as individual discoveries, the record company as musical explorer bringing back a gem to share with the discriminating public; and, on the other hand, exchanged as a currency to link together a community of enthusiasts—record company bosses being at the same time promoters, journalists, deejays, musicians.[4]

Two aspects of this interest me. First, as an ideological category, world music can only be understood by reference to the rock world from which it emerged. The eleven independent labels at the famous meeting had histories. Hannibal Records was run by Joe Boyd, pioneer producer since the 1960s of folk rock; Globestyle Records was a subsidiary of Ace, a specialist in small label rock and roll and r&b reissues; Oval Records was co-owned by deejay Charlie Gillett, whose influential 1970s Radio London show, *Honky Tonk*, had specialized in regional American music (and its British pub rock tributes). The world music house journal, *Folk Roots*, had, as *Southern Rag*, developed an eclectic but militant line on the state of contemporary folk music. World music was launched with an anthology cassette, *The World at One* (available only through the indie-rock-oriented journal *NME*), and with live performances at such roots-rock venues as the Town and Country Club and the Mean Fiddler. As live music it was initially subsidized through the multicultural policy of the socialist Greater London Council and sustained by WOMAD festivals, outdoor musical celebrations clearly modelled on similar rock events.

World music, in short, might have come from elsewhere but it was sold in a familiar package—not as global pop but as roots rock, as music like that made by British and American bands who had remained true to rock and roll's original spirit. This was music for grown-ups not adolescents, unashamedly functional (for dancing, courting), expressive of local community, emotionally robust. It featured guitars, drums, voices, sweat. Many academic commentators have since observed that while "world music" sounds like an inclusive term it is, in practice, systematically exclusive. Timothy Taylor, just to give one example, draws our attention to the exclusion of Cantopop and karaoke from *World Music: The Rough Guide.*[5] But given the rock origins of world music this is hardly surprising. Indeed, as a rock critic in the late 1980s on most world-music mailing lists, I was always more aware of the authenticity claims of the music sent to me than of its exoticism. The difference at stake wasn't between Western and non-Western music but, more familiarly, between real and artificial sounds, between the musically true and the musically false, between authentic and inauthentic musical experiences. As the back cover blurb of the book of the 1989 BBC TV series *Rhythms of the World* put it: "During the late 1980s, rock and pop have become increasingly predictable and nostalgic and an appetite has developed for stronger stuff."[6]

Note, secondly, the way in which world music depended from the start on a displayed expertise. This is most obvious in record sleeve notes (and WOMAD Festival program notes), in the explanations and descriptions of particular musical forms and their roots in local traditions and practices, their well-researched biographies of the artists involved. International pop as world music was thus marketed quite differently from international pop as tourist music (as was most obvious when old releases were reissued); proper appreciation of world music meant, it seemed, ethnomusicological knowledge rather than tourist memories. World music discourse drew here on the collecting ideology that had given most of these labels their original market niche. Folk song and rock record collecting, with its equation of obscurity and significance, its obsession with fact, its pursuit of the original, its hierarchy of experts, had long been a key route through which African American music, from jazz and r&b to soul and Motown, had been appropriated by Europeans. And such collectors' expertise had always involved a kind of academicism.[7]

The relevant academic expertise for world music marketing was ethnomusicology, and if one result was the scholar as deejay, anthologist, journalist, and writer of blurbs,[8] another was the record company boss as scholar, engaged in his or her own fieldwork, developing his or her own theories of musical movement and exchange. The coming together of academic and commercial concerns was reflected in the late 1980s development of the International Association for the Study of Popular Music (which even recruited Peter Gabriel for a while), and can be seen in the list of contributors to *World Music: The Rough Guide.*[9]

If ethnomusicologists thus helped define world music, the subsequent relationship between academic and commercial expertise has not been straightforward. World music record companies may have had little difficulty justifying their activities in terms of their musical enthusiasm, but academic enthusiasts were soon anxious about the assumptions behind and effects of world music as a sales category. The very fact that ethnomusicological expertise was needed to guarantee the authenticity of what was being sold called into question the notion of authenticity itself. It was soon clear, for example, that "the authentic" worked in retail terms as a redescription of the exotic. International pop music in the 1990s may be packaged quite differently from international pop music in the 1950s, with greater respect shown to its formal qualities and local history, but what's on offer to the consumer, the musical pleasures promised, aren't so different: in the context of the denunciation of Western pop artifice and decadence, the authentic itself becomes the exotic (and vice versa). This move is familiar enough from the long European Romantic celebration of the native (the peasant and the African) as more real (because more natural) than the civilized Westerner. The implication is that world musicians can now give us those direct, innocent rock and roll pleasures that Western musicians are too jaded, too corrupt to provide. World music thus remains a form of tourism (as *World Music: The Rough Guide* makes clear), just as "world travellers" are still tourists, even if they use local transport and stay in local inns rather than booking package tours and rooms in the national Hilton. Indeed, this musical equation of the exotic and the authentic can be traced back at least to Capitol Records' *Capitol of the World* series, launched in 1956: "\*Recorded in the country of the music's origins \* Captured in flawless high fidelity \* A remarkable series of albums for world music-travellers.\*"[10] As Keir Keightley notes, already the search for the exotic and the authentic is going hand in hand. He cites a *Holiday* magazine ad in 1957 headlined "The Real Stuff":

> The spicier Paris haunts where tourists go, and the more genuine quarters where Frenchmen go, have now been captured in pure melody by famed French conductor-composer Andre Colbert. It's the most authentic and lovely album of Parisian listening that'll come your way in a month of Tuesdays . . . here is the real stuff, the real music of Paris—romantic melody that can never be copied.[11]

From the academic point of view this equation of the authentic with the exotic calls into question the meaning of authenticity. On the one hand it can be doubted whether there is such a thing as an "authentic"—autonomous—musical form in the first place; on the other hand it is apparent that authenticity here functions as an ideological construct—a construction of commercial (and academic) discourse. It describes a process of music appropriation rather than music-making. And this leads us to a second kind of academic anxiety: the lurking problem of cultural imperialism, the suspicion that what "world music" really describes is a double process of exploitation: Third World musicians being treated as raw materials to be processed into commodities for the West, and First World musicians (in the back cover

words of *Rhythms of the World*) putting "new life into their own music by working with artists like Ladysmith Black Mambazo, Youssou N'Dour and Celia
Cruz."

As I write, Ladysmith Black Mambazo's *Greatest Hits* is riding high in
Britain's Top Ten Album charts, following the use of the group's music in a
Heinz TV advertisement; world musicians' international success is clearly an
effect of global capitalism, and if by the beginning of the 1990s there was
general academic agreement that "cultural imperialism" was no longer a term
that clarified the workings of leisure corporations, it was also agreed that these
workings did need critical analysis.[12] World music labels are highly infor-
mative about the musical source of their releases, about local musical traditions, genres, and practices, but they are highly uninformative about their
own activities—the process through which music from Mali reaches a record
store in Middlesborough is not explained. On the one hand, there is remarkably little information available about the licensing and publishing deals
involved, about copyrights and contracts, about the money flow.[13] On the
other hand, world music sleeve notes systematically play down the role of
record producers in shaping non-Western sounds for Western ears, in describing Western markets to non-Western artists. When the sales emphasis
is on local musical authenticity, the creative role of the international record
producer is best not mentioned.

In academic popular music studies the suggestion that the producer somehow interferes (whether for commercial or colonialist reasons) with the free
flow of sounds from artist to audience has by now been challenged by a more
sophisticated reading in which popular music is an effect of the relationship
between musician and producer, between musical and market considera-
tions.[14] This is, again, to challenge the concept of authenticity, and by the
early 1990s academic discussions of world music were being organized
around a different term, the hybrid. Hyunju Park summarizes current academic thinking:

> Musicians are blending together musical elements from everywhere and
> adding to them the musical possibilities afforded by new technologies. This
> process of global bricolage is still intertwined with, but no longer entirely de-
> pendent on, the core industry. In observation of this new eclecticism, the core
> industry itself has begun to look to all cultures for potential raw materials and
> consequently its former rock centre has splintered into many subgenre frag-
> ments. Even if centre dominance diminishes, however, local musicians will not
> work in a less commercialized environment. The process of hybridity is not
> one of absolute free choice but one of constant compromise between what
> might be desired creatively and what will be accepted commercially.[15]

In introducing the concept of hybridity into the discussion ethnomusicologists were not simply pointing at the value of detailed local work on music-

making processes, or trying to follow the movement of particular musics through the international trade in sounds and symbols; they were also drawing on broader academic concerns about globalization, concerns inflected by postmodern theory. On the one hand, then, world music could be seen as a site on which new sorts of (hybrid) identity are being performed.[16] On the other hand, world music could be seen as a site on which new sorts of cultural theory could be developed, new futures glimpsed. The academic concern is no longer to apply some general theory of development (the cultural imperialism thesis, say) to music as an example, but, rather, to read the meaning of globalization through world music. Jocelyne Guilbault thus claims that "world music seems far ahead of other fields of activity in its use of active social forces that are diverse and contradictory as agents of change and in its reliance on both local and international forces in the shaping of individual and social identities."[17] Edwin Seroussi writes, about popular music studies in Israel:

> The study of the forces that shaped Israel's popular music industry or the description and classification of Israeli music according to genres is certainly not the ultimate goal of this field of research. Although interpretative analysis of social and musical processes from the past will continue to guide much future research, it is also necessary to pay attention to the power of popular music to predict. Just as the emergence of *musikah mizrahit* predicted the rise of political consciousness among the second generation of North African and Middle Eastern Jewish immigrants in the early 1970s, the rich palette of popular music expression in Israel today may forecast new social configurations still in their formative stages.[18]

If for world music record companies the concept of authenticity was a way of condensing a series of arguments about how music works and why it matters, drawing on potential listeners' understandings of rock and folk, so for world music scholars hybridity has become a way of condensing a number of arguments about globalization and identity, drawing on potential readers' understandings of postmodern theory. For Seroussi, for instance, to study popular music in Israel is to study "the struggle to create a new, local culture," to examine the dialectical relationships between past Jewish cultures and present Middle Eastern cultures, between Israeli national identity and the "threatening influence" of global, Americanized dreams. And it is this sense of struggle to which the concept of hybridity draws our attention.

In using this term scholars have adopted two different analytic approaches—detailed studies of local practice on the one hand, grand theories of the global condition on the other. Local studies start from established accounts of musical syncretism, of the ways in which musical styles develop through a constant process of borrowing and quotation. As Nancy Morris suggests in a review of recent work on Latin American and Caribbean music, ethnomusicologists have long assumed that "neither identities nor traditions are static; both change with changing circumstances, and with the continuous interaction of peoples."[19] From this perspective, hybridity is a new name for a familiar process: local musics are rarely culturally pure (a genre as nationally distinct as Dominican *bachata* can thus be shown to draw on Mexican, Colombian-Ecuadorian, and Puerto Rican as well as Dominican sources). As Morris suggests such music is made in local contexts of mobility, migration, the constant writing out and blurring of class and ethnic difference; tradition is always a matter of invention and reinvention, and what's at issue here is not simply commercialization (rural music becoming urban commodity, say) but also legitimation, as styles initially despised for their association with the lower classes become nationally and internationally popular. This is not a process without tensions—it is still difficult for the Jamaican cultural establishment, for example, to come to terms with the fact that reggae is the country's most successful cultural export—but the point is that world music is shaped by responses to national/political as well to commercial/ global conditions.[20]

In local studies the most important conclusion to draw from this is that musical traditions are only preserved by constant innovation. In his study of Peruvian panpipe music, Thomas Turino quotes the charter of the Federation of Puno Musicians in Lima. These musicians, children of urban immigrants, started out by asserting that their music was "the creation of our ancestors. It is a free and natural manifestation of community that expresses the living history of our Quechua and Symara nations."[21] This sense of tradition inspired these students to teach themselves to play a music that articulated an imagined regional identity even as their urban experience shaped the way in which they conceived and played that music, and it can be contrasted to the artificial preservation of tradition by state edict, exercised through the control of radio outlets, local recording studios, education, and performance. The impact of international pop, in other words, may be as important for the preservation of music traditions as for their destruction. In the books Morris discusses, this is probably best brought out by Deborah Pacini Hernandez's study of *bachata* in the Dominican Republic. Local musicians there are clear that traditional Dominican sounds have only developed freely since the end of the thirty-year Trujillo dictatorship in 1961: "We can't forget how significant it has been to merengue as a popular music to have come into contact with the popular music of other countries."[22]

The fieldwork of Turino, Hernandez, and many other contemporary ethnomusicologists makes clear, in Morris's words, that "urbanization, modern transportation, and electronic media" have speeded up "the age-old process of musical mixing" and "with fewer intermediaries than ever before," but it does not suggest that the underlying dynamic of musical change has become qualitatively different. Today Peruvian *chicha* combines electric rock instruments, highland-mestizo *wayno* melodies and phrasings, and the rhythms of Colombian *cumbia*, musical elements absorbed by the Lima-born children of rural-born parents as much from radio, records, and *MTV Internacional* as from neighborhood performers, tutors, and rituals. In the early 1960s Jamaican popular musicians brought together the musical resources of African drumming, Afro-Protestant Revivalist hymns, European ballroom dance, Caribbean calypso and rumba, and United States rhythm and blues, pilfering from local musical events and internationally distributed and broadcast records alike. The media of global musical communication may change; the ways in which music is a mobile life form do not.

This is the optimistic view of world music: musical creativity always involves cultural borrowing; changes in musical tradition don't mean the loss of cultural identity but articulate the way it changes with circumstance. The fact that such hybrid forms become popular internationally, are traded in the global marketplace, is analytically irrelevant; the meaning of local musics must be referred to local conditions of production. This is the academic argument that best suits (and is most used by) world music companies; it defines hybridity as authenticity and implies that musical creativity depends on a free trade in sounds; "uncorrupted" music can now be seen as stagnant music, music constrained by reactionary political and cultural forces.

This argument is developed most systematically and critically in Jocelyne Guilbault's study of *zouk*. Guilbault describes the local effect in the Antilles of the international success of the *zouk* group Kassav:

> As it has acquired power through fame, Kassav has contributed to some significant changes: a revolution in local show business practices and in record production in the French Antilles; the development of ties for the first time with international markets; new collaboration between local and commercial entrepreneurs and music groups; and a transformation of social consciousness. . . . Kassav's financial success has led to the recognition that cultural changes brought about through popular music can bring economic changes, that the process of cultural identification awakened by mass-distributed music in general and zouk in particular informs new attitudes, which in turn affect the economy through consumer choices and production methods.[23]

But Guilbault also makes clear the difficulty of confining "local conditions of production" to a locality. As live music-making in the Antilles was replaced by the use of records, by mobile discos and deregulated radio stations, "Antillean music groups of the early eighties were forced to develop a 'sound' that could compete with imported foreign music," and such competition in itself transformed the frame of musical expectations. If local ethnomusicological studies tend to see the dynamics of musical change as somehow organic, Guilbault argues that once musicians enter the international music market their music is shaped by new kinds of nonlocal forces:

Popular local dance musics that reach the international market are subject to the paradox inherent in the transnational recording industry. They must comply with what is often referred to as the "international sound," that is, the use of preponderant Euro-American scales and tunings, harmony, electronic instruments now seen as standards, accessible dance rhythms, and a Euro-American-based intonation. They are also obliged to deal with subjects that are accessible to a wide audience. . . . But in contrast to the standardization of the songs' sounds and content, these musics must, at the same time, distinguish themselves from the others by featuring elements unique to their cultural elements. They must utilize in a specific way their dependence on the international markets by and through a continual process of creation/adaptation.[24]

And this has its own local effects. Kassav's choice to sing in Creole rather than French "was certainly and unapologetically a marketing device to attract attention and to be clearly identified [in the international French music market] as *Antillais*," but "it was also unmistakeably a way to show solidarity with compatriots at home and in exile," and therefore both to nurture a sense of collectivity among all Creole speakers in the Islands and to legitimate the use of Creole in public Antillean institutions.[25] Guilbault concludes,

> As do all other world musics, zouk creates much stress in its countries of origin by underscoring how its relation with the international market reformulates local traditions and creative processes. As it emphasises the workings of world political economy at the local level, zouk renders more problematic for Antilleans the definition of the "we" as a site of difference. It challenges in fact the traditional way of thinking about the "we" as a self-enclosed unit by highlighting its relational character.[26]

A similar argument has been proposed by cultural sociologists writing from the opposite direction, studying not world music as the other of Western culture but rock music as the other of non-Western cultures. Motti Regev thus argues that for many musicians and fans in the last twenty-five years,

> the presence of rock music in their own local cultures and its influence on local music is hardly seen as a form of cultural imperialism. On the contrary, they perceive rock as an important tool for strengthening their contemporary sense of local identity and autonomy. Anglo-American sub-styles of rock as they are, imitations that put local-language lyrics to the same styles, or hybrids that mix rock elements with local music traditions, proliferate in countries around the world. Italian hip hop, Polish reggae, Chinese *xibei-feng*, Algerian *pop-rai*, Israeli *musica mizrahkit*, Argentinian *rock nacional*, Zimbabwean *chimurenga* or *jit*, are a few of these sub-styles. Producers of and listeners to these types of music feel, at one and the same time, participants in a specific contemporary global-universal form of expression *and* innovators of local, national, ethnic and other identities. A cultural form, associated with American (US) culture and with the powerful commercial interests of the international

music industry, is being used in order to construct a sense of local difference and authenticity.[27]

Regev is partly arguing here that rock, as a "local authentic" music, is important for resolving the postmodern condition of occupying global/mediated and local/immediate space simultaneously. But his more specific point is that rock is a modern rather than postmodern form. Rock, that is, stands for a certain kind of self-consciousness, a particular mode of individual expressivity. "Rock music," in his words, "is used to declare a 'new'—modern, contemporary, young, often critical-oppositional—sense of local identity, as opposed to older, traditional, conservative forms of that identity."[28] Rock, to put this another way, can be seen as the authentic articulation of a local identity in its very recognition of the complexity of that identity, of the global in the local and the local in the global.

On the one hand, then, rock is a vernacular lower class version of the expressive modernity that has always "transcended" local conditions (not least in the spread of Western classical music); on the other hand, it exemplifies, in Regev's words, "one of the cultural logics of globalization"—"instead of being disparate, relatively independent musical languages, local styles of music become part of one history, variations of one cultural form—without necessarily losing a sense of difference."[29] From this postmodern perspective hybrid music is the necessary expression of a hybrid condition. This condition is partly technological. David Toop thus concludes an essay on "Exotica and World Music Fusions" with the observation:

> It is all too probable that one of the endearing, perhaps enduring, clichés of the end of the twentieth century will be the postmodern/electronic age concept of image chaos: the progressively unshocking shocks of overloaded layers, bizarre juxtapositions and oppositions, forgeries and thefts, wrenches of time and location, and dislocations of function and meaning. There are tangible models everywhere: the streetsounds of a modern Fourth World, *retronuevo* city like Miami; the recording studios of the Bombay film industry with its indiscriminate pile-ups of world music bites; the traverse of historical and religious divides and levels of technology in the music of Mali and Senegal. . . . Music history has become, to a remarkable extent, a record and tape collection. Music is composed or performed with knowledge gleaned from recordings; records are made with fragments of music lifted from other records. Unnecessary, at the end of the twentieth century, to bring forty marines and a brass band [as the Prussian ambassador brought to Japan in 1860]; a single cassette, arriving in a new geographical location, can upturn musical traditions for good.[30]

And Peter Manuel argues, also with reference to the cassette, that "the lower costs of production enable small-scale producers to emerge around the world, recording and marketing music aimed at specialized, local grassroots audiences rather than at a homogenous mass market. The net result is a remarkable decentralization, democratization, and dispersal of the music industry at the expense of multinational and national oligopolies."[31] Either way, technology makes for a new music culture, organized around neither local traditions nor global corporate trends. In Manuel's words about India, "while obscure, specialized traditional genres have come to be marketed on cassette, new syncretic styles have also emerged in close association with cassette dissemination. Such genres have been able to bypass the disapproving or indifferent control of state bureaucracies and/or formerly dominating majors."[32]

The postmodern condition is reflected both in the collapse of grand musical narratives and authorities and in the blurring of musical borders and histories. World music can thus be treated as the sound of postmodern experience, following Stuart Hall's suggestion that "the aesthetics of modern popular music is the aesthetics of the hybrid, the aesthetics of the crossover, the aesthetics of the diaspora, the aesthetics of creolization."[33] Timothy Taylor analyzes the way the British musician Apache Indian exploits "free-floating signifiers," and suggests that if Apache Indian is, as Peter Manuel suggests, "a quintessential postmodern musician," this is not just a matter of style or irony but articulates, rather, a particular experience of—and emotional response to—what Taylor calls (following Hall) "the global postmodern." In Taylor's words, "new technologies and modes of musical production allow musicians to occupy different subject positions in a kind of simultaneity never before possible; they don't move from one to the next but rather employ and deploy several at once."[34] Or as Veit Erlmann argues more abstractly:

> For the contradiction that characterizes our historical moment is this: if the truth of an individual or collective identity, the experience of an authentic rooting in a time and a place, is now inextricably bound up with the truths of other places and times, then the desire to account truthfully for this very fact in some kind of macro model amounts to missing the individual experience. But if the systemic notion of a cultural totality is to be of any value and if it is to avoid the dangers of Eurocentric monolithic representations, it must precisely capture this dilemma as one of the deepest motivating forces for a global aesthetic production.[35]

Erlmann's interest is the "wholesale disappearance of the social and of difference as such" and "the rapid loss of referentiality." World music thus "does away with time and space altogether." Developing Fredric Jameson's concept of pastiche, Erlmann suggests that in world music "difference itself becomes the signified," while global music pastiche describes the "attempt at coating the sounds of a commodified present with the patina of use value in some other time and place."[36]

The contrast between these positions is clear enough: Erlmann is considering the weight world music has to carry for its listeners in the West, Taylor the meaning it has for the musicians themselves. Either way, the differ-

ence between the West and its other is preserved: Erlmann sees it in the constantly reinstated nostalgia of the world music consumer; Taylor suggests that
only world musicians express the postmodern condition authentically. Their
music is, paradoxically, a critique of Erlmann's postmodern despair: "Just as
the subordinate groups in US culture have always done more than the dominant groups to make radical positions available through new sounds, new
forms, new styles, it looks as though it is the subordinate groups around the
world who are doing the same, perhaps even showing us how to get along
on this planet. If we would only listen."[37] Taylor's argument draws here from
cultural, or rather subcultural, studies of "resistance," of the ways in which
"subordinate" consumers turn commodities back on themselves, and mar-
ginalized communities define their own social spaces, their own centers and
peripheries, in the process of stylization.[38] The problem here (as in the original youth subcultural studies) is that "resistance" describes such a variety of
activities, from day-to-day communal sociability to full scale political mobilization. In his study of a typical hybrid youth form, German hip hop, Dietmar Elflein distinguishes between the music made by "Krauts with attitudes,"
German rappers using the German language to express (however ironically)
a nationalist resistance to U.S. leisure culture, and the music made by the
children of "guest workers," rap used to explore critically the complexities
of German immigrant experience. But he also cautions against reducing either kind of rap simply to an ideological or ethnic position (a position of
more interest to the record companies marketing the music than to the musicians making it):

> The music these bands produce is hip hop and nothing more. There is no
> need to propose different ethnically defined subgenres on the basis of the ori-
> gin of particular musical samples. . . . In the end, the issue is this: anyone who
> wants to gather up musicians under an ethnically defined flag (as did *Cartel*
> and *Krauts with Attitude*) is, in practice, trying to become the dominant musi-
> cal, political and commercial power in a scene which is, by its nature, various
> and pluralistic.[39]

To treat world music as postmodern resistance is to beg questions about music's significance for identities and social mobilization, questions that are better answered in the particular than the general.[40] A rich source of such particular discussion can be found in *Retuning Culture,* a collection of essays on
"musical changes in Central and Eastern Europe" edited by Mark Slobin.[41]
What concern these authors are the ways in which "music shapes politics and
economics and social life as well as being shaped by them."[42] The question
is how does such shaping work?

Effectively, according to these studies, through processes of social identity formation. On the one hand, music plays a role in turning a class-in-
itself into a class-for-itself. Vague feelings of ethnic affiliation become a self-

conscious ethnic identity, as shared myths and memories are articulated musically, given instrumental, rhythmic and lyric form. On the other hand, people are mobilized by music materially, as crowds brought together to make events; concerts offer, in themselves, the experience of collective power. Under certain circumstances, then, music becomes a source of collective consciousness which promotes group cohesion and social activities that in turn have political consequences.

These Eastern European studies suggest first (unsurprisingly) that music is particularly significant for the politics of national and ethnic identity; music becomes politically significant, that is, when issues of national and ethnic identity are the prime sites and sources of political dispute—whether at moments in the creation and dissolution of states or in terms of diasporic mobilization around the rights of minorities and migrants. Secondly (and more tellingly), these studies suggest that the music at issue in these situations is "folk" music, music precisely defined in terms of collective identities. It is when the validity of a social group is in dispute that music becomes politically important, as a way of authenticating it. It follows that aesthetic arguments—what makes for good music?—are ethical arguments—what makes for the good life? In this context, music articulates a way of being-in-society both representationally (in its subject matter) and materially (in its lived-out relationships between musicians and between musicians and audience). This is a process of idealization both in formal terms (the way in which music provides a narrative, an experience of wholeness and completion) and as a matter of staging, in events in which solidarity is made physical.

Catherine Wanner thus describes a Ukrainian nationalist song festival which took place (shortly before the collapse of the Soviet empire) in a football stadium in Zaporizhzhia. This was a rock concert that began with a religious procession ("A stream of priests solemnly entered the stadium walking along the track in long black robes carrying candles and crosses. In this way, twenty chanting priests introduced, so to speak, the first rock band") and mixed the lineup of rock bands with folk singers. If the (local) rock bands indicated that Ukrainian culture was contemporary, and not confined to officially sanctioned folklore, the folk singers (groups from the Ukrainian communities of Canada, the U.S.A., France, and Australia) suggested that the Ukraine's authentic cultural tradition had been protected from Soviet incursions.

> During the third song of the opening ceremony of the festival, as the feeling of solidarity and euphoria accelerated, most of the audience poured down from the bleachers onto the soccer field to dance. They broke the traditional segregation of performer and audience and joined hands or elbows in a human chain, encircling the singers on stage and each other. . . . The soccer stadium became the central town square as the "imagined community" of Ukrainians, at least for one night, was reified and celebrated in music and dance.

"Why," asks Wanner, "did advocates of Ukrainian independence turn to music to recast the critical relationship between Russia and Ukraine?"

> The demarcations between musical styles, genres, and performances, while nonetheless reflective of a cultural tradition, are infinitely more porous than other avenues of culture that also inform identity. Other cultural elements . . . such as religious affiliation, historical memories and myths, and language, do not command the immediate acceptance and visceral reactions that music has the power to trigger.[43]

The importance of Eastern European studies for accounts of world music is that they address questions of identity and musical change in a situation in which identity is the central political issue. In doing so they make clear that the way we feel music—respond to it emotionally and viscerally—must be analyzed as a grounded experience, grounded in a particular time and place, grounded in a particular form. Musical response involves recognition, sympathy, and commitment; it is at once free and necessary. Following a stay in Bulgaria, Tim Rice writes:

> Studying music as social life and symbolic system would have taken more time than I had, but I did observe the extraordinary staying power of tradition, which speaks if not to the autonomy of music, then to its power to make claim on us—to force us to engage with its rules—even as social, economic, and political conditions change. . . . Musicians were undoubtedly using music to construct notions of ethnic and national identity, but precisely how that is working itself out in the details of musical style will have to be studied in more careful future analyses.[44]

Meanwhile, Rice notes three developments: Gypsy musicians appropriating African American rap in the Romany language; radio programs mixing the previously segregated genres of "authentic folklore," "arranged folklore," and "wedding music"; and a new folk radio station "broadcasting a large amount of Macedonian music, along with a fair dose of Bulgarian *narodna, svatbarska* and *starogradska* ("old city") *muzika,* and Gypsy, Greek, Serbian and even Latin American music."[45] Whatever new forms of Bulgarian identity are being constructed musically, then, they are being constructed through a series of explorations of the non-Bulgarian, and to describe the resulting sounds (Romany rap, for example) as hybrid may be to miss the point: what's involved here is less a sense of subjective instability than the negotiation of new cultural alliances.

Rice concludes his essay on Bulgaria with the observation that "when viewed from the point of view of the individual practitioners, music can be understood as economic practice, as social behavior, and as a symbolic system with the powerful ability to make aesthetic sense while hiding meaning; to reference existing worlds; and to imagine new, utopian worlds."[46] When world music is viewed from this perspective the most commonly imagined utopia seems to be one in which issues of identity do not even arise. "'Stick to African music!'" writes Manu Dibango. "How many times have I heard this *diktat,* from critics as much as musicians from the continent. I have found myself stuck, labeled, locked in behind prison bars. . . . " Dibango accepts that "Weight comes from tradition. . . . But you need rhythm to move forward. . . . Talent has no race; there simply exists a race of musicians. To be part of it, you have to have knowledge. Musicians—and composers even more so—perceive pleasant sounds around them and digest them. They like the sounds; the sounds become part of them."[47]

But such a view—commonly expressed by world musicians—is not simply utopian. It reflects too the realities of the world musical life.[48] Jocelyne Guilbault has analyzed in detail how the Caribbean superstars of Calypso and Soca live as "transnationals."

> In this respect, the production of a typical album by the calypsonian Arrow offers a telling example. Arrow is a calypsonian from Montserrat, who does most of his recordings in New York City, often at the recording studio owned by Frankie McIntosh, a musician from St. Vincent. For each track, Arrow often uses two arrangers who do not necessarily originate from the same country—one for the brass parts and another for the rhythm and brass arrangements. Regularly, Arrow asks Trinidadian Leston Paul, one of the most sought-after arrangers in the English Caribbean, to fly to New York to write and direct horn parts for his songs. Arrow always uses a mix of musicians from the United States and the Caribbean to produce a special sound in the horn section. . . . The production of Caribbean recordings typically involves musicians from different nationalities and territories, and various stages of the recordings often take place in different locales.[49]

The recording process described here is familiar enough in other musical worlds, whether rock or classical, but the juxtapositions of friendship and influence seem more accidental in international pop. Take, for example, the musical background of the Ethiopian musician Mulatu Astatqé. As a teenager he studied clarinet, piano, and harmony at London's Trinity School of Music and music theory at Berklee College of Music in Boston. In London he played with the calypso musician Frank Holder and in Edmundo Ros's Latino big band; in New York he founded the Ethiopian Quintet to record an album of "Afro-Latin Soul" (the other group members were Puerto Rican); back in Ethiopia, as band leader, arranger, and teacher of "Ethio-jazz," he remains after thirty years the country's only vibraphone player, a musician regarded simultaneously as a guru and a novelty.[50]

Such lives are the stuff of world music biographies and suggest, finally, that the concept of globalization, with its intimations of the inexorable forces of history and/or capital, should be replaced in the discussion of world music by an understanding of networks—globalization from below, as it were. And this is where we came in. Those record company bosses who

*320*　　SIMON FRITH

orginally met in a pub to define world music were, self-consciously, networking; world music promoters (European radio deejays, for example), continue to pass sounds around semiformal organizations of knowledge and friendship; the World Circuit (the name of an influential world music label) is, it is implied, different from the global pop market because it is a community, its authenticity guaranteed less by the music circulated than by the relationship between the people (including the musicians) doing the circulating. And here we have the final irony: academic music studies look to world music for clues about the postmodern condition, for examples of hybridity and lived subjective instability, but to understand this phenomenon we also have to recognize the ways in which world music has itself been constructed as a kind of tribute to and a parody of the community of scholars.

## NOTES

1. I'm referring here to the British music market term. In the U.S.A. the retail label is "world beat," first used by the musician Dan Del Santo as the title for an album released in 1982—see Andrew Goodwin and Joe Gore, "World Beat and the Cultural Imperialism Debate" *Socialist Review* 20, no. 3 (July-September 1990): 65.

The epigraphs to this chapter are from Kofi Agawu, "The Invention of 'African Rhythm'" *Journal of the American Musicological Society* 48, no. 3 (1995): 389–90, and Motti Regev, "Rock Aesthetics and the Musics of the World," *Theory Culture and Society* 14, no. 3 (1997): 131.

2. Quotes taken from the first WORLD MUSIC press release (n.d.).

3. See, for example, Jocelyne Guilbault: "On Redefining the 'Local' through World Music," *The World of Music* 35, no. 2 (1993): 36; Timothy D. Taylor, *Global Pop: World Music, World Markets* (London: Routledge, 1997), 2–3.

4. Jan Fairley, "The 'Local' and the 'Global' in Popular Music," in *The Cambridge Companion to Rock and Pop,* ed. Simon Frith, Will Straw, and John Street (Cambridge: Cambridge University Press, forthcoming). Fairley is commenting in particular here on Ian Anderson's editorial arguments about world music in *Folk Roots* magazine— Anderson had been involved in the original world music discussions in his capacity as boss of Rogue Records. And see Peter Jowers, "Beating New Tracks: WOMAD and the British World Music Movement" in *The Last Post: Music after Modernism,* ed. Simon Miller (Manchester: Manchester University Press, 1993), 71.

5. Taylor, *Global Pop,* 16–17.

6. Francis Hanly and Tim May, eds., *Rhythms of the World* (London: BBC Books, 1989).

7. Charlie Gillett's classic *Sound of the City,* the first systematic account of the 1950s emergence of rock and roll, which put in place the ideology of rock as roots music, locally based, the product of independent rather than major record companies, was originally written as a master's thesis at Columbia University.

8. I'm thinking here of people in Britain like Latin music expert Jan Fairley and African music expert Lucy Duran.

THE DISCOURSE OF WORLD MUSIC    *321*

9. Simon Broughton et al., eds., *World Music: The Rough Guide* (London: Rough Guides Ltd, 1994).

10. Cited in Keir Keightley, "Around the World: Musical Tourism and the Globalization of the Record Industry, 1946–66," unpublished paper (1998).

11. Keightley, "Around the World."

12. See Goodwin and Gore, "World Beat and the Cultural Imperialism Debate," and Reebee Garofalo, "Whose World, What Beat: The Transnational Music Industry, Identity, and Cultural Imperialism," *World of Music* 35 (1993): 16–32.

13. One of the few detailed accounts of world music as trade, Rick Glanvill's "World Music Mining—The International Trade in New Music" was removed from the BBC book of *Rhythms of the World* following threats of libel action.

14. Roger Wallis and Krister Malm's concept of "transculturation" has thus been more influential on studies of world music than those models in which indigenous local music cultures are celebrated for "resisting" international cultural forces. Compare Roger Wallis and Krister Malm, *Big Sounds from Small Peoples: The Music Industry in Small Countries* (London: Constable, 1984) with Deanna Robinson et al., eds., *Music at the Margins* (London: Sage, 1991).

15. Hyunju Park, *Globalization, Local Identity and World Music: The Case of Korean Popular Music* (M.Litt thesis, John Logie Baird Centre, Strathclyde University, 1998).

16. See, for example, Jocelyne Guilbault, "Interpreting World Music: A Challenge in Theory and Practice," *Popular Music* 16, no. 1 (1997): 31–44.

17. Jocelyne Guilbault, *Zouk: World Music in the West Indies* (Chicago: University of Chicago Press, 1993), 210.

18. Edwin Seroussi, *Popular Music in Israel: The First Fifty Years* (Cambridge, Mass.: Harvard College Library, 1996), 25–26.

19. Nancy Morris, "Cultural Interaction in Latin American and Caribbean Music," *Latin American Research Review* 34, no. 1 (1999): 187–200. And see also Jorge Duany, "Rethinking the Popular: Caribbean Music and Identity," *Latin American Research Review* 17, no. 2 (1996): 176–92.

20. See Kiki Marriott, *Communications Policy and Language in Jamaica* (Ph.D. thesis, John Logie Baird Centre, Strathclyde University, 1998).

21. Thomas Turino, *Moving Away from Silence: Music of the Peruvian Altiplano and the Experience of Urban Migration* (Chicago: University of Chicago Press, 1993), 188.

22. Deborah Pacini Hernandez, *Bachata: A Social History of a Dominican Popular Music* (Philadelphia: Temple University Press, 1995), 78–79.

23. Guilbault, *Zouk*, 30.

24. Ibid., 37, 150.

25. Ibid., 166. Compare Kiki Marriott's discussion of reggae's impact on the use of patois in Jamaica—Marriott, *Communications Policy and Language in Jamaica*.

26. Guilbault, *Zouk*, 209–10.

27. Regev, "Rock Aesthetics and Musics of the World," 125–26.

28. Ibid., 131.

29. Ibid., 139.

30. David Toop, "Into the Hot—Exotica and World Music Fusions," in Hanly and May, *Rhythms of the World*, 126.

31. Peter Manuel, *Cassette Culture: Popular Music and Technology in North India* (Chicago: University of Chicago Press, 1993), xiv.

*322*   SIMON FRITH

32. Ibid., 33.

33. Quoted in Taylor, *Global Pop*, xxi.

34. Ibid., 155–65, 203, 94.

35. Veit Erlmann, "The Politics and Aesthetics of Transnational Musics," *The World of Music* 35, no. 2 (1993): 7.

36. Ibid. 8, 11, 13.

37. Taylor, *Global Pop*, 204.

38. See, for example, Sanjay Sharma et al., eds., *Dis-Orienting Rhythms: The Politics of the New Asian Dance Music* (London: Zed Books, 1996); Tony Mitchell, *Popular Music and Local Identity: Rock, Pop and Rap in Europe and Oceania* (London: Leicester University Press, 1996).

39. Dietmar Elflein, "From Krauts with Attitudes to Turks with Attitudes: Some Aspects of the German Hip Hop History" *Popular Music* 17, no. 3 (1998), 255–65.

40. For a good survey of the issues involved here see Martin Stokes, ed., *Ethnicity, Identity and Music: The Musical Construction of Place* (Oxford: Berg, 1994).

41. Mark Slobin, ed., *Retuning Culture* (Durham, N.C.: Duke University Press, 1996).

42. Carol Silverman, "Music and Marginality: *Roma* (Gypsies) of Bulgaria and Macedonia" in Slobin, *Retuning Culture*, 231.

43. Catherine Wanner, "Nationalism on Stage: Music and Change in Soviet Ukraine," in Slobin, *Retuning Culture*, 139–44, 148.

44. Timothy Rice, "The Dialectic of Economics and Aesthetics in Bulgarian Music," in Slobin, *Retuning Culture*, 195–96.

45. Ibid., 196.

46. Ibid., 198.

47. Manu Dibango, *Three Kilos of Coffee* (Chicago: University of Chicago Press, 1994), 125–26.

48. Compare the musicians' views recorded in Rehan Hyder, *Indie Bands and Asian Identity: Negotiating Ethnicity in the UK Music Industry* (Ph.D. thesis, University of Staffordshire, 1998), with the arguments made on their behalf in Sharma, *Dis-Orienting Rhythms*.

49. Jocelyne Guilbault, "World Music," *The Cambridge Companion to Rock and Pop*, ed. Frith, Straw, and Street.

50. Information taken from Francis Falceto's sleeve notes for *Ethiopiques 4: Ethio Jazz & Musique Instrumentale 1969–1974*.

# CHAPTER 11

## Pop music

The biggest selling pop single of all time is the version of 'Candle in the Wind' Elton John recorded as a tribute to Princess Diana, and his Westminster Abbey performance of the song, during Diana's funeral service in September 1997, can be considered as the ultimate British pop moment. It was controversial. Pop music is still regarded as a vernacular form unsuitable for a religious occasion, a vulgar form unfit for royalty; and Elton John was not an obvious representative of the state (though he was soon to be knighted, joining Sir Cliff Richard, Sir Paul McCartney, and Sir Andrew Lloyd Webber in the official pop pantheon). He was chosen to sing because he was an intimate of Diana and, in this respect, simply represented her social circle. But it was precisely because she was an Elton John fan that Princess Diana could be described as 'the people's princess': John was an appropriate singer at her service not just as a personal friend but also as the emotional voice of a generation.

In the 1970s Elton John and his lyricist, Bernie Taupin, perfected the musical form that came to dominate Anglo-American pop music in the last decades of the century: the rock ballad. They took the sentimental song (as commercialised in the late nineteenth century), keeping its easy melodic lines, its use of rising pitch to unleash emotion, its lyrical sense of expansive self-pity, but giving it a new rock-based dynamism (in terms of rhythm and amplification). In particular, Elton John's vocal approach was taken from soul music: he sings with a hesitancy, an introversion, an intimacy which contrasts markedly with the full, extrovert, confident vocal tone of the Victorian ballad singer. And this relates to what was most striking about his Westminster Abbey song: the crowd in Hyde Park, watching the service on television relay screens, clearly saw it as a performance. They applauded, and the applause resonated in the Abbey itself. When Earl Spencer spoke, his speech was also heard as a performance, and the applause rippled around the Abbey audience too.

Now of course everyone at Diana's service was performing one way or another, but Elton John's was a specifically pop performance. He was applauded less for being sincere than for performing sincerity: applause was necessary to confirm the skill – the effect – of the performance. Someone just being sincere – crying, say – is not applauded because this involves neither skill nor calculation; it is not an act designed for an evaluative response. Elton John's performance, by contrast, was precisely a display of what we might call emoting skill. What the audience applauded was not John's actual feeling of grief (his business alone) but his ability to provide a performance of grief in which we, as listeners, could take part. 'Candle in the Wind' was, after all, first written for Marilyn Monroe, and it became popular because its feelings were so easily transferred; it was a song through which every lost love could be remembered. It was Diana's song not because she was now its object but because she had so liked it too.

Here are clues as to the ways in which pop performers can be distinguished from rock musicians, on the one hand, and from classical musicians, on the other. Elton John is a pop not a rock star because his authenticity – the authenticity of his expressed emotions – is not an issue. 'Candle in the Wind' is not a song of self-exposure; it was not written to mark off John's difference, his unique artistic sensibility. It was, rather, a pop song, designed for public use. At the same time its pleasures are neither abstract nor in any musical sense transcendent. It is a song infused with Elton John's personality and, for its emotional effect, infused too with a kind of collective sigh. Compare John Tavener's contribution to the funeral service. This also struck an emotional chord with the public (and duly turned up in Classic FM listeners' list of favourite works); but it was clearly a spiritual piece, lifting listeners out of the mundane. It was not applauded.

## Definitions

Pop music is a slippery concept, perhaps because it is so familiar, so easily used. Pop can be differentiated from classical or art music, on the one side, from folk music, on the other, but may otherwise include every sort of style. It is music accessible to a general public (rather than aimed at elites or dependent on any kind of knowledge or listening skill). It is music produced commercially, for profit, as a matter of enterprise not art. Defined in these terms, 'pop music' includes all contemporary popular forms – rock, country, reggae, rap, and so on. But there are problems with such an inclusive definition as has become apparent when states have attempted to define pop in law. When in 1990 British legislators (concerned to regulate the content of music radio) defined 'pop music' as 'all kinds of music characterised by a strong rhythmic element and a reliance on electronic amplification for their performance', this led to strong objections from the music industry that such a musical definition failed to grasp the sociologi-

*95 Pop Music*

cal difference between pop ('instant singles-based music aimed at teenagers') and rock ('album-based music for adults').

Here pop becomes not an inclusive category but a residual one: it is what's left when all the other forms of popular music are stripped away, and it is not only rock ideologues who want to distance their music from pop, for them a term of contempt. Country music performers have objected similarly to 'pop stars' like Olivia Newton-John getting country music awards, and these days rap fans dismiss cross-over stars like Will Smith as just 'pop acts'. From this perspective pop is defined as much by what it isn't as by what it is.

### Markets

Pop does not have a specific or subcultural, communal market/culture. It is designed to appeal to everyone. Pop doesn't come from any particular place or mark off any particular taste. The partial exception to this rule is teenpop which does appeal to a specific market segment (young girls) but it is misleading to conclude from this that pop is a female form or has primarily female appeal. Much of pop could be called family music. Europop, for example, has been the sound of the summer holiday since Los Bravos's million selling 'Black is Black' in 1966. Los Bravos were a Spanish group with a German lead singer and a British producer. Their success was a model for both cross-European collaboration and commercial opportunism. The skill of the Europop producer (and this is a producer-led form) is to adapt the latest fashionable sounds to Euroglot lyrics which can be followed by everyone with a high-school foreign language, and to a chorus line which can be collectively sung in every continental disco and holiday resort. Thus Boney M, a foursome from the Caribbean (via Britain and Holland), brought together by German producer Frank Farian, sold fifty million records in 1975–8, while the Swedish group Abba, had eighteen consecutive European top ten hits following their 1974 victory in the Eurovision Song Contest. Both groups appealed (particularly through television) to listeners older and younger than the dedicated holiday disco dancers, combining child friendly chorus lines with slick choreography and a tacky erotic glamour that gave Abba, in particular, a camp appeal that was a major influence on late 1970s gay music culture. The most successful British pop production team of the 1980s, Stock, Aitken, Waterman, were clearly influenced by this pop genre, and by the promotion processes that supported it. A group like Steps, which found fame at the turn of the century under Waterman's guidance, managed to combine an up-to-date sense of the Europop sound with British seaside hoofer values which would have been familiar to musical entertainers at the end of the nineteenth century.

### Ideology

Pop is not driven by any significant ambition except profit and commercial reward. Its history is a history of serial or standardised production and, in musical terms, it is essentially conservative. Pop is about giving people what they already know they want rather than pushing up against techno-logical constraints or aesthetic conventions. The new in pop thus tends to be the novelty (an instrumental hit like the Tornados' 'Telstar', an 'exotic' number like Althia and Donna's 'Uptown Top Ranking'), and pop is marked by the continuity of its musical values. Common pop terms – easy listening, light entertainment – and the familiar image of fireside crooners like Bing Crosby and Val Doonican suggest that pop is meant to be unob-trusive: if rock involves a kind of in-your-face presence, pop aims to soothe. The contrast can be heard in, say, James Last's orchestral versions of Sex Pistols songs!

### Production

Pop is music provided from on high (by record companies, radio pro-grammers and concert promoters) rather than being made from below. Pop is not a do-it-yourself music but is professionally produced and pack-aged. Hence the pop importance of song writers and record producers, on the one hand, and singing stars, on the other. The singer–songwriter is not a common pop figure (though Barry Manilow has shown what can be done with this role). Rather, the key people are commercial songwriters from Stephen Foster and Irving Berlin to Carole King and Dianne Warren, entrepreneurial producers like Berry Gordy and Mickie Most, and versa-tile performers like Jessie Matthews and the Spice Girls.

### Aesthetics

Pop is not an art but a craft. It is not about realising individual visions or making us see the world in new ways but about providing popular tunes and cliches in which to express commonplace feelings – love, loss, jealousy. But to work pop must do this in sufficiently individualised ways to appeal to us as individual listeners. And the secret here lies in the pop singers' ability to appeal to us directly, to lay their personality on a song such that we can make it our song too. This is the paradox of pop that Noel Coward described as the 'potency' of cheap music. We can and do despise pop music in general as bland commercial pap while being moved by it in particular as a source of sounds that chime unexpectedly but deeply in our lives.

## History

From a rock perspective pop is seen as a kind of unchanging 'old' music, to be contrasted with 'progressive' rock or dance music. This is partly an

97  *Pop Music*

effect of the way generations work culturally (though the identification of rock with youth does have the odd effect that thirty-year-old tracks can still be used by advertisers and style consultants to provide a youthful ambience) but it also reflects the underlying nostalgia of pop music culture: pop songs are designed both to sound familiar and, often enough, to make one regret that times and people change. But pop itself is implicated in such change: there can be few people over twenty-five who don't agree that they don't write songs like that anymore.

One reason they don't is technological. Pop was the product of a sheet music and then a record industry; it has been shaped by its use in the cinema, on radio, by television. (The most revolutionary moment in pop's technological history was undoubtedly the development of the electrical microphone, which I discuss further below.) Another is sociological. As a mass market music, pop reflects the changing nature of its audience and, in particular, is a kind of musical measure of migration, demographic change and the breakdown of geographical sound barriers. If American pop thus became dominant globally in the twentieth century, pop in the United States was itself the music of Jewish migrants from eastern Europe and the descendants of slaves from Africa. Pop music may come from no particular place, but it absorbs musical sounds from everywhere. And there is a further point to make here. In their very determination to mark themselves off from pop, fans of focused music genres like rock and country are admitting that the lines of demarcation are blurred. It has often been remarked that anything can be rocked; anything can also be popped. The history of pop is marked by the traces of all sorts of musical form – ragtime and blues, jazz and hillbilly, reggae and disco, rock and soul. Even classical music has been popped, as it were, whether in the marketing of opera singers as stars, from Enrico Caruso through Mario Lanza to Luciano Pavarotti, or in the pilfering of classical scores for good tunes – the Boston Pops Orchestra was formed (as an offshoot of the Boston Symphony Orchestra) early in the twentieth century. The success of Classic FM suggests that in Britain, at least, classical music can provide the basic programming for pop radio.

Pop has a history, then, with key moments of change. Perhaps the most important, as I have already noted, followed the marketing of the electrical microphone in the 1930s. Technically the microphone was a way of amplifying the voice, and its immediate use was to enable singers to make themselves heard above the noise of a jazz band or swing orchestra. The amplification of the voice ran parallel to the amplification of the guitar, wind and brass instruments that transformed rural blues into urban rhythm and blues and Western Swing into honky tonk (out of which came rock'n'roll). But in pop terms the microphone's importance was not that it enabled people to sing loudly but that it let them be soft. The electric mike's immediate impact was in the radio and recording studio rather than on stage. The mike meant new vocal techniques (crooning, torch singing) and new kinds of singer whose skill was microphone technique rather than diaphragm control.

What the best of these singers (notably Frank Sinatra and Billie Holiday) quickly realised was that they could sing with a new expressive intimacy. A tone and pitch that were previously only heard in private conversation could now be reproduced publicly, and, of course, central to such intimate conversations are declarations of love and intimations of desire. Listeners could now pretend that they knew the singer, that the singer understood or, at least, articulated their own feelings. This brought a new kind of emotionalism and eroticism into pop, an eroticism most obvious in the emergence of Frank Sinatra's young female fans (who prefigured teen crushes to come), and thus a new kind of stardom: the pop singer as idol.

By the end of the 1930s pop meant vocal rather than instrumental records, and the singer (rather than band leader) dominated the stage (soon displacing the big band altogether). This process was an effect too of radio and cinema, both of which played a central role in the making of the new sort of singing personality, and by the end of the 1940s its consequences for the music industry had become far reaching. Pop songs were increasingly written to display a singer's personality rather than a composer's skill; they now had to work emotionally through the singer's expressivity (rather than the mood being determined by the score) – it was Sinatra's feelings that were heard in the songs he sang rather than their writers'. The new kind of vocal pop star thus needed simpler, more directly emotional songs than those provided by jazz or theatre-based composers, and singers (and their record companies) began to draw on the folk, country and rhythm and blues repertoires. Witty lyrics and sophisticated melodic lines were replaced by melodramatic narratives and unabashed sentimentality. The rise of television reinforced the importance of pop singers as family entertainers (Dean Martin became the biggest television draw in the United States) but brought a new kind of self-consciousness and irony into pop performance (personified most flamboyantly by Liberace).

In many ways the television version of pop that was established in the United States and (with some different national characteristics) in the United Kingdom in the mid-1950s provided a blueprint of pop performance and stardom with which we are still familiar. But two complicating factors should be noted. First, the 1950s also saw the emergence of a teenage market and a teenage taste and if one aspect of this (youth marking itself off from adult entertainment) was rock'n'roll, another

## 99 Pop Music

(youth music as a new strand of showbiz) was teen pop. Teen pop idols were manufactured (Pat Boone, Fabian) or evolved from rock'n'rollers to all-round entertainers (Cliff Richard, Tommy Steele; in the end, Elvis Presley). Adult pop conventions were adapted for the teenage market. Television was important: American teen idols appeared on *American Bandstand*, British teen idols on *6–5 Special* and *Oh Boy!* On these shows rock'n'roll songs alternated with ballads, and the most successful young performers were pretty but knowable, like the ideal boy next door. When Billy Fury, say, came on to sing 'Halfway to Paradise' he was in essence just a young and more vulnerable version of David Whitfield. Trouser shapes and hair styles change, but there are obvious musical and ideological continuities between Ricky Nelson and David Cassidy, George Michael and Robbie Williams, Pat Boone and Roland Keating, and there have always been model female teen pop singers too, from Connie Francis and Helen Shapiro to Tiffany and Britney Spears.

In commercial terms, then, the 1950s manufacture and marketing of teen pop stars was not a very different process than the manufacture and marketing of pop stars generally, and by the 1960s the pop market was predominantly the teenage market anyway. But there was significant difference in the detail. The writers and producers of teen pop, for example, tended to be young themselves, with a better grasp of teenage vernacular, a better feel for teenage emotions, a better ear for what was hip than the established Tin Pan Alley hacks. The Brill Building became the Tin Pan Alley port of call for young songwriters pitching teen pop songs, and its associated producers were much more at ease with the new technology of tape recording than the established record company studio teams. The record producer changed from being a skilled arranger like Mitch Miller, getting everything in its right place before the session started, to being an inspired sound engineer like Phil Spector, treating the musical tracks as just raw material. Most importantly of all, though, this new generation of pop song writers and producers blended African–American musical conventions into the mix in new ways. In the 1950s black singers had found a television pop niche, whether as a genius entertainer like Louis Armstrong or in the mellow, sophisticated and sexy stylings of Nat 'King' Cole and Johnny Mathis. But what interested the new class of Jewish writers and producers like Jerry Leiber, Mike Stoller and Phil Spector was not the jazz that had influenced their parents, the generation of the Gershwins, but the music they'd heard directly from their African–American neighbours when growing up: rhythm and blues, doo wop, the sound of vocal groups.

The move from pop singer to pop group (which had its ultimate commercial triumph with the Beatles) partly reflected the increasing use of multi-voices for telling teenage stories: teen emotions were seen to be an aspect of everyday conversation that adult emotions are not, and so Phil Spector and Shadow Morton made their 'little operas for kids' with the Crystals and Ronettes and Shangri-Las. But in the longer run the more important point is that multitrack recording found its aesthetic equivalent in the way in which doo-wop broke up the standard pop song into vocal parts, giving it a new rhythmic and timbrel complexity, and in the call/response structure of gospel music. While there was a white pop tradition of group singing (Barbershop groups, for example), its use of close harmony was only really developed by the Beach Boys. For pop in general the group sound came to mean a seductive lead voice (on the gospel derived model of Sam Cooke and Ben E. King) with a chorus of supporters, the sound perfected in the 1960s (and soon dominating the pop sales charts) by the Motown label and acts like Martha and the Vandellas, Smokey Robinson and the Miracles, the Supremes, Temptations and Four Tops.

These pop sounds were fed into rock by British beat groups and then dismissed as 'commercial' by the newly emergent rock fans, and in the last decades of the twentieth century musical influences worked the other way, less pop developments affecting rock, than rock sounds affecting pop. Two trends in particular should be noted: the rise of the power ballad, and the prominence of the soul diva.

Although rock was a musical form that defined itself against pop, the ballad remained central to its appeal. And if jazz performers had used ballads' melodic familiarity as the basis of improvisation – transforming a standard pop song into something quite different – rock musicians (following the Beatles' lead with 'Yesterday') wrote their own ballads but used them in familiar pop ways to bind their audiences into an emotional community. The original rock'n'rollers like Elvis Presley drew on established ballad traditions, whether Italian ('It's Now Or Never') or American (country rock balladeers like Roy Orbison, Charlie Rich and Willie Nelson gave Tin Pan Alley sentiment a new edge of melancholy). But the rock ballad as such derived from soul music and, in particular, from Ray Charles, whose gospel reading of a country song, 'I Can't Stop Loving You', became its inspiration. Charles' emotional sincerity was marked by a distinct vocal roughness and if his tempo was slow it was also insistent. He had a direct influence on such singers as Eric Burdon (of the Animals), Tom Jones and Joe Cocker who, in turn, established the conventions of the ballad as a rock form, as a vehicle for male vocal virtuosity (emotive singing at high pitch and high volume) and chorus line exhilaration. Foreigner's 'I Want To Know What Love Is' (with choral support from the New Jersey Mass Choir) and Aerosmith's 'I Don't Want To Miss A Thing'

*101 Pop Music*

(with Steven Tyler's vocals so over-the-top as to be parodic) are the classic power ballads, songs of feeling bottled up and bursting out; musical, emotional and sexual release somehow all equated.

This was balladry in a rock context, but such an amplified approach to wanting-songs soon affected pop singing conventions too, as marked initially, as I have already mentioned, by the 1970s emergence of Elton John and then by the success of Michael Bolton in the United States and Mick Hucknall and Simply Red in Britain. The best selling pop singer of the late 1990s, Céline Dion, started out as a child singing French Canadian folk songs and won the Eurovision Contest for Switzerland, but she became a superstar with a singing style that was clearly drawn from power balladry (even working with Meatloaf's producer, Jim Steinman, on one album), and this brings me to the pop importance of the soul diva. In many ways the history of female pop singing follows along the same lines as the history of male pop singing. In the 1960s the sophisticated night club approach of Dionne Warwick (mostly singing the notably adult songs of Burt Bacharach and Hal David) was overlaid by the gospel soul baring of Aretha Franklin and the more adolescent pop seductiveness of Diana Ross in the development of a new kind of vocal virtuosity (and fame) for Gladys Knight, Tina Turner and then Whitney Houston. But in other respects the role of the female pop singer has been different from that of the male pop star. Just as a matter of a wider gender ideology, women singers are heard to have a pathos or vulnerability that men lack – they can make us feel sorrier for them. And then, by this same token, they are also taken to be more skilled at the nuances of emotional expression, more powerful at emotional warfare, more confident at holding up their emotions for our exploration as it were. It is not surprising that Judy Garland, Shirley Bassey, and Dusty Springfield, for example, have had a certain camp appeal, a gay following precisely interested in the performance of emotional excess, nor that there's an element of kitsch in the sexual appeal of the biggest women pop stars – Dion, Houston, Maria Carey and, of course, Madonna.

Even more importantly, though, the very emotional impact of this singing style, its sense of raw feeling bravely dressed, has enabled its sound to be removed from its context: such strong feeling doesn't need an occasion, it can just be added into the mix. From the moment Giorgio Moroder realised that Donna Summer had the ideal voice to put over his machine music, the poppier end of the dance floor in Europe and North America has been dominated by the sound of (mostly anonymous) soul divas, by a kind of collective gospel choir of women wanting love, losing love, celebrating love, bemoaning love, boasting of love found, contemptuous of love lost. It's as if only such voices can guarantee the humanity of the electronic world.

## The sentimental song

Paul McCartney once summed pop up as 'silly love-songs', and the earliest content analysis of the American hit parade, carried out by J. G. Peatman (1942–3) in the 1940s duly found that 'all successful pop songs are about romantic love'. Indeed, Peatman claimed that he only needed three descriptive categories to characterise American pop: the happy-in-love song, the frustrated-in-love song, and the novelty song with sex interest. In historical terms, though, the popular song hasn't always been about love, and I think it makes better sense to define pop as the sentimental song and then suggest that in the twentieth century (in the West, at least) sentiment came to be applied almost exclusively to affairs of the heart.

This wasn't the case when the pop industry was first shaped in the nineteenth century. The first great commercial songwriter of the sheet music era, Stephen Foster, wrote his best-loved songs for minstrel shows. Plantation numbers like 'The Old Folks at Home' were sentimental about family, rural life and the past rather than about particular girls or boys, and the song catalogues and manuals for would-be pop composers in the 1900s suggest a range of possible lyrical topics. The pop repertoire was divided into ballad and novelty songs, and the former included not just love songs but also country or rustic songs, Irish songs, songs about Mother.

The obvious question here is what happened to pop in the first half of the twentieth century: why was it reduced to love songs? I'll come back to this. First, I just want to note that although the 1900s classification of song types is quaint it is not incomprehensible. I know what is meant by an Irish song ('Danny Boy', 'When Irish Eyes Are Smiling') and a rustic song (country songwriters like Dolly Parton were coming up with variations of 'My Old Kentucky Home' well into the 1980s). And even Mother songs or, rather, Absent Mother songs are not completely unfamiliar (in the musical *Annie*, for example), while Clive Dunn's 'Grandad' was a British hit as late as 1970. My point here, then, is that while Peatman's findings might accurately reflect the hit parade, by the 1940s the hit parade didn't accurately reflect pop. Certainly by the end of the 1950s, when singles sales charts were primarily a measure of teenage taste, 'chart pop' had become a specific and relatively insignificant strand of the pop music to which most people listened – musicals, film soundtracks, oldies, supper club songs, television-variety, jazz and country easy listening standards, and so on. It is, in short, misleading to equate pop with record sales.

One of the implications of Peatman's findings was that music that had once had resonance in a variety of social settings, for a variety of social reasons had become focused on the narcissistic feelings of one individual

103 *Pop Music*

for another. Such individualisation was obviously tied into a shift in pop music marketing: the move from a sheet music to a record industry was a move from collective to individual consumption. But again the interesting question here is not so much why people buy records but about the occasions for sentiment. Pop's history is obviously marked by moments of collective sentimentality. Twentieth-century wars, for example, were fought to the sound of songs of pathos: 'It's A Long Way To Tipperary' (an Irish song to boot!), 'We'll Meet Again'. Even the Animals' 'We've Gotta Get Out of This Place', an obvious favourite for American soldiers in Vietnam, is essentially sentimental (and a love song only in the vaguest way). Twentieth-century migration also involved the use of sentimental songs to remind people of their homelands and to idealise old ways. The Irish song thus continued to be significant throughout the century, meaning among other things that the Irish folk revival of the 1960s (and the pop success of Tommy Makem and the Clancy Brothers and the Dubliners) originated in the Irish bars of New York and that the Riverdance phenomenon started out as interval entertainment, a tourist package, for the Eurovision Song Contest. At a more mundane level, collective sentimentality remains a feature of sports spectating (whether the old Wembley tradition of 'Abide With Me' or the more recent use of Rodgers and Hammerstein's 'You'll Never Walk Alone' on the terraces at Anfield) and drinking. The *karaoke* phenomenon has certainly given new sentimental life to old sentimental songs, turning 'I Will Survive' and 'My Way' into anthems of feminist, gay and heterosexual cultures.

What's important to note about all these examples is that pop here doesn't just mean buying records but also performing them, and performing them in a particular way. Sentimentality describes not just how we listen but also how we sing, *from the heart*, and however embarrassingly we somehow all seem to know how to do that. One way of putting my argument here is to suggest that it is not strong feelings that determine how we sing, but that how we sing gives us the experience of these sorts of feeling. It's the music not the situation that makes us cry, as Hollywood film scorers have long known. To put this another way, it is the sentimental song, sentimental singing, that has come to be the public sign of sincerity. From the earliest days of the music hall, comic turns would wrap up their act with a sentimental song: forget the cynicism and humiliations of music-hall humour they seemed to say, this is the real me, the real you. This became a feature of television comics too (Ken Dodd singing 'Tears', for example) and even a much more aggressive performer like Millie Jackson brings her show to an end by moving out of her contemptuous man-mocking rap into a sentimental soul ballad .

It is perhaps not surprising then that in the latter half of the twentieth .

century the sentimental song became the sales focus of the musical, on the one hand, and the film soundtrack, on the other. Rodgers and Hammerstein's 1940s transformation of the musical into a vernacular narrative form (with *Oklahoma*, *Carousel* and *South Pacific*) also involved a new sort of show stopper, the ballad that could stand free of the story ('If I Loved You', 'Some Enchanted Evening'). Such ballads, marketed as pop songs (*West Side Story*'s 'Somewhere' being the classic example), became, in turn, a way of selling a show. This was the promotional strategy mastered by Andrew Lloyd Webber. Hit songs like 'I Don't Know How to Love Him' (*Jesus Christ Superstar*), 'Don't Cry For Me, Argentina' (*Evita*), and 'Memories' (*Cats*) drew people to his shows (rather that the show producing hits on the back of its success – as had been the case with *The Sound of Music* or *Oliver*). This is the reason, I think, that Webber works seem less like musicals than elaborately staged pop shows (one reason, perhaps, why *Cats* works best).

The big ballad has become equally important for film marketing in the last thirty years. Henry Mancini's 'Moon River', written for the opening credits of *Breakfast at Tiffany's*, is usually taken to mark a new relationship between the film and music industries. It was not just that here a song was used to sell a film (rather than vice versa) but also that the song had an accidental relationship to the plot, as it were. It might have had an obvious musical affinity to the rest of Mancini's score, captured the film's ambience, but lyrically it was quite vague and the film would lose nothing if it were removed or replaced. This use of a pop song as simply a film commercial was exploited brilliantly by the James Bond films and by the 1980s stand alone songs were being used over the closing titles too. Here the purpose wasn't just promotional. Audiences were now being sent out of the cinema uplifted by power ballads which bore little musical or lyrical relationship to the rest of the film's score. This trend gave big-voiced singers like Joe Cocker and Jennifer Warnes new careers and culminated in the simultaneous cinema and pop triumph of *Titanic* the film, James Horner's *Titanic* score, and Céline Dion's 'My Heart Will Go On'. What was most interesting here was not how film and music sold each other, but how the very meaning of the film (as a romance rather than a disaster movie) was determined by its closing sentimental song.

## Pop music and society

Pop music could be defined as the music we listen to without meaning to; the songs we know without knowing how we know them. These days we equate pop with pop records. Much of the music we hear despite ourselves is 'canned'. Pop music thus reaches us over the radio, through passing car windows, as sound around a shopping centre. Pop songs lodge themselves maddingly in the mind after holidays, children's parties, visits to the dentist; 'La Paloma Blanca', 'Barbie Girl', anything by Abba or Andy Williams. But to use the term 'pop' to describe all the music that insinuates itself into our lives and commercial music is only part of the story. We all grow up into musical cultures, collections of songs and tunes and styles that become our taken-for-granted musical knowledge. And for at least one hundred and fifty years commercially produced music has been an inescapable part of this. But only part, and with various consequences.

As children, for example, we hear lullabies, learn nursery rhymes, join in family songs. Schools teach us folk songs, children's songs; in the playground we join in skipping and jumping songs, on school outings rude songs. Most of us remember these songs throughout our lives, pass them on to children and grandchildren, and the result is a remarkably rich and jumbled repertoire, from traditional tunes which can be traced back over hundreds of years to recent pop tunes whose immediate provenance is soon forgotten. In their classic studies of the lore and language of school children, the Opies (1985) traced the wondrous 1950s journey of 'The Ballad of Davy Crockett' from American television series across English speaking playgrounds around the world, picking up a myriad of local variations along the way. Any hit pop song, it seems (Queen's 'Bohemian Rhapsody', Spice Girls' 'Wannabe'), can be given the a cappella playground treatment.

What's involved here, though, is not just the makeover of new best sellers, the translation of pop into folk, as it were. 'Children's song' is itself a commercial category. Ever since there has been a music business there has been a children's music business, and such 'children's favourites' are resold to generation after generation. BBC radio may have long since dropped its *Children's Hour* and family record request programmes, but the songs these once featured are now performed on children's television programmes (and videos), by children's entertainers like the Singing Kettle. Children's records and cassettes are still a flourishing (if little discussed) sector of the pop industry. An historian could doubtless trace the various musical origins of 'Nellie the Elephant' and 'Going to the Zoo', 'Puff the Magic Dragon' and 'The Lion Sleeps Tonight', 'The Runaway Train' and 'How Much is that Doggie in the Window?' But these songs have become, in effect, timeless, as freshly enjoyed by four-year-olds today as they were by their parents, grandparents and even great grandparents.

This process of musical absorption doesn't stop with childhood, of course, although that is when we hear the most extraordinary range of musical material, and in adult life I have often been struck by how many songs I seem to know without any idea of how I know them. Music hall songs ('My Old Man Said Follow The Van'); cabaret songs ('Mad Dogs and Englishmen'); Disney songs ('Whistle While You Work'); Gilbert and Sullivan songs ('Three Little Girls From School Are We'); film songs ('White Christmas'); songs which come from I know not where ('I Love To Go A-Wandering, A Knapsack On My Back'). What we know this way is obviously shaped by class and place and family and friends; by ethnicity and nation. Most people in Britain probably know the opening lines of 'Auld Lang Syne'; Scots people are likely to know the next lines too, and one feature of a multicultural society is an expansion of the common pop repertoire, as 'Pass the Dutchie', say, takes its place in the playground. Pop defined this way thus provides a kind of map of a changing society just as it maps our own lives, helping give emotional shape to our memories of childhood, friendship, love affairs, life changes. And pop becomes too a resource, a social storehouse from which musicians of all sorts draw and quote and sample.

My second assumption is that pop describes songs that we can and sometimes do perform as well as listen to. Much of this singing is collective – we sing at school, in the pub, at football matches, during weddings and funerals, at the end of parties. But we sing individually too – to our children, with our best friends, above all to ourselves. Indeed, I would add to the definition of pop as accessible music that it is also singable and performable music; it doesn't need the skills that classical or jazz or even rock musicians must acquire. And this argument about participation leads me to a kind of music which is not usually thought of as pop but which has some claim to have determined what pop music means. I refer, of course, to church music: even in these relatively Godless times most of us have

Pop is not usually treated so positively, so I should stress the two assumptions I'm making here. First, that a song's origin is really only of academic interest. The commercial intent behind 'How Much Is That Doggie In The Window?' is as irrelevant to a young listener now as the political intent behind nursery rhymes like 'The Grand Old Duke of York' or 'Bobby Shafto's Gone To Sea', while Davy Crockett and Tom Dooley are no more or less folk heroes than John Henry or John Barleycorn. Attempts to draw a clear distinction between authentic and inauthentic popular songs, whether using musicological or sociological criteria, are pointless. It's not where pop songs come from that matters, but where they get to. 'Jingle Bells' and 'White Christmas' are every bit as authentic Christmas songs as 'I Saw Three Ships' or 'Silent Night' simply because they are now part of everyone's musical Christmas portfolio.

My second assumption is that pop describes songs that we can and sometimes do perform as well as listen to. Much of this singing is collective – we sing at school, in the pub, at football matches, during weddings and funerals, at the end of parties. But we sing individually too – to our children, with our best friends, above all to ourselves. Indeed, I would add to the definition of pop as accessible music that it is also singable and performable music; it doesn't need the skills that classical or jazz or even rock musicians must acquire. And this argument about participation leads me to a kind of music which is not usually thought of as pop but which has some claim to have determined what pop music means. I refer, of course, to church music: even in these relatively Godless times most of us have

107  *Pop Music*

sung hymns and carols at some stage of our lives, have come to associate church music with rituals of grief and celebration.

Tim Fleming (1999) has argued persuasively that the contemporary sentimental song has its roots as firmly in the eighteenth-century senti-mental hymns of Isaac Watts and Charles Wesley as in the romantic secular songs which were the source of the first big sheet music sales. It was these hymns that gave popular song emotional tropes that we still recognise: a regret for lost innocence, a yearning for paradise as a rustic idyll, a definition of love as comfort in distress. Robbie Williams' 'Angel', to put this another way, is not so different from Isaac Watts', and the translation of gospel into soul shows how easy it is to love a man or woman musically in the same way that one loves God. It could also be said that the Church has been as significant as the music industry in the process of cultural imperi-alism, spreading Western musical forms East and South. I've always assumed that one reason for Jim Reeves' remarkable global popularity was because his singing style was familiar from years of American missionary work.

Whatever the reason for Jim Reeves' success, pop certainly doesn't work in the straightforward ways that the simpler accounts of commercialism suggest. Why did King Sunny Adé like Jim Reeves' songs so much? How did Smokie become a talisman for radical students in South Korea? Why do some songs become standards the moment they're first heard ('Yesterday', for example) while others not very different make no public mark at all? What's sure is that pop can't be sensibly analysed just in terms of musicol-ogy or aesthetics. Yes, we do respond to the song-in-itself but that song-in-itself is soon encrusted with uses and memories and references. Once a pop song is launched on the world, all sorts of things can happen to it. When Bobby Vinton was in the studio laying down 'Blue Velvet', one of his soppier tracks, could he have foreseen that the song would accompany one of the great homoerotic scenes in Hollywood cinema, in Kenneth Anger's *Scorpio Rising*, or become forever menacing, following its use by David Lynch? When Elton John and Bernie Taupin first crafted 'Candle in the Wind' could they have imagined it becoming an official state mourning song?

And if unexpected things happen to songs, so songs have unexpected effects on us. My favourite Abba song, 'The Day Before You Came', describes the wonder of falling in love by flatly documenting how banal life was before love struck. It could equally be a song about the transform-ing power of music. And so the irony remains. If pop is precisely the music we would usually include in such banality, it is also pop – more than any other form of music – that changes if not our lives then certainly the ways in which we feel about them.

*108  Simon Frith*

**Further reading**

Some of my arguments here are taken from my book *Performing Rites. On the Value of Popular Music* (Cambridge, Massachusetts: Harvard University Press / Oxford: Oxford University Press, 1996) though that deals with popular music rather indiscriminately. The best academic studies are historical. For an overview see Peter Van Der Merwe, *Origins of the Popular Style* (Oxford: Clarendon Press, 1989). Tim Fleming's doctoral thesis, cited above, is the best study I know of the origins and commercial and cultural impact of the sentimental song. For the United States see Nicholas Tawa, *The Way to Tin Pan Alley: American Popular Song 1866–1910* (New York: Schirmer Books, 1990). For the United Kingdom see Dave Russell, *Popular Music in England 1840–1914* (Manchester: Manchester University Press, 1987) and Derek B. Scott, *The Singing Bourgeois. Songs of the Victorian Drawing Room and Parlour* (Milton Keynes and Philadelphia: Open University Press, 1989). I don't know of any good pop histories covering the rest of the twentieth century though most of the biggest stars have useful biographies. From the perspective of academic research, pop seems to be that music that isn't much studied. Most books written in the last twenty years with pop in their titles are really about rock; the most suggestive studies of popular music are focused on genres like rap or country. When pop singers or composers are taken seriously it is usually in order to suggest that they transcend their commercial context, can be treated like classical composers or as jazz singers. With the exception of Henry Pleasants' fine *The Great American Popular Singers* (New York: Simon and Schuster, 1974) the resulting studies are often interesting but not often about pop, and I've yet to see an academic article on, say, Perry Como, Andrew Lloyd Webber or Cher.

For music and everyday life on the ground, as it were, see Ruth Finnegan's richly suggestive ethnography of the musical worlds in Milton Keynes: *The Hidden Musicians. Music Making in an English Town* (Cambridge: Cambridge University Press, 1989) and the engaging interviews about people's musical lives collected by Susan D. Crafts, Daniel Cavicchi and Charles Keil as *My Music* (Hanover and London, Wesleyan University Press, 1993). For illuminating if oblique approaches to pop see Mark W. Booth, *The Experience of Song* (New Haven: Yale University Press, 1981) historically arranged essays on songs from madrigals to advertising jingles, and Michael Billig, *Rock'n'Roll Jews* (Nottingham: Five Leaves, 2000) ostensibly a history of Jews in rock'n'roll, in fact a moving meditation on popular music and cultural identity.

CHAPTER 12

# Look! Hear! The uneasy relationship of music and television

**Abstract**

*Television is an essential part of the star-making machinery of the music business and music accompanies nearly all television programmes, and yet the relationship between the two is uneasy. Television does not seem to be an essential part of musical culture and adds little to music aesthetically. Music has had little impact on the form or aesthetics of television. And yet television has certainly had an impact on music and particularly on the mediation of rock and the formation of the modern pop/rock aesthetic. Here it is not music in television that is important but television in music. The 1950s was a significant turning point in popular music history not so much because of the musical revolution of rock 'n' roll but because of the impact of television.*

## I

In the popular music literature there are two broad views of television. On the one hand, it is understood as a medium of great importance. It is the most effective tool of star-making and record promotion. Television programmes from *American Bandstand* through *Top of the Pops* to *Yo, MTV Raps!* have shaped the social meanings (and our memories) of artists and genres. On the other hand, television is thought not to be very important at all. Music has not been a central part of its programming. The television audience is rarely conceived as a music audience. TV-made pop stars almost always lack musical credibility.

As I started writing this paper, the best-selling single in Britain was Will Young's 'Evergreen/Anything'. The record had more than a million sales in its first week of release, outselling all other singles combined. Young's success was the effect of a television programme, *Pop Idol*, an elaborate talent contest, based on audience votes, which Young won. Young and *Pop Idol* runner-up, Gareth Gates, were the biggest pop phenomena in Britain since Hear'Say, who in 2001 became the first band to top the UK album and singles charts simultaneously with debut releases. Hear'Say was put together in an earlier TV talent show, *Popstars* (a format that had already created new stars in Italy and Australia).

In current British TV schedules, talent shows like *Pop Idol* run alongside another kind of music programme with a more recent provenance: the instant nostalgia show. In these programmes the history of music (and television) is celebrated in lists: top tens of country music or girl groups or disco; the best 100 songs, the greatest 100 albums; viewers' favourite commercials. The basic format is the same across a variety of titles: clips from the television archives, interviews with the acts, their producers and minor celebrity fans, a mocking voiceover, an underlying sense that musical passion is ridiculous. Such programmes have little promotional effect (there's not much evidence of old records being successfully re-released to cash in on such lists) but they do suggest that television producers have found a new way of using music to get ratings.

What do programmes like *Pop Idol* and *When Disco Ruled the World* tell us about music and television? Do they confirm that television matters or that it does not? The answer, clearly, is both. Television makes pop stars and yet its treatment of music seems strangely detached. It is rare to watch a television programme without music, and just as rare to watch a programme that is really about music. Television matters for music in some ways and, *for the same reasons*, not in others. In aesthetic terms, certainly, the history of television and the history of music seem quite separate. Except in the case of rock. In this paper I will argue that while rock may, ideologically, claim to be anti-television (as articulated in many songs), it is, in fact, the only musical genre which could be said to be televisual. In arguing this I will first consider the history of music and television generally and then replay the argument with specific reference to rock. But before proceeding I want to dispose of one outstanding problem: music video.

There was a time in popular music studies (from the mid-1980s to the early 1990s) when it seemed as if the analysis of music and television would be transformed by studies of music video. Music video analysis was added to music analysis as a necessary academic skill. The MTV Corporation was studied with more interest than the record business. Scholars from other fields – film studies, cultural studies, media studies – suddenly found pop music interesting as a site for general arguments about postmodernism.[1]

Ten years on most of this literature seems curiously overblown. It has left little mark on either TV or music studies, and, more surprisingly, music videos themselves now seem to arouse little interest except from the few scholars devoted to close textual analysis. MTV these days is better understood as a youth service than a music channel, its promotional effects indicated by sales figures rather than by an account of how it has changed musical values or perceptions. There are not, to my knowledge, any systematic studies of the video audience; there is little published work on the process of video production.[2] Even music video arguments, in short, reflect the general paradox of music and television with which I am concerned. They either overestimate the significance of video clips or do not pay them any serious attention at all.

## II

If it is arguable that television was the most significant medium of political and commercial communication in the twentieth century, it is not clear that it has been a very effective means of musical communication. The instructive comparison here is with radio. Television programming was shaped by broadcasters with thirty years of radio experience behind them but there turned out to be important differences between the two media, differences that have been particularly significant musically.

In the period 1920–50 the radio and music industries developed a symbiotic relationship. Music on record became the basis of radio programming; radio play became the basis of record selling. Radio was crucial for the emergence of new popular music genres (jazz and blues and swing and hillbilly), and just as important for the making and marketing of classical records. Radio provided a livelihood for trained musicians and serious composers, and helped develop a new sort of high music culture. In commercial radio systems classical music programming was an effective weapon in the pursuit of the upmarket audience; in public service systems classical music broadcasting was an essential part of stations' perceived duty to educate as well as to entertain their listeners, to sustain the national cultural heritage as well as to promote contemporary creativity. And radio, as the first medium to bring a nation together in the simultaneous experience of the same event, also changed the experience of live music, putting performers into the home and transporting listeners into the audience, whether for a Proms or Carnegie Hall concert, for a hotel dance band, for a field recorded folk singer or club recorded crooner. If radio had not been invented, the history of music in the twentieth century would have been quite different.

The same thing could not be said immediately of television, whose significance for music makers and listeners, music promoters and scholars, has been much less clear-cut. This is not to say that TV broadcasters did not assume from the start that television would be a musical medium like radio. Europe's public service broadcasters have continued to invest heavily in the television transmission and staging of classical musical events, and in the early days of US television the gesture was still made at musically 'uplifting' programmes (Leonard Bernstein's *Young People's Concerts*, for example), even if today such classical concerts are confined to minority outlets, to niche cable and digital services like BBC4 and Artsworld.

The medium was immediately significant for popular musicians. In the USA the biggest singing stars of the 1950s (Dean Martin, Elvis Presley) came to national fame as a result of their appearances on TV variety shows, and the popular music industry realised at once that television was a potentially fundamental component of the star-making machinery whatever the music involved (whether Ricky Nelson or Van Cliburn). There is no doubt either that late 1950s pop music shows like *American Bandstand* and *Oh Boy!* helped articulate a new sort of youth music culture. That said, the subsequent emergence of rock as popular music's dominant form occurred despite and even as a critique of television culture, which became identified with the blandest sort of easy listening balladeers (Andy Williams, Val Doonican) and the most crassly commercial examples of teen idols. Far from promoting new sorts of music, television since the 1960s has always seemed to be behind the times – for European rock fans, the Eurovision Song Contest is perhaps the most obvious symbol of TV's celebration of pop archaism. It was only with the emergence of cable television in the 1980s that a music television service was developed with anything like the day-to-day significance of music radio. Music television, MTV, duly aped Top 40 radio formats, with playlists, veejays, 'hot' releases, 'breaking' singles, etc.

There are a number of overlapping reasons for television's limitations as a music medium. To begin with, most people's television sets have poor sound quality (and television sound has become relatively worse over the years as the quality of recorded and radio sound has improved with the development of hi-fi recording techniques and FM/VHF transmission). Even now that digital recording is the norm few people have – or seem to want – good television sound.

They do not want it because television is not primarily a sound medium. The musical experience is by its nature enveloping. Music may have a specific source of origin (the orchestra; the CD player) but it is heard as being everywhere (in the concert hall, in the room). As listeners we put ourselves into the music, and as radio became more portable so music became something to take with us, to change our sound environment. Television cannot offer this sort of music experience whatever its sound quality (which is why experiments with simultaneous broadcasts – pictures on the TV screen, sound from FM radio – are usually unsuccessful). To watch television is to focus on a fixed and relatively small space (compare the surround effect of the cinema screen) and to watch live concerts on television is to raise immediately the problem of what or who the camera should look at, a problem even the best editors cannot solve. At live concerts we can look at the whole (the orchestra) and the particular (the conductor, the fourth cellist) simultaneously, just as we hear them simultaneously; on television we can only see one thing at a time. Most television sets are too small for comfortable split screen editing. To engage our interest musical programmes have to offer more than music.

This is the technical factor that underlies television's peculiarity as a source of information and entertainment. Television programming is not sound-centred but picture-driven, organised around an aesthetic of immediacy (rather than reflection). Its narrative conventions depend on the concept of programme flow, on the ideology of actuality, on methods of grabbing viewers' fickle attention, on repetition and recognition, on series and soap operas and situation comedies, on news bulletins and sports events. The television composer (unlike the film scorer) has to be expert with the jingle, the theme tune, the link. Music on television is less often heard for its own sake than as a device to get our visual attention.

There have been moments when music on television has had a direct impact (Elvis Presley's comeback concert in 1968, the Live Aid show in 1985, the funeral of Princess Diana in 1997) but this has been as much an effect of the programmes' news values as of their musical quality. And the same goes for such TV rituals as *Top of the Pops*, *The Last Night of the Proms* and the *Eurovision Song Contest*, for youth music programmes from *Ready Steady Go* and *Old Grey Whistle Test* to *The Tube*, for the otherwise unexpected television interest in music competitions such as *Young Musician of the Year*. The musical moments that we remember are the ones that disrupt the flow, that become *newsworthy*. Music is omnipresent on television, in short, but the television experience is rarely just about music.

And this is true even of programmes addressing music. Music has been covered by arts magazines from *Monitor* to *The South Bank Show*; music, and musicians of all sorts are routinely the subject of documentaries. But few of these have changed the way we hear or understand a composer or composition; few have used the television medium itself in a musical way – which is why, more than thirty years on, Ken Russell's musical biographies (made for the BBC arts programme, *Monitor*) still seem extraordinary: they both changed our view of composers (Delius, for example) and suggested that television, in its technical ability to combine sound and pictures, to *dramatise* the creative process while documenting it, was, after all, an ideal medium for musical argument. Russell's achievement was to use television's own conventions to open up musical experience (rather than to try to impose a musical orthodoxy onto television); his films depended on narrative dispersal, on a sense of actuality, on emotional spectacle. As music television programmes, though, they remain unique (there is no programme on popular music with the same resonance). The only obvious comparison is with Dennis Potter's reworking of the musical as a televisual rather than theatrical form in *Pennies from*

*Heaven* and *The Singing Detective*. While other dramas have used popular music as a narrative device, they have tended to draw on film scoring (*Heartbeat, Morse*) or music video conventions (*Miami Vice*), rather than make music work televisually. And even in series influenced by Potter's experiments – *Moonlighting, Ally McBeal* – the musical interludes seem incidental to the storyline rather than integral to it. (The one US show that did seek a new way of putting music at the heart of the narrative, *Cop Rock*, was a complete failure.)

When television transmission first began, it was assumed that TV would be a medium particularly appropriate for musical theatre, for forms integrating sound and spectacle like opera and ballet. The BBC duly transmitted an opera, Gounod's *Faust*, in 1937; Leoncavallo's *I Pagliacci* was shown on American television in 1940, Menotti's 1951 *Amahl and the Night Visitors* was commissioned as a television work. But television has not turned out to be significant as a source of new musical works. Stravinsky's *The Flood* was written for TV in 1962; there have continued to be a steady series of TV dance commissions, especially in continental Europe, despite the small screen's constraint on choreographers. But such new works have had little audience appeal. Michael Tippett's *New Year*, an opera commissioned by the BBC for transmission in September 1991, had the lowest primetime viewing figures of any programme broadcast in Britain in the 1990s (next in the 'least watched' list were Judith Weir's *Blond Eckbert* and Benjamin Britten's *Turn of the Screw*). Of the forty lowest rated primetime programmes in the 1990s, more than a quarter were operas. One can understand the consequent reluctance of television executives to invest in new commissions – with fewer than 250,000 viewers these programmes were 'zero rated'. Such figures can be read a different way – Tippett's *New Year* was watched by 143,000 people, the equivalent of seventy full houses at the Royal Opera House, and the Tippett work was undoubtedly seen by a broader cross-section of the public than goes to Covent Garden.[3]

But the issue here is not so much what is meant by 'popularity' but that in high cultural terms TV has turned out to be a medium for transmitting concerts and theatrical shows to a specialist audience (this is the principle of the BBC's digital arts channel, BBC4, for example) rather than a medium which developed its own kind of high art (as in the cinema). If opera does not really work on television it is because composers have not yet created convincing aesthetic conventions for television opera, and have not felt any particular need to do so. Benjamin Britten's *Owen Wingrave*, for example, commissioned by the BBC for television transmission in 1971, was staged in Covent Garden in 1973 and the critical consensus was that its ideal performance setting was, in fact, a small theatre.

The consequences of television's extraordinary reach as a mass medium for classical music have been different. Just as a series of TV actors and actresses have had unlikely second careers as pop singers, so numerous fragments of classical music have had an unexpected second life as advertising tracks, their emotional meaning defined by products and sales talk rather than by composers and conductors.

The dominant use of music on television, one might conclude, is to sell things. Long before the classical divisions of music corporations were packaging *Relaxing Classics* or *Classic Chillouts*, they were marketing anthologies of 'classic advertisements' and these days dance albums are as likely to make their money from TV sync fees as from retail sales or air play.[4] And there is a further point to be made here. Music programmes as such tend to be conceived and presented as events that will interest the TV audience regardless of their particular tastes. Television has not, on the whole, developed specialist programmes for particular music markets (jazz or reggae, country or baroque).[5] There is an obvious economic reason for this – television advertisers do not often target music markets – and a less obvious one. Because of TV's promotional power, record companies have been willing to foot the bill for TV music programmes showcasing their acts. Television companies now take this for granted: music programmes are only made with such financial support. They do not feature acts or genres that do not have a promotional budget behind them.

The suggestion that music on television is primarily a sales device is hardly news to the music or advertising industries, but the general consequences for music and television do need spelling out. It is certainly arguable that the most common TV uses of music derive from conventions developed in commercials. I would point to three such conventions, in particular.

First, music is used to aestheticise the reality we see. This is perhaps most obvious these days in sports coverage, but has long been a feature of television documentary and is beginning to be used as a technique for news and current affairs (ITN was censured for putting music, by Gounod, to footage of the events of 11 September). Second, music is used to ground what we see, to tie a moment to a familiar song. This is perhaps most obvious in those programmes that combine archive footage with period hits, but the device has become common in dramas too. Pop songs are being used here not just to indicate a place or time or even to tug on emotional memories (as on film soundtracks) but to make historically important or dramatically intense scenes mundane (just as advertisers use familiar pop songs to imply that fantasy is routine). Third (drawing on both the previous approaches), music is used as an ironic commentary on what is seen, to distance viewers from the action and make them feel more knowing. Songs used in this way do not need to be directly related to the situation (whether historically or lyrically) – their very irrelevance can add to their effect. It is striking that when such programmes are successful – *Cold Feet, Teachers, Trigger Happy TV* – the tracks used are collected and sold as anthologies, *The Teachers CD, The Trigger Happy TV Music Collection, volumes, 1–3*. Here is the circular argument beloved of advertisers: because this is your sort of music this must be your sort of television; because this is your sort of television this must be your sort of music. The relationship of music and television is not organic but a matter of branding.

## III

When Pink Floyd appeared on *Bandstand*, singer and guitarist Syd Barrett adamantly refused to move his lips to the playback of their two British hits; he just stood there, immobile, while the rest of the band sheepishly mimed along behind him. (Shore 1985, p.110)

It is intrinsic to the ideology of rock that it is anti-television. There are a number of historical reasons for this. The development of television as the basic domestic means of entertainment in the 1950s meant the decline of radio as a family form and its pursuit of new, more narrowly defined markets. One of these markets was youth, and youth radio shaped the success of youth music. Rock 'n' roll began as a primarily radio experience and continued to be so through the 1950s and 1960s. A simple syllogism was established: rock 'n' roll was defined by youth radio; youth radio was defined against TV; rock 'n' roll was defined against TV.

Market research suggests that 'youth' is the age group that watches television least – if only because it is the age group that spends most leisure time out of the house in public spaces (and that is the most receptive to new leisure technologies – computer games, online chat rooms). Youth self-consciously differentiates itself from the rhythms of daily family life, and when TV scheduling is tied to the family audience it therefore tends to be wary of youth fads. Youth music, rock 'n' roll, was broadcast on television in the 1950s but framed by the family narrative. As Dick Clark notes about *American Bandstand*,

There were rules of dress and behaviour that had to be adhered to for the kids to get on the show. The dress code required that boys wear a jacket and tie, or a sweater and tie. Nobody dressed that way in real life, but it made the show acceptable to adults who were frightened by the teen-age world and their music. Girls couldn't wear slacks, tight sweaters, shorts or low-necked gowns – they had to wear the kind of dresses or sweaters and skirts they wore in school. No tight toreadors or upturned collars. (Clark 1976, p. 67)

And as John Hill comments about 1950s Britain:

In the cinema, 'teenpics' could be successfully marketed at the increasingly important youth audience, but television, with only two channels, had to make more of an allowance for the domestic and familial context in which it was received and hence the more heterogeneous nature of its audience. This was especially true, perhaps, of what the press had dubbed 'tea-time TV', with its implied image of the family gathered around the television set while eating. With the launch of *Six-Five Special*, it was also Saturday teatime when pop music was most likely to be seen on TV in the years which immediately followed.[6] (Hill 1991, p. 94)

*Six-Five Special* and subsequent British pop music shows were therefore also meant to appeal to parents. The youth show was the youth club show; youth music provided a bit of a laugh for grown-ups. It was this kind of packaging that rock fans and musicians came to despise. Rock 'n' roll stars might become family entertainers (like Cliff Richard and Tommy Steele); the Rolling Stones and Jimi Hendrix did not. On the one hand, rock was not easy to absorb into the routines of TV variety. It was too loud; lip-syncing was an affront to authenticity; guitarists and drummers expected as much camera attention as singers. On the other hand, TV seemed to be the defining site of the commercial pop from which rock was seeking to distinguish itself. The rock contempt for Will Young and Hear'Say (as seen in *NME* and on assorted newspaper rock pages) draws on a stream of invective that is more than thirty years old.[7]

So far so familiar. But consider the counter argument. What if the simultaneous rise of TV and rock 'n' roll was not just a matter of media reordering but also aesthetically significant? What if rock itself has to be understood as a TV product?

The issue here is actually quite straightforward. The importance of television for promoting rock 'n' roll stars from Elvis Presley onwards was that it meant potential fans *got to see them*. Rock music (like all music) is a visual as well as aural form and it certainly could be argued that the visual conventions of rock performance were shaped by television – because it was there – in ways that do not apply to musical genres which pre-dated television – classical music, opera, jazz, folk. Performers from these genres are simply shown and whatever the popularity of the *Billy Cotton Band Show* or *The Black and White Minstrel Show*, these were more about bringing stage acts into the living room than about changing their performing conventions. The most popular of such shows was, after all, *Sunday Night at the London Palladium*.

The use of television to provide a visual code for its youth audience is most obvious in shows that were designed as displays of the latest teen fashions and dance steps. Hill describes the role of the studio audience in *Six-Five Special* 'as unofficial guides to the latest fashions in clothes, haircuts and, above all, dancing' (Hill 1991, p. 95), a role which was taken from *American Bandstand* and has not really changed on youth music shows to this day.[8] But what concerns me here is something else: the effect of television on performing conventions. I assume that most rock fans have, like me, memories of TV moments that had a determining effect on their sense of a performer and their music. As a teenager I watched *Top of the Pops* to see what new acts looked like and was duly amused and appalled. But some acts (Jimi Hendrix, for example) simply defied the limits of the box in the corner. They had what can only be called television charisma. Over the years there have been other such acts – Otis Redding on *Ready Steady Go*, Freddy Mercury at the Live Aid Concert, Tracey Chapman on the Free Nelson Mandela show, Jeff Buckley on *Later* – and the question becomes this: How have the conventions of a good rock performance affected the conventions of a good television performance and vice versa?

One of the standard arguments against pop videos in the mid-1980s was that they would mean rock success in the future being determined by who was telegenic. But TV's role in the record sales process means that looking good on television has always been essential for success. I do not doubt, for example, that Elvis looked better on the screen than any of his rockabilly peers, and how else could one explain Cliff Richard's status as Britain's number 1 rock 'n' roller? The fact is that for the vast majority of people – particularly the vast majority of youth (and including the minority who themselves become performers) – rock stars are first seen on television, and what a rock star is meant to be is therefore to an extent defined by television.[9] And this is true even of those acts which seek to defy TV sales processes, from the Rolling Stones through the Sex Pistols to Nirvana and Eminem.[10]

What is the relationship between rock performance and TV performance? The question can be broken down into more specific questions. What sort of *event* is rock on television? How are viewers made to think that something special is happening? How is this event related to other television events? The central issue here is the question of *liveness*. For both television and rock the concept of live music is aesthetically crucial; both media use recording devices to give their audiences a sense of something happening here and now.[11] In the ideology of rock lip-syncing is anathema, indicating the essential inauthenticity of TV pop. But as Dick Clark observes:

Every musical motion picture ever made has used the lip-sync technique. I explained the process to the kids and they learned to distinguish between a good lip-syncer and a bad one. We used lip-sync primarily because it was cheaper, but also because it was impossible to duplicate the sound of the record – and it was the record that kids wanted to hear.[12] (Clark 1976, p. 71)

And one could say that both rock and TV performances must be seen as real, felt, exciting, happening. Both use a repertoire of technical tricks to achieve this: camera angles, amplification, lighting, editing, backing tapes, and so forth. Both address the question of audience. What audience is implied by a performance? How is it shown? How is it involved? How is it addressed? There is a clear continuity here between the way in which early TV shows framed and closed up on singers and the way in which the lead singers of rock bands are foregrounded and lit on stage. And there is continuity too between the way in which TV presenters introduce us to acts – letting us get to know them, as it were – and what we expect from live acts in terms of their own presentation, their own between-song conversation.

What I am suggesting here is that one of the reasons why the conventions of rock performance are different from those of previous pop forms is because of the effects of television. These effects are both positive (television shaped our expectations of pop performance) and negative (rock authenticity is defined against TV convention). And they have a history. The development of television, that is to say, in terms of both technology and ideology, has had its own effects on the history of rock (just as rock developments, in terms of both sound and market, have been reflected on television).[13]

On the late 1950s British show, *Oh Boy!*, for example, there was limited camera movement and unvarying lighting. What the audience saw was a stage show with no depth but an almost lurid attention to surface. Singers were seen in brightly lit close up and their feeling for their songs was mimed as they sang with what seems now an astonishing repertoire of grimaces, grins and hand and shoulder movements (they did not speak to camera at all). Editing was tight to the music (the rhythm of shots determined by the rhythm of the song) but limited to cuts between medium and close-ups, between different singing faces. The pace was fast (no breaks between numbers) and the message seemed to be that what you see is what there is – the audience in the studio (which is heard prominently on the soundtrack but is not seen) is in no sense privileged. Audience noises, the squeals and the screams, are mixed on the soundtrack to match what we see on screen, and even at this distance one can see how the performing conventions established in this TV version of a rock 'n' roll show could be directly enacted on stage, as the live version of the TV version of a live show!

By the mid-1960s, on a show like *Ready Steady Go*, what television offered was a club rather than a theatre experience. The TV viewer now saw the studio audience too, and the camera (on a dolly) was, like the crowd, in constant movement. Its view of the performance could be interrupted by dancers moving across the sightline, by performers moving out of vision. Performances in this show seemed not to be staged for the camera, but to be captured by it. Television was still presenting a happening, but now with the conventions of documentary rather than outside broadcasting. Performers sang to the audience in the studio rather than to the audience at home. TV viewers were watching a performance, but it now also included the studio audience, the studio noise, the studio movement, and even the studio cameras. Lighting was determined by the conventions of the club (the spots and the shadows) rather than by the needs of the domestic audience. The camera seemed to be trying to see things for itself (just another person in the crowd) rather than offering the TV viewer a privileged seat (as in, say, sports coverage).

If in *Oh Boy!* television dominated the music, placing it on the screen just so, in *Ready Steady Go*, music dominated television. Performing styles became more aggressive, unpredictable, and noisy. Lead singers now competed for camera attention with their surrounding musicians who had begun to develop their own visual clichés. The sense of the musical group (the defining characteristic of rock as a genre) was both cause and effect of the new editing conventions, shots determined not by the meaning of the song but by the make-up of the band – everyone had to be shown.

By the time we get to *Snub*, a low budget independent production made for BBC2's youth strand in the 1980s, performing conventions are as much about preserving the mysteries of a musical genre and its fans as about opening it up to the casual TV viewer. *Snub* combined interviews with live footage and videos (usually made specifically for the show) but it had no presenter (it used subtitles), interviewers were always off screen, and the music was presented from the musicians' point of view, with cameras usually on stage. The issue here was authenticity (this was celebrating indie music) and how to protect it *from* television. One answer was to make sure that nothing was ever really clear. Interviews were cut so that one heard only the answers (that were often cryptic, rooted in in-group laughter). Videos were relentlessly arty and experimental. Much of acts' stage performance was invisible – the lighting too dark or too bright, the close-ups too close, the camera movement too confusing. Audiences were glimpsed rather than shown; the musicians usually ignored the cameras altogether.

Here, it was suggested, were secrets that only the cognoscenti knew; here were the conventions of a genre that was formed from introversion.[14] *Snub*, in short, addressed one of the problems that TV has posed to rock: *anyone might be watching!* It is precisely this spillover effect that makes TV so important for promotion: it provides the best way for musicians to reach beyond their usual audiences. But this is also to undermine cult bands' exclusive appeal, and so *Snub* was designed to keep the casual viewer out.

What can we conclude from such case studies?[15] For most people the normal experience of rock music is an experience of records and TV not live shows, and my argument here is that the understanding and expectation of live performance is more likely to be determined by our experiences of record and TV rather than vice versa. This may be most obvious at shows for children and young teenagers – the live shows of pop acts like Steps and S Club 7 have much in common with the live shows of children's TV acts like the Tweenies (using, indeed, large TV screens). But as case studies suggest, this is true of other sorts of acts and audiences too, and there are general reasons why rock and TV may have a more symbiotic relationship than is usually assumed.

For all the ideological importance of its live performance, rock is the first popular musical form to be constructed in the studio.[16] The challenge for both record and TV producer is to create an event, a sense of something alive, from a series of takes and edits. To be commercially successful a record has to cut through the distracted listening of everyday life and a TV performance has to reach out from the TV flow. Record and TV producers all have to deal with issues of authority, audience and history. The performers must seem authoritative, even as their impact is being created by the TV and record producers, who determine how we see and hear them. We must believe that the performers are presenting themselves, even as their presence is determined by technology, by lighting, amplification, sound balance, editing, etc. For both TV and record producers, audiences, similarly, are both there and not there, an imaginary presence.[17] Producers thus have to construct a visual/aural space that we enter and complete in the act of viewing/listening; they have to find modes of address that oblige us to respond. And all this has to be done in historical context, according to performing conventions that are already known. *Ready Steady Go* knew about *Oh Boy!*. *Snub* knew about *RSG*. Rock's continual hostility to convention (in the name of authenticity) means a continual construction of performing style against convention – hence the peculiar status of *Unplugged*, an MTV show constructed as a critique of MTV.

## IV

This ITV production [*Cool for Cats*], which *illustrated* the records played with witty, imaginative and extraordinarily apposite routines by modern dancers, has never been equalled since it finished its run some years ago. All that television can offer instead is a dreary keyhole peep at the teenage clan in action. The absurdity of the whole convention that it makes entertainment when a singer mimes to one of his own gramophone records – simply because the television people cannot reproduce the sound on the record, and the singer cannot sing it well while jigging about – is not even noticed anymore. (Leslie 1965, p. 167)

The suggestion that television should illustrate or interpret records, rather than show their performance, has always seemed to miss the point. I do not remember *Cool for Cats* (which did not have the impact of *Six-Five Special* or *Oh Boy!*) but I do remember Legs and Co on *Top of the Pops*, whose interpretative dance routines seemed ludicrous, and the meanderingly irrelevant visual clips that accompanied selected album tracks on *The Old Grey Whistle Test*. It seemed obvious to me that the visuals that television could most usefully bring to music were not about reading music but displaying it.

One consequence of this is that the history of music and television told from the perspective of music is rather different from the history told from the perspective of television. My argument in this paper has been that while the twentieth century history of classical or jazz or folk music can be told without reference to television, the history of rock cannot. What of the question the other way round? How should the history of television refer to music? I do not think classical music programmes have had much effect on TV aesthetics, and even pop programmes are, I suspect, more interesting for what they reveal about the demographics of television address (and the concept of youth programming) than for their influence on television's use of sound. In general the role of music has been less significant for developing new dramas of sound and vision than as a way of filling silence and leading viewers through the televisual flow. The most important use of music is as a way of signalling what is on (hence the use of theme tunes, jingles, station idents and the tracks behind the titles).

Television is rarely free of music because it is the TV producers' crucial tool in the ongoing attempt to grab and hold people's visual interest (and even MTV works like this – the opening bars of a new track pulling one's attention back to the screen). Television producers and advertisers clearly draw on genre conventions here, and the increasing importance of niche markets has meant the increasing use of existing (rather than commissioned) tracks. If this further refines the ways in which music is used to attract the right TV audience, it also means that nowadays, more than ever, *any* music can be used this way, classical and rock, rap and reggae, jazz and jungle.[18] And so we return to the music/television paradox. The very voraciousness with which television consumes all kinds of music suggests that it has little concern for music as music at all.

Television has always been organised as a series of events. Audiences are offered access to something that seems to be happening in front of them. The key question, whether in a soap opera or a football match, a quiz or a cop show is what happens next. It is the same for music programmes. Who is number 1? Is this record a hit or a miss? Who has won? Music television means charts, awards, lists, quizzes, rituals, contests. These are ways to engage viewers who might not otherwise be very interested. To be television music must not only be visualised but given a sense of occasion. Television address – as a matter of both voice and setting – means inviting audiences to be part of something *out there* (while staying in their living rooms). Music on television thus involves a combination of presence and distance that is significantly different from the music experience of radio, records or live performance. If we are normally absorbed in and by music – it draws us into its own space and time – television's account of music resists such absorption. Instant nostalgia shows work well precisely because music that once mattered to people can now be presented at a distance, as a bit of a joke. TV, for all its influence on rock performance, was never really part of its culture.

## Acknowledgements

I would like to thank Karen Lury, Jenny McKay, Keith Negus and John Street for extremely helpful comments on an earlier draft of this paper.

## Endnotes

1. See, for example, the special MTV issue of the *Journal of Communication Enquiry*, 10/1, 1986, with articles by, among others, John Fiske and E. Ann Kaplan.
2. One such study is presently being written, Carol Vernalis's *The Art of Music Video* for Columbia University Press.
3. Figures taken from Kamal Ahmed: 'A nation switches off as the fat lady sings', *The Guardian*, 19 January 1998.
4. The sync rights to the twelve tracks on Touch and Go's 2001 album, *I Find You Very Attractive* (Oval/V2), for example, were licensed to at least thirty companies globally for use on TV ads, as title music, background sound and so on. Users included the BBC (for *Gardeners World* and *Meet Jeremy Paxman*), Channel 4 (*Nigella Bites* and *Queer as Folk*), HBO (*G-String Divas*), Carlsberg Spain, Nokia Phones Israel, and Land Rover Shoes Korea.
5. At this point readers are likely to think immediately of exceptions, and there have certainly been country music programmes (*Hee-Haw*), jazz programmes (*Jazz 625*), club music programmes (Pete Waterman's *His'n'Hers*), and so on. What is striking about such programmes, though, is their uneasy relationship with the relevant fans. In the very process of bringing a musical world to a television audience, such specialist programmes seem to render the music itself faintly (or, in the case of *Hee-Haw*, not so faintly) ridiculous, a point brilliantly made by *The Fast Show* parody of TV jazz. When I've asked genre fans

for TV memories they do not usually cite specialist shows but music heard in non-music programmes – baroque music on the soundtrack of Kenneth Clark's *Civilisation*, jazz on *Peter Gunn*.
6. *Top of the Pops* continued to be such Thursday tea-time TV until well into the 1990s.
7. Peter Leslie notes that teenagers were already dismissing TV pop presenters (in this case, David Jacobs) as 'too commercial' by the early 1960s (Leslie 1965, p. 167). It is interesting that shows in which talent really is an issue – Will Young was hardly faking it – should have become the symbol of commercial trickery. One reason why TV pop programmes may be offensive to rock fans is that they seem to pander to the self-love of music industry figures who claim to be the real source of musical talent – Simon Cowell and Pete Waterman's role in *Pop Idol* was thus a reprise of Mickey Most and Tony Hatch's role in *New Faces* and was prefigured long before that by the music biz panellists on *Juke Box Jury*. A show like *Stars in their Eyes*, a talent contest for people whose talent is to sing/perform like a star, also implies that anyone could have been Scott Walker or Tina Turner, if only they'd had the right record company break.
8. That is not to say one can comfortably dance to a TV set. Displays of pop dancing, from *American Bandstand* to Steps, work, rather, as instructional videos, routines to be precisely observed for later practice. One reason why 1990s dance music should be treated as a quite

different genre from rock is that television was quite irrelevant to its development and success.

9. Dick Clark points out that in the late 1950s and early 1960s, 'rock'n'roll had little acceptance as a form of live entertainment. In 1959 I put together the first "Dick Clark's Caravan of Stars"' (Clark 1976, p. 230). Hill suggests that in Britain *Oh Boy!* 'sought to generate the excitement of a live stage show' in contrast to *Six-Five Special's* party atmosphere (Hill 1991, p. 96). But it could be argued that the rock 'n' roll package shows that toured Britain in the early 1960s were designed to generate the excitement of *Oh Boy!*. Like Dick Clark's *Bandstand* shows they featured a fast turnover of singing stars playing with a house band and co-ordinated by an MC, just like the TV shows. For a later generation of young viewers, Don Kirshner's *Rock Concert* similarly provided a guide as to what to expect from a live show.

10. The most striking example of this is rap. Rap's commercial success – its appeal to the white suburban rock market – was an effect of *Yo, MTV Raps* which formalised the performing conventions of gangsta rap, in particular. Street style and video style fed off each other (and into Hollywood) and the most 'realist' of genres is simultaneously the most artificial.

11. My suggestion here that rock and TV share an approach to live music is obviously to challenge the usual view that their aesthetics are quite different (see, for example, Tasker 1983). The flaw of such TV critiques is that they treat 'live' performance as uncomplicatedly naturalistic.

12. For the showbiz establishment of the time, rock 'n' roll records were clearly fake precisely because of their dependence on studio technology (of which lip-syncing was just another example). This argument is best exemplified by Stan Freberg's satirical records.

13. The definitive history of popular music on television is still to be written. One problem here is that despite the best efforts of MTV or, more recently, the BBC's attempts to turn *Top of the Pops* into an international brand, television is an essentially local medium. Formats like *Popstars* and *Pop Idol* may be globally popular, but each country needs its own version, and Will Young is no more likely than Hear'Say to be successful in the USA. I know far less about television programmes in Sweden or Germany, Canada or Australia than I know about those countries' music, and I am uneasily aware than many of my references in this article will mean little to people who were not brought up in the UK. I am not even very clear about the history of music programmes on US television since the 1950s (just as American work on MTV rarely appreciates what a different place MTV occupies in other countries' TV landscapes).

14. If *Ready Steady Go*, in the end, drew its conventions from the British documentary movement, from such 1950s films as *Mama Don't Allow* and *We Are the Lambeth Boys*, films that involved outside observers trying to present youth culture on its own terms, *Snub's* references were to low-budget American avant-garde documentaries, to subcultures' accounts of themselves.

15. I am aware that my choices are somewhat random and dependent on what is easily available to view. A detailed history of popular music and television in Britain would reveal, I think, a complicated organic structure rather than a straightforward linear development. The early youth shows bifurcated into teen shows and children's shows (the latter evolving from *Crackerjack* into the various Saturday morning magazines that remain crucial for certain kinds of pop success). Teen shows in turn split into lifestyle shows, semi-political (*20th Century Box*, *The Oxford Road Show*) and entirely entertaining (*The Tube* and *The Word*), consumer shows (*Top of the Pops*), serious music shows (*OGWT*, *Later with Jools Holland*), etc. A complete chart would be extremely complicated. For a useful initial map, see Tasker (1983).

16. Gary Burns has shown that *Your Hit Parade*, *Bandstand*'s predecessor on American TV, had quite different performance conventions not simply because it was less concerned with youth but more importantly because it featured songs not records. It now seems archaic, while there is a path that can be followed from *American Bandstand* to video clips (see Burns 1998; Wolfe 1985). There are useful comparisons to be made between the relationship of records and TV in the 1950s and 1960s and the relationship of big band music and radio broadcasting and crooning and cinema sound in the 1920s and 1930s.

17. See Hennion (1990). Hennion's focus is the recording studio. TV studios may have real audiences but they are subject to such producer control as to be, in effect, constructs.

18. Keith Negus asks whether there is such a thing as TV-unfriendly music. Yes. Music that has to be listened to with complete concentration, *with one's eyes shut!*

290     *Simon Frith*

## References

Burns, G. 1998. 'Visualising 1950s hits on *Your Hit Parade*', *Popular Music*, 17, pp. 139–51.
Clark, D. 1976. *Rock, Roll & Remember* (New York)
Hennion, A. 1990. 'The production of success. An antimusicology of the pop song', in *On Record*, ed. S. Frith and A. Goodwin (New York)
Hill, J. 1991. 'Television and pop. The case of the 1950s', in *Popular Television in Britain*, ed. J. Corner (London)
Leslie, P. 1965. *Fab. The Anatomy of a Phenomenon* (London)
Shore, M. 1985. (with Dick Clark) *The History of American Bandstand* (New York)
Tasker, P. 1983. 'Pop music and television', *Stills*, September–October, pp. 20–3
Wolfe, A. 1985. 'Pop on video: Narrative modes in the visualisation of popular music on *Your Hit Parade* and *Solid Gold*', in *Popular Music Perspectives 2*, ed. D. Horn (Exeter and Göteborg), pp. 20–3

# CHAPTER 13

## *Music and Everyday Life*

In the British House of Commons on March 15, 2000, Robert Key, the Conservative MP for Salisbury, begged to move "That leave be given to bring in a Bill to prohibit the broadcasting of recorded music in certain public places" (Hansard [Parliamentary Debates]. Sixth Series, 1999–2000, vol. 346, p. 326–27)).

Key was speaking on behalf of Pipedown, the Campaign for Freedom from Piped Music, but suggested that there would be widespread public support for the measure. He cited a 1997 *Sunday Times* survey that found piped music to be number three in the list of things most hated about modern life. He noted that following a survey of its users, Gatwick Airport had stopped playing canned music. He drew on medical findings. "All uninvited noise raises the blood pressure and depresses the immune system." He added information from the Chartered Institute of Environmental Health. "The commonest type of offending noise is not pneumatic drills, cars or aircraft but music."

The bill was greeted enthusiastically in the media, perhaps because everyone knew it wouldn't get anywhere. But as a solution to the problem of public music, Key's bill was actually quite modest. He didn't seek to ban piped music from places where people choose to go (stores, hotels, sports clubs). His measure was meant to regulate involuntary listening. It covered hospitals and surgeries, local authority swimming pools, bus and railroad stations and journeys, and the streets. He didn't propose, as he might have, that in the future no one should listen to music except in premises licensed for that purpose.

It is not as if private places are free of musical pollution. How many people now travel by car in silence? Who now doesn't shave or bathe to music, cook or iron to music, read or write to music? Thanks to the radio and the record player and the tape recorder, music is now the soundtrack of everyday life, and no law is going to change that. And our ears are as likely to be assaulted these days by classical music as by pop. It's not just that music is everywhere but that all music is everywhere. Works composed for specific secular or religious occasions (marches, masses), in specific places (Thailand, Texas)—can turn up as if at random on TV commercials and restaurant tape loops. There's no longer any necessary connection between the occasion for making music and the occasion of listening to it. Hence the peculiarity of our present situation: If music was once that organization of sounds that could be distinguished from noise, it has become the epitome of noise itself, more offensive, if Robert Key is to be believed, than the sound of jackhammers.

One theme of twentieth-century composition was to make music out of noise, to reclaim the everyday for art, as it were, to write works *for* jackhammers. Noise-as-music has as many instances as music-as-noise: Cage and Stockhausen wrote works including "live" radio (*Imaginary Landscape No 4* and *Kurzwellen [Short Waves]*). Avant-garde composers took up Pierre Schaeffer's and Pierre Henry's idea of *musique concrète* in a variety of genres. Eric Satie, following a different strategy, proposed *musique d'ameublement*, furniture music, which would be unnoticed in the everyday hubbub, an idea followed up much later by Brian Eno in his *Music for Airports*. And, of course, many rock musicians—in heavy metal bands and their offshoots, in the postpunk industrial and noise scenes—have made electronic amplification and the distorting effects of high volume and feedback a central part of their aesthetic.

But what concerns me here is another of John Cage's contributions, his question: What now is silence?

Two points are striking here. First, silence is so rare that it has become, in itself, increasingly valuable. We live now not just with the permanent sense of traffic roar, the routine interruption of sirens and car alarms and mobile phones, but also with the ongoing electric hum of the refrigerator, the central heating, the neon lights, the digital clock. Silence has become the indicator of an unusual intensity of feeling—emotional intensity in the Hollywood film; public solemnity in the two-minute silence on Veterans' Day; the one-minute silence before kickoff in which to honor someone's death. It was, presumably, this that prompted the Independent

Television Commission in Britain to censure Independent Television News (ITN) for broadcasting a "sick and tasteless" sequence of news in which "the collapse of the World Trade Center in New York was set to music." The music (from Charles Gounod's *Judex*) may have been, as ITN claimed, suitable, with "a sombre, funereal tone," but the very attempt to show these images in time to music "was inappropriate and breached the programme code." And silence, as something valuable, to be bought, means not complete silence, but the absence of human or electronic or artificial sounds. Nature—the country retreat, the unspoiled beach or bush or jungle, the mountain wilderness—is the most precious holiday resource.

Because we seem to value silence, to covet it, it is perhaps surprising that silence is also now something to be feared—on radio, in seminars, on the telephone. Here silence becomes something to be *filled*, and music becomes not that which isn't noise, but that which isn't no noise (i.e., silence). Popular music, something once used to drown out other sounds—on the streets, in the music hall and variety theater, in the pub and parlor singsong—is now used to ensure that there is never no sound at all. If the BBC were to reintroduce Lord Reith's rule that programs should be followed by silence, to allow listeners to reflect on what they had heard, I have no doubt that the switchboard would be jammed with complaints: Has something gone *wrong*?

In the House of Commons, Robert Key suggested that there is an important difference between choosing to listen to music in public places and having to listen to it, and given people's apparent need to fill their lives with music, the implication is that the problem is *what* we have to hear: other people's music, not our own. And certainly the routine use of the term *muzak* to dismiss a certain sort of light instrumental arrangement suggests that what's involved here is a matter of taste. But this may be misleading. People are equally upset by what seems to be the *inappropriate* use of music they do like: Mozart as we wait for a plane to take off; Credence Clearwater or the Clash on a commercial; Miles Davis in a bank. I don't know of any systematic research into what most offends people about the use of music in public places but an unscientific survey of friends and newspaper columnists suggests that what is played matters less than its circumstances.

On the one hand, people seem less offended by live music: children singing in a playground, a brass band or choir in the park, an Andean troupe or reggae guitarist in the shopping mall. A busker singing "Wonder-

wall" or "Hey! Mr Tambourine Man" badly is less offensive than the original record. The issue here is not aesthetics but sociability. Live music
is music as a social event, an aspect of a social situation—play, display,
celebration, begging. It is an organic, a living aspect of public life (hence
the term *live music*), whatever its technical or aesthetic qualities. Canned
music, piped music (terms almost always used with negative connotations of the mechanical) has been removed from its social origins. Like
some alien force it moves relentlessly forward regardless of any human
responses to it.

On the other hand, anecdotal polling suggests that there are experiences of public music that are particularly offensive whatever the music
involved. Music while a telephone is on hold; Walkman leak on trains and
buses; the bass boom from a car at traffic lights; the endless loop of
Christmas songs in December; the sound of other people's parties. The
offense here is against one's sense of one's own space—it is being invaded;
but it reflects too, I think, resentment, resentment at being so obviously
excluded by other people. Music, that is to say, has become a defensive as
well as an offensive weapon (just as it has become a way of negotiating
shared space, as in the club or on the dance floor).

The question of how and why music got implicated in our sense of
personal space is fascinating and has been little explored. It is not just a
matter of music in public places; music is equally important in organizing
domestic space. From a sociological perspective, that is, we can better
understand the domestic relations of intimacy and distance, power and
affection, by mapping patterns of musical use than we can explain musical
tastes by reference to social variables. How is family space regulated musically? Family members (teenagers most notoriously) mark off their own
space with their music—volume as a barrier. But what happens in communal spaces—the kitchen, the car? Who decides what plays? What
music is ruled out *tout court* and why?

I doubt if there's anyone nowadays who couldn't map the history of
family relationships along musical lines. It's a moot point whether changes
in domestic ideology meant new markets for new kinds of domestic electrical goods, or whether it was the new musical possibilities that changed
families, but I have no doubt that a sociology of contemporary courtship,
romance, sex, and friendship could start with the role of music in these
relationships: the exploration of each other's tastes, the shifting degrees of
tolerance and intolerance for other people's records, the importance of the
musical gift, the attempts to change other people's music habits, to resist

changing one's own. I'll come back to this. First I want to digress into some brief remarks about the role in all this of music radio.

I believe that radio was the most significant twentieth-century mass medium. It was radio that transformed the use of domestic space, blurring the boundary between the public and the private, idealizing the family hearth as the site of ease and entertainment, establishing the rhythm of everydayness: the BBC "Children's Hour," "Breakfast Time," "Friday Night Is Music Night!" It was radio that shaped the new voice of public intimacy, that created Britain as a mediated collectivity, that gave ordinary people a public platform (creating the concept of "ordinary people" in the first place). It was radio that made sport a national symbol, that created the very idea of "light entertainment." Where radio led, television simply followed. And it was radio (rather than film) that established the possibility of music as an ever-playing soundtrack to our lives.

If television in all its varieties were to be abolished, it would make little difference to a classical music world that is, though, almost entirely dependent on radio not just for broadcasts, but also for the support of orchestras and concerts, for commissions and record sales. And while the pop world would have to adapt its ways if television no longer played a part in star making, radio is still the most important source of popular musical discourse, defining genres and genre communities, shaping music history and nostalgia, determining what we mean by "popular" music in the first place.

It was radio that created the musical map that we now use to distinguish high and low music, youth and older people's music, the specialist musical interest, and the mainstream. Radio is important not least as a means of access to music otherwise inaccessible, whether in the BBC's systematic policy of musical education or in the furtive teenage use of Radio Luxembourg, the American Forces network, and pirate radio stations as windows on another world.

But here I want to use radio to address another issue: the question of musical choice. In the early days of the music industry, it was assumed that the phonograph and the radio were competing for domestic attention, and it is often suggested that the U.S. record industry only survived the Depression years of the 1930s because of the success of the jukebox (an interesting example of a technological device for imposing private musical choices on a public). It seemed a matter of common sense that if someone owned a record they could play at will, they wouldn't turn on the radio to hear it. Or, alternatively, if they knew the radio would be routinely playing the latest hits, why would they spend money on getting the records for themselves?

In practice, though, this is not how radio choice works. From the 1950s' rise of top 40 radio in the United States to the 1990s British success of Classic FM, it has become accepted industry wisdom that people are more likely to stay tuned to a radio station the more likely it is to play music that is familiar to them, records that they already own or have just bought. It is much harder to maintain listening figures for programs or stations that routinely play the odd or unfamiliar. And radio remains, of course, the essential tool for selling music of all sorts: The more a track is played, the more likely it is that listeners will buy it.

What seems to be involved in radio listening, then, is a constant movement between predictability and surprise. On "our" station we expect to hear our kind of music, without ever being quite sure what will come next. It's as if we're happy to let someone else have the burden of choice. And radio is also a way of suggesting a broader taste community. Our personal musical likes and dislikes are publicly confirmed, and deejays and presenters have a particularly important role in treating music as a form of social communication. The only kind of radio that acquires the condition of muzak is that deejayless ambient format in which no voice is heard (unless it is selling something).

Radio has also been important in developing the skill of switching attention, moving back and forth between hearing music and listening to it, treating it as background or foreground. It's a skill that is taken for granted by film scorers, and one that we exercise everyday without thought as we walk down the street or sit in the pub. Public music irritates, one could say, when what should be in the background forces itself on us as foreground, but the question that interests me and to which I will return, is why it is, when we are now so skilled at screening out music that doesn't much interest us, that some songs or voices or melodies or beats just reach out and grab our attention anyway.

For Adorno "all contemporary music life is dominated by the commodity character" and it is the resulting "fetish character in music" that explains "the regression in listening" (Adorno [1938] 1991). Or, as we would say these days, music is a matter of brand and lifestyle. Take this report from the music industry trade paper *Music Week*:

> There was further good news for Classic FM last week when its TV-advertised Time to Relax entered the compilation chart at number nine. "Getting listeners to buy into the Classic brand is at the heart of what we do," says [Roger] Lewis [Classic FM program controller]. "As well as the albums we have the magazine, a credit card and even a dating agency. We

are seeing a classical music phenomenon in the UK, as suddenly it's cool to be classical." (*Music Week*, November 3, 2001)

But underlying such brash commercialism are two broader transformations in how music now works in society, the transformations to which Adorno is in part referring when he uses the term *commodity character*. On the one hand, we primarily think of music in terms of its *use*; on the other hand, usefulness means *individual* use.

It is the use of music as a commercial tool to which we mostly object these days: its use to manipulate us in the market. There can be few people who are unaware of how music is used by advertisers and retailers. But it is equally important to note that people nowadays routinely use music to manipulate their moods and organize their activities *for themselves.*

The pioneering researchers of music and everyday life in Britain, sociologist Tia DeNora and psychologist John A. Sloboda, both emphasize the extent to which people now regard music as a personal tool, something to be used, in DeNora's terms, for "emotional self-regulation" (DeNora 2000). As a "technology of self," music has become crucial to the ways in which people organize memory, identity, their autonomy. Both writers suggest that the driving force of people's everyday use is the need to be in control, and that today this means integrating emotional and aesthetic control: creating the setting for the appropriate display of feeling (whether to oneself or to others). Sloboda's research also shows that people are more likely to use music to accompany chores than pleasures, tasks done as duties rather than enjoyed for their own sake (Sloboda and O'Neill 2001). Joggers routinely wear a Walkman; walkers do not. Once the dinner party conversation comes to life no one bothers to put on a new CD.

In many societies, as ethnomusicologists have told us, the functions of music could be described in almost exclusively social terms: Music was used in games and for dancing; to organize work and war; in ceremonies and rituals; to mark the moments of birth, marriage, and death; to celebrate harvest and coronation; and to articulate religious beliefs and traditional practices. People might have enjoyed music individually, but its purpose was not to make them feel good. Compare assumptions now about the use of music. In a survey of 210 works on "the power of music" (commissioned by The Performing Right Society), Susan Hallam notes how contemporary research is focused on the use of music for therapy and medical treatment, for enhancing children's learning abilities, and for influencing individual behavior. Among her "key points" are these:

Music can promote relaxation, alleviate anxiety and pain, promote appropriate behaviour in vulnerable groups and enhance the quality of life of
those who are beyond medical help.

People can use music in their lives to manipulate their moods, alleviate
the boredom of tedious tasks, and create environments appropriate for
particular social events.

The easy availability of music in everyday life is encouraging individuals to use music to optimise their sense of well being. (Hallam 2001, 1)

And she concludes her survey of research by suggesting that

[t]here is also need for more systematic investigation of the ways that
music can impact on groups of people in social settings. To date, research
has tended to focus on commercial and work environments. The way that
music may affect behaviour in public places has been neglected. Such
research, for instance, might explore whether particular types of music
might stimulate orderly exits from large public functions, reduce the inci-
dence of disorder in particular settings, increase tolerance when people
have to queue for relatively long periods of time or engender feelings of
well being and safety in public places. (Hallam 2001, 19)

There are, in fact, already reports of music being used for such social
engineering—classical music played in railroad stations to make them
unsuitable as youth hangouts, for example—and what I want to note
about this is less dismay that music should have become a technology of
discipline rather than delight, than that it marks a significant shift in our
understanding of *how* music is powerful. While the Taliban outlawed
music with the traditional anxiety that it is a source of collective disorder,
a challenge to religious authority, in modern societies discipline is inter-
nalized. What's at stake is not what people want to do but usually (until
released by music) don't, but what they don't want to do in the first place.
Music remains "a powerful medium of social order," but its power is exercised less through group psychology, the orchestration of crowds, than
through individual psychology, the articulation of self.

Tia DeNora concludes her book on *Music in Everyday Life* by suggesting that

[f]urther explorations of music as it is used and deployed in daily life in
relation to agency's configuration will only serve to highlight what

> Adorno, and the Greek philosophers, regarded as a fundamental matter in relation to the polis, the citizen and the configuration of consciousness; namely, that music is much more than a decorative art; that it is a powerful medium of social order. Conceived in this way, and documented through empirical research, music's presence is clearly political, in every sense that the political can be conceived. (DeNora 2000, 163)

I want to conclude by reiterating DeNora's suggestion that music is much more than a decorative art. In *The Sociology of Rock*, published in 1978, I began with the observation that while recorded music was usually included in a list of the contemporary mass media in textbooks, it was rarely otherwise examined. Twenty and more years on and the situation hasn't really changed. The cinema, television, newspapers, magazines, and advertising are still regarded in the academy as more socially and politically significant than records. And so it needs stressing that what people listen to is more important for their sense of themselves than what they watch or read. Patterns of music use provide a better map of social life than viewing or reading habits. Music just *matters* more than any other medium, and this brings me back to my starting point and the ways in which music is now heard as offensive. It is because music is now used to mark private territory that it can also "invade" it; it is because music has become so deeply implicated in people's personas that it can be misused; and it is because music is now so widely employed as an emotional tool that its misuse is genuinely upsetting.

But there are two further points I want to make. First, DeNora and Sloboda tend to refer musical meaning to its emotional function for individuals, but music remains equally important as a means of communication and as a form of sociability. Most academic research on everyday music focuses, as I have focused here, on music listening. But what is equally remarkable is the sheer amount of *music making* in which people are engaged, and my point here is not just that people do, in large numbers, join choirs, form rock and pop groups, play around with record decks, and set up home studios, but also that these musical activities are central to their understanding of who they are. Music making provides, as Ruth Finnegan argues, critical pathways through life (Finnegan 1989). And music making is less about managing one's own emotional life than about enjoying being together in groups, real and imagined. Future research in music and the everyday needs to integrate the study of music making with the study of musical use. To my mind, ongoing investigation of people's tastes and the current research focus on issues of identity are much less interesting projects than an ethnography that would try to map in detail people's *timetable of engagement*, the reasons why particular music gets particular attention at particular moments, and how these moments are, in turn, imbricated in people's social networks.

Second, and to register finally my unease at treating music in simple functional terms, we need to balance accounts of how people use music to manage their emotions with accounts of how music still has the unexpected power to disrupt us emotionally. The ancient myths of musical power—the stories of the Sirens, Orpheus, the Pied Piper—have a continued force not primarily because of advertisers' ceaseless attempts to lead us astray but because of the much more mysterious power of music *in itself.* How is it that a voice suddenly reaches us, out of the background, whether we are paying attention or not? Whatever the strength of those commercial and technological forces that turn the transcendent into the trite, I don't think we have lost the sense that music, the musical experience, is *special,* that it is a way of one person reaching another without deceit. There's still no better way than through music to be surprised by life.

## Further Reading

Bennett, Tony, M. Emmison, and John Frow. 1999. *Accounting for tastes. Australian everyday cultures.* Cambridge, U.K.: Cambridge Univ. Press.

Booth, Wayne. 1999. *For the love of it. Amateuring and its rivals.* Chicago: Univ. of Chicago Press.

Deleuze, Gilles, and Felix Guattari. 1988. *A thousand plateaus. Capitalism and schizophrenia.* Minneapolis: Univ. of Minnesota Press.

Hargreaves, D. J., and A. C. North, 1997. *The social psychology of music.* Oxford: Oxford Univ. Press.

Hennion, Antoine, Sophie Maisonneuve, and Emilie Gomart. 2000. *Figures de L'Amateur. Formes, objets, pratiques de l'amour de la musique aujourd'hui.* Paris: La Documentation Française.

Lanza, Joseph. 1994. *Elevator music: A surreal history of muzak, easy-listening and other moodsong.* London: Quartet.

Scannell, Paddy. 1996. *Radio, television and modern life.* Oxford: Blackwell.

## References

Adorno, Theodor Wiesengrund. [1938] 1991. On the fetish character in music and the regression of listening. Pp. 26–52 in *The culture industry. Selected essays on mass culture*. Edited by J.M. Bernstein. London: Routledge.

De Nora, Tia. 2000. *Music in everyday life*. Cambridge, UK: Cambridge University Press.

Finnegan, Ruth. 1989. *The hidden musicians: Music-making in an English town*. Cambridge, UK: Cambridge University Press.

Hallam, Susan. 2001. *The power of music*. London: The Performing Right Society.

Sloboda, John A., and Susan O'Neill. 2001. Emotions in everyday listening to music. *Music and emotion. Theory and research*. Edited by Patrik N. Juslin and John A. Sloboda. Oxford: Oxford University Press.

# CHAPTER 14

# Why do songs have words?

In 1918 the chairman of Chappell & Co., Britain's largest music publishing company, wrote a letter to the novelist Radclyffe Hall. She had complained of receiving no royalties after a song for which she had been the lyricist, 'The Blind Ploughman', 'swept the country.' William Davey replied,

> Dear Miss Radclyffe Hall,
>      I yield to no one in my admiration of your words for 'The Blind Ploughman'. They are a big contributing factor to the success of the song. Unfortunately, we cannot afford to pay royalties to lyric writers. One or two other publishers may but if we were to once introduce the principle, there would be no end to it. Many lyrics are merely a repetition of the same words in a different order and almost always with the same ideas. Hardly any of them, frankly, are worth a royalty, although once in a way they may be. It is difficult to differentiate, however. What I do feel is that you are quite entitled to have an extra payment for these particular words, and I have much pleasure in enclosing you, from Messrs Chappell, a cheque for twenty guineas.[1]

Davey had commercial reasons for treating lyrics as formula writing, but his argument is common among academics too. In the 1950s and 1960s, for example, the tiny field of the sociology of popular music was dominated by analyses of song words. Sociologists concentrated on songs (rather than singers or audiences) because they could be studied with a familiar cultural research method, content analysis, and as they mostly lacked the ability to distinguish songs in musical terms, sociologists, by default, had to measure trends by reference to lyrics. It was through their words that hit records were taken to make their social mark.

*Simon Frith*

The focus on lyrics didn't just reflect musical ignorance. Until the mid-1960s British and American popular music was dominated by Tin Pan Alley. Tin Pan Alley's values derived from its origins as a publishing centre and the 'bland, universal, well-made song' (Whitcomb's description) remained central to its organisation even after rock 'n' roll.[2] In concentrating on pop's lyrical themes in this period, sociologists were reflecting the way in which the songs were themselves packaged and sold. Most of these songs did, musically, sound the same; most lyrics did seem to follow measurable rules; most songwriters did operate as 'small business-men engaged in composing, writing or publishing music' rather than as 'creative composers'.[3] Etzkorn, one of the few sociologists to research lyricists not lyrics, discovered in 1963 that

> The composing activity of songwriters would seem to be constrained by their orientation towards the expectations of significant 'judges' in executive positions in the music business whose critical standards are based on traditional musical clichés. In their endeavour to emulate the norms of successful reference groups, songwriters (even with a variety of backgrounds) will produce compositions virtually homogeneous in form and structure, thereby strengthening the formal rigidity of popular music.[4]

And this simply confirmed what analysts anyway took for granted – that it was possible to read back from lyrics to the social forces that produced them.

**Content analysis**

The first systematic analyst of pop song words, J.G. Peatman, was influenced by Adorno's strictures on 'radio music' and so stressed pop's lyrical standardisation: all successful pop songs were about romantic love; all could be classified under one of three headings – the 'happy in love' song, the 'frustrated in love' song, and the 'novelty song with sex interest'.[5]

For Peatman, this narrow range reflected the culture industry's success in keeping people buying the same thing, but most subsequent content analysts, writing with a Cold War concern to defend American commercial culture, have taken pop market choices seriously. Thus in 1954 Mooney accepted Peatman's starting point – pop as happy/sad love songs – but argued that they

78

*Why do songs have words?*

'reflected, as love songs always do, the deepest currents of thought; for as values change, so change the ideas and practice of love'.[6]

Mooney's argument was that pop song lyrics reflect the emotional needs of their time. The history of the American 'mood' can thus be traced through the shifting themes of popular songs: from 1895 to 1925 song lyrics were 'abandoned and unorthodox' and reflected the patriotism, proletarianism and hedonism of the rising American empire; from the 1920s to the 1940s songs were 'negativistic and rather morbid' and reflected the disillusion, the quiet despair of the Depression; in the 1950s pop reflected a new zeal, as 'the mass mood' invested the post-war consumer boom with Cold War fervour; and, in a later article, Mooney continued his readings into the 1960s, putting stress on songs' importance as a record of new sexual mores.[7]

Mooney related changing images of sex to changes in the class origins of pop – in the 1930s songs expressed the middle-class attitudes of their middle-class authors, by the 1960s they expressed the freer mores of their working-class performers – but his general point is that songs can be read as examples of popular ideology. Tin Pan Alley, he suggested in 1954,

> has responded to and revealed the emotional shifts of its public:
> sheet music and phonograph records are among the few
> artefacts which afford insight into the inarticulate Americans of
> the twentieth century.[8]

'The people' in a mass society may no longer make their own music, but choosing which songs and records to buy is still a means of cultural expression. Hits meet a popular need and so pop lyrics have changed over the century, despite corporate control of their production.

Mooney's survey of American cultural history is unsystematic, and he seems to choose his songs to support his thesis rather than vice versa, but his 'reflection theory' of pop lyrics has been shared by most of the more scientific content analysts who followed up his work. American sociologists have used song words, in particular, to chart the rise of a youth culture, with new attitudes to love and sex and fun, and to document the differences between 1950s and 1960s romance. In both eras the love drama passed through four acts – search, happiness, break-up, isolation – but 1960s pop stressed hedonism, movement, freedom (not dependence), choice

*Simon Frith*

(not fate). Courtship no longer led to marriage (relationships had a natural history, died a natural death); happiness meant sexual happiness; love was no longer an 'elusive quarry' but a passing, to-be-seized opportunity.[9]

The theoretical assumption here is that the words of pop songs express general social attitudes, but such song readings depend, in practice, on prior accounts of youth and sexuality. Content analysts are not innocent readers, and there are obvious flaws in their method. For a start, they treat lyrics too simply. The words of all songs are given equal value; their meaning is taken to be transparent; no account is given of their actual performance or their musical setting. This enables us to code lyrics statistically, but it involves a questionable theoretical judgment: content codes refer to what the words describe – situations and states of mind – but not to how they describe, to their significance as language.

Even more problematically, these analysts tend to equate a song's popularity with public agreement with its message – the argument is that songs reflect the beliefs and values of their listeners. This is to ignore songs' ideological work, the way they play back to people situations or ideas they recognise but which are inflected now with particular moral lessons. The most sophisticated content analysts have, therefore, used lyrics as evidence not of popular culture as such, but of popular cultural confusion.[10] Songs, from this perspective, articulate the problems caused by social change, so that Di Maggio, Peterson and Esco, for example, analyse post-war Southern history by looking at the tensions revealed by country music lyrics since the 1950s: country love songs continued to take the ideal of romantic love for granted, but increasingly explored the argument that 'a battle between the sexes is inevitable'; country drink songs described alcohol as both a solution to and a cause of emotional problems; country work songs celebrated 'the strong self-reliant worker', while despairing at the effects of the factory routine – 'by day I make the cars/and by night I make the bars.' Country lyrics, in short, reflected contradictions, as old communal values were used to measure the quality of the lives of the urban working class. The authors conclude that songs 'reflect' their listeners' concerns at the level of fantasy – such reflection means, in fact, giving people *new* shapes, new symbolic forms for their hopes and anxieties.[11]

Mike Haralambos has treated the history of black American song in this period similarly. Blues lyrics, he suggests, were

*Why do songs have words?*

essentially passive, bitter, sorrowful and fatalistic; soul words concern activity, pride, optimism and change:

> Whereas blues concentrates almost entirely on experience, usually the experience of failure, soul songs state the ideal. Moral principles are laid down, rules of conduct advocated, right and wrong involved. Blues merely states this is the way it is, and this is how I am suffering. By comparison, soul music implies life is not to be accepted as it comes, hardship is not to be borne, but life is to be made worth living.[12]

Haralambos argues that soul represented a lyrical as well as a musical merging of blues and gospel, as the free-flowing language and imagery of the church were applied to the socially realistic narratives of the blues. The resulting songs both drew on and gave shape to the new mood and vocabulary of 1960s ghetto streets. In the words of disc jockey Job Cobb:

> 'We're Rolling On' and songs like that gave a lot of people, and even a lot of civil rights organisations, hope and great strength, and made people believe in it, because actually within the record itself, it was telling you like what to expect, and what happened thus far, so like hold your head up high and keep on going, your day will come.[13]

This interpretation of lyrics as a form of ideological expression – asserting ideas in order to shape them, describing situations in order to reach them – complicates the concept of 'reflection' (these songs reflect ideals as well as realities) but retains the assumption that popular songs are significant because they have a 'real closeness' with their consumers.[14] The implication, in short, is that such readings only make sense of 'folk' forms; only in country music, blues, soul, the right strands of rock, can we take lyrics to be the authentic expression of popular experiences and need. In the mainstream of mass music something else is going on.

### Mass culture

Most mass cultural critiques of pop songs words derive from 1930s Leavisite arguments. Pop songs are criticised for their banality, their feebleness with words, imagery and emotion; the problem is

*Simon Frith*

not just that lyrics picture an unreal world, but also that pop ideals
are trite: 'One and all these refer to the world where June rhymes
with moon, where there is no such thing as struggle for existence,
where love does not have to be striven for through understanding.'[15]

In *The Uses of Literacy*, Richard Hoggart argues, similarly, that
real needs to dream are being satisfied by debilitatingly thin
fantasies, concepts of well-being defined in terms of conformity.
Mass culture has turned visions of the extraordinary into clichés of
the ordinary, and pop song lyrics have been subordinated to the
performing conventions of 'forced intimacy' – 'the singer is
reaching millions but pretends he is reaching only "you".' Love,
the dominant topic of pop songs is represented now as a solution to
all problems, 'a warm burrow, a remover of worry; borne on an
ingratiating treacle of melody, a vague sense of uplift-going-on'.[16]

For Leavisites, the evil of mass culture is that it corrupts real
feelings. Wilfrid Mellers (*Scrutiny*'s original commentator on
popular music) notes that pop songs 'do insidiously correspond
with feelings we have all had in adolescence'.

> Though these songs do not deny that love will hurt, they seek a
> vicarious pleasure from the hurt itself. So they create an illusion
> that we can live on the surface of our emotions. Sincere, and
> true, and touching though they may be, their truth is partial.[17]

The critical task is, therefore, to discover 'the amount of "felt
life" in specific words and music', and Mellers and Hoggart agree
that pop songs should not be dismissed without a proper hearing.
Other Leavisites have been less generous. Edward Lee, for
example, denounces the romantic banality of pop lyrics in terms of
its social effects (citing the divorce rate in his disdain for silly love
songs) and this argument about the corrupting consequences of the
hit parade has been taken up by Marxist critics in their accounts of
pop's 'class function'.[18] Dave Harker, for instance, reads Tin Pan
Alley lyrics as straightforward statements of bourgeois ideology.
Take 'Winter Wonderland': 'In the meadow we can build a
snowman/Then pretend he is Parson Brown/He'll say "Are you
married?" We'll say "No man/But you can do the job when you're
in town."' This song, writes Harker, 'articulates the key fantasies
not only about the Christmas period but, crucially, about the
pattern of sexual relations felt to be most appropriate for a
particular social order.'[19]

Love and romance, the central pop themes, are the 'sentimental

## Why do songs have words?

ideology' of capitalist society. Like Lee, Harker stresses the importance of pop romance for marriage – it is thus that songs work for the reproduction of social relations. Love lyrics do express 'popular' sexual attitudes, but these attitudes are mediated through the processes of cultural control. Harker makes this Leavisite comment on Elvis Presley's 'It's Now Or Never':

> Of course, the song was popular in a commercial context precisely because it did articulate certain key strands in the dominant ideology. The denial of female sexuality, the reduction of love to ejaculation, the inability to come out with emotion honestly, the habit of implying intercourse is a 'dirty little secret', the acceptability of emotional blackmail on the part of man, and so on, tell us a good deal about the paradigms of femininity in the late 1950s, *and* about the paradigms of masculinity, for all those men who had to try, presumably, to imitate Elvis Presley.[20]

Songs are, in this account, a form of propaganda. As Goddard, Pollock and Fudger put it, from a feminist perspective, 'lyrics constantly reflect and reinforce whatever ethos society currently considers desirable.'[21] They express dominant sexual ideologies through their recurrently exploitative images of women, their stereotypes of sexual subjugation, their treatment of femininity as at once 'mysterious' and 'dependent', and, above all, through their systematic denial of the material reality of sexual exploitation. As Germaine Greer once wrote,

> The supreme irony must be when the bored housewife whiles away her duller tasks, half-consciously intoning the otherwise very forgettable words of some pulp lovesong. How many of them stop to assess the real consequences of the fact that 'all who love are blind' or just how much they have to blame that 'something here inside' for? What songs do you sing, one wonders, when your heart is no longer on fire and smoke no longer mercifully blinds you to the banal realities of your situation? (But of course there are no songs for that.)[22]

Most critics of mass music assume that there are, nonetheless, alternatives to commercial pop. Hoggart, for example, praises pre-war pop songs by reference to their *genuineness*:

*Simon Frith*

> They are vulgar, it is true, but not usually tinselly. They deal
> only with large emotional situations; they tend to be open-
> hearted and big-bosomed. The moral attitudes behind them are
> not mean or calculated or 'wide'; they still just touch hands with
> an older and more handsome culture. They are not cynical or
> neurotic; they often indulge their emotions, but are not
> ashamed of showing emotion, and do not seek to be
> sophisticatedly smart.[23]

Harker praises the 'muscular compactness' of Bob Dylan's
language, and makes a telling comparison of the Beatles' 'She
Loves You' and Dylan's thematically similar 'It Ain't Me Babe':

> The Beatles' song drips with adolescent sentiment. It is
> structured around the person of a go-between, and cheerfully
> reinforces the preferred mode of courtship in a capitalist
> society, using guilt-invoking mindlessness ('you know you
> should be glad', 'you know that can't be bad'), and generally
> relying on emotional blackmail at the shallowest of levels. To
> their inane 'Yeh, yeh, yeh' Dylan counterposed a full-throated
> 'No, no, no'. Instead of their emotional tinkering and patching
> up, Dylan insists on breaking the conventions of bourgeois
> courtship, refusing to accept anything less than full-hearted
> love. Instead of their magic 'solution', he reminded us that it's
> sometimes better to call it a day. While they denied
> individuality he celebrated it – even in those forms with which
> he could not agree. While they underwrote the surface chatter
> of socially acceptable but emotionally stifling forms of
> interpersonal behaviour, Dylan raises a wry pair of fingers at
> the conventions, *not* at the woman.[24]

For Harker, 'authentic' lyrics express 'authentic' relationships,
and expose bourgeois conventions with an honest vital language –
a language which reflects experience directly and is not ideologically
mediated. A similarly argument underpinned Hayakawa's classic
1955 critique of American pop songs. He analysed lyrics in terms
of

> the IFD disease – the triple-threat semantic disorder of
> Idealisation (the making of impossible and ideal demands upon
> life), which leads to Frustration (as the result of the demands

*Why do songs have words?*

not being met), which in turn leads to Demoralisation (or Disorganisation or Despair).[25]

Hayakawa compared pop lyrics with blues lyrics, in which there was no 'chasing rainbows', no search for the ideal partner, no belief in love as magic, but an exploration of all the problems of sex and romance, 'a considerable tough-mindedness', and 'a willingness to acknowledge the facts of life'. Francis Newton wrote in parallel terms about the corruption of blues lyrics by pop publishers in what he called the 'mincing process'.

> Essentially it consists of a rigid restriction of themes which excludes the controversial, the uncomfortable, or unfamiliar, and above all the exclusion of reality. For the main industrial innovation of the pop-music business is the discovery that the day dream, or the sentimental memory (which is the day dream reversed) is the single most saleable commodity.[26]

In the 1960s this process was reversed as young musicians and audiences rejected Tin Pan Alley for rhythm 'n' blues – pop's vapidity was replaced by blues 'realism'. The function of rock lyrics became the exposure of false ideology so that, for Harker, Bob Dylan's lyrics ceased to matter (and Dylan himself 'sold out') when they ceased to be true, when (with the release of *John Wesley Harding*) they began to 'sentimentalise the family, legalised sex and the home, in ways wholly supportive of the dominant ideology'. The implication here – an implication embedded deep in rock criticism – is that all songs have to be measured against the principles of lyrical realism. The problem for Dylan and the other 1960s rock stars arose when they began to make music according to the logic of commercial entertainment, for, as Eisler had put it, entertainment music

> expresses a mendacious optimism that is absolutely unjustified, a flat pseudo-humanity, something like 'Aren't we all?' a stuffy petit-bourgeois eroticism to put you off. Feeling is replaced by sentimentality, strength by bombast, humour by what I would call silliness. It is stupid to the highest degree.[27]

**Realism**

At its simplest, the theory of lyrical realism means asserting a

85

*Simon Frith*

direct relationship between a lyric and the social or emotional condition it describes and represents. Folk song studies, for example, work with a historical version of reflection theory: they assume that folk songs are a historical record of popular consciousness. Thus Roy Palmer describes orally transmitted folk songs as 'the real voice of the people who lived in the past', and folk ballads as 'a means of self-expression; this was an art form truly in the idiom of the people'. With the development of industrial capitalism, according to A.L. Lloyd, 'the song-proper becomes the most characteristic lyrical form through which the common people express their fantasies, their codes, their aspirations', and folk realism was not just a matter of accurate description and convincing narrative. Songs were about hopes as well as facts.

> Generally the folk song makers chose to express their longing
> by transposing the world on to an imaginative plane, not trying
> to escape from it, but colouring it with fantasy, turning bitter,
> even brutal facts of life into something beautiful, tragic,
> honourable, so that when singer and listeners return to reality
> at the end of the song, the environment is not changed but they
> are better fitted to grapple with it.[28]

The question is: how does folk 'consolation' differ from pop 'escapism'? The answer lies in the modes of production involved: folk songs were authentic fantasies because they sprang from the people themselves; they weren't commodities. If certain folk images and phrases recur ('lyrical floaters', Lloyd calls them) these are not clichés (like the equivalent floaters in pop songs) but mark, rather, the anonymous, spontaneous, communal process in which folk songs are made. Lloyd continually contrasts the 'reality and truth' of folk lyrics with the 'banal stereotype of lower-class life and limited range of sickly bourgeois fantasies that the by-now powerful entertainment industry offers its audiences to suck on like a sugared rubber teat', but such comparisons rest almost exclusively on an argument about production.[29]

The problem of this 'sentimental socialist-realist' argument is its circularity: folk 'authenticity' is rooted in folk songs' 'real' origins, but we recognise these origins by the songs' authenticity and, in practice, the assessment of a song's realism is an assessment of its use of assumed *conventions* of realism. Folk song collections are folk song selections, and, to be chosen as authentic, songs have to

*Why do songs have words?*

meet literary or political criteria – authenticity lies in a particular use of language, a particular treatment of narrative and imagery a particular ideological position. The problem, then, is not whether folk songs *did* reflect real social conditions, but why some such reflections are taken by collectors to be authentic, some not. Whose ideology is reflected in such definitions of folk 'realism'?[30]

Authenticity is a political problem, and the history of folk music is a history of the struggle among folk collectors to claim folk meanings for themselves, as folk songs are examined for their 'true working-class views', for their expressions of 'organic community', for their signs of nationalism. For a Marxist like Dave Harker, some 'folk' songs are inauthentic because they obviously (from their use of language) weren't written or transmitted by working-class people themselves; others are judged inauthentic because of their ideological content, their use not of bourgeois language but of bourgeois ideas. Left-wing intellectuals can write authentic working-class songs (though not working-class themselves) as long as they represent the *real* reality of the working class – Alex Glasgow, for example, penetrates 'the elements of bourgeois ideology which have penetrated working-class culture'.[31]

This argument challenges the usual measure of folk realism, its relationship to common sense, and raises a crucial question: is lyrical realism a matter of accurate surface description or does it mean getting behind appearances, challenging given cultural forms? Taylor and Laing argue that 'cultural production occurs always in relation to ideology and not to the "real world"', and I want to examine the implications of this by looking at the blues.[32]

The original blues analysts assumed, like folk theorists generally, that the blues could be read as the direct account of their singers' and listeners' lives. Paul Oliver, for example, treated blues lyrics as a form of social history. The blues reflected American social conditions and personal responses to those conditions. They gave 'a glimpse of what it must mean to be one among the many rejected; homeless migrants – to be one single unit in the impersonal statistics that represent millions of rootless men and women.'[33]

Charles Keil read post-war urban blues lyrics similarly, as the direct expression of their singers' attempts to handle conditions in the new urban ghettos. He suggested that

> a more detailed analysis of blues lyrics might make it possible to describe with greater insight the changes in male roles within

87

*Simon Frith*

the Negro community as defined by Negroes at various levels of
socio-economic status and mobility within the lower class.
Certainly, the lyric content of city, urban and soul blues also
reflects varying sorts of adjustment to urban conditions
generally. A thorough analysis of a large body of blues lyrics
from the various genres would help to clarify these patterns of
adjustment and the attitudinal sets that accompany those
patterns.[34]

The blues, according to Oliver, was 'a genuine form of
expression revealing America's gaunt structure without a decorative facade'. In its treatment of love and sex the blues was
'forthright and uncompromising. There is no concealment and no
use of oblique references.' Blues were expressed in realistic words,
uninhibited words, words which were 'a natural transposition of
the everyday language of both users and hearers'. Even blues'
fancy terms, its rich store of imagery, were derived from everyday
life – the blues was a 'tough poetry', a 'rough poetry'. In the words
of Francis Newton, blues songs are not poetic 'because the singer
wants to express himself or herself in a poetic manner', but
because 'he or she wants to say what has to be said as best it can'.
The poetic effects 'arise naturally out of the repetitive pattern of
ordinary popular speech.'[35]

Linton Kwesi Johnson makes similar points about Jamaican
lyrics. Jamaican music, he writes,

is the *spiritual expression* of the *historical experience* of the
Afro-Jamaican. In making the music, the musicians themselves
enter a common stream of consciousness, and what they create
is an invitation to the listeners to be entered into that
consciousness – which is also the consciousness of their people.
The feel of the music is the feel of their common history, the
burden of their history; their suffering and their woe; their
endurance and their strength, their poverty and their pain.[36]

Johnson stresses the spiritual aspects of this process – 'through
music, dreams are unveiled, souls exorcised, tensions canalized,
strength realised', and notes the way in which shared religious
metaphors of hope and damnation enable Jamaican lyricists to
intensify their political comment. (Rastafarian songs draw on the
store of religio-political imagery accumulated by black American

*Why do songs have words?*

spirituals – 'Babylon' as a symbol of slavery and white oppression, for example.)[37]

Black songs don't just describe an experience, but symbolise and thus politicise it. For Newton, the lyrical world of the blues was 'tragic and helpless' – 'its fundamental assumption is that men and women live life as it comes; or if they cannot stand that they must die.' Johnson, by contrast, argues that in Jamaican music, 'Consciously setting out to transform the consciousness of the sufferer, to politicise him culturally through music, song and poetry, the lyricist contributes to the continuing struggle of the oppressed.'[38]

We're back to the original question in a new form: does 'realism' mean an acceptance of one's lot or a struggle against it, the imagination of alternatives? And there is a new question too. If blues lyrics express the suffering of an oppressed people, express them realistically, why do we enjoy them? In the words of Paul Garon, 'how is it that we gain definite pleasure by identifying with the singers' *sadness*?'[39]

Garon suggests that the blues, like all poetry, gives pleasure 'through its use of images, convulsive images, images of the fantastic and the marvellous, images of *desire*'. Blues power comes from its 'fantastic' not its 'realistic' elements. What makes a blues song poetic is not its description 'without facade', but the game it plays with language itself. Take a simple erotic blues like 'You Can't Sleep In My Bed':

You're too big to be cute, and I don't think you're clean,
You're the damnest looking thing that I have ever seen.

What you got in mind ain't gonna happen today
Get off my bed, how in the world did you get that way?
                    (Mary Dixon, 'You Can't Sleep In My Bed')

The point of this song is not its acceptance of the 'non-ideal' sexuality of real life, but its humour – the humour of its tone of voice, its descriptive terms – and humour involves not just the acceptance of reality, but also its mockery. Humour is a form of *refusal*. The blues singer, in short, 'functions as a poet through his or her refusal to accept the degradation of daily life.' In Bessie Smith's 'Empty Bed Blues', to give another example, her emotional plight is described 'realistically', but this description is

89

*Simon Frith*

invigorated, made pleasurable, by the fanciful pursuit of a sexual language:

> Bought me a coffee grinder,
> The best one I could find.
> Bought me a coffee grinder,
> The best one I could find.
> Oh, he could grind my coffee,
> 'Cause he had a brand-new grind.
>
> He's a deep, deep diver,
> With a stroke that can't go wrong.
> He's a deep, deep diver,
> With a stroke that can't go wrong.
> Oh, he can touch the bottom,
> And his wind holds out so long.
>
> He boiled first my cabbage,
> And he made it awful hot.
> He boiled first my cabbage,
> And he made it awful hot.
> When he put in the bacon,
> It overflowed the pot.
>
> (Bessie Smith, 'Empty Bed Blues')

Refusal doesn't have to be expressed in political, ideological or even collective terms and, indeed, for Garon, individualism is the essence of blues poetry: 'the essence of the blues is not to be found in the daily life with which it deals, but in the way such life is critically focused on and imaginatively transformed.' Blues lyrics work not as spontaneous expression and natural language but through individual imaginations. Garon attacks the argument that 'it is only through "realism" ("socialist" or otherwise) that human desires find their most exalted expression'. The blues is poetry, rather, in so far as it is *not* simply documentary, 'for it is poetry that seeks to illuminate and realise the desires of all men and women.'[40]

Ames had earlier argued that

> regardless of the attitudes of any individual singer, the objective social necessity of American Negro songs over a period of time was to create forms, patterns, habits and styles which would conceal the singer. Perhaps the commonest technique of

*Why do songs have words?*

concealment has been to disguise meaning in some kind of fantastic, symbolical or nonsensical clothing.[41]

Irony, rather than direct description, is the essence of blues realism, and Garon suggests that the techniques involved give blues lyricists their poetic potential, their ability to 'eroticise everyday life', to use language itself to shock and shake the dominant discourse:

New modes of poetic action, new networks of analogy, new possibilities of expression all help formulate the nature of the supersession of reality, the transformation of everyday life as it encumbers us today, the unfolding and eventual triumph of the marvellous.[42]

Ian Hoare makes a related point about soul songs. The soul singer, like the blues singer, expresses 'personal feelings in a very public manner, stating the problems and drawing the audience together in a recognition that these problems are in many ways shared', and soul is, again, a form of realism – 'the grassroots strength of soul love lyrics lies partly in the fact that the most indulgent pledges of devotion are characteristically accompanied by a resilient sexual and economic realism.' But Hoare goes on to suggest that soul lyricists' 'realism' is simply a frame for their use of pop's romantic conventions – 'the containment of the other-worldly in the worldly is close to the essence of the soul tradition.' Soul songs are not simple statements – life is like *this* – but involve a commentary on the terms of pop romanticism itself.[43] A song like the Temptations' 'Papa Was A Rollin' Stone' gets its punch (and its pleasure) from its punning use of language rather than from its descriptive truth:

Papa was a rollin' stone,
Wherever he lay his hat was his home,
And when he died,
All he left us was
Alone.
                    (The Temptations, 'Papa Was A Rollin' Stone')

One of Britain's first jazz critics, Iain Lang, threw away the remark in 1943 that 'there is much material in the blues for a Cambridge connoisseur of poetic ambiguity', and his point was

*Simon Frith*

that it was precisely blues realism, its use of everyday black talk, that made it so poetically interesting – the blues is popular music's most literary form, contains the most sophisticated explorations of the rhythmic, metaphoric and playful possibilities of language itself. And blues singers' use of the vernacular doesn't make them simply vehicles for some sort of spontaneous collective composition – if the blues are a form of poetry, then blues writers are poets, self-conscious, individual, more or less gifted in their uses of words.[44]

There's a tension in jazz criticism, then, between theorists who root blues power in the general, diffuse social realism of black popular culture, and critics who search out individual writers for particular praise or blame. It is a tension which has re-emerged, more recently, in white critical commentaries on 'rap', the contemporary Afro-American use of the rhythms of street-corner gossip, threat and argument. Rap is rooted in a long history of jousting talk, formalised in a variety of names – 'signification', the Dozens, the Toast, the Jones.[45] These are rituals of name calling, boasting and insult, in which rhyme, beat and vocal inflection carry as much meaning as the words themselves, and the irony is that while the participants are clearly engaged in individual competition – some people are simply better at the Dozens than others – white fans admire rap as a spontaneous, 'natural' black youth form. Unless acts claim specifically to *be* poets (like some Jamaican dub performers or a relatively arty New York act like the Last Poets) they are not heard to write poetry, and rock fans have always gone along with the idea that 'naturally' realistic forms (folk, blues, soul, rap) have to be distinguished from 'art' forms, which are 'original', elaborate, and rooted in personal vision and control.[46]

From the start, rock's claim to a superior pop status rested on the argument that rock songwriters (unlike the Brill Building hacks and folk and blues circuit 'primitives') were, indeed, poets. Beginning with Richard Goldstein's *The Poetry of Rock* in 1969, there has been a slew of pompous rock anthologies, and while Goldstein had the grace to include rock 'n' roll writers like Chuck Berry and Leiber/Stoller, subsequent anthologists have been quite clear that 1960s rock lyrics represented something qualitatively remarkable in pop history:

Despite the fertile sources on which rock music of the 1950s drew, it was musically innovative and vibrant but lyrically almost unrelievedly banal and trivial. If it contained any poetry at all, that poetry was pedestrian doggerel full of unrefined

92

*Why do songs have words?*

slang and trite neoromantic convention. But in the early 1960s there burst upon the scene a number of exceptionally talented artists, perhaps even poets, who managed to bring together in various degrees all the many elements of what we now call rock and to make something of quality.[47]

What is most striking about anthologies of rock poetry, though, is their consensus – no black songs, no country music, no Lou Reed even. Rock 'poets' are recognised by a particular sort of self-consciousness; their status rests not on their approach to words but on the types of word they use; rock poetry is a matter of planting poetic clues. Ian Hoare compares the Four Tops' 'Reach Out I'll Be There' and Bob Dylan's 'Queen Jane Approximately'. The Four Tops sang:

When you feel hurt and about to give up
'Cause your best just ain't good enough . . .
. . . Reach out, I'll be there.
                    (The Four Tops, 'Reach Out I'll Be There')

Dylan sang:

When all of your advisers heave their plastic
At your feet to convince you of your pain . . .
. . . Won't you come see me, Queen Jane?
                    (Bob Dylan, 'Queen Jane Approximately')

Dylan is the poet because his images are personal and obscure rather than direct or commonplace – his words are not plain, and the rock singer/songwriters who emerged from folk clubs in the 1960s followed his seminal example, drawing words from classic balladry, from the beat poets, from 150 years of Bohemian romantic verse.[48]

Rock 'poetry' opened up possibilities of lyrical banality of which Tin Pan Alley had never even dreamt, but for observing academics it seemed to suggest a new pop seriousness – 'the jingles and vapid love lyrics' had evolved into a genuinely 'mystical vision'.[49] This was to suggest a new criterion of lyrical realism – truth-to-personal-experience or truth-to-feeling, a truth measured by the private use of words, the self-conscious use of language. And truth-to-feeling became a measure of the listener too. 'True songs', wrote *Rolling Stone* record editor Paul Nelson, are 'songs

*Simon Frith*

that hit me straight in the heart'. Nelson quotes the opening stanza
of Jackson Browne's 'Farther On':

> In my early years I hid my tears
> And passed my days alone,
> Adrift on an ocean of loneliness
> My dreams like nets were thrown,
> To catch the love that I'd heard of
> In books and films and songs,
> Now there's a world of illusion and fantasy
> In the place where the real world belongs.
> (Jackson Browne, 'Farther On')

This song of illusion and disillusion illustrates numerous singer/
songwriter techniques – Browne uses 'poetic' terms like 'adrift', an
extended self-consciously literary metaphor, the 'ocean of loneliness', and an intimate mode of address – but for Nelson the point
of the song is not its technique but its effect. Alan Lomax had once
written that the 'authentic' folk singer had to 'experience the
feelings that lie behind his art'. For Nelson the good rock singer
made the listener experience those feelings too. He treasured the
Jackson Browne song because 'when I first heard it I was
absolutely unable to put any space between myself and someone
else's childhood'.[50]

## Making meaning

All comparisons of lyrical realism and lyrical banality assume that
songs differ in their effects – effects which can be read off good and
bad words. For mass culture critics, as we've seen, the problem of
pop is that fans treat *all* songs as if they were real and have a false
view of life accordingly. Pop lyricists themselves have always
found this suggestion bemusing. Ira Gershwin, for example, made
his own mocking reply to his critics:

> 'Every night I dream a little dream,/And of course Prince
> Charming is the theme . . . .' One is warned that this sort of
> romantic whimwham builds up 'an enormous amount of
> unrealistic idealisation – the creation in one's mind, as the
> object of love's search, of a dream girl (or dream boy) the
> fleshly counterpart of which never existed on earth'. Sooner or
> later, unhappily, the girl chances on a Mr Right who, in turn, is

*Why do songs have words?*

certain she is Miss Inevitable; and, both being under the influence of 'My Heart Stood Still' (which even advocates love at first sight) they are quickly in each other's arms, taxiing to City Hall for a marriage license. On the way he sings 'Blue Room' to her – she 'My Blue Heaven' to him. But, alas, this enchanted twosome is wholly unaware of the costs of rent, furniture, food, dentist, doctor, diaper service, and other necessities. There is no indication in the vocalising 'that, having found the dream-girl or dream-man, one's problems are just beginning'. It naturally follows that soon the marriage won't work out, when 'disenchantment, frustration' and 'self-pity' set in. Shortly after, they buy paper dolls, not for each other, but ones they can call their own. This comfort is, however, temporary. Subsequently, he, helpless, is in the gutters of Skid Row; she, hopeless, in a mental institution.[51]

Back in 1950 David Riesman had argued that 'the same or virtually the same popular culture materials are used by audiences in radically different ways and for radically different purposes'. Riesman accepted the critics' description of pop's lyrical message ('a picture of adolescence in America as a happy-go-lucky time of haphazard behaviour, jitterbug parlance, coke-bar sprees, and "blues" that are not really blue') but distinguished between the majority of pop fans, who took the message for granted but didn't listen to it, and a minority of 'rebels', who heard the message but rejected it.[52]

Subsequent empirical research has confirmed Riesman's scepticism about the importance of song words, and by the end of the 1960s Norman Denzin was arguing that pop audiences only listened to the beat and melody, the *sound* of a record, anyway – the 'meaning of pop' was the sense listeners made of songs for themselves; it could not be read off lyrics as an objective 'social fact'.[53]

This argument was the norm for the sociology of pop and rock in the 1970s. Frith, for example, ignored lyrical analysis altogether and simply assumed that the meaning of music could be deduced from its users' characteristics. In the USA empirical audience studies measured pop fans' responses to the words of their favourite songs quantitatively. Robinson and Hirsch concluded from a survey of Michigan high school students that 'the vast majority of teenage listeners are unaware of what the lyrics of hit protest songs are about', and a follow-up survey of college

*Simon Frith*

students suggested that the 'effectiveness' of song messages was limited: the majority of listeners had neither noticed nor understood the words of 'Eve of Destruction' or 'The Universal Soldier', and the minority who did follow the words weren't convinced by them.[54]

The implication of this sort of research (which continues to fill the pages of *Popular Music and Society*) is that changes in lyrical content cannot be explained by reference to consumer 'moods', and American sociologists have turned for explanations instead to changing modes of lyrical production, to what's happening in the record industry, the source of the songs. Paul Hirsch, for example, argues that during the period 1940 to 1970 song performers gained control of their material while the music industry's censors lost it, and Peterson and Berger extend this analysis (looking at 'the manufacture of lyrics' since 1750!), concluding that 'the outspoken rock lyric of the 1960s (and the counter-culture it animated) were largely unintended byproducts of earlier mundane changes in technology, industry structure and marketing'. In the rock era airwaves and studios had been opened to competition, and

> the proliferation of companies competing for audience attention together with the broadening range of radio programming formats of the 1950s reversed the process which had created the Tin Pan Alley formula tune in the previous era of oligopoly. With competition, there was a search for lyrics that would be ever more daring in exposing the old taboo topics of sex, race, drugs, social class, political commentary, and alternatives to middle-class standards generally.[55]

The changing music did change the audience too ('by gradually creating a self-conscious teen generation') but the general point is that 'the amount of diversity of sentiments in popular music lyrics correlates directly with the number of independent units producing songs', and more recent research has shown how a tightening of corporate control (in the country music industry) leads to a narrowing range of song forms.[56]

In this account of pop the banality of Tin Pan Alley words is taken for granted and explained in terms of the organisation of their production, but pop is defended from charges of corruption on the grounds that nobody listens to the words anyway. This became one way in which 'authentic' rock was distinguished from its commercial, degenerate versions – real rock lyrics matter

96

*Why do songs have words?*

because they can be treated as poetry or politics, involve social commentary or truth-to-feeling; bad rock words are just drivel. What most interests me about this position, though, are the questions it begs. Mainstream, commercial pop lyrics – silly love songs – may not 'matter' to their listeners like the best rock words do, but they're not therefore insignificant. Popular music is a song form; words are a reason why people buy records; instrumental hits remain unusual – to paraphrase Marilyn Monroe in *Seven Year Itch*, you can always tell classical music: 'it's got no vocals!' People may not listen to most pop songs as 'messages' (the way they're presented in all that American empirical research) and the average pop lyric may have none of the qualities of rock realism or poetry, but the biggest-selling music magazine in Britain by far is still *Smash Hits*, a picture paper organised around the words of the latest chart entries, and so the question remains: why and how do song words (banal words, unreal words, routine words) work?

### The poetry of pop

In songs, words are the sign of a voice. A song is always a performance and song words are always spoken out, heard in someone's accent. Songs are more like plays than poems; song words work as speech and speech acts, bearing meaning not just semantically, but also as structures of sound that are direct signs of emotion and marks of character. Singers use non-verbal as well as verbal devices to make their points – emphases, sighs, hesitations, changes of tone; lyrics involve pleas, sneers and commands as well as statements and messages and stories (which is why singers like the Beatles and Bob Dylan in Europe in the 1960s would have profound significance for listeners who didn't understand a word they were singing).[57]

I don't have the space here to describe how these techniques work in particular songs but from the work that has been done it is possible to draw some general conclusions.[58] First, *in analysing song words we must refer to performing conventions which are used to construct our sense of both their singers and ourselves, as listeners*. It's not just what they sing, but the way they sing it that determines what a singer means to us and how we are placed, as an audience, in relationship to them. Take, as an example, the way sexual identities are defined in pop songs. All pop singers, male and female, have to express emotion. Their task is to make public performance a private revelation. Singers can do this because the

97

*Simon Frith*

voice is an apparently transparent reflection of feeling: it is the sound of the voice, not the words sung, which suggests what a singer *really* means. In fact, there's nothing natural about the singing voice at all (compare the popular vocal sounds of Britain and Italy, say, or the USA and Iran), and so the conventions of male and female pop singing are different, reflect general assumptions about the differences between women and men.

The female voice in Anglo-American pop has usually stood for intimacy and artlessness – this is the link which has given women access to pop (they have been excluded from most other productive roles). We hear women as better able than men to articulate emotion because femininity is defined in emotional terms. The public world is masculine and there is no agreement about how public, unemotional women should sound (which is why the tone of Margaret Thatcher's voice keeps changing). By the same token, the intimate male voice is unmasculine, unnatural. In pop this is registered by the recurrent use of the falsetto, by the high-pitched, strained vocal that has been a feature of mainstream rock singing from Yes to the Police.

The conventions of female pop singing have both reflected and shaped the idea of femininity as something decorative and wistful secret and available, addressed, by its very nature, at men. The voice is so intimately connected with the person that sound and image cannot be separated in this respect. As a man, I've always taken it for granted that rock performances address male desires, reflect male fantasies in their connections of music and dance and sexuality. The first time I saw a women's band perform for women I was made physically uneasy by the sense of exclusion, became suddenly aware how popular music works as a social event. Its cultural (and commercial) purpose is to put together an audience, to construct a sense of 'us' and 'them'. Such pop consciousness depends primarily on the use of voices to express the identity at issue.

In raising questions of identity and audience I am, implicitly, raising questions of genre – different people use different musics to experience (or fantasise) different sorts of community; different pop forms (disco, punk, country, rock, etc.) engage their listeners in different narratives of desire – compare, for example, the different uses of male/female duets in soul and country music: the former use the voices to intensify feeling, the latter to flatten it. In soul music realism is marked by singers' inarticulacy – they are overcome by their feelings – and so duets, the interplay of male

*Why do songs have words?*

and female sounds, add a further erotic charge to a love song. In country music realism is marked by singers' small talk – the recognition of everyday life – and so duets, domestic conversations, are used to add further credibility to the idea that we're eavesdropping on real life (an effect heightened when, as is often the case, the couples *are* lovers/married/divorced).

The immediate critical task for the sociology of popular music is systematic genre analysis[59] – how do words and voices work differently for different types of pop and audience? – but there is a second general point to make about all pop songs: *they work on ordinary language*. What interests me here is not what's meant by 'ordinary' (as different genres draw on different communal terms and images and codes) but what's meant by 'work'. Songs aren't just any old speech act – by putting words to music, songwriters give them a new sort of resonance and power. Lyrics, as Langdon Winner once put it, can 'set words and the world spinning in a perpetual dance'.[60]

'In the best of songs,' according to Christopher Ricks, 'there is something which is partly about what it is to write a song, without in any way doing away with the fact that it is about things other than the song.' Sociologists of pop have been so concerned with these 'other things' – lyrical content, truth and realism – that they have neglected to analyse the ways in which songs are about themselves, about language. Tin Pan Alley songs are customarily dismissed as art (in those anthologies of rock poetry, for example), but they have their own literary importance. Bernard Bergonzi describes the resonance that pop lyrics had for writers in the 1930s, for example. W.H. Auden, Louis McNeice and Graham Greene all wrote and used such songs for their own purposes. Brecht was similarly concerned to draw on 'the directness of popular songs', and for him the appeal of pop lyrics lay in their ability to open up language – Brecht used the rhymes and rhythms of popular clichés to say significant things *and* to expose the commonsense phrases in which such things are usually said. As David Lodge writes of slang generally,

> Slang is the poetry of ordinary speech in a precise linguistic sense; it draws attention to itself *qua* language, by deviating from accepted linguistic norms, substituting figurative expressions for literal ones, and thus 'defamiliarises' the concept it signifies.[61]

99

*Simon Frith*

'What could a popular song be which scorned or snubbed cliché?' asks Ricks, and Clive James, another literary pop critic, answers that the best lyricists are bound to celebrate common speech. The Beatles' genius, for example, was that they 'could take a well-worn phrase and make it new again'. They could spot the 'pressure points' of language, 'the syllables that locked a phrase up and were begging to be prodded'.

> The sudden shift of weight to an unexpected place continually brought the listener's attention to the language itself, engendering a startled awareness of the essentially poetic nature of flat phrases he'd been living with for years.[62]

The songwriter's art, suggests James, is to hear 'the spoken language as a poem', to cherish words 'not for their sense alone but for their poise and balance', and this is a matter of rhythm too – the rhythm of speech. If, in many pop songs, the regularity of the beat seems to reduce the lyrics to doggerel, on the other hand, as Roy Fuller puts it, music can 'discover subtleties in the most commonplace of words'. Fuller gives the example of George Gershwin's setting of the line, 'how long has this been going on?'

> When he has to set that, a line of regular iambic tetrameter, surely he sees how banal it would be to emphasise the word 'this' as the underlying stress pattern of the words requires:
> 'Hŏw lóng hăs thís bĕen góiňg ón?'
> What he does is to give the line three beats only – on 'long', the first syllable of 'going' and on 'on'. The three middle words, including the word 'this', are unaccented, giving the effect of a little skip in the middle of the line –
> 'Hŏw lońg hăs thĭs bĕen góiňg ón?'
> It is the action itself and the action's duration that Gershwin brings out, and how right it seems when he does it.[63]

### Last words

In his study of Buddy Holly, Dave Laing suggests that pop and rock critics need a musical equivalent of the film critics' distinction between *auteurs* and *metteurs en scene*:

> The musical equivalent of the *metteur en scene* is the performer who regards a song as an actor does his part – as something to

100

*Why do songs have words?*

be expressed, something to get across. His aim is to render the lyric faithfully. The vocal style of the singer is determined almost entirely by the emotional connotations of the words. The approach of the rock *auteur* however, is determined not by the unique features of the song but by his personal style, the ensemble of vocal effects that characterise the whole body of his work.[64]

Ever since rock distinguished itself from pop in the late 1960s, *auteurs* have been regarded as superior to *metteurs* and lyrics have been analysed in terms of *auteur* theory. But Laing's point is that the appeal of rock *auteurs* is that their meaning is *not* organised around their words. The appeal of Buddy Holly's music, for example, 'does not lie in what he says, in the situations his songs portray, but in the exceptional nature of his singing style and its instrumental accompaniment.' My conclusion from this is that song words matter most, as words, when they are *not* part of an *auteur*-ial unity, when they are still open to interpretation – not just by their singers, but by their listeners too. Billie Holiday, the greatest *metteur* Tin Pan Alley pop had, wrote:

Young kids always ask me what my style derived from and how it evolved and all that. What can I tell them? If you find a tune and it's got something to do with you, you don't have to evolve anything. You just feel it, and when you sing it other people feel something too.[65]

The pleasure of pop is that we can 'feel' tunes, perform them, in imagination, for ourselves. In a culture in which few people make music but everyone makes conversation, access to songs is primarily through their words. If music gives lyrics their linguistic vitality, lyrics give songs their social *use*.

This was, indeed, the conclusion that Donald Horton reached from his original content analysis of the lyrical drama of courtship. 'The popular song,' he wrote, 'provides a conventional language for use in dating.' The 'dialectic' of love involved in pop songs – the conversational tone, the appeal from one partner to another – was precisely what made them useful for couples negotiating their own path through the stages of a relationship. Most people lacked skill in 'the verbal expression of profound feelings' and so a public, impersonal love poetry was 'a useful – indeed a necessary alternative'. The singer became a 'mutual messenger' for young

101

*Simon Frith*

lovers, and pop songs were about emotional possibilities. The singer functioned 'in dramatising these songs to show the appropriate gestures, tone of voice, emotional expression – in short the stage directions for transforming mere verse into personal expression'.[66]

Pop love songs don't 'reflect' emotions, then, but give people the romantic terms in which to articulate and so experience their emotions. Elvis Costello once suggested that

> Most people are confused regarding their identities, or how they feel, particularly about love. They're confused because they're not given a voice, they don't have many songs written for or about them. On the one hand there's 'I love you, the sky is blue,' or total desolation, and in between there's a lack of anything. And it's never that clear-cut. There's a dishonesty in so much pop – written, possibly with an honest intent – all that starry stuff. I believe I fulfill the role of writing songs that aren't starry eyed all the time.[67]

Pop song lyrics have been criticised in these terms since the 1920s; they've been condemned for their romantic fictions, their 'exclusion of reality'. But that doesn't mean that we must, like the mass culture critics, listen to pop songs as if they were sociology. Costello's point is that what is at issue is fantasy – the problem of romantic ideology is not that it is false to life, but that it is the truth against which most people measure their desires. We need still to heed, therefore, the words of Marcel Proust:

> Pour out your curses on bad music, but not your contempt! The more bad music is played or sung, the more it is filled with tears, with human tears. It has a place low down in the history of art, but high up in the history of the emotions of the human community. Respect for ill music is not in itself a form of charity, it is much more the awareness of the social role of music. The people always have the same messengers and bearers of bad tidings in times of calamity and radiant happiness – bad musicians . . . . A book of poor melodies, dog-eared from much use, should touch us like a town or a tomb. What does it matter that the houses have no style, or that the gravestones disappear beneath stupid inscriptions?[68]

102

*Why do songs have words?*

## Notes

1 Lovat Dickson: *Radclyffe Hall at the Well of Loneliness*, Collins, London, 1975, pp. 45–6.
2 See Ian Whitcomb: *After the Ball*, Penguin, Harmondsworth, 1972, and Charlie Gillett: *The Sound of the City*, Souvenir Press, London, 1971.
3 Terms used by an American congressional Committee on song publishing, cited in K. Peter Etzkorn: 'On esthetic standards and reference groups of popular songwriters', *Sociological Inquiry*, vol. 36, no. 1, 1966, pp. 39–47.
4 K. Peter Etzkorn: 'Social context of songwriters in the United States', *Ethnomusicology*, vol. VII, no. 2, 1963, pp. 103–4.
5 J.G. Peatman: 'Radio and popular music', in P.F. Lazersfeld and F. Stanton (eds): *Radio Research*, Duell, Sloan & Pearce, New York, 1942–3.
6 H.F. Mooney: 'Song, singers and society, 1890–1954', *American Quarterly*, vol. 6, 1954, p. 226.
7 H.F. Mooney: 'Popular music since the 1920s', *American Quarterly*, vol. 20, 1968.
8 Mooney, op. cit., 1954, p. 232.
9 See D. Horton: 'The dialogue of courtship in popular song', *American Journal of Sociology*, vol. 62, 1957; J.T. Carey: 'Changing courtship patterns in the popular song', *American Journal of Sociology*, vol. 74, 1969; R.R. Cole: 'Top songs in the sixties: a content analysis', *American Behavioural Scientist*, vol. 14, 1971. In recent years the most prolific content analyst, B. Lee Cooper, has traced a variety of ideological issues through pop and rock songs, though he seems less concerned to chart changing values than to point to the recurring problems of American ideology. For a summary account of his work see his *A Resource Guide to Themes in Contemporary American Song Lyrics*, Greenwood, London, 1986. Very little similar work seems to have been done in Britain but for the 1950s/1960s contrast see Antony Bicat: 'Fifties children: sixties people', in V. Bogdanor and R. Skidelski (eds): *The Age of Affluence 1957–64*, Macmillan, London, 1970, and for the rock/punk contrast in the 1970s see Dave Laing: *One Chord Wonders*, Open University Press, Milton Keynes, 1985, pp. 63–73.
10 For an interesting use of music hall material this way see G. Stedman Jones: 'Working-class culture and working-class politics in London 1870–1900', *Journal of Social History*, vol. 7, no. 4, 1974.
11 P. Di Maggio, R.A. Peterson and J. Esco: 'Country music: ballad of the silent majority', in R.S. Denisoff and R.A. Peterson (eds): *The Sounds of Social Change*, Rand McNally, Chicago, 1972.
12 M. Haralambos: *Right On: From Blues to Soul in Black America*, Eddison, London, 1974, p. 117.
13 Ibid., p. 125.
14 'Real closeness' is a term used by Richard Hoggart to distinguish authentic from commercial working-class ballads – see *The Uses of Literacy*, Penguin, Harmondsworth, 1958, pp. 223–4.
15 D. Hughes: 'Recorded music', in D. Thompson (ed.): *Discrimination and Popular Culture*, Penguin, Harmondsworth, 1964, p. 165.
16 Hoggart, op. cit., p. 229.
17 W. Mellers: *Music in a New Found Land*, Faber & Faber, London, 1964, p. 384.
18 E. Lee: *Music of the People*, Barrie & Jenkins, London, 1970, p. 250. For a Marxist reading of the 'genteely romantic' bourgeois ideology of British pop music until rock 'n' roll began to use blues and folk idioms that expressed 'bottom dog consciousness' and to 'speak for the excluded and rebellious', see

## Simon Frith

Eric Hobsbawm: *Industry and Empire*, Penguin, 'Harmondsworth, 1968, p. 284.

19 Dave Harker:*One for the Money*, Hutchinson, London, 1980, p. 48.

20 Ibid., p. 61.

21 T. Goddard, J. Pollock and M. Fudger: 'Popular music', in J. King and M. Stott (eds): *Is This Your Life?*, Virago, London, 1977, p. 143.

22 Germaine Greer: *The Female Eunuch*, Paladin, London, 1971, p. 164.

23 Hoggart, op.cit., p. 163.

24 Harker, op.cit., p. 129.

25 S.I. Hayakawa: 'Popular songs vs. the facts of life', *Etc.*, vol. 12, 1955, p. 84.

26 Francis Newton: *The Jazz Scene*, Penguin, Harmondworth, 1961, p. 162.

27 Hans Eisler: *A Rebel in Music*, International Publishers, New York, 1978, p. 191.

28 R. Palmer: *A Touch of the Times*, Penguin, Harmondsworth, 1974, pp. 8, 18, and A.L. Lloyd: *Folk Song in England*, Baladin, London, 1975, pp. 158, 170.

29 Lloyd, op.cit., p. 369.

30 For full discussion of these issues see Dave Harker: *Fake Song*, Open University Press, Milton Keynes, 1985, and Vic Gammon: 'Folk song collecting in Sussex and Surrey, 1843–1914', *History Workshop*, no. 10, 1980.

31 See Harker, op.cit., p. 189.

32 J. Taylor and D. Laing: 'Disco-pleasure-discourse', *Screen Education*, no. 31, 1979, p. 46.

33 Paul Oliver: *Meaning of the Blues*, Collier, New York, 1963, p. 68. And see Iain Lang: *Background of the Blues*, Workers' Music Association, London, 1943, and Samuel Charters: *The Poetry of the Blues*, Oak, New York, 1963.

34 Charles Keil: *Urban Blues*, University of Chicago Press, Chicago, 1966, p 74.

35 Oliver, op.cit., pp. 133–4, 140 and Newton, op.cit., pp. 145–6.

36 Linton Kwesi Johnson: 'Jamaican rebel music', *Race and Class*, no. 17, 1976, p. 398.

37 See R. Ames: 'Protest and irony in Negro folk song', *Science and Society*, vol. 14, 1949.

38 Newton, op.cit., p. 150 and Johnson, op.cit., p. 411.

39 Paul Garon: *Blues and the Poetic Spirit*, Eddison, London, 1975.

40 Ibid., pp. 21, 26, 76, 64.

41 Ames, op.cit., p. 197.

42 Garon, op.cit., p. 167.

43 Ian Hoare: 'Mighty Mighty Spade and Whitey: black lyrics and soul's interaction with white culture', in I. Hoare (ed.): *The Soul Book*, New York, 1975, pp. 157, 162.

44 Lang, op.cit., p. 39. For a suggestive general study of 'oral poetry' see Ruth Finnegan: *Oral Poetry*, Cambridge University Press, Cambridge, 1977.

45 See Claude Brown: 'The language of soul', in R. Resh (ed.): *Black America*, D.C. Heath, Lexington, 1969; Ulf Hannerz: *Soulside*, Columbia University Press, New York, 1969; Geneva Smitherman: *Talkin' and Testifyin'*, *The Language of Black America*, Houghton Mifflin, Boston, 1977; David Toop: *The Rap Attack*, Pluto, London, 1984.

46 For an unusually intelligent version of this argument see Peter Guaralnick: *Feel Like Going Home*, Vintage, New York, 1971, pp. 22–3.

47 David Pichaske: *Beowulf to the Beatles and Beyond*, Macmillan, New York, 1981, p. xiii (quoting the 1972 edition). And see Richard Goldstein: *The Poetry of Rock*, Bantam, New York, 1969; B.F. Groves and D.J. McBain: *Lyric Voices: Approaches to the Poetry of Contemporary Song*, John Wiley, New York, 1972; Bob Sarlin: *Turn It Up (I Can't Hear the Words)*, Simon & Schuster, New York, 1973; Matt Damsker (ed.): *Rock Voices! The Best Lyrics of an Era*, St Martins Press, New York, 1980.

*Why do songs have words?*

48  For a brilliantly detailed discussion of Dylan's poetic sources see Michael Gray:
    *Song and Dance Man: The Art of Bob Dylan*, Hamlyn, London, 1981.
49  R.R. Rosenstone: '"The Times they are A-Changing": the music of protest',
    *Annals of the American Academy of Political and Social Science*, no. 382, 1969.
      The English poet Thom Gunn, writing in 1967, suggested that the Beatles
    represented a completely new pop sensibility, and had at last seen off Tin Pan
    Alley, 'the fag-end of the Petrarchan tradition'. The change had come with the
    line 'I've been working like a dog'. 'As soon as that line had been written
    immense possibilities became apparent. For what lover in a Sinatra song *ever
    works at a job?*' (*The Listener*, 3 August 1967)
50  Paul Nelson: 'The pretender' in G. Marcus (ed.): *Stranded*, Knopf, New York,
    1979, p. 120.
51  Ira Gershwin: *Lyrics on Several Occasions*, Elm Tree Books, London, 1977,
    pp. 112–13.
52  David Riesman: 'Listening to popular music', *American Quàrterly*, vol. 2, 1950,
    pp. 360–1.
53  Norman Denzin: 'Problems in analysing elements of mass culture: notes on the
    popular song and other artistic productions', *American Journal of Sociology*,
    vol. 75, 1969. And see J. Johnstone and E. Katz: 'Youth and popular music: a
    study of taste', *American Journal of Sociology*, vol. 62, 1957.
54  J.P. Robinson and P.M. Hirsch: 'Teenage responses to rock and roll protest
    songs', in Denisoff and Peterson, op.cit., p. 231; R.S. Denisoff and M. Levine:
    'Brainwashing or background noise? The popular protest song', in the same
    colection; S. Frith: *The Sociology of Rock*, Constable, London, 1978.
55  Paul Hirsch: 'Sociological approaches to the pop music phenomenon',
    *American Behavioural Scientist*, vol. 14, 1971, and R.A. Peterson and
    D.G. Berger: 'Three eras in the manufacture of popular music lyrics', in
    Denisoff and Peterson, op.cit., pp. 283, 296.
56  Ibid., p. 298, and see J. Ryan and R.A. Peterson: 'The product image: the fate
    of creativity in country music songwriting', *Sage Annual Review of
    Communication Research*, vol. 10, 1982.
57  For a very interesting discussion of Bob Dylan's 'meaning' in Germany see
    Dennis Anderson: *The Hollow Horn: Bob Dylan's Reception in the US and
    Germany*, Hobo Press, Munich, 1981, chs 9, 20.
58  For detailed readings of lyrics in performance see, for example, the comparison
    of Kate Bush's 'The Kick Inside' and Millie Jackson's 'He Wants to Hear the
    Words', in S. Frith and A. McRobbie: 'Rock and sexuality', *Screen Education*,
    no. 29, 1978, and the psychoanalytic account of Buddy Holly's 'Peggy Sue' in B.
    Bradby and B. Torode: 'Pity Peggy Sue', *Popular Music*, vol. 4, 1984. For
    general discussions see S. Frith: *Sound Effects*, Pantheon, New York, 1981,
    pp. 34–38; Alan Durant: *Conditions of Music*, Macmillan, London, 1984,
    pp. 186–95, 201–11; and the introduction to Mark Booth: *The Experience of
    Song*, Yale University Press, New Haven, 1981.
59  This approach has been developed most interestingly in the Italian work of
    Franco Fabbri and Umberto Fiori. See, for example, Fabbri's 'A theory of
    musical genres: two applicatons', in D. Horn and P. Tagg (eds): *Popular Music
    Perspectives*, IASPM, Gothenburg and Exeter, 1982.
      From a continental European perspective one of the more intriguing aspects of
    contemporary pop lyrics is their use of a 'foreign' language, English. One of the
    defining features of the punk music that swept Europe in the late 1970s was its
    use of the different performers' 'native' tongues – the question rose as to what,
    in pop and rock, is a native tongue. Dave Laing suggests that even in Britain it
    meant bands determinedly *not* singing in 'American' – see Laing, op.cit.,
    pp. 54–9.
60  See L. Winner: 'Trout mask replica', in Marcus (ed.), op.cit.

*Simon Frith*

61  D. Lodge: 'Where it's at: California language', in L. Michaels and C. Ricks
    (eds): *The State of the Language*, University of California Press, Berkeley,
    1980, p. 506; and see C. Ricks: 'Clichés' in the same collection; B. Bergonzi:
    *Reading the Thirties*, Macmillan, London, 1978, ch. 6; and C. Ricks: 'Can this
    really be the end?', in E.M. Thompson (ed.): *Conclusions on the Wall: New
    Essays on Bob Dylan*, Thin Man, Manchester, 1980.
62  Clive James: 'The Beatles', *Cream*, October 1972.
63  Roy Fuller: *Professors and Gods*, André Deutsch, London, 1973, p. 86.
    Compare Ace's solution to the same problem in their hit song, 'How Long'.
    Their more maudlin emphasis is on the initial syllable: 'Hów lŏng, hăs this beĕn
    góiňg ŏn.'
      Stephen Sondheim suggests another example of the precise attention to words
    necessary in good lyric writing:

    > The opening line of *Porgy and Bess* by Dubose Heyward is 'Summertime
    > and the livin' is easy' – and that 'and' is worth a great deal of attention. I
    > would write 'Summertime when' but that 'and' sets up a tone, a whole poetic
    > tone, not to mention a whole kind of diction that is going to be used in the
    > play; an informal, uneducated diction and a stream of consciousness . . . .
    > The choices of 'and's and 'but's become almost traumatic as you are writing
    > a lyric – or should anyway – because each one weighs so much. (S. Sondheim:
    > 'Theatre Lyrics', in G. Martin (ed.): *Making Music*, Muller, London, 1983,
    > p. 75)

64  D. Laing: *Buddy Holly*, Studio Vista, London, 1971, pp. 58–9.
65  Quoted in Mellers, op.cit., p. 379.
66  Horton, op.cit., p. 577.
67  Elvis Costello interview in *New Musical Express*, 21 August 1982, p. 10. And
    see Steve Coombes: 'In the mood', *Times Educational Supplement*, 12 February
    1982, p. 23. He writes:

    > Writing for shows, thirties lyric writers were in both the best and worst
    > senses of the word in the business of creating fictions. The moods of their
    > lyrics do not reflect emotions they had actually felt nor that they expected
    > anyone to think that they had felt nor even that they expected anyone else to
    > feel for that matter. Nothing would have disturbed the cosmopolitan Cole
    > Porter more than the idea that people might think that he actually did sit and
    > moon over lost love – that emphatically was not his style. The moods of
    > thirties lyrics are about what you ought to have felt or more accurately what
    > you might like to have felt given the chance to think about it. Paradoxically,
    > then, the tone is at the same time extremely sophisticated yet highly
    > idealised.

68  Quoted in Eisler, op.cit., pp. 189–90.

# CHAPTER 15

# Hearing secret harmonies

The Polish musicologist Zofia Lissa has written that 'silent' films needed, in fact, to be accompanied by music for a variety of reasons – to cover the noise of the projector and the passing traffic, to maintain or switch moods more smoothly than early cutting and editing devices could, to give early cinema a veneer of respectability – but the point she makes that most interests me is that silence in a cinema is embarrassing.[1] This is obviously true nowadays – to show students silent films on a course is to call forth a shuffle of nervous feet, stifled giggles, stagy whispers – and it suggests one of the central use of popular music in this century: to conceal the furtive pleasure of indulging in private fantasies in public places.

In this chapter, I want to examine some of the ways in which film music works, but I must begin by setting my remarks in the framework of a more general comment on popular culture.

'Popular culture' describes culture in capitalist societies (elsewhere, 'folk culture' or even just 'culture' are adequate terms) and the most common way of looking at popular culture is therefore in terms of the production and consumption of commodities. The recurring twentieth-century question has been what is the relationship of 'art' and the market place; the recurring answer has been in terms of the opposition between high culture and mass culture – the place of popular culture in this couplet is unclear. One reason for this is that the high/mass culture typology actually muddles two

## 54 HIGH THEORY/LOW CULTURE

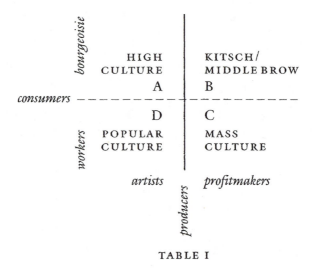

TABLE I

issues, production and consumption. This can be clarified by Table 1.

Most sociology is focused on A (high culture) and C (mass culture) but boxes B and D are equally interesting, especially given how thin most of the dividing lines really are. High culture very easily becomes middlebrow culture (the general move of the classical music tradition this century); mass culture and middlebrow culture are no more easily distinguished (how should Andrew Lloyd Webber's *Requiem* be classified?) than mass culture and popular culture, the usual focus for left-wing debate. At first glance the distinction between A and D, high and popular culture, seems sharper, but even here there are problems – how should post-war jazz be classified? the popular avant-garde more generally? All this table does is reveal how confident aesthetic judgements (A and D are good; B and C are bad) rest on muddled aesthetic categories.

My approach to popular culture depends, then, on scrapping this typology entirely. The concept 'mass culture', in particular, is supect both theoretically and historically. I prefer the notion of 'capitalist culture' – culture defined, that is, not in terms of the production and consumption of commodities (though this is involved) but as the way in which people deal with/symbolise/articulate/share/resist the *experience* of capitalism (including, but not exclusively, the ideological experience of capitalism). From this perspective the most important quality of capital is that it is in a state of premanent crisis; the experience of capitalism means, as Marshall Berman has argued, the experience of modernity. The logic of capital accumulation is a logic of cultural dynamism; divisions of labour and the labour process itself keep changing, as live labour is replaced by the dead labour embodied in machines; a constant flow of new products means the continual arousal of new needs. The contradiction of capitalist culture is that the need for social reproduction means a simultaneous emphasis on ideological stability, on tradition, history, established morality, common sense (hence the key significance of the family). For individuals living with capitalism, three 'issues of experience' need constant handling: (a) *issues of change and continuity* (think of the role of nostalgia in the mass media, from pop records to video games, its combination with fashion, novelty and 'progress'. Popular memory is one of the most important products of popular culture; popular pleasures involve experiences of both integration and disintegration); (b) *issues of identification and difference;* and (c) *issues of activity and passivity.*

Following up issues (b) and (c) it is clear that both high and popular culture are aspects of capitalist culture (and can only be understood in relationship to each other). Their distinction is not clean-cut and shifts historically – if high culture

## 56 HIGH THEORY/LOW CULTURE

has, on the whole, been used to articulate ruling class and bourgeois identity, popular culture has not generally just expressed working-class concerns – the *petit-bourgeoisie* and middle classes have had a crucial role in developing popular forms, in determining, that is, the ways in which culture produces poeple's sense of identity, their sense of who they are, where they belong. Popular culture produces 'the people', not vice versa, and, in subjective terms, what seems to be involved here is not identification as such (between fan and star, say) but a process of *recognition,* in which cultural form – tones of voice, jokiness, parody, a self-conscious dis-tancing, *play* with relationships of fantasy and reality – is as important as cultural content (this is certainly apparent in British popular culture, from children's comics to rock music to television 'soaps' and the daily press).

'Taste' involves, by definition, the idea of shared taste; to choose a programme or a record is to be like other people who choose that programme or record – this is part of what such choices are about (and choice differentiates one from people with different tastes too). All popular culture involves shared experience, however 'privatised' it seems; the tired contrast between the collective activity of watching a football match and the individual activity of watching television is indeed meaningless. It is through popular culture that we discover what shared experience means – hence the *Minder* effect (in south London, everyone now talks like Terry and Arthur) and more generally, the recurring phenomena of media cults. The most important ideological role of capitalist culture is to mobilise people to vote or to buy by 'placing' them, giving them a social identity through popular taste. What we need, as socialists, is a much clearer understanding of how this mobilisation works *and* fails, under what circum-stances cultural forms have an oppositional effect.

In this context the public/private distinction common in cultural sociology is hard to maintain. People do not have 'private' knowledge, particularly not private emotional knowledge, knowledge independent of public cultural meanings and experiences (think again, of the concept of 'taste', something that is not exactly public or private). The active/passive distinction (as in active production/passive consumption) is equally problematic. Popular culture involves choices, reasons, arguments – low theory – even in moments of consumption, and pleasure industries have more often responded to emerging organisations of taste then created them – most recently, for example, in the fad for health and fitness.

High culture critics traditionally put themselves on the side of the artist – their job is to explain the artist's vision/work from the artist's point of view (hence the cultural television programmes like the *South Bank Show*); popular culture critics identify with the consumers, ar openly involved in the struggle for the meaning of goods once they have reached the market. The resulting politics of pleasure cannot easily be separated, historically, from the politics of leisure, from struggles over education, time and space, cultural capital or from the question of signifying power – who can make meanings stick? Consider current debates about pornography, 'video nasties', and censorship. What does it mean when the BBC bans a record like 'Relax'?

It is a recent convention among left-wing cultural commentators, at least in the fields of film and popular music, to celebrate the works that are seen as most disruptive (punk, for example). Good art means art which promotes change; bad art confirms the status quo. Culture is identified with ideological reproduction; anything which makes such reproduction difficult – the avant-garde! – is dandy. But if it is capitalism that disrupts people's lives, reorganises their desires, then popular culture may articulate its most political class consciousness, its most revolutionary forms in its resistance to change, its statement of 'traditional' human values. This is to return us to the old-left folk argument but with a new twist: the question is how the constant cultural need to

58 HIGH THEORY/LOW CULTURE

look back to hold on, comes to be enmeshed, excitingly, dismayingly, with the drive towards *new* consumption?

I am not going to answer that question here, just use it to signal a plea that writers in popular film and television (and music) should take seriously their own experinces of the texts, their own contradictory positionings – should move, that is, from a high cultural to a popular cultural mode of analysis.

I will begin, then, with the Barry Manilow problem.[2] My question is not why is Manilow so successful, but why does his music have an *emotional* impact when he seems so personally anonymous, so uninteresting in terms of vocal style or arrangement? The first clue to his pop appeal is that he started his career as a commercial jingle writer, but I am sure that the reason for his impact – even the wariest listeners can feel their 'heart strings pulled' – is that he makes the sort of music that these days come at the end of a Hollywood film, writes the sort of song that plays as we leave the cinema and re-arrange our feelings.

Theme songs (rather than soundtrack excerpts) have been an important source of pop hits since the 1950s ('High Noon' is an obvious example, or Henri Mancini numbers like 'Moon River'), and this is clearly an aspect of how Hollywood film music is planned – part of the promotional drama surrounding a new James Bond film, for example, concerns who is going to be chosen to write and sing the theme tune, and in the 1960s traditional film scorers like Bernard Herrmann denounced the degeneration of film music into pop song. But if such songs have a straight commercial object – there is extra money to be made from pop (the American charts, in particular, have been dominated by film themes in recent years)[3] and a well-timed theme record release is an extremely effective film trailer – they have a filmic significance too, particularly given their function of closing a film. Theme songs work, first, as *summary,* they reprise a melody we have been hearing all through the film. Secondly, the songs capture the *mood* of an ending – romantic harmony, new wisdom, social uplift. And thirdly, theme songs often seem to have a built-in sense of sadness or *nostalgia:* the film is over, we have to withdraw from its experience, get 'back to reality'.

What interests me here, though, is not these musical functions as such, but the fact that *songs* are now conventionally used to perform these functions – music, that is, with voices and words neither of which need have anything to do with characters or dialogue in the film (usually, indeed, the only obvious link between a film and its song is the shared title and even that is becoming less common). The effect of this is that the song become a kind of *commentary* on the film: the singers represent us, the audience, and our response to the film, but also become our teachers, making sure we got the film's emotional message.

These songs do this by using pop's own emotional conventions and thus place films in a much wider framework of pop romance and pop common sense. The 1983 norm for such songs, for example, was the male/female duet, which enabled the music both to articularte vocally the male/female basis of Hollywood love and also to stylise emotional intimacy. Hit examples are Joe Cocker's and Jennifer Warnes's 'Up Where We Belong' (from *An Officer and a Gentleman*) and James Ingrams's and Pattie Austin's 'How Do You Keep the Music Playing?' (from *Best Friends*). Both songs draw on black musical techniques of emotional expression (which have nothing to do with the films in question) and both make generalised reference to the future – 'who knows what tomorrow will bring?' 'how do you keep the music playing, how do you make it last?' – which link the mood of the end of the film to the mood of the end of watching the film. (And both songs reveal how useful the synthesiser is in preserving the Hollywood equation of love and the sound of massed strings.)

My conclusion from these example is that we cannot

## 60 HIGH THEORY/LOW CULTURE

develop an explanation of how music works in film without reference to an explanation of how popular music works more generally. From this perspective, it is surprising how often in film studies it is asserted, in Schoenberg's words, that 'music never drags a meaning around with it', that it is non-representational, 'abstract art par excellence' (Eisler), 'useless' (Adorno). Such assertions are the basis of numerous accounts of how a film's 'musical system' supports or counters its 'visual system'. My sense of pop music is that, in fact, it drags all sorts of meanings into and out of films. There is a standard musicological exercise, for example, in which people are played pieces of instrumental music and asked to write down their 'associations'. The results (when I gave the paper on which this chapter is based in Birmingham, I played pieces of the soundtracks of *The Big Country, Psycho, A Summer Place* and *American Gigolo*) suggest both that there are widely shared conventions of musical meaning and that these conventions are partly derived from people's shared experiences of film soundtracks.

Claudia Gorbman (who has written the best essay on narrative film music) suggests that we should think in terms of three sorts of musical code: (a) pure musical codes, generating musical discourse, music referring to music itself; (b) cultural musical codes, music referring to the usual cultural context of its production and consumption; and (c) cinematic musical codes, music in formal relationship to co-existent elements in a film.[4]

In practice, though, these different 'levels' are hard to separate. Take the distinction between pure and cultural musical codes. The concept of a pure musical code draws on an account of 'classical' music, on the possibility of a formal, structural analysis of rational, tonal music organised by certain compositional regulations. But this is a peculiar form of music, music without words or direct social function, which is, Eisler suggested, specific to bourgeois culture and has to be understood as such. The 'purity' of the music is,

HEARING SECRET HARMONIES 61

in other words, itself a cultural code and, in fact, music in the classical tradition is heard to express the 'soul' of its composer and to convey or invoke particular sorts of imagery. Both these readings of classical music are important for the continuous use the cinema has made of nineteenth-century romantic music. One early use of film, for example, was to show the images taken to lie in the accompanying music (just like rock videos now). Miklos Rozsa provides an entertaining account of the possible complexity of the inter-pay between musical and film images:

Billy Wilder approached me at a party and said he loved my violin concerto, and that he had worn out his copy of the record and wondered if I had another one. I was as intrigued as much as flattered but all he would say was, 'I've got an idea'. Some months later he called me into his office and revealed the idea: he had written a screenplay called *The Private Life of Sherlock Holmes* and he had written it around my concerto, inspired by the fact that Holmes liked playing the fiddle. The theme of the first movement is somewhat nervous and this apparently suggested to Wilder Holmes' addiction to cocaine. The theme of the second movement of the concerto brought a lady spy to Wilder's mind, and the tur-bulent third movement conjured up for him the Loch Ness mons-ter. He said, 'This is perfect monster music'. I wasn't flattered but he was right, it did work out quite well. I agreed to score the film for him using the concerto. He seemed to think this would be easy because I wouldn't have to think up any new themes. Actually it was very difficult. The concerto was not written with any images in mind and the timings had to be altered to fit the film sequences. It would have been much easier to invent something fresh.[5]

The most interesting current approach to musical 'mood' conventions is being developed in Sweden by the musicologist Philip Tagg. He cites an experiment performed by one of his Gothenburg colleagues in a postgraduate seminar:

A psychologist from Lund read what a patient had said while listening to a particular piece of music under hypnosis (the instruc-

## 62 HIGH THEORY/ LOW CULTURE

tions to the patient had been to say what the music made him/her
see, like in a daydream). The seminar knew neither the identity
nor anything else about the piece of music which had given rise
to the patient's associations which were roughly as follows. Alone
out in the countryside on a gently sloping field or meadow near
some trees at the top of the rise where there was the view of a lake
and the forest on the other side. Using this information only, the
seminar was asked to make a rough score of the sort of music they
thought might have evoked such associations. The seminar's sketch
consisted of high notes (perhaps flageolets) sustained in the violins
and a low pedal point in the cellos and basses. These two pitch
polarities were in consonant (either octave or fifth) relations to
each other. A rather undecided, quiet but slightly uneasy figure
was put into the viola part now and again while a solo woodwind
instrument (either flute, oboe or clarinet) played a quasi-modal
legato melodic line which wandered slowly and slightly aimlessly
piano over the rest of the almost static sounds (pianissimo). The
seminar's quick sketch proved to correspond on most counts with
the original musical stimulous which was the taptoe from Vaughan
Williams's *Pastoral Symphony*.[6]

Tagg's own research interest is in the 'mood music collections' that are used by companies making film commercials,
industrial documentaries, government promotions and a
variety of cinema entertainments. The coding of musical
moods dates back to the ways in which nineteenth-century
music was taken to carry meanings, and Tagg suggests that
there were material reasons why the cinema took over these
'classical' conventions:

there was no technically, economically, socially or culturally viable
music for use in the early years of the capitalist film industry other
then that provided by the bourgeois musical tradition. There was
no other storable music, neither in graphic, mechanical, optical
nor electronic form, neither was there any other sort of transcultur-
ally viable 'nature music' other than that of the bourgeoisie (p. 8).

Tagg's point here is that such 'nature music' is ideologically
loaded; the music represents a particular account of 'nature'.

HEARING SECRET HARMONIES 63

Today the mood music catalogues cross reference 'nature' themes and sounds with various emotional labels, such that 'nature is mainly viewed as a positive, pleasant source of relaxation and recreation, as a leisure facility, as a backcloth for romance, as a historical-meditative retreat' (p. 24).

Similar assumptions lay behind the use of cue sheets in silent film accompaniment, pioneered by Max Winkler, a music publisher's clerk with an exceptional musical memory, whose catalogue 'listed all the compositions under categories – action music, animal music, church music – sinister, chaste, sad, mysterious, majestic, furious etc., etc.'[7] In this context (especially as Winkler later confessed to 'dismembering the great masters. We murdered the works of Beethoven, Mozart, Grieg, J. S. Bach. . .') it is difficult to lay bare 'pure musical codes'. The question becomes how we come to have associations for sounds and structures, how the pure and cultural musical codes relate to each other.

Cultural and cinematic musical codes are similarly entangled, if only because our 'cultural' understanding of musical meanings is, by this stage of cultural history, so dependent on their recurring film contexts. As film composer George Antheil put it in 1945:

Hollywood music is very nearly a public communication, like radio. If you are a movie fan (and who isn't?) you may sit in a movie theatre three times a week listening to the symphonic background scores which Hollywood composers concoct. What happens? Your musical tastes become molded by these scores, heard without knowing it. You *see* love, and you *hear* it. Simultaneously. It makes sense. Music suddenly become a language for you, without your knowing it.[8]

This is to raise a number of historical questions. How, for example, did silent film pianists develop their sense of 'appropriate' accompaniment? How significant were cue sheets? To hear someone play for a silent film today, is to hear someone drawing on the expectations of solo piano (whether

## 64 HIGH THEORY /LOW CULTURE

Chopin or Russ Conway) and on implicit assumptions about how silent films *should* sound – the piano now is played to connote the piano then. The interplay of music's cultural and cinematic meanings has its own history (and it would be interesting in this context to compare Hollywood's effect on popular music with the development of popular film and music in India). In cinema's early history, accompanying music was part of the process in which cinema became 'respectable'; nowadays the absence of music is taken as the sign of a film's seriousness. Music may carry a meaning in film, in short, by drawing attention to the 'cultural conventions of its cinematic use', by drawing on genre rules, for example, which may or may not be confirmed by other aspects of the film.

If popular forms (jazz and country music, rock and roll and disco) first get used in films to signal their 'outside' social source (black culture, southern culture, youth culture, and so on ), their use is often soon so stylised as to refer, rather, to their place in previous films. Early 1970s black action films, for example (*Shaft, Superfly, Trouble Man,* etc.), so encoded the 'wah wah' guitar that its use in a film score now (in 1982's *Vortex,* say) inevitably appeals to our ability to draw on *film* references. (Rock has often been taken to be a problematic form for film scorers – its very *presence* can swamp surrounding visual images. Rock videos, though, reveal that rock's musical meanings can soon be closed down by the systematic use of visual clichés.) The most interesting film composers (I am particularly intrigued by Bernard Herrmann and Ennio Morricone) draw on music's ability to cross and *confuse* cinematic and cultural codes in their construction of sound 'narratives'.[9]

One paradox of film music is that while 'high theorists' have paid much less attention to aural than to visual codes, 'ordinary' film viewers (low theorists?) take the complications of musical reference for granted. In the Birmingham weekend (see note 2) discussion of television commercials, for instance, I noted the following casual musical descriptions: 'middle-of-the-road', 'background', 'up-beat', 'Close Encounters climactic', 'new-exciting-world-just-around-the-corner', 'youth music', 'homely, healthy, folky'. Everyone present seemed to understand and agree with such descriptions even though they draw on a remarkable jumble of references and assumption, and fuse musical, cultural, historical and cinematic allusions. I want to keep this in mind in addressing the three issues that have most fruitfully occupied more systematic approaches to film music.

## Realism

In common-sense terms it might seem that music is the 'non-realist' aspect of films, yet audiences take it for granted that strings accompany a clinch. Indeed, a clinch without strings may seem *less* real, though another film convention is to climax a sex scene with silence, as if to register its 'privacy' (and our voyeuristic embarrassment). The point of this example is to stress that music is as essential to the perceived 'truth' of a film as everything else, but the reality music describes/refers to is a different sort of reality than that described/referred to by visual images. Film composers themselves often take their cue on this from Wagner, who argued that the purpose of music was 'to amplify what can't be shown' – and what cannot be shown is regularly called 'atmosphere' or 'mood'. Broadly speaking, two strands of reality seem to be involved here: First, *emotional reality*. Music, it seems can convey and clarify the emotional significance of a scene, the true 'real' feelings of the characters involved in it. Music, in short, reveals what is 'underneath' or 'behind' a film's observable gestures. Thus, for composer Jerry Goldsmith, the aim of film music is 'emotional penetration', while in Elmer Bernstein's words:

## 66 HIGH THEORY/LOW CULTURE

The job of the composer is really very varied. You must use your art to heighten the emotional aspects of the film – music can tell the story in purely emotional terms and the film by itself cannot. The reason that it can't is that it's a visual language and basically intellectual. You look at an image and you then have to interpret what it means, whereas if you listen to something or someone and you understand what you hear – that's an emotional process. Music is particularly emotional – if you are affected by it, you don't have to ask what it means.[10]

Secondly, *reality of time and place*. Another recurring point made by the film scorers interviewed by Tony Thomas is how much research they do. In writing music for a film set in a particular historical period or in a particular geographical place, they must produce sounds which current audiences believe relate to what people in that time or place would have 'really' heard. This is a more complicated matter than it might seem. The 'reality' of film musical settings actually refers to historical and geographical myths (themselves constructed, in part, by previous music in previous films set in these places and times). Thus the music for *Zorba the Greek* became so powerfully connotative of Greece that Greek restaurants (even those in Greece itself) have to use the music to convince customers of their 'Greekness'. And a time and a place can have an emotional meaning too (this is one of the functions of 'nature music'). The Australian *Picnic at Hanging Rock* thus conveyed the 'mystery' of the rock by using Gheorghe Zamfir's eastern European pan pipes (underscored by a cathedral organ), while Michael Nyman's score for *The Draughtsman's Contract* used the appropriate historical musical form but scored instrumentally according to the rules of contemporary minimalism, thus making the apparent celebration of 'order' distinctly unsettling.

All these examples of musical realism raise the question of how audiences *recognise* musical authenticity. It is easy to move (like Elmer Bernstein) from the directness of music's emotional impact to an assertion of its 'natural' meaning, so

HEARING SECRET HARMONIES 253

it is worth citing another cautionary musicological story: a group of African musicians, invited to tour the US folk festival circuit, found that their music was getting a decidedly cool response, was being dismissed as 'commercial'. After a few weeks the musicians sat down and worked out a new arrangement of their material, designed specifically to signal 'authenticity' in American folk terms. With this 'fake' sound (it bore little relationship to the music they played in their home country) they became widely praised for their 'ethnic' flair. More recently, Jeremy Marre's series of films for Channel Four on popular music in Asia was criticised by critics because, in the words of the *Sunday Times* (18 March 1984) it didn't include 'enough indigenous melody as opposed to processed western pop'. Marre's point, of course, was to show that this distinction is nowadays meaningless.

## Diagesis

The most systematic theoretical approach to film music begins by distinguishing its diagetic use (when it has a place in 'the narratively implied spatio-temporal world of the actions and characters', when it is made by the band in a night-club scene, for exmple) and its non-diagetic use (when the music heard has no source within the film's own world). The important point here, as Claudia Gorbman has made clear, is that in pratice music straddles this apparently clear divide. How, for example, do we classify the moment when someone remembers a tune and we hear it on the soundtrack – the physical production of the music is non-diagetic, but its emotional production is diagetic. Is the character 'really hearing something'?

More generally, it seems that our classification of music in terms of diagesis depends on an implicit sense of sounds' *appropriateness* to a scene, in terms, that is, of musical realism (which, as I have already suggested, is not the same thing as visual realism). If, for example, the diagetic/non-diagetic dis-

## 68 HIGH THEORY / LOW CULTURE

tinction refers to the source of a sound, then this is not just a question of what we can actually see in a scene but of what we might *expect to see* as part of the film's realistic 'sound-scape'. In *The Godfather,* for example, Nino Rota's score uses and makes deliberate reference to Italian street music, to 'live' sounds, even when the musicians could not possibly be present in the narrative. This is a non-diagetic use of music, but one which is drawing our attention to the music's previous 'real' presence. In youth films from *American Graffiti* to *The Big Chill,* to give a different sort of example, rock and roll is so much part of the 'diagesis' (and we do indeed see radios and record-players turned on, even records being played by Wolfman Jack himself) that it is misleading to assert that in those scenes when such music has no 'real' source that it suddenly becomes non-diagetic. Disco music is used similarly in *Saturday Night Fever:* in the love scene, 'How Deep Is Your Love' is the sort of song that *could* have been on the radio or record-player – the implication is that the film characters are 'hearing' it as clearly as we are in the audience. By the time we get to a film like *Blade Runner* we find that the 'reality' of this future Los Angeles is guaranteed precisely by the invisibility of the ever-present synthesised sounds – outside the cinema too we are increasingly surrounded by music which has no apparent source.[11]

### Subjectivity

The third important question raised by theoretical debate is how music works to position film spectators (or auditors), and this is to address the question of emotional realism from a slightly different perspective: one function of film music is to reveal our emotions as the *audience*. Film music is often said to have physical effects – sending shivers down the spine, bringing a lump to the throat – and sounds, more obviously than visions, have collective effects – we hear a beat and tap our feet (or march or work) together. Film scores are thus

HEARING SECRET HARMONIES 69

important in representing *community* (via martial or nationalistic music, for example) in both film and audience. The important point here is that as spectators we are drawn to identify not with the film characters themselves but with their emotions, which are signalled pre-eminently by music which can offer us emotional experience *directly*. Music is central to the way in which the pleasure of cinema is simultaneously individualised and shared; like political rhetoric it can cue responses through the application of general rules of crowd arousal to particular circumstances.

There is, in this context, another sort of approach to musical meaning – the Barthian analysis of music as a *sensuous* pleasure, in which we are overwhelmed by sound (as in *Blade Runner?*). Barthes himself raised the question of why certain sorts of voice give pleasure (speaking as well as singing voices), why we take delight in the experience of meaning *being made*. This is to widen the question of film music in two directions – first by linking it to non-musical but human sounds; secondly by referring us to films, musicals, which are explicitly about music making. In the long run any analysis of music in film will have to cover all this ground, but in this chapter I have been specifically concerned with music's coded pleasures and so my closing questions is this: where do emotional codes come from? This is to go back to the issue of the clinch and the strings: to have meaning, emotions must be shaped, and this is as much a public as a private process, one in which music (and music making) seems central. Do people 'hear harmonies' when they kiss outside films too? To develop the theory of film music we need, in Antoine Hennion's words, 'not so much a sociology of music as a musicology of society'.[12]

## Notes

1 Zofia Lissa, *Asthetik der Filmmusik* (Berlin: Henschelvelg, 1965).

2 What follows was first presented as a talk at the SEFT Sound Cinema weekend, Triangle Arts Centre, Birmingham, 29-30 October 1983 and appeared in a slightly different form in *Screen* 25, 1984. Thanks to Philip Tagg for his help.

70 HIGH THEORY/ LOW CULTURE

3 In Britain, by contrast, television themes are more likely to have chart success – like the themes from *Minder, Hill Street Blues* and *Auf Wiedersehen Pet,* or more bizarrely, the arrangement of Ravel's *Bolero* used by Torvill and Dean in their skating triumphs.

4 Claudia Gorbman, 'Narrative film music', *Yale French Studies* 60, 1980, p. 185.

5 Quoted in Tony Thomas, *Music for the Movies* (New York: A. S. Barnes, 1973), pp. 96-7.

6 Philip Tagg, *'Nature' as a Musical Mood Category* (Gothenburg: IASMP, 1983), p. 31.

7 Thomas, *op. cit.,* p. 38.

8 Quoted in Thomas, *op. cit.,* p. 171.

9 For a fuller discussion of this point see Simon Frith, 'Sound and Vision', *Collusion* 1, 1981, pp. 7-9.

10 Quoted in Thomas, *op. cit.,* p. 193.

11 *Blade Runner* has an interesting score for other reasons. Its composer, Vangelis, refused to allow the release of his electronic performance and so it was reproduced, remarkably accurately, by the strings of The New American Orchestra.

12 Antoine Hennion, 'Music as social production', in David Horn and Philip Tagg eds., *Popular Music Perspectives* (Gothenburg and Exeter: IASMP, 1982), p. 40.

# CHAPTER 16

# *Towards an aesthetic of popular music*

## Introduction: the 'value' of popular music

Underlying all the other distinctions critics draw between 'serious' and 'popular' music is an assumption about the source of musical value. Serious music matters because it transcends social forces; popular music is aesthetically worthless because it is determined by them (because it is 'useful' or 'utilitarian'). This argument, common enough among academic musicologists, puts sociologists in an odd position. If we venture to suggest that the value of, say, Beethoven's music can be explained by the social conditions determining its production and subsequent consumption we are dismissed as philistines – aesthetic theories of classical music remain determinedly non-sociological. Popular music, by contrast, is taken to be good only for sociological theory. Our very success in explaining the rise of rock 'n' roll or the appearance of disco proves their lack of aesthetic interest. To relate music and society becomes, then, a different task according to the music we are treating. In analyzing serious music, we have to uncover the social forces concealed in the talk of 'transcendent' values; in analyzing pop, we have to take seriously the values scoffed at in the talk of social functions.

In this paper I will concentrate on the second issue; my particular concern is to suggest that the sociological approach to popular music does not rule out an aesthetic theory but, on the contrary, makes one possible. At first sight this proposition is unlikely. There is no doubt that sociologists have tended to explain away pop music. In my own academic work I have examined how rock is produced and consumed, and have tried to place it

ideologically, but there is no way that a reading of my books (or those of
other sociologists) could be used to explain why some pop songs are good
and others bad, why Elvis Presley is a better singer than John Denver, or
why disco is a much richer musical genre than progressive rock. And yet for
ten years or more I have also been a working rock critic, making such
judgments as a matter of course, assuming, like all pop fans, that our musical choices matter.

Are such judgments spurious – a way of concealing from myself and
other consumers the ways in which our tastes are manipulated? Can it really
be the case that my pleasure in a song by the group Abba carries the same
aesthetic weight as someone else's pleasure in Mozart? Even to pose such a
question is to invite ridicule – either I seek to reduce the 'transcendent'
Mozart to Abba's commercially determined level, or else I elevate Abba's
music beyond any significance it can carry. But even if the pleasures of
serious and popular musics are different, it is not immediately obvious that
the difference is that between artistic autonomy and social utility. Abba's
value is no more (and no less) bound up with an experience of transcendence than Mozart's; the meaning of Mozart is no less (and no more)
explicable in terms of social forces. The question facing sociologists and
aestheticians in both cases is the same: how do we make musical value
judgments? How do such value judgments articulate the listening
experiences involved?

The sociologist of contemporary popular music is faced with a body of
songs, records, stars and styles which exists because of a series of decisions,
made by both producers and consumers, about what is a successful sound.
Musicians write tunes and play solos; producers choose from different
sound mixes; record companies and radio programmers decide what should
be released and played; consumers buy one record rather than another and
concentrate their attention on particular genres. The result of all these
apparently individual decisions is a pattern of success, taste and style which
can be explained sociologically.

If the starting question is why does this hit sound this way, then sociological answers can be arranged under two headings. First, there are answers
in terms of technique and technology: people produce and consume the
music they are capable of producing and consuming (an obvious point, but
one which opens up issues of skill, background and education which in
pop music are applied not to individual composers but to social groups).
Different groups possess different sorts of cultural capital, share different
cultural expectations and so make music differently – pop tastes are shown
to correlate with class cultures and subcultures; musical styles are linked to

specific age groups; we take for granted the connections of ethnicity and sound. This is the sociological common sense of rock criticism, which equally acknowledges the determining role of technology. The history of twentieth-century popular music is impossible to write without reference to the changing forces of production, electronics, the use of recording, amplification and synthesizers, just as consumer choices cannot be separated from the possession of transistor radios, stereo hi-fis, ghetto blasters and Walkmen.

While we can thus point to general patterns of pop use, the precise link (or homology) between sounds and social groups remains unclear. Why is rock 'n' roll youth music, whereas Dire Straits is the sound of Yuppie USA? To answer these questions there is a second sociological approach to popular music, expressed in terms of its functions. This approach is obvious in ethnomusicology, that is in anthropological studies of traditional and folk musics which are explained by reference to their use in dance, in rituals, for political mobilization, to solemnize ceremonies or to excite desires. Similar points are made about contemporary pop, but its most important function is assumed to be commercial – the starting analytical assumption is that the music is made to sell; thus research has focused on who makes marketing decisions and why, and on the construction of 'taste publics'. The bulk of the academic sociology of popular music (including my own) implicitly equates aesthetic and commercial judgments. The phenomenal 1985 successes of Madonna and Bruce Springsteen are explained, for example, in terms of sales strategies, the use of video, and the development of particular new audiences. The appeal of the music itself, the reason Madonna's and Springsteen's fans like them, somehow remains unexamined.

From the fans' perspective it is obvious that people play the music they do because it 'sounds good', and the interesting question is why they have formed that opinion. Even if pop tastes are the effects of social conditioning and commercial manipulation, people still explain them to themselves in terms of value judgment. Where, in pop and rock, do these values come from? When people explain their tastes, what terms do they use? They certainly know what they like (and dislike), what pleases them and what does not. Read the music press, listen to band rehearsals and recording sessions, overhear the chatter in record shops and discos, note the ways in which disc jockeys play records, and you will hear value judgments being made. The discriminations that matter in these settings occur *within* the general sociological framework. While this allows us at a certain level to 'explain' rock or disco, it is not adequate for an understanding of why one rock record or one disco track is better than another. Turn to the explanations of the fans or musicians (or even of the record companies) and a familiar argument appears. Everyone in the pop world is aware of the social forces that determine 'normal' pop music – a good record, song, or sound is precisely one that transcends those forces!

The music press is the place where pop value judgments are most clearly articulated. A reading of British music magazines reveals that 'good' popular music has always been heard to go beyond or break through commercial routine. This was as true for critics struggling to distinguish jazz from Tin Pan Alley pop in the 1920s and black jazz from white jazz in the 1930s as for critics asserting rock's superiority to teen pop in the late 1960s. In *Sound effects*[1] I argued that rock's claim to a form of aesthetic autonomy rests on a combination of folk and art arguments: as folk music rock is heard to represent the community of youth, as art music rock is heard as the sound of individual, creative sensibility. The rock aesthetic depends, crucially, on an argument about authenticity. Good music is the authentic expression of something – a person, an idea, a feeling, a shared experience, a *Zeitgeist*. Bad music is inauthentic – it expresses nothing. The most common term of abuse in rock criticism is 'bland' – bland music has nothing in it and is made only to be commercially pleasing.

'Authenticity' is, then, what guarantees that rock performances resist or subvert commercial logic, just as rock-star quality (whether we are discussing Elvis Presley or David Bowie, the Rolling Stones or the Sex Pistols), describes the power that enables certain musicians to drive something individually obdurate through the system. At this point, rock criticism meets up with 'serious' musicology. Wilfrid Mellers' scholarly books on the Beatles and Bob Dylan,[2] for example, describe in technical terms their subjects' transcendent qualities; but they read like fan mail and, in their lack of self-conscious hipness, point to the contradiction at the heart of this aesthetic approach. The suggestion is that pop music becomes more valuable the more independent it is of the social forces that organize the pop process in the first place; pop value is dependent on something outside pop, is rooted in the person, the *auteur*, the community or the subculture that lies behind it. If good music is authentic music, then critical judgment means measuring the performers' 'truth' to the experiences or feelings they are describing.

Rock criticism depends on myth – the myth of the youth community, the myth of the creative artist. The reality is that rock, like all twentieth-

[1] Simon Frith, *Sound effects: youth, leisure and the politics of rock 'n' roll* (New York, 1981).
[2] Wilfrid Mellers, *Twilight of the gods: the Beatles in retrospect* (London, 1973), and *A darker shade of pale: a backdrop to Bob Dylan* (London, 1984).

century pop musics, is a commercial form, music produced as a commodity, for a profit, distributed through mass media as mass culture. It is in practice very difficult to say exactly who or what it is that rock expresses or who, from the listener's point of view, are the authentically creative performers. The myth of authenticity is, indeed, one of rock's own ideological effects, an aspect of its sales process: rock stars can be marketed as artists, and their particular sounds marketed as a means of identity. Rock criticism is a means of legitimating tastes, justifying value judgments, but it does not really explain how those judgments came to be made in the first place. If the music is not, in fact, made according to the 'authentic' story, then the question becomes how we are able to judge some sounds as more authentic than others: what are we actually listening for in making our judgments? How do we know Bruce Springsteen is more authentic than Duran Duran, when both make records according to the rules of the same complex industry? And how do we recognize good sounds in non-rock genres, in pop forms like disco that are not described in authentic terms in the first place? The question of the value of pop music remains to be answered.

### An alternative approach to music and society

In an attempt to answer these questions I want to suggest an alternative approach to musical value, to suggest different ways of defining 'popular music' and 'popular culture'. The question we should be asking is not what does popular music *reveal* about 'the people' but how does it *construct* them. If we start with the assumption that pop is expressive, then we get bogged down in the search for the 'real' artist or emotion or belief lying behind it. But popular music is popular not because it reflects something, or authentically articulates some sort of popular taste or experience, but because it creates our understanding of what popularity is. The most misleading term in cultural theory is, indeed, 'authenticity'. What we should be examining is not how true a piece of music is to something else, but how it sets up the idea of 'truth' in the first place – successful pop music is music which defines its own aesthetic standard.

A simple way to illustrate the problems of defining musical popularity is to look at its crudest measure, the weekly record sales charts in the British music press and the American *Billboard*. These are presented to us as market research: the charts measure something real – sales and radio plays – and represent them with all the trimmings of an objective, scientific apparatus. But, in fact, what the charts reveal is a specific definition of what can be counted as popular music in the first place – record sales (in the right shops), radio plays (on the right stations). The charts work not as the detached measure of some agreed notion of popularity, but as the most important determination of what the popularity of popular music means – that is, a particular pattern of market choice. The charts bring selected records together into the community of the market place; they define certain sorts of consumption as being collective in certain sorts of ways.

The sales charts are only one measure of popularity; and when we look at others, it becomes clear that their use is always for the creation (rather than reflection) of taste communities. Readers' polls in the music press, for example, work to give communal shape to disparate readers; the Pazz 'n' Jop poll in *The Village Voice* creates a sense of collective commitment among the fragmented community of American rock critics. The Grammy awards in the United States and the BPI awards in Britain, present the industry's view of what pop music is about – nationalism and money. These annual awards, which for most pop fans seem to miss the point, reflect sales figures and 'contributions to the recording industry': measures of popularity no less valid than readers' or critics' polls (which often deliberately honor 'unpopular' acts). In comparing poll results, arguments are really not about who is more popular than whom empirically (see rock critics' outrage that Phil Collins rather than Bruce Springsteen dominated the 1986 Grammys) but about what popularity means. Each different measure measures something different or, to put it more accurately, each different measure constructs its own object of measurement. This is apparent in *Billboard*'s 'specialist' charts, in the way in which 'minority' musics are defined. 'Women's music', for example, is interesting not as music which somehow expresses 'women', but as music which seeks to define them, just as 'black music' works to set up a very particular notion of what 'blackness' is.

This approach to popular culture, as the creation rather than the expression of the people, need not be particular to music. There are numerous ways in our everyday life in which accounts of 'the people' are provided. Turn on the television news and notice the ways in which a particular mode of address works, how the word 'we' is used, how the word 'you'. Advertisers in all media are clearly in the business of explaining to us who we are, how we fit in with other people in society, why we necessarily consume the way we do. Each mass medium has its own techniques for addressing its audience, for creating moments of recognition and exclusion, for giving us our sense of ourselves. Pop music does, though, seem to play a particularly important role in the way in which popular culture works. On the one hand, it works with particularly intense emotional experiences – pop songs and pop stars mean more to us emotionally than other media events or performers, and this is not just because the pop business sells music to us through individual market choices. On the other hand, these musical experiences always contain social meaning, are placed within a social context – we are not free to read anything we want into a song.

The experience of pop music is an experience of placing: in responding to a song, we are drawn, haphazardly, into affective and emotional alliances with the performers and with the performers' other fans. Again this also happens in other areas of popular culture. Sport, for example, is clearly a setting in which people directly experience community, feel an immediate bond with other people, articulate a particular kind of collective pride (for a non-American, the most extraordinary aspect of the 1984 Olympics was the display/construction of the Reagan ideology of both the United States and patriotism). And fashion and style – both social constructions – remain the keys to the ways in which we, as individuals, present ourselves to the world: we use the public meanings of clothes to say 'this is how I want to be perceived'.

But music is especially important to this process of placement because of something specific to musical experience, namely, its direct emotional intensity. Because of its qualities of abstractness (which 'serious' aestheticians have always stressed) music is an individualizing form. We absorb songs into our own lives and rhythms into our own bodies; they have a looseness of reference that makes them immediately accessible. Pop songs are open to appropriation for personal use in a way that other popular cultural forms (television soap operas, for example) are not – the latter are tied into meanings we may reject. At the same time, and equally significant, music is obviously rule-bound. We hear things as music because their sounds obey a particular, familiar logic, and for most pop fans (who are, technically, non-musical) this logic is out of our control. There is a mystery to our musical tastes. Some records and performers work for us, others do not – we know this without being able to explain it. Somebody else has set up the conventions; they are clearly social and clearly apart from us.

This interplay between personal absorption into music and the sense that it is, nevertheless, something out there, something public, is what makes music so important in the cultural placing of the individual in the social. To give a mundane example, it is obviously true that in the last thirty years the idea of being a 'fan', with its oddly public account of private obsessions, has been much more significant to pop music than to other forms of popular culture. This role of music is usually related to youth and youth culture, but it seems equally important to the ways in which ethnic groups in both

Britain and the United States have forged particular cultural identities and is also reflected in the ways in which 'classical' music originally became significant for the nineteenth-century European bourgeoisie. In all these cases music can stand for, symbolize *and* offer the immediate experience of collective identity. Other cultural forms – painting, literature, design – can articulate and show off shared values and pride, but only music can make you *feel* them.

### The social functions of music

It is now possible to move back to the starting point of this essay – the social functions of music and their implications for aesthetics. I will begin by outlining the four most significant ways in which pop is used and then suggest how these uses help us to understand how pop value judgments are made.

The first reason, then, we enjoy popular music is because of its use in answering questions of identity: we use pop songs to create for ourselves a particular sort of self-definition, a particular place in society. The pleasure that pop music produces is a pleasure of identification – with the music we like, with the performers of that music, with the other people who like it. And it is important to note that the production of identity is also a production of non-identity – it is a process of inclusion and exclusion. This is one of the most striking aspects of musical taste. People not only know what they like, they also have very clear ideas about what they don't like and often have very aggressive ways of stating their dislikes. As all sociological studies of pop consumers have shown, pop fans define themselves quite precisely according to their musical preferences. Whether they identify with genres or stars, it seems of greater importance to people what they like musically than whether or not they enjoyed a film or a television program.

The pleasure of pop music, unlike the pleasures to be had from other mass cultural forms, does not derive in any clear way from fantasy: it is not mediated through day-dreams or romancing, but is experienced directly. For example, at a heavy metal concert you can certainly see the audience absorbed in the music; yet for all the air-guitar playing they are not fantasizing being up on stage. To experience heavy metal is to experience the power of the concert as a whole – the musicians are one aspect of this, the amplification system another, the audience a third. The individual fans get their kicks from being a necessary part of the overall process – which is why heavy metal videos always have to contain moments of live performance

*Towards an aesthetic of popular music*                    **141**

(whatever the surrounding story line) in order to capture and acknowledge the kind of empowerment that is involved in the concert itself.

Once we start looking at different pop genres we can begin to document the different ways in which music works to give people an identity, to place them in different social groups. And this is not just a feature of commercial pop music. It is the way in which all popular music works. For example, in putting together an audience, contemporary black-influenced pop clearly (and often cynically) employs musical devices originally used in religious music to define men's and women's identity before God. Folk musics, similarly, continue to be used to mark the boundaries of ethnic identity, even amidst the complications of migration and cultural change. In London's Irish pubs, for example, 'traditional' Irish folk songs are still the most powerful way to make people feel Irish and consider what their 'Irishness' means. (This music, this identity, is now being further explored by post-punk London Irish bands, like the Pogues.) It is not surprising, then, that popular music has always had important nationalist functions. In Abel Gance's 'silent' film, *Napoleon*, there is a scene in which we see the *Marseillaise* being composed, and then watch the song make its way through the Assembly and among the crowds until everyone is singing it. When the film was first shown in France, the cinema audience rose from their seats and joined in singing their national anthem. Only music seems capable of creating this sort of spontaneous collective identity, this kind of personally felt patriotism.

Music's second social function is to give us a way of managing the relationship between our public and private emotional lives. It is often noted but rarely discussed that the bulk of popular songs are love songs. This is certainly true of twentieth-century popular music in the West; but most non-Western popular musics also feature romantic, usually heterosexual, love lyrics. This is more than an interesting statistic; it is a centrally important aspect of how pop music is used. Why are love songs so important? Because people need them to give shape and voice to emotions that otherwise cannot be expressed without embarrassment or incoherence. Love songs are a way of giving emotional intensity to the sorts of intimate things we say to each other (and to ourselves) in words that are, in themselves, quite flat. It is a peculiarity of everyday language that our most fraught and revealing declarations of feeling have to use phrases – 'I love/hate you', 'Help me!', 'I'm angry/scared' – which are boring and banal; and so our culture has a supply of a million pop songs, which say these things for us in numerous interesting and involving ways. These songs do not replace our conversations – pop singers do not do our courting for us – but they make our feelings seem richer and more convincing than we can make them appear in our own words, even to ourselves.

The only interesting sociological account of lyrics in the long tradition of American content analysis was Donald Horton's late 1950s study[3] of how teenagers used the words of popular songs in their dating rituals. His high school sample learned from pop songs (public forms of private expression) how to make sense of and shape their own inchoate feelings. This use of pop illuminates one quality of the star/fan relationship: people do not idolize singers because they wish to be them but because these singers seem able, somehow, to make available their own feelings – it is as if we get to know ourselves via the music.

The third function of popular music is to shape popular memory, to organize our sense of time. Clearly one of the effects of all music, not just pop, is to intensify our experience of the present. One measure of good music, to put it another way, is, precisely, its 'presence', its ability to 'stop' time, to make us feel we are living within a moment, with no memory or anxiety about what has come before, what will come after. This is where the physical impact of music comes in – the use of beat, pulse and rhythm to compel our immediate bodily involvement in an organization of time that the music itself controls. Hence the pleasures of dance and disco; clubs and parties provide a setting, a society, which seems to be defined only by the time-scale of the music (the beats per minute), which escapes the real time passing outside.

One of the most obvious consequences of music's organization of our sense of time is that songs and tunes are often the key to our remembrance of things past. I do not mean simply that sounds – like sights and smells – trigger associated memories, but, rather, that music in itself provides our most vivid experience of time passing. Music focuses our attention on the feeling of time; songs are organized (it is part of their pleasure) around anticipation and echo, around endings to which we look forward, choruses that build regret into their fading. Twentieth-century popular music has, on the whole, been a nostalgic form. The Beatles, for example, made nostalgic music from the start, which is why they were so popular. Even on hearing a Beatles song for the first time there was a sense of the memories to come, a feeling that this could not last but that it was surely going to be pleasant to remember.

It is this use of time that makes popular music so important in the social organization of youth. It is a sociological truism that people's heaviest

---

[3] Donald Horton, 'The dialogue of courtship in popular songs', *American Journal of Sociology*, 62 (1957), pp. 569–78.

personal investment in popular music is when they are teenagers and young adults – music then ties into a particular kind of emotional turbulence, when issues of individual identity and social place, the control of public and private feelings, are at a premium. People do use music less, and less intently, as they grow up; the most significant pop songs for all generations (not just for rock generations) are those they heard as adolescents. What this suggests, though, is not just that young people need music, but that 'youth' itself is defined by music. Youth is experienced, that is, as an intense presence, through an impatience for time to pass and a regret that it is doing so, in a series of speeding, physically insistent moments that have nostalgia coded into them. This is to reiterate my general point about popular music: youth music is socially important not because it reflects youth experience (authentically or not), but because it defines for us what 'youthfulness' is. I remember concluding, in my original sociological research in the early 1970s, that those young people who, for whatever reasons, took no interest in pop music were not really 'young'.

The final function of popular music I want to mention here is something more abstract than the issues discussed so far, but a consequence of all of them: popular music is something possessed. One of the first things I learned as a rock critic – from abusive mail – was that rock fans 'owned' their favorite music in ways that were intense and important to them. To be sure, the notion of musical ownership is not peculiar to rock – Hollywood cinema has long used the clichéd line, 'they're playing our song' – and this reflects something that is recognizable to all music lovers and is an important aspect of the way in which everyone thinks and talks about 'their' music. (British radio has programs of all sorts built around people's explanations of why certain records 'belong' to them.) Obviously it is the commodity form of music which makes this sense of musical possession possible, but it is not just the record that people think they own: we feel that we also possess the song itself, the particular performance, and its performer.

In 'possessing' music, we make it part of our own identity and build it into our sense of ourselves. To write pop criticism is, as I have mentioned, to attract hate mail; mail not so much defending the performer or performance criticized as defending the letter writer: criticize a star and the fans respond as if you have criticized them. The biggest mail bag I ever received was after I had been critical of Phil Collins. Hundreds of letters arrived (not from teenyboppers or gauche adolescents, but from young professionals) typed neatly on headed notepaper, all based on the assumption that in describing Collins as ugly, Genesis as dull, I was deriding their way of life, undermining their identity. The intensity of this relationship between taste and self-definition seems peculiar to popular music – it is 'possessable' in ways that other cultural forms (except, perhaps, sports teams) are not.

To summarize the argument so far: the social functions of popular music are in the creation of identity, in the management of feelings, in the organization of time. Each of these functions depends, in turn, on our experience of music as something which can be possessed. From this sociological base it is now possible to get at aesthetic questions, to understand listeners' judgments, to say something about the value of pop music. My starting question was how is it that people (myself included) can say, quite confidently, that some popular music is better than others? The answer can now be related to how well (or badly), for specific listeners, songs and performances fulfill the suggested functions. But there is a final point to make about this. It should be apparent by now that people do hear the music they like as something special: not, as orthodox rock criticism would have it, because this music is more 'authentic' (though that may be how it is described), but because, more directly, it seems to provide an experience that transcends the mundane, that takes us 'out of ourselves'. It is special, that is, not necessarily with reference to other music, but to the rest of life. This sense of specialness, the way in which music seems to make possible a new kind of self-recognition, frees us from the everyday routines and expectations that encumber our social identities, is a key part of the way in which people experience and thus value music: if we believe we possess our music, we also often feel that we are possessed by it. Transcendence is, then, as much a part of the popular music aesthetic as it is of the serious music aesthetic; but, as I hope I have indicated, in pop, transcendence marks not music's freedom from social forces but its patterning by them. (Of course, in the end the same is true of serious music, too.)

### The aesthetics of popular music

I want to conclude with another sort of question: what are the factors in popular music that enable it to fulfill these social functions, which determine whether it does so well or badly? Again, I will divide my answer into four points; my purpose is less to develop them in depth than to suggest important issues for future critical work.

My first point is brief, because it raises musicological issues which I am not competent to develop. The most important (and remarkable) feature

*Towards an aesthetic of popular music* 145

of Western popular music in the twentieth century has been its absorption of and into Afro-American forms and conventions. In analytical terms, to follow the distinction developed by Andrew Chester at the end of the 1960s, this means that pop is complex 'intentionally' rather than, like European art music, 'extensionally'. In the extensional form of musical construction, argues Chester, 'theme and variations, counterpoint, tonality (as used in classical composition) are all devices that build diachronically and synchronically outwards from basic musical atoms. The complex is created by combination of the simple, which remains discrete and unchanged in the complex unity.' In the intentional mode, 'the basic musical units (played/sung notes) are not combined through space and time as simple elements into complex structures. The simple entity is that constituted by the parameters of melody, harmony and beat, while the complex is built up by modulation of the basic notes, and by inflexion of the basic beat.'[4] Whatever the problems of Chester's simple dichotomy between a tradition of linear musical development and a tradition of piled-up rhythmic interplay, he does pose the most important musicological question for popular music: how can we explain the *intensity* of musical experience that Afro-American forms have made possible? We still do not know nearly enough about the musical language of pop and rock: rock critics still avoid technical analysis, while sympathetic musicologists, like Wilfrid Mellers, use tools that can only cope with pop's non-intentional (and thus least significant) qualities.

My second point is that the development of popular music in this century has increasingly focused on the use of the voice. It is through the singing voice that people are most able to make a connection with their records, to feel that performances are theirs in certain ways. It is through the voice that star personalities are constructed (and since World War II, at least, the biggest pop stars have been singers). The tone of voice is more important in this context than the actual articulation of particular lyrics – which means, for example, that groups, like the Beatles, can take on a group voice. We can thus identify with a song whether we understand the words or not, whether we already know the singer or not, because it is the voice – not the lyrics – to which we immediately respond. This raises questions about popular non-vocal music, which can be answered by defining a voice as a sign of individual personality rather than as something necessarily mouthing words. The voice, for example, was and is central to the appeal of jazz, not through vocalists as such, but through the way jazz people played

---

[4] Andrew Chester, 'Second thoughts on a rock aesthetic: The Band', *New Left Review*, 62 (1970), pp. 78–9.

146    SIMON FRITH

and heard musical instruments – Louis Armstrong's or Charlie Parker's instrumental voices were every bit as individual and personal as a pop star's singing voice.

Today's commercial pop musics are, though, song forms, constructing vocal personalities, using voices to speak directly to us. From this perspective it becomes possible to look at pop songs as narratives, to use literary critical and film critical terms to analyze them. It would be fairly straightforward, for example, to make some immediate genre distinctions, to look at the different ways in which rock, country, reggae, etc. work as narratives, the different ways they set up star personalities, situate the listener, and put in play patterns of identity and opposition. Of course, popular music is not simply analogous to film or literature. In discussing the narrative devices of contemporary pop in particular, we are not just talking about music but also about the whole process of packaging. The image of pop performers is constructed by press and television advertisements, by the routines of photo-calls and journalists' interviews, and through gesture and performance. These things all feed into the way we hear a voice; pop singers are rarely heard 'plain' (without mediation). Their vocals already contain physical connotations, associated images, echoes of other sounds. All this needs to be analyzed if we are going to treat songs as narrative structures; the general point, to return to a traditional musicological concern, is that while music may not represent anything, it nevertheless clearly communicates.

The third point is an elaboration of the suggestion I have just made: popular music is wide open for the development of a proper genre analysis, for the classification of how different popular musical forms use different narrative structures, set up different patterns of identity, and articulate different emotions. Take, for example, the much discussed issue of music and sexuality. In the original article on rock and sexuality I wrote with Angela McRobbie at the end of the 1970s,[5] we set up a distinction between 'cock' rock and teenybop narratives, each working to define masculinity and femininity but for different audiences and along different contours of feeling. Our distinctions are still valid but we were looking only at a subdivision of one pop genre. Other musical forms articulate sexuality in far more complicated ways; thus it would be impossible to analyze the sexuality of either Frank Sinatra or Billie Holiday, and their place in the history of crooning and torch singing, in the terms of the 'cock' rock/teenybop contrast. Even Elvis Presley does not fit easily into these 1970s accounts of male and female sexuality.

[5] Simon Frith and Angela McRobbie, 'Rock and sexuality', *Screen Education*, 29 (1978/9), pp, 3–19.

*Towards an aesthetic of popular music* 147

The question these examples raise is how popular musical genres should be defined. The obvious approach is to follow the distinctions made by the music industry which, in turn, reflect both musical history and marketing categories. We can thus divide pop into country music, soul music, rock 'n' roll, punk, MOR, show songs, etc. But an equally interesting way of approaching genres is to classify them according to their ideological effects, the way they sell themselves as art, community or emotion. There is at present, for example, clearly a form of rock we can call 'authentic'. It is represented by Bruce Springsteen and defines itself according to the rock aesthetic of authenticity which I have already discussed. The whole point of this genre is to develop musical conventions which are, in themselves, measures of 'truth'. As listeners we are drawn into a certain sort of reality: this is what it is like to live in America, this is what it is like to love or hurt. The resulting music is the pop equivalent of film theorists' 'classic realist text'. It has the same effect of persuading us that this is how things really are – realism inevitably means a non-romantic account of social life, and a highly romantic account of human nature.

What is interesting, though, is how this sort of truth is constructed, what it rests on musically; and for an instant semiotic guide I recommend the video of *We are the world*. Watch how the singers compete to register the most sincerity; watch Bruce Springsteen win as he gets his brief line, veins pop up on his head and the sweat flows down. Here authenticity is guaranteed by visible physical effort.

To approach pop genres this way is to look at the pop world in terms rather different from those of the music industry. Against the authentic genre, for instance, we can pitch a tradition of artifice: some pop stars, following up on David Bowie's and Roxy Music's early 1970s work, have sought to create a sense of themselves (and their listeners) as artists in cool control. There is clearly also an avant-garde within popular music, offering musicians and listeners the pleasures of rule breaking, and a sentimental genre, celebrating codes of emotion which everyone knows are not real but carry nostalgic weight – if only they were! What I am arguing here is that it is possible to look at pop genres according to the effects they pursue. Clearly we can then judge performers within genres (is John Cougar Mellencamp's music as truthful as Springsteen's?), as well as use different genres for different purposes (the sentimental genre is a better source of adult love songs than the avant-garde or the artificers). To really make sense of pop genres, though, I think we need to place this grid of ideologies over the industry's grid of taste publics. To understand punk, for example, we need to trace within it the interplay of authenticity and artifice; to understand country we need to follow the interplay of authenticity and sentiment.

In everyday life we actually have a rather good knowledge of such conventional confusions. To know how to listen to pop music is to know how to classify it. One thing all pop listeners do, whether as casual fans or professional critics, is to compare sounds – to say that A is like B. Indeed, most pop criticism works via the implicit recognition of genre rules, and this brings me to my final point. Our experience of music in everyday life is not just through the organized pop forms I have been discussing. We live in a much more noisy soundscape; music of all sorts is in a constant play of association with images, places, people, products, moods, and so on. These associations, in commercial and film soundtracks, for example, are so familiar that for much of the time we forget that they are 'accidental'. We unthinkingly associate particular sounds with particular feelings and landscapes and times. To give a crude example, in Britain it is impossible now for a ballet company to perform the *Nutcracker Suite* for an audience of children without them all, at the key moment, breaking into song: 'Everyone's a fruit and nut case', has been instilled into them as a Cadbury's jingle long before the children hear of Tchaikovsky. Classical or 'serious' music, in short, is not exempt from social use. It is impossible for me, brought up in post-war popular culture, to hear Chopin without immediately feeling a vaguely romantic yearning, the fruit of many years of Chopinesque film soundtracks.

There is no way to escape these associations. Accordions played a certain way mean France, bamboo flutes China, just as steel guitars mean country, drum machines the urban dance. No sort of popular musician can make music from scratch – what we have these days instead are scratch mixers, fragmenting, unpicking, reassembling music from the signs that already exist, pilfering public forms for new sorts of private vision. We need to understand the lumber-room of musical references we carry about with us, if only to account for the moment that lies at the heart of the pop experience, when, from amidst all those sounds out there, resonating whether we like them or not, one particular combination suddenly, for no apparent reason, takes up residence in our own lives.

## Conclusion

In this paper I have tried to suggest a way in which we can use a sociology of popular music as the basis of an aesthetic theory, to move, that is, from a description of music's social functions to an understanding of how we can and do value it (and I should perhaps stress that my definition of popular

*Towards an aesthetic of popular music* 149

music includes popular uses of 'serious' music). One of my working assumptions has been that people's individual tastes – the ways they experience and describe music for themselves – are a necessary part of academic analysis. Does this mean that the value of popular music is simply a matter of personal preference?

The usual sociological answer to this question is that 'personal' preferences are themselves socially determined. Individual tastes are, in fact, examples of collective taste and reflect consumers' gender, class and ethnic backgrounds; the 'popularity' of popular music can then be taken as one measure of a balance of social power. I do not want to argue against this approach. Our cultural needs and expectations are, indeed, materially based; all the terms I have been using (identity, emotion, memory) are socially formed, whether we are examining 'private' or public lives. But I do believe that this derivation of pop meaning from collective experience is not sufficient. Even if we focus all our attention on the collective reception of pop, we still need to explain why some music is better able than others to have such collective effects, why these effects are different, anyway, for different genres, different audiences and different circumstances. Pop tastes do not just derive from our socially constructed identities; they also help to shape them.

For the last fifty years at least, pop music has been an important way in which we have learned to understand ourselves as historical, ethnic, class-bound, gendered subjects. This has had conservative effects (primarily through pop nostalgia) and liberating ones. Rock criticism has usually taken the latter as a necessary mark of good music but this has meant, in practice, a specious notion of 'liberation'. We need to approach this political question differently, by taking seriously pop's individualizing effects. What pop can do is put into play a sense of identity that may or may not fit the way we are placed by other social forces. Music certainly puts us in our place, but it can also suggest that our social circumstances are not immutable (and that other people – performers, fans – share our dissatisfaction). Pop music is not in itself revolutionary or reactionary. It is a source of strong feelings that because they are also socially coded can come up against 'common sense'. For the last thirty years, for example, at least for young people, pop has been a form in which everyday accounts of race and sex have been both confirmed and confused. It may be that, in the end, we want to value most highly that music, popular and serious, which has some sort of collective, disruptive cultural effect. My point is that music only does so through its impact on individuals. That impact is what we first need to understand.

# CHAPTER 17

# ADAM SMITH AND MUSIC

I

When I first gave a version of this paper, at a conference on the Scottish Enlightenment, someone stood up to say that while he accepted that there was a place for the well-meaning amateur among scholars *in* the eighteenth century, he was not convinced that there was a place for the well-meaning amateur among scholars *of* the eighteenth century. At the time (given the context), I took his point – I'm no expert on either Adam Smith or the history of musicology. But I was also dimly aware that this response was ironic – part of the point of the paper was to question interpretative authority. Certainly as far as music is concerned (if not in the world of eighteenth-century Scottish studies), the concept of expertise is problematic. It's not just that music scholarship is no guarantee of musical creativity, nor that many of the most gifted musicians are quite unschooled, but also that, from a listening perspective, the relationship of knowledge and pleasure is unclear. As Nicholas Cook puts it:

> What I find perplexing, and stimulating, about music is the way in which people – most people – can gain intense enjoyment from it even though they know little or nothing about it in technical terms.[1]

The question of musical judgement has perplexed me ever since I became a rock critic and realized that I had no hesitation about pronouncing authoritatively on new releases while, academically, I could offer no convincing theoretical account of musical value at all. For the last ten years I have stumblingly been trying to develop an aesthetics of popular music.[2] How do people come to value and assess particular sounds and styles and stars? How does popular music give pleasure (or pain)? In what terms do people make sense of their musical experiences? Where do these terms come from? 'To understand music,' suggests Peter Kivy, 'seems in significant part to be able to describe it.'[3] What, then, do people's descriptions of their favourite records reveal of their musical understanding?

To get from these questions to Adam Smith was a matter of serendipity, a coincidental reading of two rather different texts. First, an interview in *Melody Maker* with Green from Scritti Politti. Green is an intellectual kind of pop star – he named his publishing company *Jouissance* in honour of Roland Barthes, and early in his career put out a single called 'Jacques Derrida'. In his *Melody Maker* interview, he recalled meeting the great man:

1. Nicholas Cook, *Music, Imagination and Culture*, Clarendon Press, Oxford 1990, pp1-2.

2. See 'Towards an Aesthetic of Popular Music', R. Leppert and S. McClary (eds), *Music and Society*, Cambridge University Press, Cambridge 1987; and 'What is Good Music?', *Canadian Universities Music Review*, vol. 10, no.2, 1990.

3. Peter Kivy, *Music Alone*, Cornell University Press, Ithaca 1990, p97.

He said that what I was doing was part of the same project of undoing and unsettling that he's engaged in. He said that what sets the musician apart is the possibility of meaninglessness.[4]

4. *Melody Maker*, 12 May 1990.

Second, Kevin Barry's *Language, Music and the Sign*. Barry subtitles his book 'A Study in Aesthetics, Poetics and Poetic Practices From Collins to Coleridge', but this is misleading in two respects: on the one hand, Barry's concern is narrower than might be thought – he is primarily interested in writings on music; on the other hand, it is much broader – Barry celebrates an aesthetic tradition which is neglected in contemporary debates about signification. In his own words,

5. Kevin Barry, *Language, Music and the Sign*, Cambridge University Press, Cambridge, 1987, p2.

6. Adam Smith, 'Of the Nature of that Imitation which takes place in what are called the Imitative Arts', *Essays on Philosophical Subjects*, (ed. W.P.D. Wightman and J.C. Boyne), Clarendon Press, Oxford 1980, p189.

much attention has been given to the interaction between concepts of the pictorial and the poetic. Little attention has been given to the ways in which eighteenth-century thinking also includes another interaction: that between a concept of language and a concept of the 'empty' sign.[5]

The latter concept, taken from theories of music, provided poets like Blake, Wordsworth and Coleridge with a non-representational account of meaning which Barry traces back to writers like Alexander Gerrard, James Usher, Sir William James, Dugald Stewart, Thomas Twining and Adam Smith.

7. James Beattie, 'An Essay on Poetry and Music as they affect the Mind' (1776), reprinted in P. le Huray and J. Day (eds), *Music and Aesthetics in the Eighteenth and Early-Nineteenth Centuries*, Cambridge University Press, Cambridge 1981, pp154-5.

In 'pictorial' theories of signification, the signifier 'stands for' the signified, however arbitrary the relationship of sign and referent may be (written language, for example, was taken to have evolved from 'imitative' hieroglyphics through symbols to letters). The assumption is that the meaning of a sign is what it signifies. What, then, does music signify? For Lockean empiricists, the difficulty of answering this question indicated the inferiority of music to pictorial art, the ears to the eyes. Seeing depends on the distance between perceiver and perceived; it is this which enables us to measure objects, to acquire 'clear and distinct ideas'. Hearing is a much more messy affair. 'In the power of expressing a meaning with clearness and distinctness,' wrote Adam Smith, 'Dancing is superior to Music and Poetry to Dancing.'[6] Smith was making a familiar enough point here. As his contemporary, James Beattie, had pointed out, the meaning of 'music without poetry' can only be 'vague and ambiguous'. A ballad could thus shift mood lyrically without requiring a change of tune; the association of sounds and scenes was either a matter of circumstance (military music and troop movements, religious music and church ceremony) or convention – a foreigner, as Beattie put it, would not be able to hear the glens in a so-called 'Scottish' tune.[7]

8. Smith, *op.cit.*, p204; Barry, *op.cit.*, p181.

The sound object cannot be easily separated, then, from the hearing subject. The question becomes *when* do the various noises made by the instruments in an orchestra become 'music', something more, in Smith's words, 'than the effects of the particular sounds which ring in our ears at every particular instant?' Or perhaps the question is *where* do sounds become music – Barry remarks that in the Gothic novel the sound of music is a sign of the uncanny: the question is not what does it mean but, more frighteningly, where does it come from?[8]

Rousseau, an author, according to Smith, 'more capable of feeling strongly than analysing accurately', suggested that even if music could not represent nature as such, it did so indirectly, by arousing in its listeners those feelings that would have been induced by direct perception:

> The musician will sometimes not only agitate the waves of the sea, blow up the flames of a conflagration, make the rain fall, the rivulets flow and swell the torrents, but he will paint the horrors of a hideous desert, darken the walls of a subterranean dungeon, calm the tempest, restore serenity and tranquillity to the air and the sky, and shed from the orchestre a new freshness over the groves and the fields. He will not directly represent any of these objects, but he will excite in the mind the same movements which it would feel from seeing them.[9]

But even in this formulation what is being 'represented' is an absence, a landscape or a phenomenon that isn't there. 'I must observe,' says Smith,

> that without the accompaniment of the scenery and action of the opera, without the assistance either of the scene-painter or of the poet, or of both, the instrumental Music of the orchestre could produce none of the effects which are here ascribed to it; and we could never know, we could never even guess, which of the gay, melancholy, or tranquil objects above mentioned it meant to represent to us; or whether it meant to represent any of them, and not merely to entertain us with a concert of gay, melancholy or tranquil Music.[10]

Music only 'represents', that is, if listeners respond to it properly — its meaning depends on their interpretation.[11]

Kevin Barry suggests that for an increasing number of late eighteenth-century philosophers music thus gave poets a better aesthetic model than painting. At the very least, musical appreciation seemed a more democratic matter than an aesthetic perception dependent on scholastic pictorial conventions. People could take pleasure in music — be moved by a melody, know that a harmony was wrong — without needing to know anything about the notes with which melodies and harmonies are constructed.

What are the aesthetic implications of 'active' listening, the apparent freedom we have to interpret sounds? One eighteenth-century answer was that as music can only be about itself, so musical appreciation must be an appreciation of our own response to it. It is therefore dependent neither on a formal correspondence between sound and nature, as Rousseau suggested, nor on our empathy with the music's composers or players, as some Romantic theories of musical expression were to argue. Musical appreciation does, though, reflect our previous experience of music — both Hume and Burke argued that good taste was a matter of refining one's sensibility, not one's reason.

9. Quoted in Smith, *op.cit.*, p199.

10. *Ibid.*

11. This is the argument that would later underpin reader-response theory. See, for example, Roman Ingarden, 'Aesthetic Experience and Aesthetic Object', *Selected Papers in Aesthetics*, Catholic University of America Press, Washington DC 1985, p110.

## II

Adam Smith made as astute a contribution as anyone to eighteenth-century arguments about aesthetics, and one reason for drawing attention to his remarks on music (probably written in the 1770s though not published till after his death, in 1790) is that they have been neglected in musical theory, which is still taken to be, in William Austin's words, 'a German speciality'.[12] In Carl Dalhaus' history of music aesthetics, for example, Smith is not listed in the bibliography; neither is he mentioned in Peter Kivy's important study of eighteenth-century musical thought, *The Corded Shell*. His name does appear in le Huray and Day's comprehensive collection of eighteenth-century musical arguments but, tellingly, only in an 1820 letter written anonymously to the *Quarterly Musical Magazine and Review*, complaining about the editors' failure to take British philosophers of music seriously.[13] More surprisingly, Smith is not discussed either in Roger Scruton's music theory entries in the *New Grove Dictionary of Music*, even though Scruton's own approach to musical meaning is not dissimilar:

> Understanding music involves the active creation of an intentional world, in which inert sounds are transfigured into movements, harmonies, rhythms – metaphorical gestures in a metaphorical space.

To hear music, in Scruton's words, is 'to transfigure sound into figurative space, so that "you are the music while the music lasts" '.[14]

Despite his neglect by music historians, Smith's arguments anticipated not only those of an Anglo-Saxon analytic philosopher like Scruton, but also those within the German tradition itself (attention to Smith's critique might have tempered Kant's use of Rousseau's aesthetic assumptions, for example). These arguments concerned music's place in the hierarchy of the arts, and, more particularly, the relative value of instrumental and vocal or operatic works. The problem of instrumental music, as I have already noted, lay in its apparent inadequacy as a means of 'imitation':

> Instrumental Music, though it may, no doubt, be considered in some respects as an imitative art, is certainly less so than any other which merits that appellation; it can imitate but a few objects, and in even those so imperfectly, that without the accompaniment of some other art, its imitation is scarce ever intelligible: imitation is by no means essential to it, and the principal effects which it is capable of producing arise from powers altogether different from those of imitation.[15]

In the mid-eighteenth century it was still taken for granted by most commentators that instrumental music was inferior to music accompanied by words or gestures because it could not clearly represent (or imitate) anything – which was why Rousseau first dismissed it as 'rubbish' and later sought to

12. William Austin, 'Translator's Introduction' to Carl Dalhaus, *Esthetics of Music*, Cambridge University Press, Cambridge 1982 (1967), px.

13. See Dalhaus, *op.cit.*; Peter Kivy, *The Corded Shell*, Princeton University Press, Princeton NJ 1980; le Huray and Day, *op.cit.* – this letter is not included in the abridged paperback edition.

14. Roger Scruton, *The Aesthetic Understanding*, Methuen, London 1983, p100.

15. Smith, *op.cit.*, pp206-7.

validate it as imitating feelings.[16] It took the Romantic move – from theories of imitation to theories of expression – to reverse this judgment. In the nineteenth century instrumental music came to be valued above vocal music for its ability to *release* feeling 'from the confinements of prosaic everyday reality', that is, from its attachment to particular objects or states. By 1826, in his *Lectures on Music*, Hans Georg Nageli was celebrating instrumental music *because* it neither represents nor imitates. Music, he suggested, has no content but is simply 'a being at play', and it is this which enables it to move the listener, to invoke 'indefinite and ineffable feelings'.

> The soul hovers, carried along by this play of forms, in the whole immeasurable realm of emotions, now ebbing, now flowing up and down, plunging with the gently echoing breath of tones to the utmost depths of the heart and then soaring again with the rising impetus of tones to supreme feelings of bliss.[17]

Compare this passage to Smith's earlier, pre-Romantic description of the same experience:

> In a concert of instrumental Music the attention is engaged with pleasure and delight, to listen to a combination of the most agreeable and melodious sounds, which follow one another, sometimes with a quicker, and sometimes with a slower succession; and in which those that immediately follow one another sometimes exactly or nearly resemble and sometimes contrast with one another in tune, in time, and in order of arrangement. The mind being thus successively occupied by a train of objects, of which the nature, succession, and connection correspond, sometimes to the gay, sometimes to the tranquil, and sometimes to the melancholy mood or disposition, it is itself successively led into each of these moods or dispositions; and is thus brought into a sort of harmony or concord with the Music which so agreeably engages its attention.[18]

After the evocation of bliss, the coolness of reason. In Smith's aesthetics, the perception of beauty, the appreciation of art, seems to be as much an intellectual as a sensual matter. He thus rejected not only Francis Hutcheson's suggestion that music aroused emotion through its resemblance to a speaker's voice, but also Thomas Reid's argument that there was a *direct* 'fitness' of certain sounds 'to produce certain sentiments in our minds' and David Hartley's speculation that there is an *imitative* 'association' of sounds and sentiments. For Smith the effect of music is a matter of understanding; we don't so much feel its emotional meaning as appreciate its emotional shape.[19]

Even when we contemplate a painting, Smith suggests, something clearly representational, we don't simply see what's represented; rather, we see how the picture differs from its object while suggesting it. We marvel, that is, at the skill with which one thing has been made to represent another. In

16. See Dalhaus, *op.cit.*, p24.

17. Quoted in *ibid.*, p28.

18. Smith, *op.cit.*, pp197-8.

19. In this respect Smith anticipates Peter Kivy – the expressiveness of music is explained by 'the congruence of musical "contour" with the structure of expressive features and behaviour'. See *The Corded Shell, op.cit.*, pp22-30, 50-2, 77.

contemplating instrumental music, which is not representational, we marvel, then, at its order and method – and thus at the order and method of the mind itself:

> Whatever we feel from instrumental music is an original and not a sympathetic feeling: it is our own gaiety, sedateness or melancholy; not the reflected disposition of another person.[20]

20. Smith, *op.cit,* p198.

21. *Ibid.*, p204; and see Barry, *op.cit.,* pp60-1.

22. Barry, *op.cit.,* p148.

23. Smith, *op.cit.,* p185.

As Kevin Barry shows, Adam Smith followed other eighteenth-century philosophers in valuing music for those qualities that discredited it to the empiricists – its obscurity, instability and incompleteness. Because music is experienced temporally, what we perceive is always in a state of becoming. For James Usher this was why music, rather than painting, is sublime. In his terms, the aesthetic experience is constituted by desire, a state of mind in which an object is known by its absence, in which the contemplation of perfection is not tainted by the flaws of its material presence. Music expresses this contemplative principle best. Its significance also depends on absence, on sound already gone or yet to come; its 'perfection' is always a matter of memory and anticipation. In Smith's words:

> Time and measure are to instrumental Music what order and method are to discourse; they break it into proper parts and divisions, by which we are enabled both to remember better what is gone before, and frequently to foresee somewhat of what is to come after ...[21]

The debate, then, concerned the materiality of music, the tension between sounds heard in the abstract, made meaningful by their place in composition, and the physical sounds produced immediately by specific instruments. For Thomas Twining, the 'roughness' of the piano was aesthetically preferable to the precise notes of the harpsichord because it left the listener more to do to 'complete' the harmonics. For Coleridge, by contrast, music could be overwhelmed by materiality, its sublime potential unrealized because of the insistency of the body.[22]

Smith himself was less interested in the sublime than in the beautiful. The value of instrumental music (like the value of art in general) thus lay in its integration of the intellectual and the sensual. If music was the highest form of art, this was because it offered the most complete experience of the harmony of thought and feeling. The difference between the 'nobler works of Statuary and Painting and the phenomenon of Nature', Smith wrote, is that the former 'carry, as it were, their own explication along with them, and demonstrate, even to the eye, the way and manner in which they are produced.'[23]

Similarly,

> a well composed concerto can, without suggesting any other object, either by imitation or otherwise, occupy, and as it were fill up, completely the whole

capacity of the mind, so as to leave no part of its attention vacant for thinking of anything else. In the contemplation of that immense variety of agreeable and melodious sounds, arranged and digested, both in their coincidence and in their succession, into so complete and regular a system, the mind in reality enjoys not only a very great sensual, but a very high intellectual pleasure, not unlike that which it derives from the contemplation of a great system in any other science.[24]

Smith is anticipating here one strand of Romantic thought – the belief in 'absolute music'. 'Must not purely instrumental music create its own text?' asked Friedrich von Schlegel in 1798. 'And is not its theme developed, confirmed, varied and contrasted, just as is the object of a sequence of philosophical speculation?' Music, summarized Jules Cambarieu a hundred years later, 'is the art of thinking in sounds'.[25]

## III

In her recent study of the rise to dominance of the nineteenth-century concept of the 'musical work', Lydia Goehr suggests that Adam Smith's writings 'mark a transitionary phase'.[26] The transition was from the analysis of music as rhetoric to the analysis of music as art. Central to this change in perception were two metaphorical shifts. First, music began to be described in terms of space rather than time. Second, aesthetic attention moved from the listening subject to the musical object.[27] Both these changes meant the elevation of the intellectual over the sensual response. For Eduard Hanslick, the most influential champion of the new approach, 'aesthetic value in music' meant 'experiencing a piece of music as a kind of beautiful object through "the voluntary and pure act of contemplation which alone is the true and artistic method of listening" '.[28]

Hanslick argued – and this took him beyond Smith's position – that the value of music lay in the formal qualities of the work itself, and not in the quality of the listener's experience. Musical appreciation is thus a matter of reason (or, in Hanslick's terms, science): it means knowing what to listen to, rather than how to feel about it. In his words, 'Certainly with regard to beauty, imagining is not mere contemplating, but contemplating with active understanding, i.e. conceiving and judging.'[29]

This argument has had two obvious consequences. First, it has moralized the musical experience: it is now customary to distinguish 'good' and 'bad' listeners; musicology in the nineteenth century became a study not of how people did listen to music, but of how they ought to. Second, this moral distinction was rooted in a distinction of mind and body, which became, in turn, a way of distinguishing between 'serious' and 'popular' forms. Adam Smith had suggested that rhythm is a more 'primitive' musical quality than melody.

The time or measure of a song are simple matters, which even a coarse and unpracticed ear is capable of distinguishing and comprehending: but to

24. *Ibid.*, p204.

25. Friedrich von Schlegel, 'Fragments from *Das Athenaum*' (1798-1800), reprinted in le Huray and Day, *op.cit.*, p247; Jules Cambarieu, 'Music, its Laws and Evolution' (1907), reprinted in Bojan Bujic, *Music in European Thought 1851-1912*, Cambridge University Press, Cambridge 1988, p211.

26. Lydia Goehr, *The Imaginary Museum of Musical Works*, Clarendon Press, Oxford 1992, p154.

27. For the best account of this, see Mark Evan Bonds, *Wordless Rhetoric: Musical Form and the Metaphor of the Orator*, Harvard University Press, Cambridge MA 1991; and cf. Donald M. Lowe, *History of Bourgeois Perception*, Chicago University Press, Chicago 1982.

28. Cook, *op.cit.*, p15.

29. Eduard Hanslick, *On The Musically Beautiful*, Hackett Publishing, Indianapolis 1986 (1854; 1891), p4.

30. Smith, *op.cit.*, pp211-12.

31. Hanslick, *op.cit.*, pp61, 64.

32. See, for example, Pinchas Noy, 'The Psychodynamic Meaning of Music: A Critical Review of the Psychoanalytic and Related Material', Part II, *Journal of Music Therapy*, vol. 4, no.1, 1967, pp14-16.

33. Rose Rosengard Subotnik, 'Towards a Deconstruction of Structural Listening: A Critique of Schoenberg, Adorno and Stravinsky', in E. Narmour and R.A. Solie (eds), *Explorations in Music, the Arts and Ideas*, Pendragon Press, Stuyvesant NY 1988, p.120. And see Cook, *op.cit.*, and Sandra Kemp, 'Conflicting Choreographies: Derrida and Dance', *New Formations*, no.16, 1992.

distinguish and comprehend all the variations of the tune, and to conceive with precision the exact proportion of every note, is what the finest and most cultivated ear is frequently no more than capable of performing.[30]

Hanslick pushed this argument further by suggesting that to be 'moved' by the intellectual elements of music, by 'harmony and melody', is no different in principle from being moved by 'sensuous rhythm'.

> [N]either proceeds out of free self-determination: neither is yielding to the promptings of spirit or of love for beauty, but both are stirred as a result of neural stimulation ... When people surrender themselves so completely to the elemental in art that they are not in control of themselves, then it seems to us that this is not to the credit of the art and is still less to the credit of those people.

After all, as he then points out (before denouncing the Italians for mental indolence) 'as is well known, music exercises the strongest effect upon savages.'[31]

What's involved here is not simply a mapping of the intellectual/sensual distinction onto the difference between the 'civilized' and the 'primitive' – a mapping which has enabled psychoanalysts to equate 'primitive', 'rhythmic' and 'infantile' music – but also a binary opposition between the aesthetic response and 'sensual stimulation'.[32] This is a familiar enough argument in the other arts, but in music has led to a particularly odd line being drawn between the ideology and the reality of listening. Nicholas Cook has explored in detail the gap between musicological accounts of musical meaning and listeners' musical experiences – what Sandra Kemp calls the 'translatability' problem – and Rose Subotnik has graphically described the material effects of being taught to listen 'structurally':

> In my college harmony course, use of piano was forbidden. Whereas scoreless listening was unheard of in my university education, soundless keyboards were fairly common ... In numerous seminars on early music I transcribed reams of manuscripts of which I never heard a note or discussed the musical value. As a music major, and later as a teacher, listening to scratched and otherwise dreadful monophonic recordings, I developed a strategy of listening which I have never entirely shaken, whereby I mentally 'correct' for inadequacies of sound or performance that distract from my structural concentration ... Yet I am not at all sure that any of this structural discipline has made me a more competent listener than my brother, who travels eight hours a week to the opera houses of New York to hum the tunes and listen to certain sopranos.[33]

The shift from music as rhetoric to music as art marked, then, a specific devaluing of the *listener's* authority in musical judgment. As Mark Bonds shows, in the eighteenth century the purpose of music had been to 'elicit an intended emotional response', 'to move, persuade and delight the listener', and musical 'form' thus referred to qualities of 'coherence and persuasiveness'. In this context, the listener was 'the only true arbiter' of musical value. Now the arbiter became the work (and its composer).

> As an organism, the musical work is an object of contemplation that exists in and of itself. As an oration, the musical work is a temporal event whose purpose is to evoke a response from the listener. We can be moved by both modes of experience; but the metaphor of the oration necessarily emphasizes the temporality of the work, the role of the listener, and the element of aesthetic persuasion, whereas the model of the biological organism has no need to account for a work's effect upon its intended audience. Indeed, the audience, for all practical purposes, is irrelevant to the organic model. The organic metaphor implies that the standards by which any given work is to be judged will be found within the work itself.[34]

Lydia Goehr suggests that we must understand the nineteenth-century definition of the musical work as a 'regulative concept', that is, it not only meant a rewriting of musical history (to turn eighteenth-century composers into artists) but also the formulation of behavioural rules for both musical performers and audiences.[35] But while there is certainly plenty of evidence that such regulation was indeed an aspect of developing bourgeois cultural practice (as audiences were taught, for example, to listen silently and not to express musical pleasure physically), the difficulty of enforcing such rules also suggests that hard as they might try to repress their feelings, even the most respectable listeners were still hearing music sensuously.[36]

It is not even clear that the claims of pure music were fully acknowledged by classical musicians. Robert Frances notes that the most extensive psychological study of European musicians (in 1918) found that only half thought that 'music was just music'. The rest referred to 'a coherent extramusical message that in its variety sustained their interest in listening'. Frances had no reason to believe that such findings wouldn't be replicated forty years later.[37]

No doubt it is the sheer aesthetic obstinacy of both listeners and players which accounts for the contemptuous tone that musicologists so often adopt. Hanslick, again, set the pattern:

> Slouched dozing in their chairs, these enthusiasts allow themselves to brood and sway in response to the vibrations of tones, instead of contemplating tones attentively. How the music swells louder and louder and dies away, how it jubilates or trembles, they transform into a nondescript state of awareness which they naively consider to be purely intellectual. These people make up the most 'appreciative' audience and the one most likely to bring music into disrepute. The aesthetic criterion of intellectual pleasure is lost to them; for all they would know, a fine cigar or a piquant delicacy or a

34. Bonds, *op.cit.*, p145, and see pp54, 68, 95, 133.

35. Goehr, *op.cit.*, pp121, 178.

36. The most entertaining account of the education of the bourgeois audience is to be found in Lawrence Levine, *Highbrow/Lowbrow*, Harvard University Press, Cambridge MA 1988.

37. Robert Frances, *The Perception of Music*, Lawrence Erlbaum Associates, Hillside NJ 1988 (1958), p227.

38. Hanslick, *op.cit.*, p59.

39. Kant quoted in le Huray and Day, *op.cit.*, p163; Adorno in Subotnik, *op.cit.*, pp104-5; Ives in Goehr, *op.cit.*, p229.

40. Quoted in Goehr, *op.cit.*, p210.

41. Quoted in Cook, *op.cit.*, p182.

42. Heinrich Adolf Kostlin, *Die Tonkunst* (1879), reprinted in Bujic, *op.cit.*, p154. The most ambitious – and to my mind wrong-headed – attempt to show (following Chomsky) that people have a 'structurally innate' ability to grasp music analytically is Fred Lerdahl and Ray Jackendoff, *A Generative Theory of Tonal Music*, MIT Press, Cambridge MA 1983.

43. Robin Maconie, *The Concept of Music*, Clarendon Press, Oxford 1990, pp116-7.

warm bath produces the same effect as a symphony.[38]

In its materiality, music, in Kant's words, 'lacks good breeding', and the final logic of the music-as-music position is that it should be neither heard nor played. Sound, mused Adorno, is a 'layer of music' using historically conditioned resources – instruments and technology and performing conventions – which 'bear the imprint of social ideology and allow the "neutralization" of structural individuality'. 'Why can't music go out the same way it comes into a man,' wondered Charles Ives, 'without having to crawl over a fence of sounds, thoraxes, catgut, wire, wood and brass?'[39]

Ives sounds here the note of Romantic individualism that originally undermined accounts of music as oration and helped define the 'serious' as the 'unpopular'. Thus in his 1802 life of Bach, Johann Forkel suggested that

The public merely asks for what it can understand, whereas the true artist ought to aim at an achievement which cannot be measured by popular standards. How, then, can popular applause be reconciled with the true artist's aspirations towards the ideal?[40]

And Schoenberg believed that

Those who compose because they want to please others and have audiences in mind, are not real artists ... They are merely more or less skilful entertainers who would renounce composing if they did not find listeners.[41]

Popularity is defined here generally, not just by reference to quantity (the size of the audience), but to also to quality (the nature of the response). The proper listener – the listener paying aesthetic attention – has to translate a temporal experience into a spatial one. Music has to be appreciated organically, in terms of its internal structure, and the question becomes how we can grasp an architecture from the immediate *flow* of sounds. 'The listener,' Heinrich Kostlin declared sternly in 1879, 'needs a firm observation post from which he can review the march-past of those harmonies, like a general reviewing his troops on parade.'[42]

Structural listening is necessarily dependent, then, on its spatial representation, on the *score*. 'By legislating for pitch,' notes composer Robin Maconie, 'notation could be said to have freed musical invention from the tyranny of the ear,' just as 'regulation of time values in its turn liberated player and composer from the limitations of memory and the tyranny of succession.'[43]

But the score isn't the music, and in what is still the most interesting analytic exploration of musical 'autonomy', Roman Ingarden suggests that the nineteenth-century argument involved two elements: the score, which fixes the work but does not constitute a musical experience nor even part of it; and an infinite set of performances, each a distinct and unique experience, but nevertheless drawing its meaning from its 'truth' to the score. Given that, in practice, no single performance is judged to be 'the absolute, faultless, genuine embodiment of the score', least of all the first performance or the composer's own version, the musical work can only be said to exist in its potential. As Ingarden puts it, a musical work is an *intentional object* – it originates in a creative act which gives the score its purpose; and a *schematic object* – the score leaves open different possibilities of completion, aesthetically significant areas of indeterminacy.[44]

A musical work, in short, is neither real (~~not~~ defined simply by its performances), nor ideal (brought into existence by material processes of composition and realization); it is neither the score nor its realization, but the relationship between the two. Bringing music into aesthetic line with the other arts in the nineteenth century meant, then, building an 'imaginary museum of musical works', a concert hall equivalent of the galleries in which the meaning of painting and sculpture was being redefined.[45] And the power of this metaphor is reflected in the musicological approach to popular music – the first task is, inevitably, transcription, the translation of sound into score, whether the score of an imaginary event (most contemporary recorded music is not performed, but constructed) or an improvised one (Ornette Coleman is said to have looked aghast at a transcription of one of his solos, knowing that he would be quite unable to play it).[46]

From this perspective, musical listening is, by definition, a double process, involving both the immediate experience of sound and an abstract, comparative exercise of judgment. Music turns out to be, after all, an imitative art: a performance is an imitation of a score. But the possibility of such imitative listening depends on certain material conditions. To put it simply, a musical work must be heard repeatedly, and it was both a cause and effect of the new approach to music in the nineteenth century that people began to think in terms of the musical repertoire (the imaginary museum), to take it for granted that 'great' music was regularly performed music. In the eighteenth century even the most committed listener would not have expected to hear any particular piece more than once – it had to do its aesthetic work immediately.

It is not surprising, then, that the twentieth-century threat to musical autonomy is not the rise of mass music as such, but the development of recording technology. There was once 'an enduring set of instructions and a succession of interpretations', now there can be 'a specific performance which constitutes the work'. Roman Ingarden argues that for classical music this is not a major problem: a record is just another version of the score and does not mean 'perfection' even if it is, in the composer's view, 'definitive'. But, as his translator notes, once we broaden our perspective to other forms of music a paradox appears: if the Romantic ideology of the original work guaranteed the 'genius' of composers, it also challenged it – their own realization of their work is not necessarily any more valuable than anyone else's. Recording, by contrast, confers absolute authority on popular performers: their performance is their work.[47]

It is not surprising, either, that the aesthetics of popular music (despite the

44. Roman Ingarden, *The Work of Music and the Problem of its Identity*, Macmillan, London 1986, pp117 and 151-2, and see the introduction by the translator, Adam Czerniawski, pxii.

45. For this term see Patricia Carpenter, 'The Musical Object', *Current Musicology*, no.5, 1967, p68; and Goehr, *op.cit.*, p173.

46. For an ingenious attempt to transcribe – and so analyze – a studio track, see Stan Hawkins, 'Prince: Harmonic Analysis of Anna Stesia', *Popular Music*, vol.11, no.3, 1992; the Coleman story is cited in Cook *op.cit.*, pp158-9.

47. Ingarden, *op.cit.* ppxiv-xv. Pre-recorded folk music can, in fact, be accommodated to Ingarden's argument – here the listener compares and assesses each performance against the memory of the 'traditional ideal'. But, again, such comparison depends on the repetition of traditional song. Cf. Hanslick's account of 'naive art', *op.cit.*, p74.

best efforts of 'serious' critics) should relate more obviously to eighteenth-century interests in oration, performance and gesture than to the nineteenth-century concern with structure. Adam Smith had suggested that one difference between singing and speaking was that the singing voice could meet the structural demands of the score in a way in which the speaking voice could not. This was one reason, he argued (as a transitory figure) that the source of the musical beauty was structural not rhetorical:

> As the sounds or tones of the singing voice, therefore, can be ascertained or appropriated, while those of the speaking voice cannot; the former are capable of being noted or recorded, while the latter are not.[48]

48. Smith, *op.cit.*, p213.

49. Derrick F. Wright, 'Musical Meaning and its Social Determinants', *Sociology*, vol.9, no.3, 1975, p428.

50. Hanslick, *op.cit.*, p51.

51. John A. Sloboda, *The Musical Mind: The Cognitive Psychology of Music*, Clarendon Press, Oxford 1985, p153.

Now, of course, we pick up a different inflexion from the term 'recorded'.

But there is one final point to be made here. If recording has transformed our sense of the musical text, it has had an even more dramatic effect on musical context. All that work done in the nineteenth century to ritualize music, to confine it to special places, special moments, special moods, has been undone (and I write as BBC Radio 3 is changing format to compete with Classical FM; one of the first things to go is any commitment to the 'integrity' of the musical work). Any music may now be heard any time anywhere – on radio, cassette and CD player, as film and TV soundtrack, as muzak and jingle. And anyone might be listening to it. Now, from a sociological perspective, musical culture obviously means 'knowledge not just of musical forms and interpretative schemes, but also of rules of behaviour in musical settings', rules of 'how, when and where to hear music'.[49] The problem of 'recorded music culture' is that it is, in these terms, anarchical.

## IV

The question underlying the last 250 years' debate about music has been a simple one: what does a listener to music actually do? Adam Smith wrote at a time when there was confidence – at least among intellectuals – that this question could be answered by systematic self-analysis, and it is, perhaps, unfortunate that since then experimental psychology has displaced the philosophy of the mind. 'The intense influence of music upon the nervous system is fully accepted as fact by psychology as well as physiology,' wrote Hanslick in 1854. 'Unfortunately an adequate explanation of this is still lacking.'[50] And as John Sloboda comments, it is an obvious limitation now that musical reception, 'the one area of music psychology in which research is flourishing, should be characterized by a relative insensitivity to the problem of relating research findings to normal musical listening.'[51]

So what is 'normal' listening? It is noteworthy that the two great European rationalists of the early twentieth century, Freud and Lenin, were both disturbed by their response to music. Lenin was reluctant to listen to Beethoven because the music made him want to pat people on the head; Freud remarked that his pleasure in art lay in comprehension.

> Whenever I cannot do this, as for instance with music, I am almost incapable of obtaining any pleasure. Some rationalistic, or perhaps analytic, turn of mind in me rebels against being moved by a thing without knowing why I am thus affected, and what it is that affects me.[52]

Laurence Kramer has suggested that to call music 'meaningless' is a response 'less to an absence of thought than to the presence of danger'.[53] The danger – the threat posed by music and dance to aesthetics – is less the absence of mind than the presence of body. The ideology of the musical work leads, as we've seen, towards the *repression* of the sensual. In the words of one psychoanalyst, 'it is a prerequisite to the *aesthetic* response to musical art work that we free ourselves of [such] sensuous feelings and let the work exert its influence unimpeded, in the full beauty of its aesthetic form.'[54]

But, in the words of another, the musical experience is an *essentially* sensual 'pleasure in motion'.

> The joyous freedom and inexplicable obedience to will in the play of musical movement is, according to my opinion, a regressive repetition and idealized intensification of bodily pleasure in that early period of infancy, when the discovery of limbs is followed by the gradual mastery of the whole body.[55]

The obvious solution to the contradiction here is somehow to integrate the intellectual and the sensual. This strategy lay behind Adam Smith's denial that the value of music could be referred to anything extra-musical. Hence his belief in the superiority of instrumental music to what would later be called 'programme' music.

> Such imitations resemble those of painted Statuary, they may surprise at first, but they disgust ever after, and appear evidently such simple and easy tricks as are fit only for the amusement of children and their nurses at a puppet-show.[56]

Music, argued Smith, may evoke feelings, but only as objects for contemplation. To feel music directly is to understand it less well than to concentrate on how those feelings are produced. To put it another way, music which is designed simply to *arouse* feeling (through collective participation, for example) is clearly inferior to music which stimulates feelings *through* thought. The latter, superior music works by suggesting nothing 'that is different from its melody and harmony'.[57]

There are a number of strands in this argument (it clearly individualizes musical experience, for example) but, most importantly, it defines the 'sensuality' of music as the effect of following musical 'thoughts'. Rather than an immediate sensual response, and then its contemplative interpretation,

52. Lenin quoted by Maxim Gorky in *Lenin on Literature and Art*, Lawrence & Wishart, London 1967, p270; Freud in Noy, *op.cit.*, Part 1, *Journal of Music Therapy*, vol.3, no.4, 1966, p127.

53. Laurence Kramer, *Music as Cultural Practice, 1800-1900*, University of California Press, Berkeley CA 1990, p4.

54. G. Revesz quoted in Noy, *op.cit.*, part II, p11.

55. Richard Sterba, 'Toward the Problem of the Musical Process', *The Psychoanalytic Review*, no.33, 1946, p41.

56. Smith, *op.cit.*, p201.

57. *Ibid.*

musical listening means grasping a piece intellectually and then taking sensual pleasure in the 'movement' of the mind. Music offers, then, the experience of *feelings under control*. This model has become the norm (in various guises) of classical music ideology. It is central, for example, to both Hanslick's and Nietzsche's accounts of the 'Musically Beautiful', and is still evident in, say, Roger Scruton's distinction between art and fantasy or Nelson Goodman's description of musical pleasure as a form of cognition. One version of the argument is summed up by Deryk Cooke:

> We may say then that, whatever else the mysterious art known as music may eventually be found to express, it is primarily and basically a language of the emotions, through which we directly experience the fundamental urges that move mankind, without the need of falsifying ideas and images – words or pictures. A dangerous art in fact ... But under the guidance of the intellect and enlightened moral sense, it is surely as safe as anything human can be – as safe at least, shall we say, as religion or science.[58]

58. Deryk Cooke, *The Language of Music*, Oxford University Press, Oxford 1959, p272. And see Roger Scruton, *The Politics of Culture and Other Essays*, Carcenet Press, Manchester 1981, pp69, 87; and Nelson Goodman, *Languages of Art*, Oxford University Press, Oxford 1969, pp255-65.

Two questions remain. First, why should following the motion of music be described as *emotional*? And, second, if 'the musical experience' is so clearly rooted in subjectivity (for all Hanslick's theoretical efforts) how can we say that anyone's response to music is 'wrong'? It simply *is*. The fact that most people don't hear (or describe) the movement of sounds that is represented by the score does not mean that they don't hear (and reflect pleasurably upon) music – sounds moving.

59. Cooke, *op.cit.*, p205.

'When we come down to the fundamental musical experience,' concedes Cooke, 'the transformation of the sound into emotion, the professional is as tongue-tied as the layman.'[59] It was established in the eighteenth century that there couldn't be a *direct* link between sound and feeling. Sir William James pointed out that 'no man, truly affected with love or grief, ever expressed the one in an acrostic, or the other in a fugue.' James Beattie asked:

60. Sir William James, 'Essays on the Poetry of Eastern Nations' (1772), reprinted in le Huray and Day, *op.cit.*, p145; Beattie, *op.cit.*, p151.

> What is the natural sound of devotion? Where is it to be heard? What resemblance is there between Handel's 'Te Deum' and the tone of voice natural to a person expressing, by articulate sound, his veneration of the Divine Character and providence?[60]

On the other hand, neither can it be denied that music does make us feel, nor that we can label those feelings – as gaiety, tranquillity or melancholia, in Smith's example. The eighteenth-century move was, then, to distinguish between general and specific feelings. Music, suggested Archibald Alison, was

> limited indeed in the reach of its imitation or expression and far inferior to language, in being confined to the expression only of general emotions, but powerful within these limits beyond any other means we know, both by the variety which it can afford, and the continued and increasing interest which

it can raise.[61]

For Hanslick, who believed that the content of music was simply 'tonally moving forms', it thereby embodied 'the motion of feeling, abstracted from the content itself, i.e. from what is felt'. Music concerns the 'dynamics of feeling' rather than feeling itself, and Hanslick made a telling analogy with dance: 'The more it abandons the beautiful rhythmicity of its forms, in order to become gestures and mimicry to express specific thoughts and feelings, the more it approaches the crude significance of mere pantomime.'[62]

Two different sorts of distinction are being made in these attempts to define emotion abstractly. In the first instance, the suggestion is that musical emotion is profound but vague – we have the feeling without its occasion; in Adam Smith's terms, music doesn't make us sad but makes us feel sadness; in von Hartmann's words,

> Music reveals ineffable depths of the emotional life, such as poetry simply cannot express, whereas poetry presents not only the emotion itself but a perception of the situations, characters and actions that determine the emotions.[63]

This is, interestingly enough, the working assumption of film-scorers, who use music to arouse the general (and profound) feelings which the audience can then place according to the film's narrative; we are both made to feel and given a reason to do so. For Hollywood pragmatists, it doesn't much matter why certain instrumental sounds cause certain feelings, it's enough that they do. But the question remains as to how the analogy between musical and emotional shapes works – and whether there is anything more to this than analogy. The second way of approaching the argument is to suggest not that music somehow expresses the shape of feelings, but, rather, that in describing musical experiences we are obliged to apply adjectives, that we therefore attach feeling words conventionally and arbitrarily to what is, in fact, a purely aural experience. This would explain why, for example, in music (unlike the other arts) a child prodigy can move us. As Max Dessoir says,

> Children of eight can perform prodigies of understanding, performing, even creating music ... There is virtually no parallel to this in the other arts, since even the most gifted can only gradually acquire that understanding of the world and of humanity which is needed by the poet and the painter. Music, on the other hand, has no essential need of any relationship with reality.[64]

But what interests me here is another point – not music's possible meaninglessness, but people's continued attempts to make it meaningful, to name their feelings, supply the adjectives. Rose Subotnik notes the suggestion that modern dance, even when accompanied by a 'difficult' score, has a

61. Archibald Alison, *Essays on the Nature and Principles of Taste* (1790), reprinted in le Huray and Day, *op.cit.*, p151.

62. Hanslick, *op.cit.*, p23 and see pp20, 29.

63. Eduard von Hartmann, *The Philosophy of the Beautiful* (1887), reprinted in Bujic, *op.cit.*, p174.

64. Max Dessoir, 'Aesthetics and General Theory of Art' (1906), reprinted in Bujic, *op.cit.*, p383. The best account of all these issues remains Kivy's *The Corded Shell*.

relatively large public (compared to modern music) 'because ballet is sufficiently abstract that audiences do not feel tempted to panic if they fail to understand the "meaning" '. I would put this slightly differently: the reason is that the 'meaning' of ballet is felt to be more open to each person's own interpretation; dance has, on the whole, escaped the tyranny of the musically correct (and 'difficult' music has, after all, long featured without panicked reaction in the cinema).[65]

The comfort of meaning is, I suppose, why Derrida relates the possibility of meaninglessness to a process of unsettling, and why postmodernism in music has been defined experientially,

> where the anxiety of the listener to 'make sense of' the piece is either perpetually frustrated by pure randomness – Cage's music of chance – or assuaged and dissipated by a bland, 'easy-listening' surface with changes happening only in a Californian *longue durée*, as in the music of la Monte Young, Philip Glass, Terry Riley, or Steve Reich.[66]

Such attempts to frustrate or dissipate audience response may be postmodern, but they also smack of conventional Romanticism (avant-garde division), and there is something decidedly self-deceptive about Derrida (object of a thousand exegeses) and Green (product of the most elaborate star-making machinery) talking about 'the project of undoing'.

Music does not have a content – it can't, for example, be translated – but, as Peter Kivy points out, this does not mean that it is not 'an object of the understanding'.[67] Or, to put it another way, the gap in music between the nature of the experience (sounds) and the terms of interpretation (adjectives) may be more obvious than in any other art form, but this does not mean that the pleasure of music doesn't lie in the ways in which we can – and must – fill the gap. 'After playing Chopin,' wrote Oscar Wilde,

> I feel as if I had been weeping over sins that I had never committed, and mourning over tragedies that were not my own. Music always seems to me to produce that effect. It creates for one a past of which one has been ignorant, and fills one with a sense of sorrows that have been hidden from one's tears. I can fancy a man who has led a perfectly commonplace life, hearing by chance some curious piece of music, and suddenly discovering that his soul, without his being conscious of it, had passed through terrible experiences, and known fearful joys, or wild romantic loves, or great renunciations.[68]

## V

To read Adam Smith, to read the history of music theory since Adam Smith, is to follow an attempt to constitute both a definition of music and a way of listening. The peculiarity of this history is that it has been, by and large, successful discursively and unsuccessful materially – people talk about 'music'

65. Herbert Landberger quoted in Subotnik, *op.cit.*, p115.

66. John Beverley, 'The Ideology of Postmodern Music and Left Politics'. *Critical Quarterly*, vol. 31, no.1, 1989, p47.

67. Kivy, *op.cit.* p66.

68. Quoted in Jan Mukarovsky, *Aesthetic Function, Norm and Value as Social Facts*, University of Michigan, Ann Arbor MI 1970, pp76-77.

in ways which make little sense of how they listen to it. We take it for granted, for example, that a clear distinction can be made between 'serious' music and music as entertainment (or, perhaps, between serious listening and listening as entertainment). But, as a listener, I'm much less clear. Can I really distinguish between the pleasure that I take in Bartok and the pleasure that I take in Hüsker Dü? Am I describing something quite different when I say that I'm moved by Fauré's *Requiem* and by Kool and the Gang's 'Get Down On It'?

The debate about musical meaning in which Smith took part was, in fact, a debate about what we should say about music. Aesthetic argument has been, ever since, a matter of lexical regulation. 'We may doubt,' writes Roman Ingarden, 'whether so-called dance music, when employed only as a means of keeping the dancers in step and arousing in them a specific passion for expression through movement, is music in the strict sense of the word.'[69] But (and this is the Green Line) the point of music, whether in club or concert hall is, precisely, to flout the strict sense of the word.

69. Ingarden, *op.cit.*, p46.

# CHAPTER 18

# Music and Identity

Henry Rollins once said that music exists to put furniture in your mind, 'because life is so cruel and TV is so mean.'

Gina Arnold[1]

Becoming what one is is a creative act comparable with creating a work of art.

Anthony Storr[2]

It is not easy, however, to be evil when music is playing.

John Miller Chernoff[3]

The academic study of popular music has been limited by the assumption that the sounds must somehow 'reflect' or 'represent' the people. The analytic problem has been to trace the connections back, from the work (the score, the song, the beat) to the social groups who produce and consume it. What's been at issue is homology, some sort of *structural* relationship between material and musical forms.

The search for homology is most commonly associated these days with subculture theory, with accounts of punk or heavy metal, for example;[4] but the supposed fit (or lack of it) between aesthetic and social values has a much longer history in the study of popular culture. This is T.S. Eliot on Marie Lloyd:

It was her understanding of the people and sympathy with them, and the people's recognition of the fact that she embodied the virtues which they genuinely most respected in private life, that raised her to the position she occupied at her death . . . I have called her the expressive figure of the lower classes.[5]

More recently the rise of identity politics has meant new assertions of cultural essentialism, more forceful arguments than ever that, for example, only African-Americans can appreciate African-American music, that there is a basic difference between male and female composition, that the 'globalization' of a local sound is a form of cultural 'genocide'.[6]

The assumptions in such arguments about the necessary flow from social identity (whether defined in terms of race or sexuality or age or nation) to musical expression (and appreciation) seem straightforward enough in the abstract (who could possibly deny that African-American music is music made by African-Americans; that the difference between male and female experience will be embedded in male and female music; that Phil Collins is an imposition on the soundscape of the Australian outback?). But they are less convincing in the everyday practice of music making and listening: how do we make sense of the obvious *love* of European listeners and players for the music of the African diaspora? Who is expressing what when, say, Ella Fitzgerald sings Cole Porter? When Yothi Yindi *rocks*?[7]

The problem here is not just the familiar postmodern point that we live in an age of plunder in which musics made in one place for one reason can be immediately appropriated in another place for quite another reason, but also that while music may be *shaped* by the people who first make and use it, as experience it has a life of its own. Marx remarks somewhere that it is easy enough to move analytically from the cultural to the material, easy enough, that is, to *interpret* culture, to read it ideologically, to assign it social conditions. The difficult trick is to do the analysis the other way round, to show how the base produced *this* superstructure, to explain why an idea or experience takes on *this* artistic or aesthetic form, and not another, equally 'reflective' or 'representative' of its conditions of production.[8] After the cultural event, as a historian might agree, we can say why expression had to happen this way; before it there is no creative necessity at all. And if art is therefore, so to speak, originally accidental, then there is no particular reason to accept its makers' special claims on it. The interesting question, rather, is how art comes to make its own claims, in other circumstances, for itself.

In examining the aesthetics of popular music, then, I want to reverse the usual academic and critical argument: the issue is not how a particular piece of music or a performance reflects the people, but how it produces them, how it creates and constructs an experience – a musical experience, an aesthetic experience – that we can only make sense of by *taking on* both a subjective and a collective identity. The aesthetic, to put this another way, describes the quality of an experience (not the quality of an object); it means experiencing *ourselves* (not just the world) in a different way. My argument here, in short, rests on two premises: first, that identity is *mobile*, a process not a thing, a becoming not a being; second, that our experience of music – of music making and music listening – is best understood as an experience of this *self-in-process*. Music, like identity, is both performance and story, describes the social in the individual and the individual in the social, the mind in the body and the body in the mind; identity, like music, is a matter of both ethics and aesthetics. In exploring these themes I will, among other things, touch critically on their treatment under the label of 'postmodernism', but my main concern is to suggest that if music is a metaphor for identity, then, to echo Marx, the self is always an imagined self but can only be imagined as a particular organization of social, physical and material forces.

## The mobile self

What's at stake has become clear in the debate about postmodernism and the unstable or 'decentred' subject, a debate which has been dominated by the problems of signification and structure. Postmodernism, that is to say, is taken to describe a 'crisis' of signification systems: how can we now tell the difference between the 'real' and the 'simulated'? The postmodern problem is the threat to our sense of place – hence the mapping metaphors, the use of terms like depth and surface. What is underplayed in such discussions is the problem of process – not the positioning of the subject as such, but our experience of the movement between positions. This is where music becomes an important area for study: what happens to our assumptions about postmodern identity when we examine a form in which sound is more important than sight, and time more important than space; when the 'text' is a performance, a movement, a flux; when nothing is 'represented'?[9]

The broad argument that I want to make here, in short, is that in talking about identity we are talking about a particular kind of experience, or a way of dealing with a particular kind of experience. Identity is not a thing but a process – an experiential process which is most vividly grasped *as music*. Music seems to be a key to identity because it offers, so intensely, a sense of both self and others, of the subjective in the collective. As Mark Slobin puts it,

> Music seems to have an odd quality that even passionate activities like gardening or dog-raising lack: the simultaneous projecting and dissolving of the self in *performance*. Individual, family, gender, age, supercultural givens, and other factors hover around the musical space but can penetrate only very partially the moment of enactment of musical fellowship. Visible to the observer, these constraints remain unseen by the musicians, who are instead working out a shared vision that involves both the assertion of pride, even ambition, and the simultaneous disappearance of the ego.[10]

The experience of identity describes both a social process, a form of interaction, and an aesthetic process; as Slobin argues, it is the 'aesthetic rather than organizational/contextual aspects of performance' that 'betray a continuity between the social, the group, and the individual'.[11] It is in deciding – playing and hearing what sounds *right* (I would extend this account of music from performing to listening, to listening as a way of performing) – that we both express ourselves, our own sense of rightness, and suborn ourselves, lose ourselves, in an act of participation.[12]

The implication of this argument is that we need to rethink the usual sociological approach to aesthetic expression. My point is not that a social group has beliefs which it then articulates in its music, but that music, an aesthetic practice, articulates *in itself* an understanding of both group relations and individuality, on the basis of which ethical codes and social ideologies are understood.[13]

What I want to suggest, in other words, is not that social groups agree on values which are then expressed in their cultural activities (the assumption of the homology models) but that they only get to know themselves *as groups* (as a particular organization of individual and social interests, of sameness and difference) *through* cultural activity, through aesthetic judgement. Making music isn't a way of expressing ideas; it is a way of living them. As John Miller Chernoff concluded from his study of drumming in Ghana,

> African music is a cultural activity which reveals a group of people organizing and involving themselves with their own communal relationships – a partici- pant-observer's comment, so to speak, on the processes of living together. The aesthetic point of the exercise is not to reflect a reality which *stands behind it* but to ritualize a reality that is *within* it.[14]

And this is not just a characteristic of African music, Philip V. Bohlman concludes his study of the role of chamber music in the lives of the *Yekkes*, the German-speaking Jews in Israel, as follows:

> But this essay is not really about an ethnic group. Nor is it about the music per se of that group [though] I am here concerned with the music history resulting from the response of a group with a shared value system to a musical repertory that articulated those values. Such groups have long populated the history of Western music. Sometimes we call them ethnic groups or communities, sometimes national cultures, and sometimes we label by coupling place with abstraction, for example in 'Viennese classicism'. All these acts of labelling suggest the process of standing outside a group and looking in to see what sort of music is to be found. Suppose the group is really the product of its musical activities and the cultural values bound to them? What if excessive concern with the musical text deflects one from seeing the formation of diverse groups and music histories. What if one looked at the Yekkes, with their devotion to chamber music, as just another justification for the conditions of absolute music?[15]

Bohlman's target here is musicology. As an ethnomusicologist he is arguing that the meaning of classical music, as an experience, is not to be found in the text, but in the performance of the text, in the process in which it is realized. The Yekke chamber music groups don't have an abstract belief in 'absolute' (or transcendent) music; rather the concept of 'absolute music' is dependent on a particular way of being – playing – together.

Bohlman's argument is particularly interesting because it is applied to 'high' music making. His suggestion, with which I strongly agree, is that in terms of aesthetic process there is no real difference between high and low music. As he notes, from his perspective, 'Western art music functions not unlike styles and repertories most commonly accepted as the ethnomusicologist's field, namely folk and non-Western music.' And I would add, from my perspective, not unlike commercial popular music either. In short, different sorts of musical activity may produce different sorts of musical identity, but *how* the musics work to form identities is the same. The distinction between high and low culture, in other words, describes not something caused by different (class-bound) tastes, but is an effect of different (class-bound?) social activities.[16]

Let me make the point in a different way, by quoting two music critics, one low and one high, and then considering the difference between them. First the low critic, Frank Kogan, writing about Spoonie Gee in a fanzine in the mid-1980s.

'Spoonin Rap' and ' Love Rap' by Spoonie Gee are my favourite American-made records of the last ten years. They came out about five years ago, 'Spoonin Rap' in late '79 and 'Love Rap' in '80. I've never read a review of either.

On the basis of his voice alone, the way it balances coolness with angry passion while keeping a dance beat, Spoonie is a major artist; in addition, he's a writer. His lyrics are as intense as his singing, and embody the same tensions. Example: both 'Spoonin Rap' and 'Love Rap' start with detailed and explicit bragging – about how cool and sexy he is, about how girls go for him, how they're impressed with his rapping and his car. He puts on his eight-track. He makes love to the girl in his car. In his Mercedes. The seat's so soft, just like a bed. At the moment of sexual triumph the lyrics make a jarring change, as if there's a second song hidden behind the first, as if the bragging were a set-up for something else. . . . And then it's like the first part of the song, but turned inside out – the guys and girls are drawn to his flashy clothes and car only so they can rip him off and leave him in the gutter. The girls are gonna play him for a fool. . . . Then it shifts back to what a great lover he is, nice descriptions of his girl friends. 'Spoonin Rap' shifts around in the same way. It's about how cool he is, about how sexy women are; then it's about don't do dope, don't steal, you'll go to jail and they'll fuck you in the ass. Then it's about jumping the turnstile and the cop pulls a gun but he doesn't shoot.

There's a lot of precedent in black lyrics for jarring emotional juxtapositions – in the blues particularly, also in Smokey Robinson's deliberate paradoxes. But the nearest emotional equivalent isn't in black music, it's in punk – early Stones, Kinks, Velvets, Stooges, Dolls – where a song will seem to be one thing, then be another. The ranting part of 'Love Rap' could be Lou Reed in one of his bad moods – except that, unlike a Jagger or a Reed, Spoonie hasn't calculated – may not even be aware of – his juxtapositions. Which adds to his power. The feelings have great impact because they come from an unexpected source. If Spoonie were in punk or rock his alienation and rage would fill an expectation of the genre. In disco, they seem truer. . . .

Spoonie Gee has made some great records and an equal number of mediocre ones. I think he's a genius, but I don't think he knows what he's doing. He's drawn to a vision of the world as a fake and treacherous place. Maybe something's bugging him. Maybe unconsciously he feels that it's not only the world that's fake, or women that are fake – it's himself.

Spoonie's not one of us. He has nothing to do with punk culture or post-punk culture. I don't know if I could carry on an interesting conversation with him, if we could find any cultural or moral common ground. But there is a common ground, that part of the intellect called the 'emotions', where I do my deepest analysis of life. However much I admire current heroes like Mark E. Smith and Ian Mackaye, people I identify with, I know they don't make music as strong as this. Listening to Spoonie is like hearing my own feelings, and I have to confront my own fear. This means maybe that I'm not really unlike him. Maybe I'm more like him that I am like you.[17]

I've quoted this at length because this is how the piece works as criticism – in the steady move from description to emotion to identity, via questions of voice and genre, text and performance, knowledge, truth and feeling, all here focused on one artist, on a couple of tracks.

Now compare high criticism: Gregory Sandow on Milton Babbitt:

> Like any Babbitt piece, *Dual* is a labyrinth of closely packed information: every detail means something, or – which to me is the awe and almost the horror if it – could mean something. The F sharp, E flat, and B natural isolated in the highest register of the piano in the first two measures return in measure six as the first three notes of a melodic phrase, accompanied by the B flat, G natural, and C natural that were the next notes heard in the highest register at the end of measure two and the start of measure three – and these are just the most obvious connections that could be made between two parts of the piece chosen almost at random. Babbitt likes to say that moments in his music can be memories of what came before, and presentiments of what is to come. Serial technique produces ever-new associations of familiar elements giving everything that happens the power of an omen. Following a Babbitt piece in close detail is like reading entrails or tea leaves: every rearrangement in every bar might mean something. So many rearrangements are possible that you never know what the omens really mean; new developments seem, if not arbitrary, then at least wilful. This is a sort of higher-order zaniness, something unpredictable and even wild that transcends Babbitt's logic, and finds its way into something I haven't mentioned yet, which I'll call Babbitt's mode of musical speech. . . .
>
> For in the end I do find Babbitt eccentric. He's a superb musical craftsman, and, I think, an authentically great composer, though in some ways hard to take, but he's also zany, wild, and – I say this again with admiration – more than a little bit mad. His music, and the whole school he represents, are products of the 1950s, as much the symptoms of the eruption of tumultuous subterranean forces into above ground life as monster movies, rock and roll, the beat generation, and abstract expressionism. But in Babbitt's case the eruption is controlled, disguised, and unmentioned, the secret nobody will acknowledge or even name. In a videotaped interview with Ann Swartz of Baruch College, Babbitt calls himself 'a man of the university', whose music 'reflects the life of the academy, in the best sense of the word'. That's partly true, of course, but there's much more there. There's no point in thinking that Babbitt should do or think anything but what he does. . . . But I can't help thinking that he's sold himself short by trying both to extend the boundaries of his art and to remain academically respectable, and by acknowledging only the verifiable (and therefore trivial) aspects of his amazing work. If – like Joyce, Jackson Pollock, or John Cage – so passionate a man had chosen to define himself as an artist and not as an academic, what might he have achieved?[18]

The descriptive terms here are different (the language of notational rather than lyrical analysis), the genre distinction draws attention to a different context (the academy rather than the market), but the overall shape of the review is the same – the move from describing the music to describing the listener's response to the music to considering the relationship of feeling, truth and identity. And Kogan's and Sandow's judgements are, in fact, much the same: both Spoonie Gee and Milton Babbitt show flawed genius; in both cases the critics seem to know better than the artists what they are – or should be – doing.

What links these responses, in other words, is the assumption that music, the experience of music for composer/performer and listener alike, gives us a way of being in the world, a way of making sense of it. And if both critics begin by stressing their distance from the musicians – both Spoonie Gee and Milton Babbitt are set up as decidedly odd; both critics also end up in a sort of collusion with them: musical appreciation is, by its very nature, a process of musical identification, and the aesthetic response is, implicitly, an ethical agreement.

## Postmodernism and performance

The blurring of the high/low cultural boundary (here between critics) is, of course, a sign of the postmodern, and in bringing Kogan and Sandow together I need to distinguish my position from the one usually adopted. The confusion of the high and low is conventionally indicated by quotation (or appropriation) across the divide: the pop recycling of classical music and the art re-use of pop are taken to mark an underlying shift of aesthetic sensibility. In practice, as Andrew Goodwin has pointed out, such arguments mostly concern a relationship between the artistic avant-garde and certain pop forms (pop art remains the model): the most cited postmodern musicians are people such as Laurie Anderson, David Byrne and Brian Eno, who are clearly 'artists' rather than 'pop stars'. The institutional boundary between high and mass art seems intact – there remains a clear difference between a Philip Glass and a Madonna in terms of packaging, marketing, performance space, recording sound, and so forth; just as we can continue to distinguish between the pop Eno (producer of U2 and James) and the art Eno (producer of ambient video). The *frisson* of blurring of the art/mass boundary depends on the boundary still being clearly drawn.[19]

And if we go back to eighteenth-century debates about musical meaning, and to the origins of the Romantic view of art that underpins high cultural arguments (the view which was duly appropriated by would-be artist rock musicians in the 1960s), it becomes apparent that the high/low distinction doesn't really concern the nature of the art object, or how it is produced, but refers to different modes of *perception*. The crucial high/low distinction is that between contemplation and 'wallowing', between intellectual and sensual appreciation, between hard and easy listening (which is why a comparison of high and low critics becomes interesting).

To add low cultural goods to lists of 'art' objects available for intellectual (or 'serious') appreciation (which is what postmodern theorists tend to do) is not, then, to get rid of the traditional boundaries between the high and the low, and the much more interesting issue is whether we can really continue to sustain the implicit separation of emotion and feeling, sense and sensuality, body and mind. (This is the issue raised, for example, by the ambient house music of groups like Future Sound of London and the Aphex Twin, music which draws simultaneously on rave culture and minimalism.) The question, in fact, is whether musical experience has ever really been mapped by the high/low, mind/body distinction. The nineteenth century ideologues of absolute music may have worked hard to make musical appreciation a purely mental experience, but this was hard work precisely because most listeners didn't listen to music this way, however much they wanted to. Even high music making and listening remained a physical as well as a 'spiritual' activity, a sensual as well as a cognitive experience; to enjoy music of all sorts is to feel it.

At the same time, musical pleasure is never just a matter of feeling; it is also a matter of judgement. Take the postmodern reading of contemporary pop in terms of pastiche. Digital technology has certainly speeded up the process in which composition means quotation, but what we need to consider here are not so much the specific texts that result, as the way our attention is drawn to the *performance* of quotation. On rap tracks, for instance, far from musical authority being dissipated into fragments and second-hand sounds it is enhanced by the attention drawn to the quoting act itself. As Paul Gilroy suggests, 'the aesthetic rules that govern it are premised on a dialect of rescuing appropriation and recombination that creates special pleasures'. Pleasures in which 'aesthetic stress is laid upon the sheer social and cultural distance that formerly separated the diverse elements now dislocated into novel meanings by their provocative aural juxtaposition', and in which the continuing importance of performance is 'emphasised by [tracks'] radically unfinished forms'.[20]

Hip-hop, in other words, with its cut-ups, its scratches, breaks and samples, is best understood as producing not new texts but new ways of performing texts, new ways of performing *the making of meaning*. The pleasure of montage comes from the act of juxtaposition rather than from the labour of interpretation – and for the listener and dancer too, the fun lies in the process not the result. Not for nothing is rap a voice-based form with an exceptionally strong sense of presence. The aesthetic question about this postmodern music, at least, concerns not meanings and their interpretation – identity translated into discursive forms which have to be decoded – but *mutual enactment*, identity produced *in* performance.

## Space, time and stories

It is conventional, nowadays, in the academy at least, to divide the arts into separate categories such that the performing arts (theatre, dance and music) are differentiated from the fine arts (literature, painting, sculpture) and, on the whole, the performing arts are taken to be inferior to the fine arts, incapable of providing such rich aesthetic experience or social commentary. This is a relatively recent hierarchy, an effect of nineteenth-century conventions, the impact of Romanticism, the simultaneous emphases on art as individual expression and as private property. 'High' art was thus institutionalized by the bourgeoisie as a transcendent, asocial, experience (in the contemplative bank-like setting of the gallery and the concert hall, the museum and the library).

In the eighteenth century, with its concern for rhetoric and oratory, the distinction between the performing and the fine arts was not so clear and there were ways in which the former were clearly superior to the latter. One way of thinking about the contrast here is to see the fine arts as being organized around the use of space, and the performing arts as organized around the use of time. In spatial arts value is embodied in an object, a text; the analytic emphasis is on structure – a detached, 'objective' reading is possible, and artistic meaning can be extricated from the work's formal qualities. In temporal arts the value of the work is experienced as something momentary, and the analytical emphasis is on process; 'subjective' reading is necessary – a reading taking account of one's own immediate response – and the work's artistic meaning lies in that response, the work's rhetorical qualities.

The first point to make about such distinctions is that they do not, in fact, describe different art forms so much as different approaches to art forms, different ways of framing 'the aesthetic experience', different assumptions about what is artistically valuable or meaningful. The nineteenth century argument that art was 'timeless' meant, then, an attempt to objectify all art, the performing arts too; one effect was to redefine music as a musical object, to put the analytic emphasis on the work, the score, rather than on its performance. And, given that to be 'music' the score had to be performed, the performance itself was also objectified, made the object of repeated performance, such that the tradition, the history of performance could be claimed as defining music's meaning, rather than the immediate effect, which was, by its nature, inevitably distorted by social, historical and material exigencies.

This process of objectification was also a process of academicization (hence, eventually, Milton Babbitt), as art became an object of study, and scholars became guardians of its traditional meaning, as they had always been in matters of religion and law. Here too the emphasis was, by necessity (the necessity of what can be stored and taught), on the qualities of a work in space, structural qualities, rather than on the qualities of a work in time, the qualities of immediacy, emotion, sweat – suspect terms in both the library and the classroom.

It should be stressed too, though, that what I'm describing here is a discursive process, an idealistic attempt to grasp an experience through a particular evaluative framework which was not, and perhaps could not be, entirely successful. In the end, how people (or, rather, critics and scholars) talked about music became detached from how people (musicians and listeners) felt about it. There was always an excess in musical experience, something unreasonable, something that *got away*. And if it is relatively easy to illustrate the problems of treating temporal arts in spatial terms (analysing a score or a playscript is not, in the end, to treat the experience of music or drama), it is just as important to note that the 'spatial' arts also have temporal elements. We do, after all, experience books in time; poems too have a beginning, a middle and an end. Reading is a process, and an emotional process at that; oratory is an aspect of the fine art experience too.[21]

The linking concept here is narrative – structured time, temporal space: if narrative gives the fine arts their dynamism, it gives the performing arts their structure. Musical pleasure is also a narrative pleasure, even when the music is at its most abstract – compare Greg Sandow's response to Milton Babbitt cited earlier to Greg Tate's appreciation of Cecil Taylor:

> Someone once said that while Coleman Hawkins gave the jazz saxophone a voice, Lester Young taught it how to tell a story. That is, the art of personal confession is one jazz musicians must master before they can do justice by their tradition. I couldn't relate to Cecil's music until I learned to hear the story he was shaping out of both black tradition and his complex 'life as an American Negro'.[22]

For Tate, as for other jazz writers, the 'story' in music describes an entanglement of aesthetics and ethics; such a narrative is necessary to any claim that art has something to do with life. A good jazz performance, that is to say (like any good musical performance), depends on rhetorical truth, on the musicians' ability to convince and persuade the listener that what they are saying matters. This is not a matter of representation or 'imitation' or ideology but draws, rather, on the African-American tradition of 'signifying'; it puts into play an emotional effect, a collusion between the performer and an audience which is engaged rather than detached, knowing rather than knowledgeable.

This is the reason why popular music (and I don't believe the argument is confined to African-derived forms, though it does help to explain their remarkable global impact) must be understood not to represent values but to embody them. The point is well made in Christopher Waterman's study of *jùjú:*

> Jùjú history suggests that the role of musical style in the enactment of identity makes it not merely a reflexive but also a potentially *constitutive* factor in the patterning of cultural values and social interaction. Yoruba musicians, responding creatively to changes in the Nigerian political economy, fashioned a mode of expression that enacted, in music, language, and behaviour, a syncretic metaphoric image of an ideal social order, cosmopolitan yet firmly rooted in autochthonous tradition. This dynamic style configuration, consonant with Yoruba ideologies of the 'open hierarchy' as an ideal pattern of aesthetic and social organization, allowed jùjú performance to play a role in the stereotypic reproduction of 'deep' Yoruba values during a period of pervasive economic and political change.[23]

This echoes Paul Gilroy's comments on the ways in which in the history of black culture, 'the politics of trans-figuration strives in pursuit of the sublime, struggling to repeat the unrepeatable, to present the unpresentable'. If the politics of fulfilment, in pursuit of rational western politics, seeks to 'assimilate the semiotic, verbal and textual', the politics of transfiguration 'pushes towards the mimetic, dramatic and performative'. Hence 'the traditions of performance that continue to characterize the production and reception of African diaspora musics'.[24] Gilroy notes that

> The power of music in developing our struggles by communicating information, organising consciousness and testing out, deploying, or amplifying the forms of subjectivity which are required by political agency, individual and collective, defensive and transformational, demands attention to both the formal attributes of this tradition of expression and its distinctive *moral* basis. . . . In the simplest possible terms, by posing the world as it is against the world as the racially subordinated would like it to be, this musical culture supplies a great deal of the courage required to go on living in the present.[25]

Gilroy thus suggests that 'the history of black music enables us to trace something of the means through which the unity of ethics and politics has been reproduced as a form of folk knowledge', and if music thus may 'conjure up and enact the new modes of friendship, happiness and solidarity that are consequent on the overcoming of the racial oppression on which modernity and the duality of rational western progress as excessive barbarity relied', it also conjures up and enacts dialogue, argument, call and response: 'lines between self and other are blurred and special forms of pleasure are created as a result'. Gilroy quotes Ralph Ellison on jazz:

> There is in this a cruel contradiction implicit in the art form itself. For true jazz is an art of individual assertion within and against the group. Each true jazz moment . . . springs from a contest in which the artist challenges all the rest; each solo flight, or improvisation, represents (like the canvases of a painter) a definition of his identity; as individual, as member of the collectivity and as a link in the chain of tradition. Thus because jazz finds its very life in improvisation upon traditional materials, the jazz man must lose his identity even as he finds it.[26]

But while music is thus particularly important in the complex history of black identities, this use of music, as that aesthetic process through which we discover ourselves by forging our relations to others, is not confined to black cultures. In Britain, for example, white listeners have long been engaged in their own enactments of black musical values. Take Brian Jackson's 1960s description of the importance of the Huddersfield Jazz Club to its displaced working-class grammar school girls and boys:

> If the life of New Orleans was an exaggerated image of working-class life, the stimulating generalized emotions of jazz were a hazy image of what the world of art could offer.

Jackson notes the importance of the jazz 'solo' for these self-conscious individualists as they struggled to make music for themselves (solos in which no one else in the club even feigned interest), but he also notes how jazz was used in Huddersfield as a musical practice in which to stage an understanding of collectivity:

> It didn't lead to social promotion or to high art – there was no 'transfer' at all from jazz to classical music. Its function was to hold together and sustain a steady stream of post–1944 Act pupils. As a floating community, it became admirably and intricately designed for that purpose – and the feeling of how to do *this*, was the real inheritance from working-class Huddersfield.[27]

To turn to a different world altogether, Philip Bohlman explores the role of chamber music – another form of small-scale making-music-together – in shaping German Jewish identity in Israel, in both articulating cultural values and enacting collective commitment to them (from the audience as much as from the performers). In this context the scored basis of 'absolute music' was as ethically binding as the improvised basis of jazz:

> Viewed from a performative perspective, the absence of specific meaning within the text allows meaning to accrue only upon performance, thus empowering any group – for example, an ethnic community – to shape what it will from absolute music. A gap therefore forms between the content of chamber-music repertoires and the style of performance situations. It is within the mutability allowed by style that differences in meaning and function of music arise, thereby transforming chamber music into a genre that can follow numerous historical paths. These paths may be as different as, say, the ethnic associations in Israel and the practices of amateur music making found in many American academic communities. Clearly, such cases reflect different attitudes towards both the repertoires of chamber music and the communities that lend the music its distinctive functions and form its different histories.[28]

## From aesthetics to ethics

Underlying all the other distinctions critics continue to draw between 'serious' (European-derived) and 'popular' (African-derived) music is an assumption about the sources of musical value. Serious music, it seems, matters because it transcends social forces; popular music is aesthetically uninteresting because it is determined by them (because it is 'functional' or 'utilitarian'). The sociological approach to musical value has thus meant uncovering the social forces concealed in the talk of 'transcendent' values; the populist reversal of the high/low hierarchy has meant praising the 'functional' at the expense of the 'aesthetic'.

My concern is the opposite: to take seriously the aesthetic value (the aesthetic function, as one might say) of all musics, popular music too. The sociologist of contemporary popular music is faced with a body of songs, records, stars and styles which exist because of a series of decisions, made by both producers and consumers, about what is 'good'. Musicians write tunes and play solos and program computers; producers choose from different mixes; record companies and radio and television programmers decide what will be released and played; consumers buy one record rather than another and concentrate their attention on particular genres. The result of all these apparently individual decisions is certainly a pattern of success, taste and style which can be explained sociologically, but it is also a pattern that is rooted in individual judgement.

We can, as I suggested earlier, trace such judgements back to material conditions easily enough, by way, for example, of Pierre Bourdieu's concept of taste. We can point to the cultural capital embedded in technique and technology: people produce and consume the music they are capable of producing and consuming; different social groups possess different sorts of knowledge and skill, share different cultural histories, and so make music differently. Musical tastes do correlate with class cultures and subcultures; musical styles are linked to specific age groups; we can take for granted the connections of ethnicity and sound. This is the sociological common sense of rock criticism and the idea of authenticity:

> There is not a British rocker on earth who could ever turn Jack Scott's chorus-line,
>
> > Lonesome Mary's cuttin' out
> > Hate to be around when Johnnie finds this out
>
> into anything approximating a convincing statement.[29]

But while we can thus describe (or assume) general patterns of musical taste and use, the precise fit (or homology) between sounds and social groups remains unclear, which is why commonsense sociology has had to deploy its second set of arguments, about the match of music's *formal* and social functions. This approach is most sophisticated in ethnomusicology, in anthropological studies of traditional and folk musics which are explained musically (in terms of their formal and sonic qualities) by reference to their use – in dance, in rituals, for political mobilization, to solemnize events. Similar points are made about contemporary popular music, though its most important social function is assumed to be commercial – the starting analytical assumption is that the music is made to sell; research focuses on who makes marketing decisions and why, on the construction of taste and 'taste publics'. The appeal of the music itself, the reason why people like it, and what, more importantly, 'liking it' means, is buried under an analysis of sales strategies, demographics, the anthropology of consumption.

From the 'consumers' perspective, though, it is obvious that people play the music they do because it 'sounds good', and even if musical tastes are, inevitably, an effect of social conditioning and commercial manipulation, people still explain them to themselves in terms of something special. Everyone in the pop world is aware of the social forces that determine 'normal' pop music and 'normal' pop tastes, but a good record or song or sound is precisely one that transcends those forces.

From this perspective, pop music becomes the more valuable aesthetically the more independent it is of the social forces that organize it, and one way of reading this is to suggest that pop value is thus dependent on something outside pop, is rooted in the person, the *auteur*, the community or the subculture that lies behind it. Critical judgement means measuring performers' 'truth' to the experience or feelings they are describing or expressing. The problem is that it is, in practice, very difficult to say who or what it is that pop music expresses or how we recognize, independently of their music, the 'authentically' creative performers. Musical 'truth' is precisely that which is *created* by 'good music'; we hear the music as authentic (or rather, we describe the musical experience we value in terms of authenticity) and such a response is then read back, spuriously, on to the music-making (or listening) process. An aesthetic judgement of effect is translated into a sociological description of cause: good music must be music made and appreciated by good people. But the question we should be asking is not what does popular music reveal about the people who play and use it but how does it create them as a people, as a web of identities? If we start from the assumption that pop is expressive, then we get bogged down in the search for the 'real' artist or emotion or belief lying behind it. But popular music is popular not because it reflects something or authentically articulates some sort of popular taste or experience, but because it creates our understanding of what 'popularity' is, because it places us in the social world in a particular way. What we should be examining, in other words, is not how true a piece of music is to something else, but how it sets up the idea of 'truth' in the first place – successful pop music is music which defines its own aesthetic standard.

## The imagined self

The experience of pop music is an experience of identity: in responding to a song, we are drawn, haphazardly, into emotional alliances with the performers and with the performers' other fans. Because of its qualities of abstractness, music is, by nature, an individualizing form. We absorb songs into our own lives and rhythm into our own bodies; they have a looseness of reference that makes them immediately accessible. At the same time, and equally significantly, music is obviously collective. We hear things as music because their sounds obey a more or less familiar cultural logic, and for most music listeners (who are not themselves music makers) this logic is out of our control. There is a mystery to our own musical tastes. Some records and performers work for us, others do not – we know this without being able to explain it. Somebody else has set up the conventions; they are clearly social and clearly apart from us. Music, whether teenybop for young female fans or jazz or rap for African-Americans or nineteenth century chamber music for German Jews in Israel, stands for, symbolizes *and* offers the immediate experience of collective identity.

If narrative is the basis of music pleasure, to put this another way, it is also central to our sense of identity. Identity, that is to say, comes from the outside not the inside; it is something we put or try on, not something we reveal or discover. As Jonathan Ree puts it,

> The problem of personal identity, one may say, arises from play-acting and the adoption of artificial voices; the origins of distinct personalities, in acts of personation and impersonation.[30]

And Ree goes on to argue that personal identity is therefore 'the accomplishment of a storyteller, rather than the attribute of a character'. He draws on Sartre and Ricoeur in suggesting that narrative is 'the unity of a life', not something achieved through some essential continuity but rather through a 'recurring *belief* in personal coherence, a belief necessarily 'renewed in the telling of tales'.

> The concept of narrative, in other words, is not so much a justification of the idea of personal identity, as an elucidation of its structure as an inescapable piece of make-believe.[31]

This argument has two immediate implications. First, identities are, inevitably, shaped according to narrative forms. As Kwame Anthony Appiah points out,

> Invented histories, invented biologies, invented cultural affinities come with every identity; each is a kind of role that has to be scripted, structured by conventions of narrative to which the world never quite manages to conform.[32]

But if identity is always somehow constrained by imaginative forms, it is also freed by them: the personal is the cultural, and, as Mark Slobin suggests, we are not necessarily restricted in terms of such cultural imagination by social circumstances: 'We all grow up with *something*, but we can choose just about *anything* by way of expressive culture.'[33]

In broad terms we may be able to relate social and cultural identities, to finger social and cultural 'theft'. 'The blackface performer,' writes Eric Lott, 'is in effect a perfect metaphor for one culture's ventriloquial self-expression through the art forms of someone else's.'[34] But at an individual level, biology, demography and sociology seem less determining. As I have argued elsewhere, with reference to literary forms and social identities (black writing, women's writing, gay writing, etc.), the question is not 'simply whether such writing can be mapped back onto the reader (reading as a woman, a man, a black) but whether literary transformation – the process of writing *and* reading – doesn't subvert all sociological assumptions about cultural position and cultural feeling'.[35]

And this seems an even more obvious question about popular music, of which the dominant forms in all contemporary societies have originated at the social margins – among the poor, the migrant, the rootless, the 'queer'.[36] Anti-essentialism is a necessary part of musical experience, a necessary consequence of music's failure to register the separations of body and mind on which such 'essential' differences (between black and white, female and male, gay and straight, nation and nation) depend. Hence Paul Gilroy's scepticism about rap nationalism: 'How does a form which flaunts and glories in its own malleability as well as its trans-national character become interpreted as an expression of some authentic Afro-American essence?'[37]

If Gilroy remembers that growing up he was 'provided by black music with a means to gain proximity to the sources of feeling from which our local conceptions of blackness were assembled', he also realizes that 'the most important lesson music still has to teach us is that its inner secrets and its ethnic rules can be taught and learned'.[38] And as a child and young man I also learned something of myself – took my identity – from black music (just as I did later, in the disco, from gay music). What secrets was I being taught?

First, that an identity is always already an ideal, what we would like to be, not what we are. And in taking pleasure from black or gay or female music I don't thus identify as black or gay or female (I don't actually experience these sounds as 'black music' or 'gay music' or 'women's voices') but, rather, participate in imagined forms of democracy and desire. The aesthetic, as Colin Campbell has argued, these days describes a quality of experience rather than a state of being, and the popular aesthetic experience is an effect of 'modern autonomous imaginative hedonism':

> The pleasures which self-illusory hedonism supplies are largely aesthetic and emotional, the scenes created in imagination having the characteristics of both works of art and drama.[39]

In his classic account of *The Presentation of Self in Everyday Life*, Erving Goffman thus emphasizes Simone de Beauvoir's point that in dressing and making up, a woman

> does not present *herself* to observation; she is, like the picture or the statue, or the actor on stage, an agent through whom is suggested someone not there – that is, the character she represents, but is not. It is this identification with something unreal, fixed, perfect as the hero of a novel, as a portrait or a bust, that gratifies her; she strives to identify herself with this figure and thus to seem to herself to be stabilized, justified in her splendour.[40]

But if musical identity is, then, always fantastic, idealizing not just oneself but also the social world one inhabits, it is, secondly, always also real, enacted in musical activities. Music making and music listening, that is to say, are bodily matters, involve what one might call *social movements*. In this respect, musical pleasure is not derived *from* fantasy – it is not *mediated* by daydreams – but is experienced directly: music gives us a real experience of what the ideal could be. In his discussion of black identity, Paul Gilroy thus argues that it is neither 'simply a social and political category' nor 'a vague and utterly contingent construction' but 'remains the outcome of practical activity: language, gesture, bodily significations, desires'.

> These significations are condensed in musical performance, although it does not, of course, monopolise them. In this context, they produce the imaginary

effect of an internal racial core or essence by acting on the body through the specific mechanisms of identification and recognition that are produced in the intimate interaction of performer and crowd. This reciprocal relationship serves as a strategy and an ideal communicative situation even when the original makers of the music and its eventual consumers are separated in space and time or divided by the technologies of sound production and the commodity form which their art has sought to resist.[41]

And once we start looking at different musical genres we can begin to document the different ways in which music works *materially* to give people different identities, to place them in different social groups. Whether we're talking about Finnish dance halls in Sweden, Irish pubs in London, or Indian film music in Trinidad, we're dealing not just with nostalgia for 'traditional sounds', not just with a commitment to 'different' songs, but also with experience of alternative modes of social interaction. Communal values can only thus be grasped, as musical aesthetics *in action*.[42] Helen Myers, for example, quotes Channu, a village singer in Felicity, Trinidad:

> Indian music sounds much sweeter. Whatever the Indian sing and whatever music they play, they don't do it of a joke. It's serious thing for whoever understand it. It brings such serious feelings to you. Calypso they only sing. You might hear calypso. You will just feel happy to jump up. But if you hear a real technical piece of Indian music, you might sit down stiff and still, and you might be contrasting so much that you mightn't know when it start or when it finish.[43]

For these Trinidadians, 'Indianized pieces, borrowed from a twentieth-century urban Hindi culture' are therefore heard as 'more authentic than the local Westernized repertory, a reflection of their New World heritage'. Authenticity in this context is a quality not of the music as such (how it is actually made), but of the story it's heard to tell, the narrative of musical interaction in which the listeners place themselves.[44]

## Conclusion

Music constructs our sense of identity through the direct experiences it offers of the body, time and sociability, experiences which enable us to place ourselves in imaginative cultural narratives. Such a fusion of imaginative fantasy and bodily practice marks also the integration of aesthetics and ethics. John Miller Chernoff has thus eloquently demonstrated how among African musicians an aesthetic judgement (this sounds good) is necessarily also an ethical judgement (this is good), The issue is 'balance': 'the quality of rhythmic relationships' describes a quality of social life. 'In this sense, style is another word for the perception of relationships.'

> Without balance and coolness, the African musician loses aesthetic command, and the music abdicates its social authority, becoming hot, intense, limited, pretentious, overly personal, boring, irrelevant, and ultimately alienating.

And

> As the dance gives visible form to the music, so too does the dance give full and visible articulation to the ethical qualities which work through the music, balance in the disciplined expression of power in relationship.[45]

Identity is thus necessarily a matter of ritual, it describes one's place in a dramatized pattern of relationships – one can never really express oneself 'autonomously'. Self-identity *is* cultural identity; claims to individual difference depend on audience appreciation, on shared performing and narrative rules. As Appiah puts it:

> The problem of who I really am is raised by the facts of what I appear to be: and though it is essential to the mythology of authenticity that this fact should be obscured by its prophets, what I appear to be is fundamentally how I appear to others and only derivatively how I appear to myself.[46]

In her study of music making in (the very white) Milton Keynes, *The Hidden Musicians*, Ruth Finnegan persuasively argues that these days people's voluntary, leisure activities are more likely to provide their 'pathways' through life than their paid employment. It was in their musical activities that her city dwellers found their most convincing narratives; it was in their aesthetic judgements that they expressed their most deep-seated ethical views.[47]

This is, perhaps ironically, to come back to music via a spatial metaphor. But what makes music special – what makes it special for identity – is that it defines a space without boundaries (a game without frontiers). Music is thus the cultural form best able both to cross borders – sounds carry across fences and walls and oceans, across classes, races and nations – and to define places; in clubs, scenes, and raves, listening on headphones, radio and in the concert hall, we are only where the music takes us.

## Notes

1 Gina Arnold, *Route 666. On the Road to Nirvana*, St Martin's Press, New York, 1993, p. 228

2 Anthony Storr, *Music and the Mind*, Harper Collins, London and New York, 1992, p. 153.

3 John Miller Chernoff, *African Rhythm and African Sensibility*, Chicago University Press, Chicago, 1979, p. 167.

4 Although the best version of the argument remains the earliest, Paul Willis's *Profane Culture*, Routledge & Kegan Paul, London, 1978.

5 Quoted in Eric Lott, *Love and Theft. Blackface Minstrelsy and the American Working Class*, Oxford University Press, New York and Oxford, 1993, p. 91.

6 For the debate about race and rap see, for example, Greg Tate, *Flyboy in the Buttermilk. Essays on Contemporary America*, Simon & Schuster, New York, 1992. For the debate about gender and music see Susan McClary, *Feminine Endings. Music, Gender and Sexuality*, University of Minnesota Press, Minneapolis, 1991. For discussion of national musical identities see Deanna Robinson, Elizabeth Buck and Marlene Cuthbert, *Music at the Margins*, Sage, London, 1991.

126        *Questions of Cultural Identity*

7 For an interesting answer to the last question see Tony Mitchell, 'World music and the popular music industry: an Australian view', *Ethnomusicology*, 37, 3, 1993, pp. 309–38.

8 Or, as Charles Rosen put it more recently (and with reference to sexuality rather than class): "I presume – or I should like to presume – that a rapist and a foot fetishist would write very different kinds of music, but I am not sure how we would go about confirming this". ('Music à la mode', *New York Review of Books*, 23 June 1994, p. 60).

9 For an interesting answer to these questions, see Richard Shusterman, *Pragmatic Aesthetics*, Basil Blackwell, Oxford, 1992, Chapter 8. Shusterman, like many commentators, takes rap to be the postmodern articulation of popular music. He argues (p. 202) that rap is 'postmodern' in its appropriation, recycling and eclectic mixing of previously existing sounds and styles; in its enthusiastic embrace of technology and mass culture; in its emphasis on the localized and temporal rather than the universal and eternal. By this definition, though, other pop forms besides rap could be suitably labelled postmodern, and Shusterman's most interesting argument about rap does not really raise the spectre of postmodernism at all! Rap, he suggests (pp. 212–13) is unusual in uniting the aesthetic and the cognitive, the political-functional and the artistic-expressive; rap is dynamic culturally (p. 235) because of the *formal* tension it expresses between innovation and coherence.

10 Mark Slobin, *Subculture Sounds. Micromusic of the West*, Wesleyan University Press, Hanover and London, 1993, p. 41.

11 Ibid., p. 42.

12 I develop this argument at much greater length in my *Performing Rites*, Harvard University Press, Cambridge, MA, forthcoming.

13 For an influential and pioneering approach to music in this way see Steven Feld, *Sound and Sentiment: Birds, Weeping, Poetics and Song in Kaluli Expression*, University of Pennsylvania Press, Philadelphia, 1982.

14 Chernoff, *African Rhythm and African Sensibility*, p. 36. (original emphasis).

15 Philip V. Bohlman, 'Of *Yekkes* and chamber music in Israel: ethnomusicological meaning in western music history', in Stephen Blum, Philip V. Bohlman and Daniel M. Neuman (eds), *Ethnomusicology and Modern Music History*, University of Illinois Press, Urbana and Chicago, 1991, pp. 266–7.

16 See ibid., p. 255.

17 Frank Kogan, 'Spoonie Gee', *Reasons for Living*, 2, June 1986.

18 Gregory Sandow, 'A fine madness', *Village Voice*, 16 March 1982, pp. 76, 93.

19 For an excellent discussion of the issues here see Andrew Goodwin, 'Popular music and postmodern theory', *Cultural Studies*, 5, 2, 1990, pp. 174–90.

20 See Paul Gilroy, 'Sounds authentic: black music, ethnicity, and the challenge of a *changing* same', *Black Music Research Journal*, 10, 2, 1990, pp. 128–31.

21 This is most obvious in poetry, but for an interesting argument about painting picking up on some of the points raised here see Mieke Bal, *Reading Rembrandt*, Cambridge: Cambridge University Press, 1991 and the useful review by Sandra Kemp in *Journal of Literature and Theology*, 7, 3, 1993, pp. 302–5.

22 Tate, *Flyboy in the Buttermilk*, p. 25.

23 Christopher A. Waterman, 'Jùjú history: toward a theory of sociomusical practice', in Blum et al. (eds), *Ethnomusicology*, pp. 66–7.

24 Gilroy, 'Sounds authentic', p.113. Gilroy suggests that the concepts of 'dramaturgy, enunciation and gesture' ('the Pre- and anti-discursive constituents of black metacommunications') thus need to be added to concerns for textuality and narrative in black cultural history.

25 Paul Gilroy, 'It ain't where you're from, it's where you're at . . .', *Third Text*, 13, 1990–1, pp. 10, 12.

26 Quoted ibid., pp. 13–14. And see Chernoff, *African Rhythm and African Sensibility*, Chapter 2, for an extensive discussion of what he calls 'the conversational mode' of African music.

27 Brian Jackson, *Working Class Community*, Routledge & Kegan Paul, London, 1968, pp. 129, 131.

*Music and Identity*                                            127

28  Bohlman, 'Of *Yekkes* and chamber music', pp. 259–60. For the practices of amateur music making in American academic communities, see Robert A. Stebbins, 'Music among friends: the social networks of amateur musicians', *International Review of Sociology*, 12, 1976.

29  Timothy D'Arch Smith, *Peepin' in a Seafood Store. Some Pleasures of Rock Music*, Michael Russell (Publishing), Wilby, Norwich, 1992, p. 23.

30  Jonathan Ree, 'Funny voices: stories, "punctuation" and personal identity', *New Literary History*, 21, 1990, p. 1055.

31  Ibid., p. 1058.

32  Kwame Anthony Appiah, *In My Father's House*, Methuen, London, 1992, p. 283.

33  Slobin, *Subculture Sounds*, p. 55.

34  Lott, *Love and Theft*, p. 92.

35  Simon Frith, *Literary Studies as Cultural Studies. Whose Literature? Whose Culture?*, University of Strathclyde, Glasgow, 1991, p. 21.

36  I take this point from Veronica Doubleday's review of Martin Stokes's *The Arabesk Debate* in *Popular Music*, 13, 2, 1994, pp. 231–3.

37  Gilroy, 'It ain't', p. 6.

38  Gilroy, 'Sounds authentic', p. 134.

39  Colin Campbell, *The Romantic Ethic and the Spirit of Modern Consumerism*, Basil Blackwell, Oxford, 1987, p. 246.

40  Quoted (from *The Second Sex*) in Erving Goffman, *The Presentation of Self in Everyday Life*, Allen Lane, London, 1969 [1959], p. 65.

41  Gilroy, 'Sounds authentic', p. 127.

42  This point is emerging in interesting ways from Sara Cohen's current research on ethnic musical communities in Liverpool. See, for example, Sara Cohen, 'Localizing sound: music, place and social mobility', in Will Staw (ed.), *Popular Music: Style and Identity*, Centre for Research in Canadian Cultural Industries and Institutions, Montreal, 1995, pp. 61–7.

43  Myers, 'Indian music in Felicity', in Blum et al. *Ethnomusicology*, p. 236.

44  Ibid., p. 240.

45  Chernoff, *African Rhythm and African Sensibility*, pp. 125, 140, 144.

46  Appiah, *In My Father's House*, p. 121.

47  Ruth Finnegan, *The Hidden Musicians*, Cambridge University Press, Cambridge, 1989. And cf. Robert A. Stebbins, *Amateurs. On the Margin between Work and Leisure*, Sage, Beverly Hills and London, 1979.

# CHAPTER 19

# What is Bad Music?

From my scrapbook.

> First there is the *innocently stupid*, the insipid song; then the *intentionally stupid*, the song ornamented with all the stupidities that the singer takes into his head to make . . . Next comes the *vicious song* which corrupts the public and lures it into bad musical paths by the attraction of certain capricious methods of performance, brilliant but with false expression, which is revolting to both good sense and good taste. Finally we have the *criminal song*, the wicked song, that unites with its wickedness a bottomless pit of stupidity, which proceeds only by great howls and enjoys adding noisy melees to the long drum rolls, to the sombre dramas, to the murders, poisonings, curses, anathemas, to all the dramatic horrors that provide the occasion to show off the voice. It is this last which, I am told, reigns supreme in Italy . . .
>
> HECTOR BERLIOZ C1840

> Sloppy versification, sophomoric diction, clichés, maudlin sentiments and hackneyed verbiage.
>
> LORENZ HART ON 1920S POP

> If Sibelius' music is good music, then all the categories by which musical standards can be measured . . . must be completely abolished.
>
> T. W. ADORNO C1940

> The Stones are fake-simple, without gift. The design of their 'Devil' lacks arch, the sonic element is without sensibility, much less invention, and the primary harmonies are not simple but simplistic. Neither does the melody flow anywhere, nor does its stasis invite hypnotism rather than boredom . . . Misfired

**16**                                                    **Bad Music**

simplicity, then, makes this music bad. The words, too, pretend . . . What makes Jagger's lyrics bad is their commercial up-
to-date before-the-fact intent . . . The vocal performance is
doubly false . . . Jagger's inability to revamp plagiarism into
personal style because of superficial (even dishonest: he's a
white Englishman) instinct for choice (of vocal models—
'parents') makes his performance bad . . .

NED ROREM 1969

It's a contributory factor to epilepsy. It's the biggest destructor in
the history of education. It's a jungle cult. It's what the Watusis
do to whip up a war. What I see in the discos with people
jogging away is just what I've seen in the bush.

HARVEY WOOD, DIRECTOR GENERAL OF THE RHODESIAN
BROADCASTING CORPORATION, ON DISCO, 1979

No single song has done more for the pro-choice movement than
this sexist piece of wretchedness.

CITATION FOR PAUL ANKA'S "(YOU'RE) HAVING MY BABY,"
NUMBER 1 IN *THE BOTTOM FIFTY. SONGS THAT MADE
THE WHOLE WORLD CRINGE*, GANNETT NEWS SERVICE, 1991

There are six main reasons why unrestrained pop music is a
grave social evil. First, with very few exceptions it is artistically
worthless. The intolerable amplification which is essential to
projecting it, and which is one of the chief reasons for its appeal,
makes musical creativity impossible. It destroys the aural
perception of the children who grow up accustomed to it, makes
it difficult for them to cast off its spell, and thus denies them the
love of true music . . .

PAUL JOHNSON 1995

Kissin has been appearing in Britain for 14 years, since he was
17. His platform appearance now is just as mechanical as it has
ever been—one suspects the back of his tailcoat hides the hole
for a giant wind-up key—and his fingers are as stunningly
accurate as ever, but all traces of spontaneity have been progressively obliterated . . . On Thursday he rampaged through
his programme in a totally repellent and scarcely credible
manner . . . the paeans of the final Great Gate of Kiev carried no
weight or majesty because all the sound and fury that preceded
them had generated no tension or excitement, except of the most
primitive kind . . . [Kissin] started out on his career as a musical

**Simon Frith** **17**

talent of apparently limitless potential, and has turned into the biggest pianistic circus act since David Helfgott; there's nothing there but technique.

ANDREW CLEMENTS 2002

**L**ike Nicolas Slonimsky, editor of the *Lexicon of Musical Invective*, I have long been a collector of musical abuse, but I should make it clear at the beginning of this chapter that I am not going to answer my question—what is bad music?—directly.[1] I did think about this: rather than prepare a chapter, I could compile a list of bad records, a guide to dreadful songs. I decided not to for two reasons. First, what intrigues me is not music I don't like (and other people might) but music I do like (and other people don't).[2] Day-to-day bad music is music that my family and friends beg me to take off or turn down, to stop playing because it is so ugly or dull or incompetent.[3] Second, there is no point in labelling something as bad music except in a context in which someone else thinks it's good, for whatever reason. The label "bad music," that is to say, is only interesting as part of an argument. There is no purpose (and it would be no fun) to discuss music which everyone agrees is bad (a tape of me singing in the shower, for example). And this is not an argument we can have blind. I can't, in other words, persuade someone that the music they like is bad (and this is the most common setting for the use of the concept) unless I know their tastes, the way they make sense of their listening pleasures (which is not to say that the arguments here are *just* a matter of taste).

In short, I'm more interested in examining ways of arguing about music (good *versus* bad) than in setting up a taxonomy, this is bad music of one sort, this is bad music of another sort. I'll come back to this momentarily; first, an aside on taxonomies.

There are, by now, various albums (and radio and TV shows) featuring "bad music." The first I can remember is a 1970s K-Tel anthology of the *Worst Records Ever Made*, selected and introduced by the British disk jockey, Kenny Everett. There are three sorts of tracks featured in such collections and shows:

- Tracks which are clearly incompetent musically; made by singers who can't sing, players who can't play, producers who can't produce. Such acts (Tiny Tim springs to mind) used to be the stuff of certain sorts of television variety shows.

- Tracks organized around misplaced sentiments or emotions invested heavily in a banal or ridiculous object or tune. Jess Conrad's "My Pullover" is much anthologized in Britain, for instance.
- Tracks involving a genre confusion. The most common examples are actors or TV stars recording in the latest style: Telly Savalas sings Bob Dylan, Steven Seagal ("extending his creativity") writes and performs his own songs.[4] I'd add almost any opera singer performing almost any rock song. And, come to that, the Kiri Te Kanawa/José Carreras recording of *West Side Story*.

Bad music here means essentially *ridiculous* music, and the sense of the ridiculous lies in the gap between what performers/producers think they are doing and what they actually achieve. Such recordings reflect a complete musical misunderstanding: this is bad music as naïve or foolish music (rather than immoral or corrupting music). Anthologies of bad music thus offer listeners tracks at which to laugh, to regard with affection, and above all about which to feel *knowing*: we, as listeners, understand this music—and what's wrong with it—in a way in which its producers do not.

Rock critical lists of the worst records ever made, which nowadays feature routinely in the press and in books of rock ephemera, rest on a rather different approach to musical taxonomy. The tracks cited here are usually well known and commercially successful (rather than being oddities or commercial flops); the object of such lists is a critique of public taste, and the judgment involves the explicit assertion that these records are simply *heard too often*, as staples on classic pop or oldies radio stations, at weddings and in shopping malls.

There seem to be two sorts of tracks on these lists:

- Tracks that feature sound gimmicks that have outlived their charm or novelty (from "Disco Duck" to "The Ketchup Song" via "Bohemian Rhapsody"; Christmas and summer holiday hits generally).
- Tracks that depend on false sentiment (like Paul Anka's "(You're) Having My Baby"), that feature an excess of feeling molded into a radio-friendly pop song (songs about birth and death generally, in fact; most 9/11 songs, for example).

There's still a knowingness here, but the critical contempt seems less for the recordings than for the people who like them, who take them seriously, who still find them funny or sad. And while one could imagine buying a bad record collection and playing it to friends as a camp gesture (re-framing kitsch as art), these critical lists of bad records are intentionally identifying tracks that are irredeemable. These are, it seems, records that no one could want to play who has any sense of good music at all![5]

I'll come back to this argument. What I want to do immediately, moving back from taxonomy to analysis, is to make clear the premises of what follows. First, then, I am going to assume that there is no such *thing* as bad music. Music only becomes bad music in an evaluative context, as part of an argument. An evaluative context is one in which an evaluative statement about a song or a record or performer is uttered communicatively, to persuade someone else of its truth, to have an effect on their actions and beliefs (the quotes that introduce this chapter are all arguments in this sense).

There are more or less appropriate circumstances for musical evaluation, but probably the most significant (significant in that evaluations here have the most effect materially) involve music making rather than music listening: the judgments made at the piano or the keyboard, in rehearsal rooms and recording studios, at run throughs and sound checks.[6] Musicians, interestingly, are more likely to use the term "wrong" than the term "bad": "that's the wrong chord, the wrong tempo, the wrong sound, the wrong mix." One question that arise here is what is the relation, if any, between *wrongness* and *badness?*[7]

Second, I am going to assume that even if bad music doesn't exist, "bad music" is a necessary concept for musical pleasure, for musical aesthetics. To put this another way, even if as a popular music scholar I can't point authoritatively to bad music (my authority will undoubtedly be rejected), as a popular music fan I do so all the time. This is a necessary part of fandom. A self-proclaimed rock or rap or opera fan who never dismissed anything as bad would be considered as not really a *fan* at all. And what interests me here is what we are doing when we make such judgments and why it is that we need to make them. My question, in short, is not what is bad music but what is "bad music"?

The first analytic problem is to clarify the discursive basis of this concept. Conceptually, that is to say, most *judgments* of bad music are

simultaneously *explanations* of bad music: the judgment is the explanation, the explanation is the judgment (and people's musical judgments often, in fact, combine or confuse explanations, or move
imperceptibly from one sort of explanation to another). In very broad
terms (making an artificial separation for analytic purposes), the most
common discourses in popular music judgment refer either to how the
music was produced or to its effects, and we can therefore note immediately that although it is music that is here being judged "bad," the
explanation is not musical but sociological. What's going on, in other
words, is a displaced judgment: "bad music" describes a bad system
of production (capitalism) or bad behavior (sex and violence). The
apparent judgment of the music is a judgment of something else altogether, the social institutions or social behavior for which the music
simply acts as a sign.

I can clarify this by going through the most common arguments
in a little more detail. First, in *arguments about production* there are
two familiar positions.

Music is judged bad in the context of or by reference to a critique
of mass production. Bad music (in the argument made most influ-
entially by T. W. Adorno) is "standardized" or "formulaic" music.
The implicit contrast is with "original" or "autonomous' or "unique"
music, and the explanation built into the judgment depends on the
familiar Marxist/Romantic distinction between serial production, production to commercial order, to meet a market, and artistic creativity,
production determined only by individual intention, by formal and
technical rules and possibilities.

Among other things, this means that "formula" or "standard"
production that is not commercial is not, in this discursive context,
usually judged bad: the fact that all disco numbers in the late 1970s
"sounded the same" is a mark of unhealthy (commercial) formulaic
production; the fact that all folk songs collected in Norfolk or Virginia
in the late 1870s sounded the same is a sign of their healthy (non-
commercial) roots in a collective history. More generally, one could
say that such formula criticism tends to be genre-dependent: minor
variations in boy band music are taken to be insignificant; minor variations in rural blues guitar tunings or madrigal polyphonics are of great
aesthetic importance.

A second sort of criticism, which refers to production but without a Marxist edge, equates bad music with *imitative* music. Again,
the implicit contrast is with "original" or, perhaps, "individual" sounds,

and I am sure that every music listener has sometime dismissed a record or artist for sounding just like someone else (or, indeed, for sounding just like themselves), for "cashing in" on a successful musical formula.

There are many variations on this sort of argument. Take, for example, shifting attitudes to the "cover version," British imitations of U.S. hits. When I first started arguing about pop, in the mid-1960s, rock fan orthodoxy was that the cover version was necessarily inferior to the original. This was obviously true of white pop versions of black r&b songs (Pat Boone's "Tutti Frutti" is probably the nearest thing to a consensual bad record in popular music history), but was soon applied in playground argument to the Beatles' versions of Chuck Berry songs (which we actually heard afterward), and I can admit now that the logic of the argument didn't always reflect my listening habits. Nearly all the records I first bought in the late 1950s and early 1960s were cover versions. And soon white British r&b versions of black American r&b songs were raising different questions again—a guitarist like Eric Clapton acquired his reputation by sounding *more* like the blues originals than anyone else.

By the end of the 1960s rock critics were making a quite different sort of argument, drawn from both folk and jazz, in which creative musicians (whether Billie Holiday or Charlie Parker, Ray Charles or Bob Dylan) were heard to make something original out of standards. A "version" of an old song could be just as original as a new song. From an academic point of view, then, particularly in this age of hiphop and sampling, there is no clear position on originals and copies; judgments can only be made on a case to case basis.[8] In lay terms, though, the old assumptions about race and authenticity, commerce and inauthenticity, still have considerable purchase. On August 15, 2002, to mark the twenty-fifth anniversary of Elvis Presley's death, the *Guardian* published an article by Helen Kolaoke dismissing his music on the grounds that "for black people Elvis more than any other performer epitomises the theft of their music and dance." This led to a flurry of correspondence in which fifty years of critical argument about race and rock'n'roll were replayed in miniature: when does "borrowing" become "appropriation," when does "cultural exchange" become "theft"?

At the core of this dispute, though, was a simple but unstated point: people who liked Presley's music were defending him from the charge of racial exploitation; people who didn't sought to develop the charge. The confusion of musical judgment and social explanation was

**22**                                                    **Bad Music**

obvious, but there is also an implicit argument here about value and intention. The fact that Pat Boone's "personal stamp" was put on "Tutti Frutti" is clearly a bad thing; the fact that John Coltrane's personal stamp was put on "These Foolish Things" is clearly a good thing. There's an assumption here about motives as well as race—Boone making a marketing decision, Coltrane an artistic judgment (years later Puff Daddy's use of Sting's "I'll Be Watching You" would equally be dismissed as cynical, commercial, bad). And so while I can't think of a rock critic who wouldn't agree that the Peter Frampton version of *Sgt. Pepper* is one of the worst albums ever made, there would be disagreement about Paul Young's version of Joy Division's "Love Will Tear Us Apart." Rip off or tribute? The judgment rests not on what Paul Young says about the record but on how it sounds.

The law, of course, has always had its own (non-aesthetic) interest in authorship and plagiarism and this is the source of another kind of argument about bad music and production. Following the 1988 Copyright Act, British law (unlike U.S. law) was brought into line with the law in other European Union countries and now acknowledges authors' moral rights in their work. Under this clause, the "integrity" of a composer's work is protected; "bad music" by this definition, illegal music, is that which in arrangement or interpretation brings a composition or its composer into "disrepute," fails to "respect" the work and its author's intentions. Few cases have been heard under this clause (though injunctions against the use of samples have referred to it) but it seems clear to me that in practice the intention of the "interpreter" will be less significant in judging the moral value of their work than its effect on listeners, on the original composer and, indeed, on the judge.

Even here, though, on the evidence of straight plagiarism cases, the musical judgment will refer to production processes and depend on particular sorts of knowledge. To condemn a record as derivative or disreputable we must know (or know about) the "original" (the kind of knowledge displayed so ostentatiously by both classical and popular music critics faced with new work, by musicological "experts' in court). To describe a song as "standardized" means that we have heard (or heard of) other songs of a similar type. Such knowledge may be more or less extensive, more or less valid; judgments here often rest on hypothetical knowledge, on unexamined assumptions about record company, studio and marketing decisions. (This was obvious in the *Guardian*'s Presley correspondence.) Listeners read from a record how they think it must have been produced, and then condemn it (or not) accordingly. Hence the familiar enough experience (to which people are often loath to admit) that we need to know who a record is by before we can evaluate it.

Production arguments do tend, then, to be deployed by fans; they depend on certain sorts of musical knowledge and engagement. At the same time, though, even the most well informed fan is still, in the end, referring "bad music" to the something "in the music itself" that led him or her down this discursive path in the first place (again the Presley point). And the recurring negative musical judgment in all these discussions of the original and the derivative, the individual and the standardized, seems to be in terms of excessive *familiarity*: a piece of music is bad because it uses musical clichés; because its development is easily predictable; because nothing unexpected happens. And the critical problem here is not just that there can be pleasure in the predictable, but that not everyone has the same expectations. Few people who bought Atomic Kitten's 2002 U.K. hit, "The Tide is High," knew the Blondie record it faithfully copied (itself a cover version).

Arguments, about musical *effects* are rather different. Bad music is, it seems, responsible for bad things, for hysteria and sexual arousal, for violence and crime. In their entertaining history of "the opposition to rock'n'roll," Linda Martin and Kerry Seagrove quote a typical 1950s editorial about this new form of bad music, this one from the worthy *Music Journal*. Teenagers listening to rock'n'roll were, the journal argued,

> Definitely influenced in their lawlessness by this throwback to jungle rhythms. Either it actually stirs them to orgies of sex and violence (as its model did for the savages themselves), or they use it as an excuse for the removal of all inhibitions and the complete disregard of conventions of decency . . . [rock'n'roll] has proved itself definitely a menace to youthful morals and an incitement to juvenile delinquency. There is no point in soft-pedalling these facts any longer. The daily papers provide sufficient proof of their existence . . . It is entirely correct to say that every proved delinquent has been definitely influenced by rock'n'roll.[9]

Such dire warnings about its effects have accompanied every popular music trend since—the twist, rock, disco, punk, rave, rap. Even as I was writing the final draft of this chapter, in January 2003, a British culture minister, Kim Howells, was denouncing rap in general and the

U.K. garage act So Solid Crew in particular, in the aftermath of a gun battle in Birmingham which left two teenage girls dead: "Idiots like the So Solid Crew are glorifying gun culture and violence." Howells was echoing comments made earlier by a senior policeman, Tarique Ghaffur, "who blamed a 'backdrop of music' for alienating young men and encouraging them to use weapons as fashion statements."[10]

The subsequent public debate about music and violence in Britain has almost exactly replayed the U.S. debate about music and violence in the early 1990s, following the success of gangsta rap. There were hearings in 1994 in both the Senate and House of Representatives to consider the problem of "violence and demeaning imagery in popular music," and, as Doug Simmons then wrote, the underlying question was this: "does reality shape rap or does rap shape reality?"[11] What is remarkable is how many politicians have so strong a belief in the power of music to shape society when music analysts themselves are ever more wary of such a description. At its most ludicrous, this political belief becomes the certainty that the most evil music (usually heavy metal) gets its effects subliminally, by including backward messages. Judas Priest had to go to court in 1990 to defend themselves from the charge of inducing two teenage boys to attempt suicide as a result of such a devilish musical ploy.[12]

The suggestion that music is evil comes from all parts of the political spectrum. In Europe, for instance, white nationalist skinhead groups like Skrewdriver have long been accused of fomenting fascism, violence and political mindlessness, while the rap and ragga acts denounced by policemen and politicians for glamorizing violence are equally condemned from the left for promoting misogyny and homophobia.[13]

Such arguments about rock's dreadful effects are familiar and I must resist the temptation to document even more outlandish examples, but some general points are worth noting here. First, musical judgments in terms of musical effects are usually made by people from outside the musical worlds concerned, and involve no informed pop or rock knowledge at all (which is why such arguments seem plain silly to the fans and musicians themselves, even if they have to take them seriously to protect their music from censorship or regulation).

Second, despite (or maybe because of) this, effect arguments, unlike production arguments, are surprisingly influential institutionally, in terms of record labelling, banning and censorship. These accounts of bad music do affect what we can hear on the radio, see on stage, buy in shops. Indeed, the moral logic of such music criticism is that *something should be done*! Ban Eminem/So Solid Crew/Buju Banton![14]

Third, there is, nonetheless, very little evidence that bad music has the effects it is purported to have, whether on crowd behavior, individual attitudes, social beliefs, or whatever. It follows, paradoxically, that the focus here is much more closely on the music itself than in production criticism. The "effects" of the music, that is to say, are deduced from the music itself because there is no independent evidence that they actually exist. (Compare the way in which Soviet officials could only determine what music was decadent, what music was not, by formal analysis.)

Opponents of rock usually reduce "the music itself" to a small number of effective elements: *rhythm; lyrics; performance.* I discuss the long association of rhythm, race, sexuality, and the "primitive" in *Performing Rites*. Here I will focus on lyrics and performance.

Nearly all indictments of "bad music" leading to censorship or airplay bans concern lyrics, as exemplified by the "parental guidance" labelling of albums following the Parents' Music Resource Centre's successful U.S. lobbying campaign in the 1980s.[15] In his account of the Mosely-Brown Senate Committee hearings on demeaning imagery in popular music, Doug Simmons describes "the sheets of graphic lyrics stacked on the press tables." The demeaning imagery was, it seems, verbal rather than musical.[16]

Are there circumstances in which a pop melody or arrangement or instrumental texture is censored? Totalitarian regimes have certainly banned whole musical genres because of their supposed political or oppositional or "foreign" implications. Religious authorities have on occasion decided that instrumental music is incompatible with godliness (I'm not just thinking here of the Taliban's denunciation of all music, but also of the way the Church of England banned all musicians except choirs and organists from its services in the late nineteenth century). The arguments here are not so much about bad music as that music— all music—is bad per se.

Music performance raises different questions. The most widely discussed examples of offensive performance over recent decades have been the pop videos condemned by right and left alike as sexist, racist, homophobic. A more interesting case of "bad music" being explained by reference to its offensive performing conventions, though, is minstrelsy, white people aping blacks, and, in particular, *The Black and*

*White Minstrel Show*, which ran on British television from 1957–1973, and which is still occasionally revived as a live attraction.[17] Even as a child I found the minstrels' show unsettling: the falseness and excess of the make-up made the musical emotions of the standard Tin Pan Alley songs seem false and excessive too (I had much the same reaction to the Rolling Stones' stage spectaculars in the late 1970s).

In retrospect, though, at least *The Black and White Minstrel Show* had the virtue of drawing attention to its performing conventions, to the problems of staging musical authenticity and inauthenticity, to what it means to *be an act*. In her illuminating account of the 1990 Florida court case in which 2 Live Crew were charged and acquitted of staging an obscene performance, Lisa Jones makes the point that 2 Live Crew are just such an act. Decidedly offensive and unpleasant, but still an act. The turning point in the trial came when the police witnesses had to "translate" to the court the meaning of what they'd seen. "After lunch there's a breakthrough. The jury has sent a note to Judge Johnson asking if they're allowed to laugh. It's a deciding moment in the case."[18]

Ten years later and we have to make the same argument about Eminem. I know of no credible rock critic who thinks Eminem makes bad music. On the contrary, his records provide some of the best popular music of the turn of the century. But then I know of no credible rock critic who's not made uneasy by their pleasure in these words, this sensibility. "He's an act," we comfort ourselves, "a brilliant act, Eminem (like James Dean or Johnny Rotten before him) is *playing* a disturbed and disaffected young white man." In denying that the rise in gun violence in the U.K. had anything to do with music, a spokeswoman for So Solid Crew suggested that their own music reflected society "just as Robert de Niro reflected American gangster society in his film roles."[19] And what's at issue in drama criticism is how well a role is played; to articulate a sensibility musically is not to endorse it.

I'm not entirely convinced that this argument describes musical (as against dramatic) performance but before dealing with that I want to take stock of my argument so far. I've been describing uses of the term "bad music" that refer more or less explicitly either to how it was produced or to its presumed effects. What is going on here, to repeat my starting point, is the entanglement of a musical judgment—the music is bad—with an explanation of why it is, and I think most day-to-day arguments about music are conducted in this way: aesthetic judgments are necessarily tangled up with ethical judgments. I suggest that what's involved here are not accounts of bad music as such but justifications for using the label, "bad music."

To clarify this point I need to discuss briefly a third kind of critical discourse, derived from the arguments used in music making. For musicians, bad music seems to fall into two broad categories. First, *incompetent* music, music that is badly played, that reflects inadequate skill, technique and so forth. But even here technical, "objective," judgments (this player is lagging behind the beat, has erratic pitch, played the wrong note) are often confused with an ideological, subjective, ones. Musicians' incompetence can be explained in two ways. Either they are *untutored* (they can't do certain things because they haven't been taught how) or they are *unprofessional* (they are unwilling to learn proper techniques). The former argument implies that bad musicians want to play differently but can't, the latter implies that there are pop genres in which "bad musicianship"—erratic pitch, wrong notes— is actually welcomed. Even in classical criticism reviewers tend to favor a "passionate" performance, wrong notes and all, over something that is technically flawless but "cold."

This argument spills over into a second sort of conception of bad music, that it is *self-indulgent*. At least three different points are conflated here. Musicians may be criticized for selfishness or ego-centricity; bad musicians are musicians who forget or deny that good music is a collective practice; they use a performance to show off their own virtuosity or character, to dominate the microphone or sound mix, to play too long or loudly. Such musicians don't listen to their performing colleagues and the resulting music is bad because it is "unbalanced." Musicians may also be criticized for emptiness; bad musicians indulge in form at the expense of content, make music that "has nothing to say" but says it elaborately anyway. Their music is not made for any reason except as a display of technical skill. Cecilia Bartoli, writes Tim Ashley,

> could be accused of unearthing second-rate music for the express purpose of showing off, for what she now presents us with is a vocal olympiad, at which we are primarily invited to marvel at her technique . . . Bartoli is always impressive but rarely moving. It is artifice rather than art."[20]

Musicians may also be criticized for their incomprehensibility; bad musicians play in a completely introverted way, for self-satisfaction or for therapeutic reasons, as a matter of private obsession. Their music is not communicative; it does not acknowledge or address an audience. This is the standard workaday musician critique of "arty" music, for example.

All the arguments here are, indeed, about communication. Bad music is music that doesn't communicate—between musician and audience, between musician and musician, between performer and composer. The implication is that musical decisions are communication decisions, and certainly one kind of judgment of bad music is that the composers'/performers' choices—to write/play this note rather than that—have been made randomly, with no communicative point at all. And this leads me to my final set of questions. What do people want from music? What it is that they're *not* getting when they describe a song or performance or work as bad music? I would suggest three rather grand answers: truth, taste and intelligence.

The most common account of bad music (of bad rock music certainly) is that it is *inauthentic*. This certainly refers to its production, but not in any coherent way. "Inauthentic," that is to say, is a term which may be applied evaluatively within genres which are straightforwardly, cynically, commercial. Fans distinguish between authentic and inauthentic Eurodisco or TV pop idols, and what is being described is not how something was actually produced, but a more inchoate feature of the music itself, a perceived quality of sincerity and commitment. It's as if people expect music to mean what it says, however cynical that meaning, and music can be heard as being false to its own premises (which is one reason why I have difficulty in treating Eminem—or Madonna—as "just an act"). How do people hear music in such ethical ways? What is it about a record that makes us say "I just don't believe it," not necessarily agreeing with anyone else on this at all. This is, I think, related to the ways in which we judge people's sincerity generally. It is a human as well as a musical judgment.

Bad music may also be described as music in *bad taste*, and this involves a different kind of judgment, in terms of its appropriateness or inappropriateness to a particular function or occasion. Post-9/11, the U.K. TV news service, ITN, was thus censured by the Independent Television Commission for broadcasting a "sick and tasteless" sequence of news in which "the collapse of the World Trade Center in New York was set to music." The music (from Charles Gounod's *Judex*) may have been, as ITN claimed, suitable, with "a sombre, funereal tone," but the very attempt to show these images in time to music "was inappropriate and breached the programme code." There are both specific and general questions here: is this piece of music suitable for this event (Elton John's "Candle in the Wind" at Princess Diana's funeral service)? Is any sort of popular commercial music suitable to deal with disease or pain in general, to deal with them *entertainingly*?

Third, bad music may be considered *stupid*. This is a common term in popular discourse even if it is not often articulated by professional critics. And it is an interesting term because it is not only applied to words or lyrics; people can and do find tunes and arrangements and sounds stupid too. What is meant here? Clearly the analogy is with the way we call a statement (or the person making a statement) stupid, a suggestion not just that their account of the world is wrong, but that it is also somehow demeaning, that it demeans us through our involvement, however unwilling, in the collusive act of listening to someone making, say, a racist or sexist remark, to *The Black and White Minstrel Show,* to Eminem. Stupid music in this (non-academic) context is offensive because it seems to deny what we're capable of, humanly, rationally, ethically, aesthetically. Which is why we can loath a tune that we can't get out of our heads.

And that brings me to my final set of arguments. I'm happy to concede that "bad music" is a matter of taste, involves a judgment that depends on the social and psychological circumstances of the person making it. I doubt if the readers of this book could come up with an agreed list of bad records and I agree that it would be foolish to try. On the other hand, whatever the individual bases of our judgments, once made we do seek to justify and explain them, and my concern here has been to survey the language that seems available to us, and to point out some of its problems.

From this perspective it is clear that we need a concept of "bad music" even if we know full well that we won't be able to agree on how the label should be applied. The marking off of some tracks and genres and artists as "bad" is a necessary part of popular music pleasure; it is a way we establish our place in various music worlds. And "bad" is a key word because it suggests that aesthetic and ethical judgments are tied together here: not to like a record is not *just* a matter of taste; it is also a matter of argument, an argument that matters. My students have always been agreed on this: other people's musical tastes have a decisive effect on friendships, courtship, love.

Throughout this chapter I've been treating the evaluative process as a matter of discourse: what is happening when we talk about music?

**30**                                                          **Bad Music**

As a music lover, though, I know that what's equally at issue is feeling: what is happening when we listen to music? "Bad music" describes to begin with an emotional not an ideological response. I don't like a record; I then try to account for that dislike, to justify it. When we label something as "bad music" it is because it is music that, if nothing else, upsets or offends us, that we don't want to listen to. *Please* play something else! Do I *have* to listen to this? It grates, hurts, bores; it's ugly, it's painful, it's driving me *mad*. Is there anything I can say as a sociologist about such responses?

Well, to begin with, I don't believe that music in itself just *is* ugly or painful or boring. What's at issue here is not the sound but the emotional response to the sound. And looking back at my schematic account of evaluative language and evaluative circumstances, at my discussion of when and why music is labelled "bad," two themes become apparent. First, musical arguments (whether referring to production or effects) call into question musical *intent*. They are judgments of musicians' motivations; they call to account the reasons *why* the music sounds as it does. They are thus judgments of performers' attitudes to their listeners; they are arguments about communication. Bad music is heard to be music made in bad faith. But this is to suggest a second theme, musical *expectation*. People don't just read off musicians' intentions from their music, they interpret what they hear in the light of what they believe music could or should be. (And certainly one difference between music critics and committed fans, on the one hand, and "ordinary" or casual listeners, on the other, is that the former have higher expectations of music in general and specific performers in particular, and are therefore more often disappointed.)

The question, then, is how to relate the emotional response to music to these understandings and expectations of the musical experience. Or, to put this the other way round, when does not *liking* a piece of music mean judging it *"bad"*? When does a piece of music make someone so angry that they have to speak their objections?[21] There can be no doubt that this happens, famously, for example, at the first performance of Stravinsky's *Rite of Spring*. One source of listeners' displeasure seems to have been a sense of sacrilege. The problem was not just that the music was difficult, that it lacked the melodic and sonic qualities the audience expected, but that it somehow ridiculed such qualities, bringing "primitive" elements to a highly serious occasion. A reading of contemporary music criticism suggests that anger at a performance is still imbued with this sense that it, the performance, is somehow making a mockery of what the critic believes music is supposed to be. I would classify such critical anger under three headings:

- Anger that other people are enjoying something that is *not worthy of enjoyment*. (This is what one might call the David Helfgott problem—critics are particularly incensed when someone they regard as musically sloppy if not meretricious is rapturously applauded for "sentimental" reasons.)[22]
- Anger that performers or composers are *betraying their talent*. (This is often seen to be in the pursuit of crowd-pleasing, whether emotionally or commercially. The most familiar version of this argument is the rock cultural concept of "selling out," but classical critics are often similarly upset—the more talented or "promising" the musician the greater the critic's anger.)
- Anger that a performer or composer or record company is dishonouring music by *corrupting its original integrity*. (This is the language, as we've seen, of moral rights, the source of legal injunctions against dance music producers "adapting" the work of Carl Orff, of ethnomusicologists' despair at the way in which local ritual and spiritual music is sampled for Western entertainment.)[23]

In all these cases the performance is heard to be insulting, and the performers to lack respect, whether for their music, its composers, or their listeners. It's the same sense of insult that makes people angry about the *inappropriate* use of music—as muzak, on advertisements, in television shows. People are most annoyed, that is to say (going by anecdotal evidence), when music they particularly *like*, whether it be Verdi or the Rolling Stones, is used to soothe nerves or sell cars, used in a way which will make it difficult for them ever to listen to this music *in their own way* again.

In all these cases a performance of music is making people angry because of what it is not. People don't just have unmet musical expectations, thwarted ideals of musical performance, occasion and experience, but feel that these ideals are being sullied. I want to note two aspects of this immediately. First, such a sense of sacrilege depends on a particular kind of musical understanding. Second, music here is making people angry because of its ethical rather than technical shortcomings (which is why we can be made angry by music in which in other circumstances we delight).

I will turn now to a related but I think different kind of anger, rooted in issues of identity. The most famous example of an angry audience in rock history (the iconic equivalent of the first *Rite of Spring*) was captured on tape at Bob Dylan's concert at the Free Trade Hall in Manchester in 1966.[24] Listen to it now and the sense of betrayal is still palpable—in the audience response to Bob Dylan playing electric rock, in Dylan's own response to his audience's disapproval. This is an example of the sheer emotional charge of the accusation of "sell out!" And for rock and pop fans the problem here seems to be less the dishonouring of an ideal or original musical concept than the betrayal of an identity, of a belief in what an artist *stood for*, and how that, in turn, reflected (and reflected back on) the identity of the listener. For Bob Dylan's folk-club followers musical taste was a key to the way they differentiated themselves from the mainstream of commercial pop consumers. Dylan going pop thus had for his folk fans something of the same emotional impact as betrayal by a lover. Their musical trust had been abused; the new Bob Dylan called their very sense of themselves into question. The source of anger here, in short, was not so much the music itself as who was playing it.

Audiences can be angered by another kind of betrayal of trust, when they feel that a musician is cheating or exploiting them. In the days when I was reviewing a lot of concerts I did occasionally see audiences get very angry indeed. This was either because they thought they had been short-changed—numbers performed perfunctorily, with mistakes and sloppiness, musicians displaying a kind of contempt. Or because they detected the use of backing tracks or drum machines or other kinds of pre-recorded assistance (in fact used by most rock bands, but usually well concealed). Here too, if without the sense of self involved in the more intense kinds of fandom, music can be seen as a relationship in which both sides have certain obligations. (My own rages at concerts were with audience members who failed to meet their obligations as listeners—talking all through the quiet bits.)

I want to turn finally to a third and rather different (if more familiar) kind of anger. I will summarize this as the problem of *noise* because, in general, it is anger expressed at music being played *too loud*! In fact, though, I think the problem is not volume as such (measured by decibels) but the feeling that someone else's music is invading our space, that we can't listen to it as music, a pleasurable organization of sound, but only as noise, an undifferentiated din.[25] This is an increasing problem in everyday life and these days musical disputes are probably more often arguments about noise than taste. "Turn it down!" is the eternal parental cry (even when the music isn't actually being played that loudly), and so, over the last few months, I've found myself being most irritated at home by one child's habit of playing Bob Dylan's *Greatest Hits* in the kitchen—too loud!—whenever he gets the chance to do so, tracks that I'll happily put on myself when I'm home alone.

"Noise" in such domestic disputes refers to people's sense of spatial integrity, and the question becomes how music works to include and exclude people from this kind of aural space, and when and why other people's music is felt to invade it. It's clear to begin with that the music itself is not really the issue, just that it is not, at that moment, *our* music. And certainly in domestic life some records come to carry traces of battles past, to symbolize particularly charged arguments not so much about good and bad music as about the personal right to make such judgments (and enforce them)!

My grand opening question—what is bad music?—has ended up with musical judgment as the banal currency of domestic squabble. But there is a grand point I want to make about this, as I draw to a conclusion. Our feelings about a piece of music are, of course, drawn forth by the music: we listen, we respond. But we listen on the basis of who we are and what we musically know and expect, and we respond according to how and where and why we're listening. I've been arguing throughout this chapter that musical judgments are also ethical judgments, concern the perceived purposes as well as sounds of music, and that judgment is, by its nature, an attempt to persuade other listeners of the rightness of one's own responses. What I want to conclude is that the aesthetics of music, therefore, involve a particular mix of individualism and sociability.

I don't think there can be any doubt that for both technological and cultural reasons the twentieth century experience of music became highly individualized. Music listening became tied up with personal identity and the sense of self; music became something through which one laid claim to and identified one's own physical and geographical space. This in turn led to a new kind of demand being placed on music: it was expected to meet its listeners' individual (and shifting) emotional needs, to confirm their sense of individuality. At the same time, music became something to which one could be, individually, more or less committed; it was no longer just a shared part of communal life.

**34**                                                              **Bad Music**

In different but related ways music critics and music fans developed evaluative positions in which greater knowledge and better taste (derived from the individual devotion to music of much time and attention) meant a superior way of *listening*. The self became invested in musical judgment as never before.

The paradox is that this egocentric aesthetic ("I" is the most common word in all forms of music criticism) is driven by a passionate desire to make other people listen differently. In both published criticism and everyday argument, "good" and "bad" music are terms used to persuade people to change their listening expectations. Even as the musical experience has been individualized, it has remained necessarily and undeniably sociable. I haven't dealt here at all with music and dance, with collective music making, with musical pleasures that are social pleasures (and therefore not subject to the same sort of aesthetic judgment). But, more pertinently, the peculiar thing about music is that even in these days of the personal sound systems, it is not, and cannot be, just an individual experience. These days, when music accompanies every conceivable public and private activity, we can't help hearing what other people are listening to and, if we think of ourselves as any sort of music lover, wanting to do something about it.

**NOTES**

1. The first version of this chapter was prepared for a seminar in the Musicology Department, University of Stockholm, in 1994, and published by the Department as part of its report on that event, *We're Only In It For The Money.* I wrote it as a companion paper to "What is Good Music," *Canadian University Music Review* 10(2), 1990. Arguments from both papers fed into my *Performing Rites. On the Value of Popular Music* (Cambridge, MA: Harvard University Press, 1996).

2. This is the everlasting appeal of Slonimsky's *Lexicon*, first published in 1953 (and kept in print by the University of Washington Press). What makes this collection of "critical assaults on composers' such compulsive reading is its examples of critics getting things wrong. It is less about bad music than about bad music criticism.

3. The original spoken version of this paper was illustrated by the following records: Dub Syndicate's *One Way System* ("boring" and "repetitious"); Midi, Maxi and Efti's "Bad Bad Boys" (unoriginal, standardized disco pop complete with tacky rap); Tommy Tune and Twiggy's "Room in Bloomsbury" from *The Boyfriend* (parody of the Tin Pan Alley heterosexual love song at its most lyrically and melodically banal); Joseph Spence's "Santa Claus is Coming to Town" ("incompetent" performance and production); an unknown country singer's "Ice Cream Cones and Soda Pops' ("bad taste" death of a child song); Meat

**Simon Frith**                                                              **35**

Loaf's "Rock and Roll Dreams Come Through" (sexist, offensive, over-produced, commercial formula white rock). I'm fond of all of these but can only play them at home when I'm alone.

4.  Savalas did sing Bob Dylan, just as Robert Mitchum sang calypso before him. Seagal's songs so far only exist as promises on his Web site. It seems somehow safe to assume that they will be dreadful—see John Sutherland's column in the *Guardian*, January 13, 2003 (G2, 5)

5.  For the last ten years I've chaired the judges of the Mercury Music Prize, which is awarded to the best British record of the year, of any genre. We sometimes consider producing a list of the worst records of the year too. There are two kinds of bad music on which we are all agreed: albums by 70s rock stars success-ful enough to indulge themselves in some religious or philosophical fad and attempts to give classical music pop appeal (Bond, Opera Babes, Planets, and the like). The former are ridiculous and therefore have kitsch potential; the latter are irredeemable.

6.  In the art music world the value judgments made by grant and commission giving bodies might be equally important materially (in determining which musicians can make a living from their music and which can't; which works are heard by audiences and which not). Such funding bodies rarely articulate publicly the reasons why somebody was *unworthy* of support.

7.  I address this question in *Performing Rites*.

8.  For two excellent recent discussions of the issues here see Dai Griffiths: "Cover versions and the sound of identity in motion," in D. Hesmondhalgh and K. Negus eds., *Popular Music Studies* (London: Arnold, 2002), 51–64; Michael Coyle: "Hijacked hits and antic authenticity: cover songs, race and postwar marketing," in R. Beebe, D. Fulbrook and B. Saunders eds., *Rock Over the Edge* (Durham and London: Duke University Press, 2002), 133–157.

9.  Quoted in Linda Martin and Kerry Seagrove, *Anti-Rock. The Opposition to Rock'n'Roll* (Hamden, Connecticut: Anchor Books, 1988), 53.

10.  Fiachra Gibbons, "Minister labelled racist for attack on rap 'idiots.'" *Guardian.* January 6, 2003, 3.

11.  Doug Simmons: "Gangsta Was the Case," *Village Voice,* March 8, 1994, 63.

12.  See Ivan Solotaroff, "Subliminal Criminals," *Village Voice,* September 4, 1990, 24–34.

13.  A campaign in Glasgow in 2001 to prevent Marilyn Manson and Eminem head-lining the annual Festival on the Green thus involved an unusual alliance of fundamentalist Christians and gay activists.

14.  For a useful recent survey of global music censorship and regulation see Mar-tin Cloonan and Reebee Garofalo eds., *Policing Pop* (Philadelphia: Temple University Press, 2003).

15.  For a good contemporary discussion of the PMRC campaign and its historical context see James R. McDonald, "Censoring Rock Lyrics," *Youth & Society*, 19, no. 3 (1988): 294–313.

16.  Simmons op. cit., 63.

17.  For a sophisticated discussion of minstrelsy as British entertainment see Michael Pickering, "John Bull in blackface," *Popular Music* 16, no. 2 (1997): 181–201.

18.  Lisa Jones: "The Signifying Monkees," *Village Voice,* November 6, 1990, 171.

**36**                                                                 **Bad Music**

19. Gibbons op. cit.
20. Tim Ashley: "Cecilia Bartoli," *Guardian,* November 7, 2002, 27.
21. Some of the arguments that follow were first presented in "Why does music make people so cross?", a paper given to the 4th Nordic Music Therapy Conference in Bergen in May 2003. Thanks to the participants for their comments.
22. David Helfgott was the Australian pianist whose story of mental breakdown and recovery was told in the emotionally and commercially effective film, *Shine*. His subsequent concert hall appearances were rapturously received by audiences but almost universally panned by critics.
23. See, for example, Steven Feld, "The Poetics and Politics of Pygmy Pop" in G. Born and D. Hesmondhalgh, eds., *Western Music and Its Others* (Berkeley: University of California Press, 2000)
24. The tape was issued as a bootleg record, misleadingly titled *Dylan Live at the Albert Hall*. For the true story of this event, see C. P. Lee, *Like the Night. Bob Dylan and the Road to the Manchester Free Trade Hall* (London: Helter Skelter, 1998).
25. For further discussion of some of the issues here see Simon Frith, "Music and Everyday Life" in M. Clayton, T. Herbert and R. Middleton, eds., *The Cultural Study of Popular Music* (New York and London: Routledge, 2003).

# Index